"Miscommunication" and Problematic Talk

"Miscommunication" and Problematic Talk

edited by

Nikolas Coupland
Howard Giles
John M. Wiemann

SAGE PUBLICATIONS
The International Professional Publishers
Newbury Park London New Delhi

For information address:

SAGE Publications, Inc.
2455 Teller Road
Newbury Park, California 91320

SAGE Publications Ltd.
6 Bonhill Street
London EC2A 4PU
United Kingdom

SAGE Publications India Pvt. Ltd.
M-32 Market
Greater Kailash I
New Delhi 110 048 India

Printed in the United States of America

Library of Congress Cataloging-in-Publication Data

Main entry under title:

"Miscommunication" and problematic talk / edited by Nikolas Coupland, Howard Giles, John M. Wiemann.
p. cm.
Includes bibliographical references.
ISBN 0-8039-4032-7. — ISBN 0-8039-4033-5 (pbk.)
1. Communication. I. Coupland, Nikolas, 1950- . II. Giles, Howard. III. Wiemann, John M.
P90.M5413 1991
302.2—dc20 90-22484
CIP

FIRST PRINTING, 1991

Sage Production Editor: Astrid Virding

Contents

1

Talk as "Problem" and Communication as "Miscommunication": An Integrative Analysis

Nikolas Coupland
John M. Wiemann
Howard Giles

The "Pollyanna" Perspective

Miscommunication is an interesting and slippery concept—perhaps interesting initially because it is slippery. The term has usually been applied, very loosely, to any sort of problem that might arise interactionally, and typically to local processes of misunderstanding. A key reason why we have traditionally failed to embrace the concept of miscommunication, its diversity and its implications, can be called the "Pollyanna" perspective that language and communication research has tended to adopt: Researchers have looked for the "good" and ignored the "bad"; communication problems were treated as aberrant behavior which should be eliminated. At the same time, we have devoted too little effort to characterizing and critiquing this evaluative dimension, and research has operated with limited and perhaps naive definitions of what good and bad might mean. Appeals to "effective," "efficient," "appropriate", or "satisfying" communication abound. Pretty much in line with the admonitions

AUTHORS' NOTE: We gratefully acknowledge Justine Coupland's critical reading of an earlier version of this chapter.

of etiquette book writers, researchers have built their interpretations of data, explicitly or implicitly, around the principle "be open, honest, and avoid miscommunication."

Communication research typically has been couched in prosocial terms with little regard for the fact that most communicators are sometimes of necessity skeptical, crafty, and less than veracious (Giles & Wiemann, 1987), and that sharing a disclosure is an inherently constrained exercise of semantic transfer and strategic selection. Intentionally hostile or dissociative strategies of talk have even been seen as the product of unskilled individuals and, in the extreme, as symptoms of psychopathology (cf. Watzlawick, Beavin, & Jackson, 1967). A variety of problems in organizations have been attributed to the "quality" of communication or "communication breakdown" among individuals and groups. Similarly, research on deception emphasizes detecting it rather than analyzing how deception is interactionally constituted and the contexts in which it may be pernicious or necessary, perhaps even desirable and a matter of skilled achievement.

Our intention in this volume is therefore to rescue "miscommunication" from its theoretical and empirical exile, and explore its rich explanatory potential in very diverse contexts. This volume does, nevertheless, have some important precursors. An issue of the journal *Social Problems* has been devoted to considering the role of interaction in the analysis of a diverse set of routinely difficult but also life-threatening social circumstances (Maynard, 1988). In sociolinguistics, Grimshaw's research (1980), like that of Pride (1985), Gumperz (1982a, 1982b), Maltz and Borker (1982), and others, has established that it is necessary and profitable to adopt less idealized perspectives on talk in context. The social psychology of language (Giles & Robinson, 1990; Giles & Coupland, 1991) has consistently adopted an explicitly applied orientation to language and interaction, with social evaluative data integrated theoretically into models of talk in context. In communication science, it has been argued that the study of communicative competence is more appropriately seen as the ability to avoid problems, to conduct encounters and relationships in a manner that is adequate or merely "good enough" rather than excellent or perfect (Wiemann & Kelly, 1981). From this standpoint, much of what gets said is neither clearly true nor false, but rather is constructed to appear to address issues at hand while actually saying very little—what Bavelas (1983) calls verbal disqualifications. Speakers and hearers appear to cooperate in constructing messages that are ambiguous, that omit as much as they reveal (see Giles & Wiemann, 1987). And Redding (1972) has shown that in organizations, clear, concise, honest communication is as frequently the *cause* of difficulties as it is the solution to them. "Miscommunication" is therefore not to be characterized simply as a deviation from some underspecified ideal.

An important starting point is the observation that language use and communication are in fact pervasively and even intrinsically flawed, partial, and problematic. To this extent, communication is itself miscommunicative, although the motivating force behind many research paradigms is the recognition that language and communication underpin and enact more specific social problems, divisions, inequalities, and dissatisfactions. Communicative interchange becomes a foregrounded rather than a taken-for-granted process most frequently when we recognize its inefficiencies and its unforeseen or undesirable consequences. But interpretations are severely limited if we gloss these rich and varied processes under simplistic evaluative labels such as *communication breakdown, communication failure,* and indeed *miscommunication* itself. By so doing, we risk under-analyzing the multiple levels and dimensions in which discourse can enact "problems" of widely varying degrees of severity: Miscommunication may be a matter of transient annoyance, or it can inhibit life-satisfaction, health, and healing. On the other hand, it is easy to overlook what "miscommunication" may positively *contribute* to ongoing interaction and social relationships. The study of language and communication processes should not avoid orienting to issues of miscommunication, but must do so far more consciously and systematically than in the past.

Therefore, this book assembles a comprehensive series of invited reviews of key research areas which have in the past made at least implicit contact with such issues as misunderstanding, misattribution, social inequality, conflict, and nonsuccess. Each chapter stands in its own right as an integrative overview of research in a defined social context—highlighting particular social groups, social situations of talk and communicative modes. But authors have in each case turned these literatures in on themselves. The 14 chapters therefore give up-to-date résumés of applied research in many of the key social contexts studied by contemporary communication science, sociolinguistics, discourse analysis, and social psychology, although reassessing them, for the first time, in terms of miscommunication rather than communication, of problematicality rather than success. Each chapter establishes what the "mis" in miscommunication appropriately designates for its own research area, and what range of phenomena and processes (cognitive, discursive, and societal) is implicated in communicative "deficiency" or "problems." Miscommunication is in some cases applied as a *moral* judgment on the uses and abuses of language and communication. In others, it designates primarily communication *mishaps,* or *mismatches* of mental states, deviations from communicative *norms,* or the consequences of low levels of communicative *competence* in specific domains. Others demonstrate that miscommunication, alternatively, is a status quo of interaction, and even the means by which some *desirable* ends are communicatively reached.

This array of approaches, necessarily from an array of disciplines, reflects radically different perspectives on linguistic, discursive, and communication activities. Some authors address local concerns with the encoding and decoding of the propositional and affective meanings of utterances; others are more concerned with the contextualization of talk, in social relationships, in particular intergroup or institutional settings. Correspondingly, we have to see miscommunication relating to several different levels and dimensions of interaction. In what follows, therefore, we highlight some recurring themes and insights that arise in the chapters, leading us to propose an integrative model of approaches to "miscommunication."

Referential/Affective Miscommunication

Many authors show how miscommunication can and regularly does surface in the ideational/informational and affective dimensions of language. At this level, we can recognize hearer-based *misunderstandings* (as outlined by Milroy, 1984) and speaker-based *mispresentations/misrepresentations* of meanings (see Bell's useful review of terminology in this volume[1]). In media contexts, for example, not least because of the many stages involved in the formulation of many media messages, supposedly factual information is liable to be miscast and misinterpreted in countless ways. Bell demonstrates these processes in the reporting of the climate change issue in New Zealand radio news broadcasts. Somewhat similarly, Aronsson opens her review of miscommunication processes in legal discourse with the observation that spoken and written representations of content are not entirely compatible. In courtroom discourse, and in the official recording of legal happenings, this incompatibility predisposes several points at which the "recycling" of legal evidence involves significant modifications of source meanings. One category of problematic outcomes is misquoting, for example in response to the pressure to construct coherent courtroom narratives from disjointed pieces of evidence. Translating across languages emerges as another source of misrepresentations of original content or emphasis in Aronsson's account, and again in

Gass and Varonis's discussion of semantic mismatches of various sorts in native/non-native speaker discourse.

These approaches demonstrate that some semantic "slippage" is common in the management of meaning transfer, and in fact there are many reasons to suppose that this is *inevitably* the case. If we acknowledge that speaking occurs (a) under real-time processing constraints and (b) within the lexical and syntactic confines of particular linguistic codes, we must doubt that there are such entities as pure, unsullied, and perfect semantic representations. In the ethnomethodological tradition, language use, the making of meaning and its reconstruction, has been viewed as inherently problematic, strategic, and effortful. Garfinkel's (1967) perspective on talk as "accomplishment" acknowledges the probability of communicative inadequacy and incompleteness. Discourse theory (van Dijk, 1987) similarly asserts that utterances are intrinsically *indeterminate.* Because meaning resides in the interaction of linguistic form and social context, exchanges of meanings operate under inherent constraints and communicative acts are creative in compensating for the inexplicitness and indirectness of speech acts and texts. Aronsson exemplifies precisely these qualities of discourse in the courtroom, where for example a witness's silence is open to being interpreted as either embarrassment or evasiveness, depending on the presuppositions and goals of listening participants (e.g., defense and prosecution counsels).

Communicative Competence Across Cultures

Reports of "things going wrong" communicatively often relate to cross-cultural encounters, and their consequences can be devastating. Mismatches may be found in the ways different communities assign meaning to linguistic forms—or for that matter to silence. Even cultural *beliefs* about the functions of talk and silence can be a major source of communication difficulties (Giles, Coupland, & Wiemann, in press; Wiemann, Aiu, & Busch, 1988; Wiemann, Chen, & Giles, 1986). Saville-Troike (1985) gives the following example of a period of military tension between Egypt and Greece:

> Egyptian pilots radioed their intention to land at an airbase on Cyprus and the Greek traffic controllers reportedly responded with silence. The Greeks intended thereby to indicate *refusal* of permission to land, but the Egyptians interpreted silence as *assent.* The result of the misunderstanding in this case was the loss of a number of lives when Greeks fired on the planes as they approached the runway. (p. 11)

The *pragmatic* implementation of interaction across cultures is an arena where we might predict recurring miscommunicative sequences, though hopefully more benign than in the above instance. Gumperz (1982a, 1982b) has pioneered the study of miscommunicative consequences stemming from varying cultural norms for language use, interaction, and conversational inferencing (see Gass & Varonis). Aronsson also gives instances of first-language-users' patterns of inference from second-language speakers during courtroom testimony. In a similar vein, Banks, Gudykunst, Ge, and Baker show how members of "individualistic" cultures may attribute the group-centered orientations and acts of "collectivist" culture-group members as hostility.

Analyses of miscommunication in intercultural research are concerned with degrees of communicative competence (in the sense of appropriate social skill, rather than as the achievement of competent relationships; Wiemann & Kelly, 1981) and the consequences of either lower levels of competence or different competencies. Communication competence is, of course, a constraint on communicative adequacy, whether to do with very minor considerations of fluency (e.g., slips of the tongue) or levels of syntactic and pragmatic proficiency (e.g., in a second language). On the other hand, it is clearly wrong to associate cross-cultural interaction with inevitable "communication breakdown" (in Milroy's [1984] sense). In cross-cultural and cross-code settings, for example, it may be that communicative problems that are analyzable linguistically may be deemed unimportant because (a) they are often easily identified and remediated; (b) the deficiencies are attributable to language or language-knowledge itself (rather than to grosser incompetence or malevolent intent); and because (c) language differences may in turn be attributed to "cultural difference." Also, (d) participants may have lower initial expectations of cross-cultural interaction, with the consequence that talk itself may be restricted to particular topics or modes that are mutually selected to be manageable (cf. Taylor & Simard, 1975). That is, when we take miscommunication to cover more territory than simply inaccuracies of meaning transfer, the ultimate degree of problematicality may actually on occasions be tempered interculturally. At the same time, this is not to underestimate the recurring, genuine difficulties that participants in intercultural contexts experience and often *fail* to attribute in the ways we suggest above.

Deceptively Adequate Communication

Correspondingly, the absence of superficial problems of meaning exchange is no indication of the absence of miscommunication at deeper levels. Talk can be deceptively adequate and because of this, insidiously problematic. For some theorists, language is intrinsically fickle, even deceitful. In his discussion of "pseudo-communication" (see Henley & Kramarae), Habermas (1970) suggests that the very sharing of a common language code is itself deceptive, since it falsely suggests a common ground and a "naturalness" of communication that binds communicators to their actual misalignments. Henley and Kramarae, in fact, challenge the *two cultures* approach to language and gender precisely because it appears to explain away the power-laden structure of cross-gender communication as "mere" and perhaps "natural" communicative difference.

In fact, it is rarely possible to operationalize miscommunication purely at the propositional level, except perhaps in circumstances such as the person-machine communication contexts reviewed by Reilly, in which relationships and affect are not a primary issue. Bell's study raises the intriguing issue of which criteria are most apt for judging the presence/absence of media mispresentation of news. Asking the initial providers of factual information, the scientists in Bell's study, to evaluate the extent and nature of inaccuracies in the way the information came to be reported, does provide valuable insights. But it also highlights the gulf between scientific and journalistic perspectives on "truth" and the value of information. The miscommunication of science in the media (and nonfactual reporting is only evidently miscommunicative from the scientists' point of view) appears to be founded in the competing goals and assumptions of two quite different social institutions, over and above the specific processes of mispresenting, misunderstanding, and misremembering scientific facts. Likewise, Aronsson concludes that legal interrogations are not merely bureaucratic procedures for extracting "facts" but also societal means for teaching moral lessons.

Anti-Idealism: A Relativist Perspective

West and Frankel, along with others in the collection, remind us of the risks of idealizing communication processes. For example, high levels of comprehension are not to be equated with communicative success; *good* need not equal *clear.* Studies of communication in medical settings reviewed by West and Frankel have shown that patients sometimes actually prefer to be addressed by doctors who use *less* easily interpretable medical jargon. In organizations, too, ambiguity carries multiple potential benefits (Redding, 1972). What appears miscommunicative at one level is either overridden or traded for some other functional outcomes. "Openness" and "sharing" ideologies of effective communication similarly appear naively idealistic because many communication settings require tolerance of differences and stable conditions of concealment. It is for these reasons that Eisenberg and Phillips favor a definition of miscommunication in terms of balance—between individual creativity and coordination/control. Brown and Rogers argue that successful relationships demand neither harmony nor discord, but rather the resources to manage *both* polarities. From this perspective, "miscommunicative" sequences in relationships are not in themselves failures but an intrinsic part of the cycle of creating a "working consensus."

A *relativist* conceptualization of communicative failure or inadequacy is therefore appropriate. In Eisenberg and Phillips's review of approaches to miscommunication in organizational settings, in addition to miscommunication as a failure to be understood (that is propositional miscommunication, as discussed earlier), they address three further general definitions: failure to achieve one's communicative goals; failure to be authentic, honest, and disclosive; and failure to establish an open dialogue. Each approach is associated with unique criteria for "effectiveness" and builds on its own assumptions of what constitutes communication. The apparently anomalous proposition that miscommunication can in fact promote desirable outcomes surfaces at several points in this book. Referential miscommunicative sequences are frequently repaired, and the repair-mechanisms have the potential to elaborate in productive ways upon shared meanings and to build on the base of earlier failed attempts. In language-learning contexts (Gass & Varonis), negative responses to learners' linguistic attempts can feed back valuable, perhaps essential, metalinguistic information into the learning process (see also Giles & Byrne, 1982). Ochs focuses on misunderstandings involving children, and likewise orients as much to the positive socializing potential of these events as to their local status as problems. For Ochs, misunderstandings are culturally-determined structuring sequences during the socialization of children, rather than points where the communicative order "breaks down."

In support of relativism, many contributors stress the inadequacy of *sender-receiver* or *conduit* models of communication. McTear and King invoke Sperber and Wilson's (1985) "inferential model" of communication, according to which miscommunication is a norm, not an aberration. Brown and Rogers offer an extended critique of the ideology that sustains conduit models. They argue that support for the "ideology of intimacy" is "a function of the practice of research itself," and perhaps predominantly a white, middle-class, Western bias. Yet this ideology has inspired a whole tradition of research on self-disclosure premised on the assumption that high levels of disclosure indicate healthy and satisfying relationships.

Similarly, Brown and Rogers argue that the uncertainty reduction literature has construed uncertainty as a miscommunicative when, for them, uncertainty in fact encapsulates many of the most vitalizing forces in relationships to do with excitement and change. Predefinitions of what in fact is "miscommunicative" about relationships and/or social interaction have in these ways proved to be a significant constraint on social scientific inquiry.

The Management of "Problems" in Conversation

The notion of communication breakdown appears to build directly on the assumption of communication as a linear flow of information, and for that reason often does not do justice to the complex, even dialectical processes through which troubles or dissatisfactions are sequenced and come to be recognized in talk. Several chapters address the issue of how language is used to define, to recount, and to manage problems. Hopper and Drummond give a conversation analytic account of how misunderstandings come to be recognized as such, often retrospectively, in on-going discourse, and how they are then acted upon, repaired, or consolidated. Similarly, Gass and Varonis trace distinct routes through misunderstanding sequences in second-language-use contexts, and consider the role such sequences play in sometimes obstructing as well as generally facilitating the language learning process. Ochs's review shows how very different cultural groups conventionally manage misunderstandings through a near-universal "discourse structure of misunderstandings," but in ways that contribute to the reproduction of particular cultural norms and local theories of how talk should be enacted. Ultimately, "what it means to be a child," across cultures, is in part determined by strategic preferences in the management of sequences of misunderstanding.

These studies can usefully cross-refer to Jefferson's work on the conversational management of troubles-telling (e.g., 1984, 1988); that is where troublesome circumstances become thematized as topics of talk and therefore as self-disclosures. Jefferson (1988) develops a *template ordering* according to which such sequences tend to develop sequentially in her (telephone-call) data. She observes that it is only through interactional work by the troubles-teller and the troubles-recipient that "troubles" do (or do not) come to be recast as "problems" (see also Maynard, 1988). Related to this, Coupland, Nussbaum, and Coupland review discourse analytic studies of elderly "painful self-disclosure." But from this perspective, talk is not only the means by which intimate troubles are disclosed as conversational "content," but also the means by which younger and older people reproduce their attitudes to aging and perpetuate patterns of cross-generation (mis)alignment. In several chapters, then, we begin to see the role of miscommunication in the reproducing of cultural beliefs, and to visualize systematic connections across levels of analysis—patterns in the local management of interaction feeding problematic social processes at "deeper" levels.

Morality, Intentions, and Prejudice

It is the *moral* dimension of miscommunication, concern with the proper treatment of individuals and groups, that is uppermost in many of the contributions to the book. Many chapters show how it is necessary to dislocate problematicality not only from purely informational concerns but also from the immediate context of interaction in the analysis of rights and obligations. Here, the question of intentionality in the definition of "miscommunication" becomes a complex one. As Banks et al. point out, instances of deliberate deception do not automatically qualify as miscommunicative, at least by the criteria of goal fulfillment and "effectiveness." In courtroom discourse (Aronsson), the use of subtly leading questions, such as predisposing witnesses' testimony through particular framings of questions, is scarcely miscommunicative from the counsel's viewpoint, although the manipulation of linguistic resources to influence testimony is possibly censurable on ethical grounds.

Where disenfranchised social groups are involved, attitudinal factors are repeatedly shown to threaten the moral acceptability of communication practices (Hewstone & Giles, 1986). Coleman and DePaulo's chapter is a careful review of how negative attitudes, stigma, and stereotyping can influence interactions between able-bodied and disabled people. Even uncertainty or curiosity on the part of the able-bodied conversation partner can generate interactional imbalance, for example in the form of reticence and inhibited communicative style, or a falsely ingratiating manner. In their various ways, these behavioral modifications can trigger discomfort, distrust, or embarrassment, and lead to further uncertainty. Disabled people's anticipations of such miscommunicative cycles can impose their own limitations, possibly leading them to misattribute gestures of friendliness as pity (cf. Markova, 1990). In clinical consultations, McTear and King likewise argue that miscommunication needs to be characterized as socially cognitive in essence—problems of alignment resulting from schemes, inferences, and attributions—rather than as a direct consequence of some linguistic or communicative dimension of impairment in the patient's competence.

Social Structure

For several authors in the collection, miscommunication is therefore ultimately grounded in social organization itself. Many dimensions of problems are associated with interaction in institutional settings (cf. Fisher & Todd, 1986) and authors focus on the communicative constraints institutions impose. Aronsson considers how the very nature of courtroom testimony is problematic because it involves "time-traveling" and complexities of referencing that we can assume will be difficult for first- as well as second-language speakers (Aiu, 1990). The notion of "social frames" (as developed in the work of Cicourel [1968] and Goffman [1974]) is appealed to at many points. For example, in the courtroom, talk can be located within a treatment frame or a punishment frame, and outcomes for particular groups of suspects (e.g., black versus white youths) can be predicted on this basis. Blacks may be systematically "misunderstood" because the legal machinery brought to bear considers their cases *ab initio* in a punishment frame. The bureaucracy of legal procedures generally, for black and white alike, can be bewildering, intimidating, and stressful.

In the gender context, Henley and Kramarae argue that miscommunication is the set of power-configuring processes that generate assumptions of what is normative (for them, men's talk), and permeate orientations to men's and women's language use, and even social science investigation itself. Our expectations of gender behaviors, and our inferences regarding them, are just as much constrained by these forces as the forms that language takes. Miscommunication can thus be said to be "founded in and . . . expressive of . . . inequality." The analysis Henley and Kramarae offer is a radical one, not least because for them the claim that miscommunication is a linguistically- or interactionally-located process is itself a subterfuge—a strategy of deflection from the social inequalities where real discrimination resides.

An Integrative Model

One important contribution that this volume therefore makes is in deconstructing conventional assumptions about communicative adequacy and in pointing out that "miscommunication" is a deceptively familiar misnomer for what is in fact a family of normal as often as exceptional communicative processes and strategies. In doing this, it starts afresh by exploring the contexts in which and the means by which interactional sequences come to be adjudged "miscommunicative," and then the sometimes positive social functions that these sequences in fact fulfill. Taken together, the chapters collected here suggest to us a structural, layered organization of perspectives on miscommunication (see Figure 1.1). A model is presented here to serve as a reference point for the reading of the chapters that follow. The organization it suggests is of course not fully and explicitly represented in each individual chapter, although we believe the model does succeed in characterizing the general groupings of analytic goals and assumptions in the book as a whole. Within this model, progressively deeper analyses speculatively reflect problems which carry increasing "weightiness" and social significance. Levels are also distinguished on the basis of how aware participants (in contrast to researchers) are likely to be of the existence of some category of problem. Therefore, the model primarily summarizes research orientations, and the assumptions researchers have made about where miscommunication resides and what its implications are for participants in social settings. The six levels of analysis that we identify also make very different assumptions about what is possible by way of "repair," and what forms repair could or should take.

At *Level I,* miscommunication is taken to be pervasive, inherently constituted in the nature of symbolic meaning-exchange. Though the term "miscommunication" would not normally be invoked at this level of analysis, it can be demonstrated (see our earlier discussion of Referential/Affective Miscommunication) that routine discourse is intrinsically constrained through (a) limited code and channel capacities; (b) the interplay between linguistic meaning and context; and hence (c) the need for cognitive heuristics in both encoding and decoding. In this vein, Hermann (1983) has discussed the *pars pro toto* principle, whereby speakers of necessity have to constrain their choices of words hopefully to trigger the larger "picture" of meanings they are attempting to "paint" lexically and grammatically for listeners. The intrinsic imperfection of communicative interchange and the inherent ambiguity and incompleteness of messages is recognized, although these constraints (because of their pervasiveness) will not typically be construed as problems, and so repair is not a relevant concern. In other words, that fallibility of human thought and action is necessarily manifest in interaction as miscommunication (see McTear's notion of "radical subjectivities"), analogous to the recognition that visual illusions are not aberrant distortions separable from the study of so-called normal vision. Rather, they are part and parcel of the phenomena and processes of everyday sight. The potential for ill-formed input because of the failure of one's "model" of a partner's repertoire (as Reilly discusses it) is enormously high. In fact Reilly's analysis of person-machine interaction provides a stringent set of criteria for assessing human communication at its most basic.

Level	Characteristics attributed to "miscommunication"	Problem status	Awareness level	Repairability
I	Discourse and meaning-transfer are inherently flawed	Unrecognized	Participants are unaware	Not relevant
II	Strategic compromise; minor misunderstandings or misreadings are routine disruptions to be expected	Possibly, not necessarily recognized	Low for participants; easily identified at local level by researchers	Relevant at local level only
III	Presumed personal deficiencies	Problems attributed to individual lack of skill or ill will (or both)	Moderate for participants; directed toward other (or sometimes self)	Deficient people can be "fixed" (e.g., by skills training)
IV	Goal-referenced; control, affiliation, identity and instrumentality in normal interactions	Problems recognised as failure in conversational goal-attainment	High; participants may be fully aware of strategic implications of behavior	Repair is an on-going aspect of everyday inter-action with relationship implications
V	Group/cultural differences in linguistic/ communication norms, predisposing mis-alignments or mis-understandings	Problems mapped onto social identities and group-memberships	Moderate; group identities taken for granted and differences seen as natural reflections of groups' statuses	Acculturation or outgroup accommodation; socio-cultural learning
VI	Ideological framings of talk; socio-stuctural power imbalances	Participants perceive only*status quo*	Participants typically unaware; researchers hyper-aware, galvanized by their own ideology	Only through critical analysis and resulting social change

Figure 1.1 Integrative Model of Levels of Analysis of "Miscommunication"

At *Level II,* participants may show some low-level awareness of the imperfection and effortfulness of interaction, which will be recognized to involve both management and compromise, although miscommunicative messages are not analyzed as strategic here. The primary goals of interactants are not the creation of perfect performances, but rather performing so as to avoid undue unclarity, unpleasantness, threat, and confrontation. Equivocations, disqualifications (Bavelas, 1983), small deceptions, minor misunderstandings, interrupted turns at talk, and slips of the tongue are not at all uncommon. The "let it pass" rule (Ragan & Hopper, 1984) is observed as often as not. The term "miscommunication" has lay currency at this level to designate some trivial communicative annoyance or misdemeanor.

The option to repair a deficiency of any of these sorts is always available, although repair itself needs to be managed through conversational action (Drummond & Hopper). Attempts at repair may, in fact, be seen as signs of goodwill or concern, though they also risk foregrounding communicative inadequacy and hence generating problems of their own.

At *Level III,* miscommunication takes on implications of personal inadequacy and therefore, perhaps, blame. Whether poor communication skills, unwillingness to communicate, bad temper, personality problems, or some other individual difference is assumed, these attributes typically lead to down-graded evaluations of misperforming participants. The behavior itself is seen as non-normal according to some implicit standard of adequacy or as behavior that easily leads to misperceptions of content and/or intent by interlocutors. The assumption is that these problematic people can be "fixed," that some form of training, education, or coercion can get them to perform appropriately on subsequent occasions. Much communication, applied linguistics, and other social scientific research has operated with concerns about miscommunication at this level. For example, the entire social skills training and research effort (e.g., Argyle, 1981) is located at this level, as is much work on communicative competence (see above), communication apprehension (cf. Daly & McCrosky, 1984), and the like.

Level IV analyses reveal the *strategic* value of commonplace activities thought to be miscommunicative at previous levels and frequently relate to goal management in everyday interaction. Communicative adequacy is defined as degrees of goal achievement in particular interpersonal contexts. Our everyday communication behavior is much too frequently construed as Level II or III miscommunication for it to be seen constructively as inconsequential or as merely deviant. In fact it is usually only deviant from some sort of etiquette-book type ideal, which is seldom achieved without great effort (Wiemann & Bradac, 1989)—and then it is often devalued because it is *too* perfect (see Goffman's [1961] essay on role distance). Again, as at Level II, interactants are less concerned with creating a perfect performance, than with performing in such a way so as to avoid communicational unpleasantness—confrontations over possible deceptions, hurt feelings, admissions that one doesn't understand or is in some other way deficient, and the like. The distinguishing feature between Levels II and IV is that at Level IV strategic use of communication enters into the analysis. At this level, the misunderstandings and misreadings of everyday conversation experienced at Level II come into full consciousness for participants. Interactionally, priority is given to cooperation between participants in creating and sustaining a working consensus in which identity and relational goals (cf. Tracy & Coupland, 1990) can be met. Conversation is construed as a matter of dialectical choices among preferred and dispreferred alternatives (see Sacks, 1987). Lies are often white here; friends protect each other's positive and negative faces (Brown & Levinson, 1978).

Starting from the observation that interaction is designed around *multiple* simultaneous goals (Tracy, 1991; Tracy & Coupland, 1990), miscommunication at this level will reflect negotiation of conversational and relational control (*relational goals*), the maintenance of preferred personas and their modification (*identity goals*), and the achievement of specific task-related outcomes (*instrumental goals*). Although participants may not always explicitly recognize and formulate goals at each of these levels, communication is subject to continual monitoring for the success or failure of goals of at least these three general types, and "miscommunication" appears to be an appropriate label for sequences that fail to achieve desired social outcomes in some salient respect. Certainly, repair will be recognized to be possible, through repeated or modified attempts to achieve goals in the same or a later interaction or through the negotiation of a new relational definition (thereby reframing the communication).

At *Level V,* miscommunication resides in group and cultural phenomena, and may be accountable in terms of code-based or other cultural differences in behaviors, beliefs, or construals. Culture is seen as having communicative consequences for participants. The salient dimensions of contexts in which interaction becomes miscommunicative are assumed to be status, one's (and one's group's) relationship to a power base or structure, and affiliation (how well one and one's group is liked). At this level, identity is defined in social rather than personal terms (Tajfel & Turner, 1979). Social group membership may be defined as ingroup/outgroup membership, giving rise to observable communication difficulties based on lack of understanding of differences, suspicion or fear of the outgroup, or threatened social identity. But from this cultural perspective, miscommunication can also be considered to offer a dimension for the positive socialization and acculturation of speakers, be they children (Ochs), linguistic minorities (Kim, 1988), immigrants being enculturated (Kim, 1986) or conversationalists reaching new depths of conversational understanding (Drummond & Hopper). What is adjudged miscommunication at this level is again amenable to repair, though by increased understanding of social processes rather than by improving skills, by learning rather than training.

At the deepest level of conceptualizing, *Level VI,* "miscommunication" is an ideological analysis. Here interaction is seen as reinforcing or even constituting a societal value system and its associated social identities (Henley & Kramarae; Coupland, Nussbaum, & Coupland). What defines interaction sequences as "miscommunication" communicatively and sociolinguistically is that they implicitly or explicitly disadvantage people or, more likely, groups, while proposing themselves as normal, desirable, and even morally correct (Ng, 1990). The ideological foundations of communication are typically invisible to participants. Yet the level of consciousness of the analysis is very high; hence, research is framed as meta-analytic or critical. There are no obvious avenues along which repair can take place, other than in and through the critique offered in the analysis itself (Billig et al., 1990) and whatever political or socio-structural reorientation it may trigger.

As we have sketched it here, the model primarily serves a heuristic function; we do not wish to defend its levels in anything like absolute terms. We suggest it may provide a preliminary template against which researchers and readers of this volume may locate their own perspectives on miscommunication, and consider others'. It is the lack of just this sort of sharing and cross-fertilization of approaches that has to date impaired our appreciation of the many faces of miscommunication.

The model certainly allows us to suggest, as the following chapters will clearly show, that the concept of miscommunication resists any simple definition. Rather, it refers to a highly diverse set of characteristics of interaction, its origins, contexts, and outcomes. The hierarchical organization of the model we have proposed is intended to reflect the variety of different perspectives available to analysts of miscommunication, and to imply that *the same* communicative acts are open to interpretation in highly *diverse* ways. For example, forms of talk being attributed to racism, ageism, sexism, and so on, suggest an analysis at Level V. But a commentator less alert to the sociocultural history and implications of, for example, racism might propose a Level III analysis of the offending sequence, glossing it as an off-hand defamatory remark that showed a lack of communicative sophistication or awareness—the remark of a fool or a bigot. A Level II interpretation might even be feasible, in terms of "normal mis-speaking," a momentary lapse of the sort to which communicators "are after all prone." Moving to a deeper level of analysis, others would argue that racism is "more than" a Level V issue, and that cultural difference alone is inadequate to explain the institutionalization of prejudice and oppression (this is the basis of Henley & Kramarae's argument in the gender context).

The levels approach shows how the goals of academic inquiry itself predispose characteristic lines of interpretation. This is a salutary observation for communication science, social psychological, discourse analytic, and sociolinguistic research, suggesting that particular traditions and disciplines may themselves contribute a dimension of miscommunication. There are certainly different levels of consciousness to be found in participants' perspectives on miscommunication, too. A comment or an episode may well only be miscommunication for an outgroup audience or from one participant's viewpoint. This in turn suggests that a further important condition of miscommunication is where participants in talk do not share a perception of what precisely *is* miscommunicative about their interaction or their relationship.

The model has also highlighted the need to extend the conversational analytic notion of repair well beyond its now-conventional domain (see Drummond & Hopper). Where repair is relevant (as it is at all but our first level of miscommunication), it designates widely varying processes: on the one hand, clarification and expansion processes local to and endemic within talk itself; at the other extreme, sociocultural change, social policy, and perhaps legislation. In some cases, "consciousness raising" about the nature of miscommunication will itself enact repair and an interactant becomes a player in the (potentially) corrective process. In others, to the extent that repair has been achieved, participants have reached a new definition of a situation, a relationship or a group and participants have been resocialized. To the extent that repair opportunities are ignored, extant social identities are potentially reinforced. But we also need to reconsider the apparently clear division between problems and repair, because we have seen how repair may on occasions be ingrained in "normal" interactional practice, and how repair may itself on occasions introduce further dimensions of problematicality.

For the moment, however, systematic explorations of communication repair processes are premature, before miscommunication across contexts and levels has been adequately documented. And it is here that the primary aim of the present volume lies. We hope that the review of processes we have considered and attempted to model in this chapter may stimulate further empirical studies and integrative theoretical efforts. But already, in their very diversity, the chapters in this book exhibit a rich appreciation of the several ways in which miscommunication can profitably be understood by interactants and researchers alike. We feel sure that they constitute a sound basis for the language and communication sciences to sharpen their evaluative focus on language and communication processes.

Note

1. Undated author-citations in this chapter refer to contributions to the present volume.

2

Gender, Power, and Miscommunication

Nancy M. Henley
Cheris Kramarae

Females and males seem to have frequent problems of miscommunication, most notably in adult heterosexual interaction. Many magazines and books, in fact, offer to teach one sex,[1] usually women, how to interpret the other. Women's reactions to men's "street talk" is another example that what is ostensibly meant by one sex may not be what is understood by the other (Gardner, 1980). An extreme form of miscommunication is sometimes said to occur in cases of date, acquaintance, and marital rape, when a frequently offered explanation is that a male has interpreted a female's "no" as part of sexual play. Problematic heterosexual communication takes place not only in verbal, but in nonverbal interaction also, as facial expressions, gestures, and other bodily expressions may be intended as one kind of signal but received as another.

Nonsexual interaction also provides the circumstances of miscommunication. Patterns of sex difference in speech interaction may lead to difficulties in communication, as evidenced in such behaviors as interruption,

AUTHORS' NOTE: A much-condensed version of this chapter was presented at the annual meeting of the National Women's Studies Association, June 1988, in Minneapolis, Minnesota. The authors wish to thank Barrie Thorne, Candace West, Vickie Mays, and Gail Wyatt for their helpful suggestions and contributions to their thinking. Nancy Henley wishes to thank members of the Southern California Language and Gender Interest Group; members of the University of California, Santa Cruz 1987-1988 Language and Gender Organized Research Activity; members of her spring 1988 graduate seminar on "Theories and Controversies in Gender and Communication"; audiences at the University of Southern California Annenberg School of Communication and Bard College; and research assistants Jennifer Murphy and Jennifer Stadler, for their discussions and sharing of ideas on these topics. Cheris Kramarae wishes to thank members of her Women and Language class at the University of Illinois and her class on Language, Gender and Social Control at the University of Oregon for their thoughtful suggestions and stimulation.

overlap, and "back-channeling," or in hedging and apologizing. There are also sex-related differences in lexical usage which may lead to miscommunication: for example, the different meanings in the terms used by women and men to evaluate, or the different understandings they may have of masculine forms used generically (e.g., *mankind*). Space limitations prevent us from offering a complete summary of these differences; however, examples appear throughout the chapter, along with their miscommunicative consequences. For those who wish further background on this topic, summaries and reviews of sex differences in language and communication are widely available, for example in Key (1975), Kramarae (1981), McConnell-Ginet, Borker, and Furman (1980), Thorne and Henley (1975), Thorne, Kramarae, and Henley (1983) and others. All miscommunication does not necessarily lead to immediate disruption and repair of the conversation: It may be unnoted or unacknowledged at the time by the interactants, only to come up, or be discovered, later when the different understandings lead to unexpected different outcomes, such as one voicing support and the other nonsupport for a proposal, or dressing up versus dressing down for a social event.

Female-male miscommunication has been interpreted in a number of ways, most notably as an innocent by-product of different socialization patterns and different gender cultures, occurring in interaction between speakers who are ostensibly social equals (Maltz & Borker, 1982). We wish to examine cross-sex miscommunication and the explanations surrounding it with special attention to the context of sexual inequality. This context creates the gender-polarized conditions that give different interpretations and different evaluations of women's and men's language usage; suggest that men and women have distinctive languages which demand interpretation to one another, and tend to create denial and reinterpretation of women's negations in the sexual realm. It is our belief that, viewed in the context of male power and female subordination, the explanation that miscommunication is the unfortunate but innocent by-product of cultural difference collapses.

This pattern of polarization, differential evaluation, denial, and reinterpretation is the same as that between different ethnic, racial, religious, age, and class groups (for example), when there is social inequality based on these differences: although cultural differences between groups are undeniable and may lead undeniably to miscommunication, that is not the end of the story. Hierarchies determine whose version of the communication situation will prevail; whose speech style will be seen as normal; who will be required to learn the communication style, and interpret the meaning, of the other; whose language style will be seen as deviant, irrational, and inferior; and who will be required to imitate the other's style in order to fit into the society. Yet the situation of sex difference is not totally parallel: sex status intercuts and sometimes contrasts with other statuses; and no other two social groups are so closely interwoven as men and women.

Theories of Female/Male Miscommunication

Explanatory theories of cross-sex miscommunication are based on expositions of gender differences in language usage, so it is to these we must first turn. The most influential theories have been *female deficit* theory and *two cultures* theory. We begin with them and present them in most detail. Then we look more briefly at other explanations that stress social power, psychological difference, language system-based problems, and cross-sex "pseudocommunication." We have found all of these explanations for miscommunication helpful and all of them limited. We next discuss some broad issues that must be addressed in an adequate theory of cross-sex miscommunication, and in the last section of the chapter propose an alternative theory, which we call a multi-determined social context approach.

Female Deficit

Despite women's supposed bilingualism in knowing both men's and women's language forms (Lakoff, 1973, 1975) and often-cited superior female language abilities (e.g., Garai & Scheinfeld, 1968; Maccoby & Jacklin, 1974), women's communication is often evaluated as handicapped, maladaptive, and needing remediation. To a notion of deviancy from a masculine norm are added assumptions and statements of the inferiority of "women's language." For example, the linguist Otto Jespersen (1922), in a widely cited book chapter, wrote that women have a less extensive vocabulary than men, have less complex sentence constructions, and speak with little prior thought and hence often leave their sentences incomplete (pp. 237-254).

Although more sympathetic to women than is Jespersen's chapter, Robin Lakoff's (1975) influential exploratory essay about the ways women's speech differs from men's still suggests that women are disadvantaged relative to men by a basically inferior, less forceful "women's language" which they learn through socialization. Lakoff emphasizes various female forms and styles conveying weakness, uncertainty, and unimportance.

Her analysis of women's language clearly identifies it as inferior to "neutral" or men's language, and as contributing to women's inferior status; for example she suggests that women who use "women's language" are "systematically denied access to power" (p. 7); she names the recognition of women as experts in making fine color distinctions linguistically "a sop," given in place of decision-making power (p. 9); and writes that women's lexicon and syntax are "peculiar" (p. 14). (Note that Lakoff's theory, besides being one of deficit, is also characterized as psychological; see that section below).

Earlier female deficit theories, like Jespersen's, seem to have been based in an unquestioned biological causation, women having naturally inferior reasoning capacity to that of men, for example, or having essential difference from men in interests, assertiveness, and so on. The more recent sociobiological theory (Tiger & Fox, 1971; Wilson, 1975) would attribute sex difference in speech to behaviors that display and exaggerate sex difference in order to help select superior mates, as a means to ensure survival of offspring.

Other recent deficit theories, such as Lakoff's, stress environmental rather than biological causation, either through women's socialization to speak "women's language" or through women's isolation from the cultural mainstream, leading to different life experiences from men's, and therefore deviant perceptions and values.

Consequences and Implications of Female Deficit Theory

Theories of female deficit, along with those of cultural difference (see below), have probably had the most consequence in our daily lives. A primary consequence of female deficit theory is the expansion of notions of male normativeness. By this we mean a view that sees female/male difference as female deviation from what is often called "the" norm, but is actually the male cultural form. The male normativeness is manifested in several ways.

1. There is a focus on female forms and female "difference." This is obvious in the many recent writings on language and gender that emphasize female speech, such as *Language and Woman's Place* (Lakoff, 1975), *The Way Women Write* (Hiatt, 1977), *Women's Language and Style* (Butturff & Epstein, 1978), and "How and Why are Women more Polite" (Brown, 1980). Although most writing about language and speech is tacitly based on men's actions, very little is written on men's language and speech forms per se, which should merit as much attention as female ones, as distinctive cultural forms. This focus on the female is found not only in recent writings, but has earlier origins in, for example, the chapter on "The Woman" in Jespersen's *Language: Its Nature, Development and Origin* (1922), and the early writings of anthropologists who observed in far-away cultures what they often called "women's languages" (e.g., Blood, 1962; Chamberlain, 1912). The focus on female difference of course emphasizes the underlying assumption that the female is a deviant (Schur, 1983) while the male is "normal" and speaks "the language." The ultimate conclusion of this view defines women as puzzling or unknowable, remaining for linguists "one of the mysteries of the universe" (Shuy, 1970, cited in Nichols, 1983).

2. There is pressure on women to use "men's" language. Lakoff takes for granted that women will want to use men's language, though she does not always call it that:

> most women who get as far as college learn to switch from women's to neutral language under appropriate situations (in class, talking to professors, at job interviews, and such) . . . if a girl knows that a professor will be receptive to comments that sound scholarly, objective, unemotional, she will of course be tempted to use neutral language in class or in conference. (1975, pp. 6-7)

In the late 1970s and early 1980s, the general problem with communication between women and men was presented as women's hesitancy in stating their interests and wishes. The basic solution presented by many "experts" was (especially in the U.S.) assertiveness training, which was to help women change their behavior and be more assertive (e.g., Baer, 1976; Butler, 1976). That is, both the blame and the potential solution were located within the woman experiencing trouble in making others understand her (Henley, 1979, 1980).

3. There is an expectation that females should (re-)interpret male expressions. Lakoff suggests that girls and women have to be bilingual, to speak both women's and men's languages. But there is no suggestion that boys or men have to be bilingual, even though she claims that young boys learn women's language as their first language, and have to unlearn it by around the age of 10 (Lakoff, 1975, pp. 6-7). Why are not men already bilingual, or why are they not too required to become bilingual?

Evaluation of Female Deficit Theory

This requirement of bilingualism, or bidialectalism, if it is true (we know of no empirical research directly on the question), would be more invidious than it might at first appear. We believe there is an implicit deficit theory underlying dominant U.S. culture, which requires (and teaches, through popular magazines) females, not males, to learn to read the silence, lack of emotional expression, or brutality of the other sex as not only other than, but more benign than, it appears. From a young girl's re-framing of a boy's insults and hits as signs that he likes her, to a woman's re-framing of her husband's battering as a perverse demonstration of caring, females are encouraged to use their greater knowledge of males' communication to interpret men's assaultive behavior, to make it in an almost magical way "not so" (Baughman, 1988).

Women, on the other hand, are not reinterpreted by men. They are in fact often characterized as uninterpretable and unfathomable by men. Yet many theorists and researchers have written about the ways that dominant groups of a social hierarchy (e.g., men) largely determine the dominant communication system of the society, and about the ways subordinate groups (e.g., women) are silenced and made inarticulate in the language (E. Ardener, 1975; S. Ardener, 1975; Kramarae, 1981). This *muted group* theory argues that women's voices are less heard than men's in part because they are trying to express women's experiences that are rarely given attention and they are trying to express them in a language system not designed for their interests and concerns; hence their language may at times seem unfathomable to men.

Although Jespersen's (1922) romp through examples of female deficit had many hearings in bibliographies, his statements and evidence are no longer given official credence. Nevertheless, the newer theories have had strong effect; a belief in women's "inferior talk" is undoubtedly still the basis for many stereotypes affecting women's lives. Lakoff's suggestions and recommendations have led to many written papers that treat her hypotheses as fact or as the most important communication factors to study; this legacy persists in advice books that caution women to, for example, avoid "weak, feminine" tag questions. These simplistic critiques too often ignore context and within-gender variation, and treat women's expressions as feeble deviations from men's stronger expressions.

We reject much in the theories of female deficit because of their biased evaluation of female and male speech styles, and we reject biologically based theories as ignoring the large and complex contributions of culture and psychology to speech differences. However, the point made by Lakoff that society differentially evaluates women's and men's speech is largely true and must be taken into account in any theory of difference and miscommunication.

Two Cultures

Daniel Maltz and Ruth Borker, in their influential 1982 paper "A Cultural Approach to Male-Female Miscommunication," apply Gumperz's (1982a) approach to the study of difficulties in cross-ethnic communication to those in cross-sex miscommunication. This was one of the first papers on sex-related differences and similarities to discuss systems of talk rather than collections of variables. Because of this, their work has served as a valuable basis for further discussion about relations between women's and men's speech.

Rejecting social power-based and psychological explanations of female/male difference (explained below), Maltz and Borker prefer to think of both cross-sex and cross-ethnic communication problems as examples of the larger phenomenon of cultural difference and miscommunication. They put forward what they consider a preferable alternative explanation, that American men and women come from different sociolinguistic subcultures which have different conceptions of friendly conversation, different rules for engaging in it, and different rules for interpreting it. Even when women and men are attempting to interact as equals, the cultural differences lead to miscommunication. Another proponent of this two-cultures view is Deborah Tannen (1987), who writes:

> Women and men have different past experiences . . . Boys and girls grow up in different worlds . . . And as adults they travel in different worlds, reinforcing patterns established in childhood. These cultural differences include different expectations about the role of talk in relationships and how it fulfills that role. (p. 125)
>
> When styles differ, misunderstandings are always rife (p. 127).

Maltz and Borker (1982) compare the situation in cross-sex communication with that in interethnic communication, in which communication problems are understood as personality clashes or interpreted through ethnic stereotypes. Gumperz's framework offers a better interpretation, they emphasize, because "it does not assume that problems are the result of bad faith, but rather sees them as the result of individuals wrongly interpreting cues according to their own rules" (p. 201). (Note that this is what Fishman's "Social power (b)" explanation, below, does too.)

Maltz and Borker see the sources of the different cultures to lie in the peer groups of middle childhood: The rules for friendly interaction and conversation are being learned at a time when peer groups are primarily of a single sex, and the two styles are quite different. The world of girls, they assert (based on their own experience and on published studies of child play), is one of cooperation and equality of power; but because of heavy emotional investment in pair friendships, girls must learn to read relationships and situations sensitively. The world of boys, on the other hand, is said to be hierarchical; dominance is primary, and words are used to attain and maintain it, also to gain and keep an audience and to assert identity. The adult extension of these group differences in speech situations is that women's speech is interactional: It engages the other and explicitly builds on the other's contributions, and there is a progressive development to the overall conversation; while men's speech is characterized by storytelling, arguing, and verbal posturing (verbal aggressiveness). They discuss six areas "in which men and women probably possess different conversational rules, so that miscommunication is likely to occur" (Maltz & Borker, 1982, pp. 212-213).

1. Minimal response. As a prime example of different rules based on gender subcultures leading to misinterpretation, they cite the finding of gender-differential use of minimal responses (Fishman, 1978/1983; Hirschman, 1973: West & Zimmerman, 1977; Zimmerman & West, 1975.) (A minimal response is something like "uh-huh" or "mm-hmm," given in response to another's talk.) Women's meaning by the positive minimal response (PMR) is said to be something like "continue, I'm listening," while men's is said to be something like "I agree, I follow you." These two different meanings of the expression and interpretation of PMRs can explain, Maltz and Borker claim, several of the sex-related differences and miscommunication findings: (a) women's more frequent use of PMRs than men's; (b) men's confusion when women give PMRs to their (men's) speech, then later are found not to agree; and (c) women's complaint that men are not listening enough when they (women) talk.

(For the other rule differences they cite [pp. 212-213], Maltz and Borker do not make direct links to research evidence. However, their reviews of boys' and girls', women's and men's conversational interaction patterns in the previous pages of their paper contain many references, and we include some pertinent ones in the following brief summaries.)

2. The meaning of questions. Women use questions for conversational maintenance; men tend to use them as requests for information (Fishman, 1978/1983; Hirschman, 1973).

3. The linking of one's utterance to the previous utterance. Women tend to make this link explicitly, but for men no such rule seems to exist, or they explicitly ignore it (Hirschman, 1973; Kalčik, 1975).

4. *The interpretation of verbal aggressiveness.* Women see verbal aggressiveness as personally directed and as negative. For men, it helps to organize conversational flow (Faris, 1966; Goodwin, 1980).

5. *Topic flow and shift.* In women's conversations, topics are developed and expanded, and topic shifts are gradual. But men tend to stay on a topic as narrowly defined, and then to make an abrupt topic shift (Hirschman, 1973; Kalčik, 1975).

6. *Problem sharing and advice giving.* Women tend to discuss and share their problems, to reassure one another and listen mutually. Men, however, interpret the introduction of a problem as a request for a solution, and they tend to act as experts and offer advice rather than sympathize or share their own problems (Kalčik, 1975; Maltz & Borker also cite anecdotal and informant information in their footnote 4, p. 216).

All of these differences which they claim in conversational rules are, according to Maltz and Borker, potential sources of misunderstanding between the sexes, as other sex-related differences in language usage may be.

Consequences and Implications of Two Cultures Theory

Although earlier "women's" problem with language was seen as nonassertiveness, more recently the basic problem has been named *miscommunication,* and the general solution advocated by many lay and professional researchers is to help everyone recognize that women and men have different cultures, different needs and experiences, which lead to different ways of understanding and relating to one another. Colette Bouchez (1987) summarizes the evidence from academic and popular media for these "different worlds." She writes that often men and women have "enormously different interpretations of some of the key emotional words," that adults in the same culture often speak "very different and often conflicting languages," and that some of the "latest psychological research" tells us that the "misguided signals" between the sexes "may in fact be the underlying problem in such serious contemporary issues as sexual harassment, some forms of job discrimination, and may also have an effect on the rising statistics of divorce and so-called 'date rape' " (p. 4).

One consequence of the cultural difference approach is this explanation of date and marital rape and other such forms of sexual aggression as extreme examples of miscommunication, in which males and females had different interpretations of their own and each others' behavior, and communication breakdown resulted. Sexual communication is an often difficult matter in western societies, complex in its layers of subtlety, indecision, game-playing, sex-specific prescription, and choices to understand or not understand. Muehlenhard and Hollabaugh (1988), though finding that over 60% of some 600 undergraduate women they questioned reported *never* saying "no" when they meant "yes," found 39% to report they had used token resistance at least once, primarily for practical reasons. To the extent that women communicate imprecisely the distinction between determined and token resistance, and/or men fail to understand the distinction, sexual miscommunication may result. Accuracy in encoding and decoding may be quite consequential here: as MacKinnon (1987) points out, men's understanding is part of the legal definition of rape. A man must both understand a woman does not want intercourse and force her to engage in it anyway, to be convicted of rape.

But is rape in such a circumstance truly a matter only of "missed" communication? No; in actuality, power tracks its dirty feet across this stage. Greater social power gives men the right to pay less attention to, or discount, women's protests, the right to be less adept at interpreting their communications than women are of men's, the right to believe women are inscrutable. Greater social power gives men the privilege of defining the situation—at the time, telling women that they "really wanted it," or later, in a court.

And greater social power gives men the ability to turn definitions of the situation into physical violation. If the problem really were cultural difference alone, would we have such scenarios? In purely cultural difference, the male's and the female's understanding of the situation would each prevail about equally. The outcome might be arguments in which either part's definition would prevail and the "losing" party would go home angry; or the couple might have sullen evenings of unexpressed expectations and disappointments; or when a man's definition of the situation won out, the woman would only be forced to agree that her interpretation of their interaction was wrong—but she would not be raped as a consequence.

Evaluation of Two Cultures Theory

We have presented two cultures theory in such detail because it is both prominent and seductive as an explanation for between-gender miscommunication (see, e.g., Aries, 1987; Tannen, 1987, 1990). For the same reasons, it is advisable to present a detailed critique of the theory. We note at the outset that authors before us have expressed dissatisfaction with this theory, though their criticisms have been brief (Coates, 1986, p. 154;

DeFranciso, 1989, pp. 185-186; Graddol & Swann, 1989, pp. 89-91; Thorne, 1986, p. 168; Treichler & Kramarae, 1983, p. 120; Whalen & Whalen, 1986, p. 48 ff.).

The first point to be made about the claim of cultural difference is that there is truth in it: Clearly there are differences in communication style between men and women, exacerbated by sex segregation in different situations, which surely are implicated in misunderstandings. As we have been among those cataloguing these differences, we would be among the last to deny them and their potential effect. Our point here is that cultural difference alone cannot adequately explain the full pattern of language difference and miscommunication; and that in fact such an explanation badly misrepresents these phenomena.

Reinterpreting differences—culture or power? We begin with the six female-male differences that Maltz and Borker cite as innocently underlying miscommunication, and argue that those differences may be interpreted in another light when the context of cultural *dominance* as well as that of cultural *difference* is taken into account.

1. Positive minimal response. First, Maltz and Borker's interpretation of positive minimal responses suggests that if, for example, women *did not* give frequent PMRs in listening to men, but instead used them only sparingly, as men do, that men would be satisfied and find women easy to understand in this regard. However, men respond to women's—and to other men's—PMRs as reinforcement—that is, they keep talking. PMRs are the basis of what is called *verbal reinforcement* (Verplanck, 1955); there is an extensive psychological literature showing that people tend to speak more, and more of any particular speech form, when reinforced with PMRs. (The question of sex-differential response to PMRs is subject to empirical test: When asked, would men say women who were giving customary PMRs were agreeing? What would be their response if women did not give PMRs?)

But beyond this, Maltz and Borker completely ignore the political use of minimal responses. Zimmerman and West (1975) found men to use *delayed* minimal response (leaving a silence before giving a minimal response) with women more than vice versa. Fishman (1978/1983) similarly reports that "male usages of the minimal response displayed lack of interest" (1983, p. 95). Such behavior can discourage interaction and lead to the failure of topics initiated by women to become joint topics of the conversation (Fishman, 1978/1983), or even extinguish a speaker's conversation (Zimmerman & West, 1975). This seemingly innocent cultural difference, then, has the effect of supporting male dominance of conversation.

2. *The meaning of questions.* Males' understanding of questions as requests for information rather than as conversational maintenance devices may alternatively be heard as taking to themselves the voice of authority.

3. *The linking of one's utterance to the previous utterance.* Men's not having, or ignoring, a rule that demands that their utterance link to and thus recognize another's contribution (Sacks, Schegloff, & Jefferson, 1974) may be seen as exercising a common prerogative of power. Those with lesser power do not have the option to ignore the other's rules, or common rules.

4. *The interpretation of verbal aggressiveness.* Men's overt use of aggressiveness against an interlocutor in organizing conversational flow may also be seen as a prerogative of power. In situations of inequality, the one of lesser power dare not show aggressiveness to the other, especially unilaterally.

5. *Topic flow and shift.* Men's tendency to make abrupt topic shifts, that is, to ignore basic conversational rules, like their tendency not to link to the previous utterance (even when on the same topic) may likewise be seen as a prerogative of power, the power to define and control a situation.

6. *Problem sharing and advice giving.* Men's tendency to take the mention of a problem as an opportunity to act as experts and offer advice rather than sympathize or share their own problems is, like the tendency to treat questions solely as requests for information, again the prerogative of authority.

In sum, the characteristics that Maltz and Borker cite for females' speech are the ones appropriate to "friendly conversation," while the ones cited for males' speech are not neutral but indicate very uncooperative, disruptive sorts of conversational interaction (e.g., see Sacks, Schegloff, & Jefferson, 1974). In addition, they tend to be self-centered, also consistent with the stance of the powerful. [For further evidence of men's greater conversational rule-violating behavior than women's (in political debate), see Edelsky & Adams, in press.]

If gender speech differences were *simply* cultural differences, there would be no pattern to them implicating dominance and power. In fact, Maltz and Borker remark that psychological differences or power differentials "may make some contribution" (p. 199). Indeed, two indications point to the *predominance* of power/dominance factors in female-male miscommunication:

a. First, as illustrated above, there is a clear pattern for language style associated with men to be that of power and dominance, and that associated with women to be that of powerlessness and submissiveness (see also, for example, Lakoff, 1973; Kramarae, Schulz, & O'Barr, 1984; Thorne & Henley, 1975).

b. Tannen (1982) states that in systematic study of couples, "certain types of communications were *particularly given to misinterpretation*—requests, excuses, explanation; in short, *verbalizations associated with getting one's way*" (p. 220; emphasis added). "Getting one's way" is a denatured term for "exercising power."

Thus the overall pattern of miscommunication is not random, but rather founded in, and we would add, expressive of, the inequality of women and men. If power differentials simply provided an overlay, as Maltz and Borker imply, they would not be the *predominant* context factor in miscommunication, but a minor one among many. Clearly, the place of power must be recognized in miscommunication problems between women and men, as it must between any two cultural groups differing in power.

Maltz and Borker's elaborate explanations of girls' and boys' worlds as the biasing factors in creating two cultures of friendly conversational speech seem to require the startling assumption that the gender-differentiated behaviors came first, alinguistically, and the speech came later, and was shaped to fit the behaviors. Rather, it stands to reason that the speech and behavior patterns developed together. This point is important because Maltz and Borker imply that they have settled the question of "why these features and not others" by the explanation of childhood single-sex groups. As the explanation only points to childhood gender cultures to explain the existence of particular forms, it cannot answer the question of why certain language features, as opposed to others, are associated with girls and women, or boys and men. The links to power and dominance made above, however, do give a rational explanation for the source of particular features.

Social Power

Two social power-based explanations that have been offered for differences in women's and men's speech in cross-sex conversation are cited by Maltz and Borker (1982):

Social power (a): This explanation states that men's conversational dominance parallels their social/political dominance, men's speech being a vehicle for male displays of power—"a power based in the larger social order but reinforced and expressed in face-to-face interaction with women" (Maltz & Borker, 1982, pp. 198-199). The chief proponent of this point of view is identified as sociologist Candace West (West, 1979; West & Zimmerman, 1977, 1987; Zimmerman & West, 1975).

Social power (b): According to this explanation, gender inequality enters conversation through the mechanism of gender role training, which serves to obscure the issue of power; the use of power by men is an unconscious consequence of gender role prescriptions. The identified proponent of this view is sociologist Pamela Fishman (1978/1983).

Evaluation of Social Power Theories

Arguments based on social power are crucial to an understanding of female/male communication and its problems—both social power (a) regarding dominance display correlating with sex hierarchy, and social power (b) regarding dominance differences in communication styles to which the genders are differently socialized. Contrary to Maltz and Borker's claim, it is the examination of dominance that tells why certain forms and not others are used by the different genders. Our evaluation of two cultures theory (above) explores the advantages of social power analysis in more detail.

Social power does not in itself tell the full story, however, if it ignores psychological difference and intercultural misunderstanding which arise from differential social power and differential socialization. A theory that integrates these different sources of gender-differentiated styles will offer fuller explanation and understanding of cross-gender miscommunication.

Psychological Difference

One psychological explanation, that of Lakoff (1973), also reviewed by Maltz and Borker, states that socialization to speak and act in feminine ways makes women "as unassertive and insecure as they have been made to sound" (Maltz & Borker, 1982, p. 199); the incompatibility of adulthood and femininity saps women's confidence and strength until their speech is not just designed to meet gender role requirements, but fits the actual personalities developed as a consequence of such requirements.

A rather different psychological theory is put forward by French structuralist/feminist psychoanalysts Luce Irigaray (1980) and Héléne Cixous (1976), who stress language as the medium that places humans in culture. These theorists argue the importance of women's different biology and sexual pleasure, distinctive sexual differences that create a different unconscious from that of men, and the potential source of new female discourses to resist conventional androcentric culture and language. These approaches focus on commonalities of psychosexual differences rather than on historical and material factors of women's lives. With this psychological approach, many of women's experiences are considered repressed or distorted when women are required to use the linguistic processes created by men in a phallocentric culture. Although the essentialist nature of these approaches have been frequently and usefully criticized, it should be noted that not only this, but most of the theoretical approaches available pay little attention to the issues of difference and dominance (e.g., in race, class, age, ethnicity, nationality) within the category called *women.*

Evaluation of Psychological Difference Theories

The psychological effects of socialization, sexuality, subordination, and societal constraints should not be ignored in any examination of sex differences in communication and cross-sex miscommunication. Psychological difference can at the least underlie contrasting meanings attached to the same utterance; at the most, if the French theorists are correct, women and men create different psyches altogether. However, as with previous explanations, a theory based solely on psychological difference is limited: Communicative interaction does not take place within a single psyche, but between individuals (with psyches) in social contexts. An important task for social scientists, including communication researchers and theorists, is the delineation of the interaction of the psychological and the societal.

Faulty Linguistic Systems

Other approaches as well as that of Irigaray (1980) and Cixous (1976) (described above) suggest that as long as the language systems we use are created and governed by men, women will not be able to speak themselves clearly—to men or women.

Ambiguous signals. Using an analysis that calls attention to our inherited linguistic systems, Deakins (1987) argues that English and other languages set the stage for ambiguity in that the same linguistic signs can be (and are) used to code both power and solidarity (see also Brown & Gilman, 1960; Henley, 1977). For example, a boss may intend to code for solidarity by saying "Good morning, Mary" and touching his secretary, but she can interpret it either as solidarity or power, especially if she is not likely to say "Good morning, Bill," but rather will use "Good morning, Mr. Jones," which may be understood as either lack of power or distance.

The indeterminacy of language systems which use the same linguistic signals for different communication function is surely a factor in many misunderstandings; however, often the ways ambiguous terms are used and understood can be explained by discussions of dominance issues.

Dominant metaphors. Although partly a corollary of the two cultures argument, and partly corollary to the *faulty linguistic system* approach, the *dominant metaphors* perspective has a distinct life of its own. For some years many articles, talks, and books about women in corporate management positions have stressed the ways managerial competence has been defined through metaphors derived from military and team-sports models (see, e.g., Harragan, 1977; Hennig & Jardim, 1977; Wheeless & Berryman-Fink, 1985). Some of the problems between women and men in management comes, it is argued, from women's not understanding, not appreciating, or not being able to use these metaphors to describe interactions.

For example, the manager who declares that "What this outfit needs is fewer tight ends and more wide receivers" may alienate employees who find the metaphor inappropriate, and confuse others who are unfamiliar with football. Ritchie (1987) believes that the use of such male-oriented, simplistic metaphors from boyhood games and dreams is decreasing. He reports hearing in specialized workplaces more use of music metaphors, with the symphony conductor coordinating the work of men and women expert at playing only one or two instruments.

Whether or not Ritchie is right about the decreased use of male-oriented metaphors, it is clear that the study of metaphors in organizations is increasing. In his book *Women, Fire, and Dangerous Things,* about what the categories we use reveal about our understandings, George Lakoff (1987) suggests that male-female interaction is governed in part by the metaphors we have for talking about lust—none of which are about a "healthy mutual lust" but instead are categories of hunger, animals, heat, insanity, machines, games, war, and physical forces.

In related work Julia Penelope (1986) argues that the "heteropatriarchal" metaphor of *control* ("being in control," "taking control") is the underlying concept that holds the sex/love/power/violence alliance together (pp. 89-90).

In her study of metaphors of conflict used in feminist organizations, Loren Blewett (1988) stresses the unchallenged ease with which metaphorical constructs are passed on within organizations, and the abundance of metaphors that encourage viewing conflict as war and violence. In focusing on women's uses of metaphors, including those that come from organizations and activities run by men, Blewett encourages discussion of problems that occur when the terminology we use undermines our desire for "non-destructive" interaction.

All of these useful discussions of metaphors recommend that we pay attention to the metaphorical concepts that often encourage violence and promote divisions.

Cross-Sex "Pseudocommunication"

Cahill (1981) adopts Habermas's (1970) term *pseudocommunication* to apply to the situation in which

> Variously categorized members of a society, because they share a common language and many common experiences, are likely to mistakenly assume that a consensus exists among them concerning the meaning of communicative behaviors. This mistaken assumption "produces a system of reciprocal misunderstandings, which are not recognized as such" or pseudocommunication. (Cahill, 1981, p. 77, quoting Habermas, 1970)

Reviewing reported verbal and nonverbal communication differences between the sexes like the ones cited here, Cahill notes that pseudocommunication is especially likely to occur in this intergroup relationship. He describes the intentions and interpretations underlying two examples of probable misunderstandings of gender displays.

In one example, a *dominance misunderstanding,* a male and female who are casually acquainted meet at an informal social gathering. He "pulls up into full posture and protrudes his chest"; she "cants her head and gives a sidelong glance" (p. 80). After a short conversation, he cups her elbow in his hand and announces the presence of a friend he wishes her to meet. She says she wants to attend to other friends, but he attempts to guide her across the room by the elbow hold. She frees her arm and protests; they have a minor dispute and separate. According to Cahill's pseudo-communication interpretation, the male understands (perhaps unconsciously) his nonverbal display at their meeting as one of dominance, and her responding display as one of submission. But the female had understood their displays as those of courting or quasi-courting (Scheflen, 1965). Thus when she did not submit to his request to meet his friend, "the male's understanding of the situated dominance alignment was violated" (p. 80). And when he attempted to enforce that alignment, the female's understanding of the terms of the contact, courting/quasi-courting, was violated. Pseudocommunication—both believing they had understood the other's signals—had occurred, a form of miscommunication—and both felt their implied agreed-upon understanding of the situation had been betrayed.

Intimacy misunderstanding may occur because of, for example, a female's greater amount of interactional gaze than a male's, which he may misinterpret as indicating intimacy. He may thus reciprocate with behavior indicating intimacy, which she may consider sexually aggressive. Her seeming forwardness followed by seeming withdrawal will likely be seen by him as the actions of a sexual tease. In another scenario, such female behavior directed at another male may provoke a proprietary male to a jealous response which she would consider unreasonable and overly possessive.

Although such description seems very much in the realm of the cultural difference approach, Cahill differentiates his pseudocommunication explanation by relating it clearly to trans-situational male dominance and privilege. The concept of cross-sex pseudocommunication provides a link between macro and micro levels of analysis (e.g., between explaining the prevalence of male violence against women societally and structurally and explaining a concrete instance of male violence biographically and situationally). It provides such a link because cross-sex pseudocommunication and trans-situational sexual inequality, he states, are reflexively interrelated:

> Trans-situational male dominance rests on the exclusion of women from culturally valued social activities. . . . this very sexual division of social activities results in cross-sex pseudocommunication. Cross-sex pseudocommunication, in turn, serves to perpetuate the segregation of the sexes. . . . Because it causes stressful communication, cross-sex pseudocommunication promotes preferences for same-sexed co-workers and, therefore, perpetuates occupational sex segregation. . . . Cross-sex pseudocommunication also promotes trans-situational male dominance more directly. By reminding women of their physical vulnerability when in the presence of males, cross-sex pseudocommunication promotes women's apparent submission to situated assertions of male dominance. (pp. 84-85)

Cahill's (1981) perspective is broader than the others in both proposing the mechanism by which cross-sex miscommunications are engendered and placing the mechanism in the specific context of cultural male dominance; and by linking micro and macro levels of analysis. However, the basic mechanism remains that of distinct female and male cultures arising from different experiences, thus it too suffers from some of the limitations of the two cultures perspective.

Some Considerations for a Better Theory of Female-Male Miscommunication

In working toward a more comprehensive theory of cross-sex miscommunication, we suggest the following broad considerations:

- Theories of female-male miscommunication have been put forward primarily by white theorists (which we are too) and are based largely on explanations of the actions of whites; to this extent their generalizability within the English-speaking, or any broader, community may be limited. (See the more extensive discussion in the next section.)
- As with all interactions, we need to recognize talk as an active process in a context that often involves speakers who may have different and changing concerns and who do not always have the conveying of information, politeness, rapport, clarity, agreement, understanding, and accommodation as primary goals. Discussions of miscommunication seldom, for example, talk about *anger* and *frustration* as emotions and expressions present *during* the conversation, not only as results of miscommunication. Women's anger in particular has frequently been denied or interpreted in terms of misunderstanding, inarticulation, and confusion.
- We might usefully consider the contemporary focus on miscommunication between women and men as a device that has encouraged thinking about oppositional spheres, as if women and men have innately quite separate interests and concerns. Attention to miscommunication is often a way to stress *difference* while ignoring *hierarchy.* Usually these discussions of miscommunication ignore the links between problems heard in female-male conversations and the inequities women experience through family policies, property laws, salary scales, and other repressive/discriminatory practices.
- We can recognize that boys and girls, women and men, belong, or are assigned by others, to particular age, sexual orientation, class, and race groups. Media attention to miscommunication pays little attention to this fact, assuming that only *gender variants* are involved. This is probably due in part to the fact that talk about "the battle of the sexes" is still often done flippantly, and casually. (In Western countries talk about the battle of the sexes still sounds much less serious and threatening than, for example, talk about the "battle of blacks and whites.") One way to trivialize the topic of female-male interaction is to simplify it, ignoring the interaction of race, class, age, sexual orientation, and sex group.
- Women and men need to be asked about what they experience as communication problems. The popular media have found it easy to talk about "miscommunication" which seems to mean primarily women and men talking past each other by unwittingly using terms or concepts not understood by the other. Blame is often equally assigned to women and men in this (popular for the mass media) battle of the sexes.

- We need to consider further the definition of ***miscommunication***. Is it an interpretive error experienced by at least one of the interactants? A mismatch between the speaker's intention and the hearer's interpretation? A response by one that indicates that she or he hasn't understood? How do we know when "misunderstandings" are intentional?
- We can recognize that all confusing talk does not involve "confusion" on the part of one or both interactants. For example, a speaker might deliberately obfuscate. Further, a speaker who says something unintelligible to another may be little interested in hearing a clarifying question; repair of misunderstandings or confusions usually requires work on the part of both speakers. *Not* acknowledging communication problems is a common strategy for speakers who try to avoid confrontation in order to avoid another's anger and laws.

The Interaction of Race/Ethnicity, Gender, and Class in Miscommunication

The types of problematic talk experienced might be quite different for white/Anglo women and women of color; and for women of different classes. In the case of race/ethnicity,[2] for example, many black women in English-speaking countries have not grown up in patriarchal, nuclear families but in matrifocal or extended families; the same is true for many Native American women. They may experience less sexist female/male interaction. They may also experience a lot of interracial "miscommunication" in talks with both white women and white men (Kochman, 1981; Stanback, 1987).

Class differences, which are well known to affect language use and values, must also interact with gender factors in creating, and affecting the nature of, miscommunication. Ethnicity, class, and gender may work either independently or interactively. The fact that race/ethnicity and class are largely confounded in multiracial societies puts special communicative strain on women of color, whose ideas, opinions, and interpretations are often not taken seriously.[3] In addition, the confounding of race/ethnicity and class sometimes causes class differences to be seen as racial ones; and the assumption of male speech as the norm may lead to taking it as an expression of a culture, rather than that of males of the culture, and ignoring females' speech, especially that of women of color.

White/Anglo middle- and upper-class cultural dominance is shown not only in the pressures on other races and classes to adapt to the dominant culture, and in the experience of those races' and classes' being wrongly interpreted, but also in the paucity of studies investigating communication within nondominant groups and between classes, races, and ethnicities.

But distorting what information there is is the fact that too often observations and studies (the few that exist) of cross-ethnic and cross-class talk ignore issues of power and dominance related to gender, race, and class (e.g., Kochman, 1981).

A basic question we need to pursue here is: Do studies of interracial/interethnic miscommunication apply equally to women and men? Is there an interaction of race/ethnicity and gender such that different races/ethnic groups have different gender differences and different gender power relations, and consequently different loci of misunderstanding? Future studies need to account for the interrelated influences of culture, class, age, and gender—and of racism, classism, ageism, sexism and so on. As Stanback (1987) writes, a systemic, feminist perspective should be concerned "with exposing and altering the underlying values of the society, values which support racist, sexist, and classist institutions and behaviors, including communication behaviors."

Same-Sex and Gay-Straight Issues in Miscommunication

Left untouched in this discussion, built as it is on a literature focused on cross-sex communication, is the question of how *same*-sex communication might be detrimentally affected by issues of male dominance. Fasteau (1974), for example, discusses obstacles to communication among men based on macho role-playing that precludes expression of feelings. A parallel might be found in talk among women based on expressions of closeness; might truthful communication be buried under obligatory expressions (feminine role-playing) of closeness?

Same-sex miscommunication may also originate from gay-straight differences and stereotypes. Many gay males and lesbians, for example, report the experience of a straight same-sex friend or acquaintance reacting oversensitively to a touch or other expression of warmth, obviously misunderstanding it as a sexual advance. Cahill (1981) notes that males' typical aversion to the touch of other males may be explained by a combination of homophobia and the equation of intimacy with sexual desire (found in the research of Nguyen, Heslin, & Nguyen, 1975): "The touch of a male would produce a homophobic reaction in another male only if it was interpreted as indicating sexual desire. Notably, females do not exhibit a similar aversion to the touch of other females" (p. 82). Here, too is the potential for miscommunication based on cultural difference and dominance—that between homosexual and heterosexual cultures. This topic certainly deserves further exploration.

Polarizing and Reifying Gender Notions

A prominent danger in examining sex differences is that of exaggerating them and ignoring sex similarity. A more insidious danger is that of accepting sex as an unproblematic category (Thorne, 1990). Similarities between the sexes are downplayed and differences exaggerated, as a general rule in Western societies, as is well evidenced by the elaboration of his-and-hers products, from pink and blue baby outfits and gender-typed children's toys to sex-customized razors, deodorants, and household tools for adults. Added to the cultural tendency to exaggerate difference is that contributed by the scholarly literature on sex difference, which has often focused uncritically on difference rather than on its underpinnings.

The exaggeration of sex difference gets much impetus from school settings, where the assumption of essential differences seems virtually institutionalized. Here children are treated as separate social categories by their teachers (e.g., made to line up in separate-sex lines, pitted as girls versus boys in many competitions such as spelling bees or undeclared races to complete group tasks like cleaning up), and addressed as separate categories even when treated as a single one ("Listen, boys and girls . . . ")

Despite the cultural emphasis on group difference, similarities of behavior between females and males, in language as in other areas, are far greater than differences, as many feminist scholars have pointed out. Maccoby and Jacklin (1974), for example, in their extensive survey of studies of sex difference, found only four out of hundreds of sex differences reported in the literature to be what they considered "fairly well established." Kramarae (1977, 1981) has demonstrated that gender stereotypes of speech are much stronger than actual speech differences. Sattel (1983) and DeFrancisco (1989), among others, make the point that males' and females' speech forms reflect strategies for usage, not restricted repertories. Thorne (1990) points out that "Gender separation among children is not as total as the "separate worlds" rendering suggests, and the amount of separation varies by situation" (p. 103). She notes, for instance, that many children are more segregated by gender when playing on school playgrounds than when in their neighborhoods, but most observational studies of children are conducted at schools.

A subtler, and therefore worse, problem is the simplistic and unthinking conception of sex and gender to be found in most writing, scholarly and popular. Thorne (1986) writes:

> Statistical findings of difference are often portrayed as dichotomous, neglecting the considerable individual variation that exists. . . . The sex difference approach tends to abstract gender from its social context, to assume that males and females are qualitatively and permanently different (with differences perhaps unfolding through separate developmental lines). These assumptions mask the possibility that gender arrangements and patterns of similarity and difference may vary by situation, race, social class, region, or subculture. (p. 168)

Thorne emphasizes the complexity of the notion of gender, and strongly criticizes the tendency to rigidify and polarize gender categories in writing on sex difference: "Gender should be conceptualized as a system of relationships rather than as an immutable and dichotomous given" (p. 168).

A Multi-Determined Social Context Approach to Female/Male Miscommunication

We envision a comprehensive approach that does not have to choose *between* the different explanations offered, but rather that recognizes the important factors of each of these as forces. The difference in feminine and masculine cultures is real, but it is not the only fact of existence for men and women in our society; differences due to race, ethnicity, class, age, sexual preference, and so on may compound and interact with gender differences; and cultural commonality exists too. Most importantly, cultural difference does not exist within a political vacuum; rather, the strength of difference, the types of difference, the values applied to different forms, the dominance of certain forms—all are shaped by the context of male supremacy and female subordination.

Furthermore, cultural segregation and hierarchy may combine to produce psychological effects in both women and men that independently engender and consolidate language forms which express superior and subordinate status. Both macrolevel power (a), based on structural male dominance, and micro-level power (b), based on individual socialization, exist and influence language use and therefore miscommunication. Structural male dominance favors the growth of faulty linguistic systems, including dominant metaphors, which express primarily male experience and further add to making women a muted group—leading to further problems in communication. At the same time, the general assumption that men's and women's words and behaviors mean the same leads to the problem of pseudocommunication, the false belief that we have understood each other, and misunderstandings may compound.

The differences and misunderstandings created by these factors are not equally engaged in all contexts: gender (like dominance) varies in meaning and prominence in different contexts. And this may be so for the different explanatory factors as well. For example, it may be that different speech cultures, to the extent that they exist, come primarily into play with marital/partner communication, as when wives/women say they want husbands/partners to engage in more emotionally sharing communication (Rubin, 1976; Tannen, 1987). Cross-sex pseudocommunication may occur especially in (hetero)sexual or potentially sexual situations. Social power may be said to enter broadly with all these factors, but may most specifically structure conversational interaction patterns. Rather than debating the merits of one factor over another, we would do well to turn our attention to ascertaining the contexts in which different factors enter to make cross-sex communication problematic.

In addition, this social context model assumes that men's as well as women's communicative behaviors are to be explained, to be studied as "caused"; that neither's speech is understood as either norm or deviant; that not only women's, but also men's psychology is seen as developing from their situation in the social structure, and as affecting their language style; that patterns of cross-sex misunderstanding may differ between racial, ethnic, age, and sexual preference groups, and the pattern in the dominant white/Anglo and straight culture cannot be taken as indicative of all. The model sees communication within the context of gender hierarchy as well as of gender segregation and socialization and assumes that not only the more noticeable (and often superficial) gender differences in speech are seen as underlying cross-sex miscommunication, but that also to be considered are deeper concerns of women's exclusion from the linguistic structuring of experience.

Conclusion

The patterns of miscommunication we have discussed occur within the cultural context of male power and female subordination: The accepted interpretation of an interaction (e.g., refusal versus teasing, seduction versus rape, difference versus inequality) is generally that of the more powerful person, therefore that of the male tends to prevail. The *metastructure* of interpretation—not what the interpretation is, but *whose interpretation is accepted*—is one of inequality. Females are required to develop special sensitivity to interpret males' silence, lack of emotional expression, or brutality, and to help men express themselves, while men often seem to be trained deliberately to misinterpret much of women's meaning. Yet it is women's communication style that is often labeled as inadequate and maladaptive, requiring remediation in which white-collar masculine norms are generally imposed.

As we have seen, miscommunication may be used to stigmatize: less powerful individuals (because of their ethnicity, class, sex, etc.) may be defined as deviant communicators, incapable of expressing themselves adequately. "Problems of communication" are often diagnosed in difficult interaction to obscure problems that arise from unequal power rather than from communication. The explanation of "separate but equal cultures" has been a means of avoiding reference to power and to racial and ethnic domination, and should be recognized for its implicit denial of sex domination as well. The complex patterns described above fit into the larger structure of female-male myths and power relations. One may in fact ask how well male dominance could be maintained if we had open and equally-valued communication between women and men. The construction of miscommunication between the sexes emerges as a powerful tool, maybe even a necessity, to maintain the structure of male supremacy.

Notes

1. In this chapter we have tried (except when quoting others) to use *sex* to refer to the two groups designated by women/girls/females and men/boys/males, and *gender* when referring to the general social structure of characteristics and relationships of those two groups. This may seem a backtracking from an earlier feminist position in which, since about the mid-1970s, many feminists have advocated reserving the term *sex* for biological distinctions and using *gender* for the more commonly referenced social ones. There are two reasons for our choice: (1) In recent years the recognition has grown that what had been seen as biological is itself so tied up with social categorization as to make the distinction problematic; and (2) at the same time, the term (*gender* has been used so frequently and ambiguously that it has lost its earlier significance, and now seems often to be used to *avoid* any reference to social constructs and hierarchical relationships. This problem with terminology requires more attention than we can give it here, but we have tried, in an admittedly imperfect way, to restore some recognition of these social/political concerns.

2. We use both terms *race* and *ethnicity* here to refer to concepts associated with persons of color. *Race* and *ethnicity* are somewhat parallel to *sex* and *gender* in their associations with biological versus social distinctions, respectively; however, it has long been acknowledged

that race is a social, not a biological, concept, and we intend its use in that way only. Nevertheless, the two terms are not co-extensive, and we use *ethnicity* as well to remind us that there are various ethnicities within races. *Ethnicity* is not used alone, however, because its singular usage often tends to obliterate issues of color.

3. Etter-Lewis (1987) suggests that black women often use indirect confrontation—"fussin' and cussin' people out under their breath"—as a response to racist and sexist interaction. (See Stanback, 1987, 1988, for discussion of the research on black women and communication.)

3

Misunderstanding Children

Elinor Ochs

Introduction

Human development is often conceptualized in terms of an evolving competence to perceive, know, feel, and act in a normal manner. Every society establishes norms of competence and all members of society, including infants and small children, are evaluated in terms of them. We may be deemed incapable, awkward, peculiar, enigmatic, able, impressive, masterful, or creative, depending on society and situation. Within the very large domain of competence is the competence to make sense out of strings of expressed propositions in the form of speaking or writing. The activity of making sense, the intellectual plaything of philosophy for centuries, has been a driving concern within the social sciences in the past several decades.

How children gain competence in sense-making has been an important research focus among developmental psycholinguists. Sense-making is discussed in terms of comprehension and noncomprehension of expressed propositions in the form of words, phrases, clauses, or strings of clauses. Each linguistic form is associated with one or more meanings which in turn a child may comprehend to different degrees and in different ways. The work of the researcher is to not only establish the nature of the child's comprehension but as well to account for its particular pattern. In most developmental paradigms, (1) the meanings assigned by the researcher are deemed normative, (2) meaning-assignment is based primarily on intentions and seen as an individual activity, and (3) degrees and avenues of

AUTHOR'S NOTE: I am grateful to Alessandro Duranti and Carolyn Taylor for their careful reading of and comments concerning an earlier draft of this discussion.

comprehension/noncomprehension are said to evidence levels of linguistic competence. With respect to (1), most developmental paradigms assume a model of communication in which meanings of particular linguistic constructions are conventional and specified. In this model, the task of the child is to acquire knowledge of these conventional meanings, that is, recognize and express meaning correctly. With respect to (2), comprehension studies presume a communication model in which meanings are conveyed from a sender (e.g., a researcher) to a receiver (a child). Within this *conduit* model of communication, there is a meaning or set of meanings intended by a sender that is or is not successfully grasped by the receiver. In this framework, the focus is on sender and receiver as individual language processors rather than on meaning-assignment as a joint psychological activity (Vygotsky in Cole, John-Steiner, Scribner, & Souberman, 1978). With respect to (3), a child who systematically assigns normative meanings (that match assigned, intended meanings) in a comprehension activity is said to have acquired an understanding of some structure within language. Contrastively, a child who assigns other than intended, normative meanings is seen as making errors or as not yet competent. Although the psycholinguistic literature focuses on dimensions of meaning children are capable of processing and on (non)comprehension as a cognitive status, this chapter examines how comprehension and noncomprehension are organized by local social orders and local theories of knowledge, communication, and competence. It visualizes relative comprehension as a social and cultural accomplishment as well as a cognitive outcome of (mis)communicative activity. The bulk of this essay is devoted to communicative activity in which one or another participant signals noncomprehension or potential noncomprehension. We refer to such activities as *misunderstandings.*

Each activity of misunderstanding—whether it takes place in the flow of daily life or in the prescribed environment of a psycholinguistic experiment—is structured in local and universal ways. The activity of misunderstanding appears universally. Further, strategies for signaling and responding to noncomprehension are common to many communities. Communities distinguish themselves, however, through their local preferences for particular forms of signaling and responding to noncomprehension. Communities do not necessarily share the same expectations regarding which forms are appropriate for a particular set of interlocutors in a particular setting. This means that in each community, competent participants to a misunderstanding bring to this activity tacit knowledge of such considerations as how noncomprehension or partial comprehension is indexed, when it is expected, when it is important, how it is anticipated, how and when it is handled by particular participants. Each enacted activity of misunderstanding perpetuates or transforms interactants' tacit knowledge of miscommunication. When children participate—even when children are audience to noncomprehension of others—the activity of misunderstanding provides an opportunity space for socialization. Children are socialized into a form of competence, namely, the competence to engage in the activity of misunderstanding. In this sense, developmentalists' interest in children's misunderstandings includes what children understand of the activity of misunderstanding in addition to their grasp of the semantic scope of linguistic constructions. Among other skills, children must come to recognize signals of misunderstanding, isolate sources of misunderstanding, and determine strategies for responding to misunderstandings.

The Language Socialization of Misunderstanding

Socialization can be considered as a process whereby one gains competence and understandings that mark membership in a social group. This process takes place in the course of daily social life through interactions with members and through the use of tools (e.g., spoken language, literacy materials) produced by or available to members. Language plays an important part in socialization, although its role relative to nonvocal modes of socialization will vary cross-culturally (cf. Rogoff, 1989). Language is the most elaborate symbolic and formal system available to the human species and humans universally exploit its symbolic and formal potential to socialize children and other novices. Cultural skills and knowledge are transmitted symbolically in part through the meaning- content of verbalized messages (e.g., "Say 'thank you' ", "The grownups get knives; the kids do not".) That is, what members say and write is a vehicle for cultural reproduction.

On the other hand, the form of a message is an important medium for socializing skills and knowledge. Every utterance displays to novices a set of linguistic forms that members of a social group conventionally use to construct particular social actions, social identities, and stances. These forms tell or *index* to those present what type of social situation is taking place. A more accurate formulation is that these forms index what type of social situation *may* be taking place, for any one form often indexes not one but a set of possible situations. For example, the use of an imperative construction may index a number of social actions (e.g., order, warning, advice, threat), social relationships (e.g., employer-employee, parent-child, friends) and stances (e.g., sympathy, irritation). To narrow the scope of possible definitions of the social situation, children and other novices learn to relate particular forms to others that co-occur and have situational meanings. They relate the imperative form, for example, to a particular intonational contour, voice quality, morphological indexes of stance, and pronominal choices. In these ways, children and other novices organize their universe through language. And in these ways, the indexical potential of grammatical and discourse forms render them powerful media for socializing culture.

How can we relate this general process, which we call *language socialization* (Ochs & Schieffelin, 1984; Schieffelin & Ochs, 1986), to the activity of misunderstanding? This chapter proposes two links:

First, every social group relies upon a set of linguistic (and gestural) forms to constitute the social and linguistic activity of misunderstanding. In this sense, the co-occurrence of these particular forms indexes that the activity of misunderstanding is taking place. Language socialization takes place when repeated co-occurrences of these forms socialize children into an understanding of how this activity is accomplished. The developmental literature indicated that misunderstandings involving children occur repeatedly in all societies and that even very young children participate with some competence in such activities. American infants 12-18 months of age display that others have misunderstood their messages (e.g., gestures and/or vocalizations) through repeating and paraphrasing their original actions (Golinkoff, 1986). Further, quite early in their development (Brown's Stage II [1973]), children are able to respond appropriately to both specific requests and global requests for confirmation, by repeating only a portion of the original utterance in response to the former and repeating the entire utterance in response to the latter (Gallagher, 1981).

Second, just as linguistic forms help to constitute the activity of misunderstanding so the activity of misunderstanding may be seen as helping to constitute other facets of the social and cultural context. For example, participation in the activity of misunderstanding may be limited to particular social identities. We know, for example, that certain societies limit who can ask questions (see below). When speakers opt for one or another strategy for engaging in the activity of misunderstanding, they are constituting their social identities. In addition to social identity, misunderstandings may be limited by local theories of how understanding is achieved. In this sense, each misunderstanding helps to instantiate and create local systems of belief. Through misunderstandings, then, children are socialized into further definitions of the *context of situation* and *context of culture* (Malinowski, 1978).

Socializing Structural Aspects of Misunderstanding

Let us now examine ways in which misunderstanding activities in which children participate are organized. We consider here misunderstandings of children's utterances by others and misunderstandings of others' utterances by children.

Misunderstanding Children's Utterances

Following the work of Cherry (1979), Corsaro (1977), Golinkoff (1986), and Ochs (1988a) on clarifying children's utterances as well as Schegloff, Jefferson and Sack's (1977) classic study of repair in adult conversation, we may analyze misunderstandings of children's utterances in terms of a discourse activity in which a verbal behavior of a child is perceived by either the child or other participant to the interaction as partially or fully unclear to others. In other words, our concern is with the activity of engaging in recognized misunderstanding rather than with misunderstanding that goes unrecognized by the participants at the time of its occurrence. Children and others involved in recognized misunderstandings have a number of alternative strategies available to them for responding to perceived unclarity. For purposes of this discussion, we focus on strategies available to those other than the child who produces the unclear utterance.

Universally, caregivers or others interacting with a young child may employ four alternative post hoc strategies to respond (overtly) to children's unintelligible utterances (Schieffelin & Ochs, 1988):

Ignore

They may ignore the child's unclear utterance. In her study of the Inuit children of Arctic Quebec, Crago (1988, p. 210) notes "In several of the tapes that were made of them, they frequently made unintelligible vocalizations. The large majority of these vocalizations went unheeded. Many times their parents did not respond, not even by looking up at the children." This characterization may apply to Athabaskan children's interactions with others, as noted by Scollon (1982, p. 87):

> Children in American middle-class society are treated as persons who have a right to be heard, even when their speech is unclear. This contrasts with the treatment of Athabaskan children whose speech is normally ignored. Although infants are treated as if their noises are meaningful, this does not usually apply to toddlers who have actually begun to speak.

Similarly, Heath (1983, p. 75) observes among working-class Black families in South Carolina that "when infants begin to utter sounds which can be interpreted as referring to items or events in the environment, these sounds receive no special attention."

Show Minimal Grasp

Others may signal that the child's utterance is unclear to them. Ochs (1988a) refers to this response as the *'minimal grasp'* strategy. Golinkoff (1986, p. 464) specifies three means of marking nonunderstanding: (1) nonverbal indicators (e.g., raised eyebrows, quizzical looks), (2) clarification requests such as "huh", "whatø, "what do you want", and (3) statements of noncomprehension (e.g., "I don't know what you want"). In addition, caregivers and others may indicate to children that their utterances are unclear through teasing (cf. Crago, 1988). Teasing along with clarification requests and the other means of indicating unclarity may promote the child to rearticulate and redesign the previously produced utterance. The rearticulation may or may not be clearer from the point of view of others co-present.

Guess

They may verbally formulate a guess at what the intended unintelligible utterance might be. Ochs (1988a) refers to this response as the *expressed guess* strategy. Golinkoff (1986) notes that guessing may be vocal or nonvocal (i.e., gestural). A caregiver, for example, may guess by holding up an object to an infant as a candidate referent. Or, a caregiver may vocally reformulate or expand what she or he believes the child to be intending (e.g., "Milk?", "You want the milk?" "Are you saying 'I want the milk'?")

In Golinkoff's observations of American mothers interacting with preverbal infants, these verbal and nonverbal reformulations accounted for almost half of mothers' signals of their failure to understand (Golinkoff, 1986). A study by Cherry (1979) of talk to American children aged two and a half to four years indicates that the proportion of maternal guesses (referred to as *requests for confirmation* versus *requests for repetition* (a type of minimal grasp strategy) increases with age of child. Presumably younger children's utterances are seen as less intelligible than the utterances of older children and hence less amenable to reformulation in the form of an explicit guess.

The apparent preference of American mothers for overtly guessing at what a child might be saying is not matched in other societies. Among the

Kaluli of Papua New Guinea, verbal guessing of what the child might possibly be saying is not done (Schieffelin, 1990), and in traditional Western Samoan communities, it is rare (Ochs, 1988a).

Provide Cultural Gloss

They may provide a culturally appropriate formulation of the unintelligible utterance (Scollon, 1982). In these cases, others are not so much concerned with the child's intended meaning as much as what the child should be meaning given the social situation at hand. More mature persons surrounding the child will provide the child with a cultural *gloss* or *translation* (Scollon, 1982). Lock (1981) has described how such glossing may address children's gestural communication long before they begin producing words. He proposes that infants' gestures come to assume a conventional meaning through a process in which initially adults systematically provide a conventional meaning to children's gestures which is eventually assumed by the infant (see also Vygotsky, in Cole et al., 1978). In other words, an infant's gestures are related to a particular goal (e.g., "more") by a co-present adult (regardless of what goals, if any, the infant had in mind) and subsequently an infant learns to use such gestures to indicate that goal. In many societies, there are conventional glosses for first words. Thus, among the Kaluli of Papua New Guinea, children's first words are conventionally glossed as "breast" and "mother" (Schieffelin, 1990). Among Samoans, children's first word is said to be the curse "shit". An interview with a Samoan mother (Ochs, 1988a, p. 160) indicates that sib and parental caregivers may be aware of this process of glossing of first words:

N64-360ff
Mother (Mo) and researcher (E) have just been talking about babbling, and E has just asked about first Samoan words.

Mo: Oh, A Samoan Word!
E: Mmm.
Mo: ((Laughs)) Well I'm ashamed! ((Laughs)) ((Coughs))
E: Don't be ashamed! ((Laughs))
Mo: They call a Samoan word ((pause)) a, you know, when the Samoan kids (([?))=
E: [uh huh
Mo: =then the Samoan ((pause)) WOMAN you know,=
E: Hmm.
Mo: =or Samoan people [said 'Oh! she said "*Tae*" ["shit"]
E: [Hmm. Yeah.

Mo: Shit! So maybe that's the FIRST word they know ((pause)).
E: Hmm.
Mo: Shit. And so the people ((emphatic particle)), we - we as adults...=

.
.
.

Mo: ((Laughs)) ((pause)) = then we know - then we know=
E: Hmm.
Mo: ((solf)) =oh my - my - my child is starting to first say the word 'shit' [or ((pause)) stupid =
E: [Yeah: ((pause)) swearing a lot ((Laughs))
Mo: =stupid. That's a first word but ((pause)) but to a kid,=
E: Hmm. ((pause)) Hmm.
Mo: =to a kid it is - ((pause)) he doesn't really mean 'shit'
E: Hmm
Mo: =He doesn't. We are translating [into that word 'shit' [
E: [Hmm. [Hmm.
Mo: =because we = we mean he says 'shit'
E: Hmm.
MO: But to a kid, NO!
E: Hmm.

Japanese mothers also make frequent use of cultural glosses, replacing children's inappropriate utterances with a culturally more acceptable paraphrase as in the interaction below:

Child: Baibai tte itta no.
"He said 'Byebye.' "
Mother: Itta no ne. Papa nante itta? Itte mairimasu tte itta deshoo. Itte mairimasu.
"He said it, didn't he. What did Papa say He said, 'I go and will come back,' didn't he. 'I go and will come back.'" Clancy, 1986, p. 236)

Children's Misunderstanding of Others' Utterances

Just as there are universal strategies for responding to children's unclear utterances, so there are universal strategies for responding to children's nonunderstanding of the utterances of caregivers and others. In these cases, either the caregiver who produces an utterance or the child who listens to an utterance perceives the utterance to be unclear. As above, the focus of the discussion is on recognized unclarity and the behavior that recognition provokes. The discussion considers caregivers' responses not only to children's displayed noncomprehension after an unintelligible utterance is produced (*post hoc unintelligibility*) but also to children's possible noncomprehension of a not yet produced, anticipated utterance (*a priori unintelligibility*).

A Priori Unintelligibility

In observing the speech of others in the presence of infants and children, researchers have noted two strategies for handling the possibility that children may not understand the talk in their presence:

Modify complexity of utterance. One strategy is to adapt the talk of others to facilitate the understanding of young children. One of the most widely reported behaviors of caregivers interacting with young children is that they modify their speech and other behavior in ways that anticipate possible misunderstanding. These modifications together constitute a distinct social register referred to as *baby talk* or *simplified register* (Ferguson, 1977), or *motherese* (Newport, 1976). Characteristics of this register include simplification of syntax, reduction of sentence length, restriction of vocabulary, exaggeration of intonation, slowing of articulation, reference to the immediate here-and-now, repetition, and paraphrases. These modifications appear to reflect a desire on the part of caregivers and others to maximize the comprehensibility of their utterances.

Simplification in many ways is the counterpart to the expressed guess strategy in that both strategies give importance to the speaker's intended meanings and organize the activity of misunderstanding around the understanding of a speaker's intentions. In the case of a priori simplification, the speaker works toward clarifying his or her intentions before any evidence that the child has misunderstood. The speaker tacitly assumes a set of cognitive and other developmental limits on the child as recipient of talk and assumes that certain modes of presentation are more likely to be understood by the child than other modes. In the case of post hoc guessing, the speaker works toward clarifying the child's intentions. The speaker tacitly assumes a set of cognitive and other developmental limits on the child producer of talk. In both simplifying and guessing, the caregiver assumes the goal of misunderstanding activity to be comprehension of the speakers' intentions and in both cases the caregiver takes on the major burden of achieving this goal. With both strategies it is the caregiver and not the child who takes on the responsibility of formulating the comprehensible utterance. In the case of simplification, the perceived "author" of the comprehensible utterance is the caregiver; in the case of expressed guessing, the perceived author of the now comprehensible utterance is the child (although the analyst could argue co-authorship quite strongly).

Simplification is a widespread strategy of caregivers across the world's societies. Indeed we might say that it is universal. Recent cross-cultural research, however, suggests that it is far more pervasive in certain societies than in others and that the type of simplification may differ across societies. In traditional Western Samoan communities, for example, sib and parental caregivers rarely simplify their utterances directed to young children (Ochs 1982, 1988a; Ochs & Schieffelin, 1984). Further, the form of simplification is much more restricted than what is reported for other communities. In Samoan communities, simplification tends to take the form of repetition of utterances (i.e., a discourse strategy). In other communities, such as in mainstream families in the United States, simplification tends to be syntactic and morphological as well as on the level of discourse.

Sustain level of utterance complexity. Although the bulk of the studies of talking to children focuses on caregivers' speech modifications, an equally important response to children's potential misunderstanding the world over is to avoid such modifications. The Kaluli of Papua New Guinea (Schieffelin, 1990) believe, for example, that children will be locked in a condition of prolonged misunderstanding and incompetence if adults and older children simplify their speech in the presence of the young. For the Kaluli, then, the route from misunderstanding to understanding is through exposing children to well-formed adult speech. Samoans, as well, rarely simplify their speech to young children. Children's development from misunderstanding to understanding is through their careful attention to the situation-appropriate words and actions of others. This world view contrasts with that of many White middle-class Europeans, who believe that the route to understanding is through a particular kind of assistance, namely assistance through utterance simplification. This is not to say that Samoan and Kaluli caregivers do not assist children in the activity of understanding. In these communities, assistance takes the form of drawing children's attention to the well-formed utterances and actions of others and sometimes post hoc strategies such as presenting the child with a repeated presentation of the well-formed utterance/action rather than a priori simplifying the complexity of any one utterance/action (cf. Rogoff, 1989; Schieffelin & Ochs, 1988).

Yet another perspective on the question of sustaining or modifying are complexity of utterances for infants and young children is that it is not always deemed important or even appropriate for children to understand the speech of others. Universally caregivers utilize strategies to make their utterances unintelligible, sometimes switching to a different code or spelling out a word. Crago (1988) describes how older generations of Inuit women feel strongly that although at times adults may simplify their speech, the talk of adults need not be always accessible to children. Indeed direct involvement may hurt them in their development. One Inuit informant comments: "(Children) should not participate in adult conversation . . . to prevent them getting involved with adult stuff before they are mature enough" (p. 166). This attitude contrasts with some European caregivers who involve their infants and young children in complex conversational activities as a means of enhancing their development. Having so involved them, these caregivers assist their charges by paraphrasing and simplifying the talk that surrounds them.

Post Hoc Unintelligibility

In addition to anticipating unintelligibility, caregivers and others universally are often faced with some evidence that a child has not understood some intended meaning behind an utterance that has been expressed (post hoc evidence).

Inappropriate/incorrect response. Children's nonunderstanding may be signaled through their inappropriate or incorrect responses to an utterance. Such responses are utilized not only by caregivers. Researchers in developmental psycholinguistics as well rely on children's verbal or nonverbal responses to index their linguistic competence.

Just as researchers vary in the emphasis that they place on comprehension versus production as a measure of language acquisition so communities vary in their reliance on comprehension versus productive ability as a measure of acquisition. In certain communities, comprehension far more than production is an index that a child has competence in his or her language. Among the Inuit, for example, a woman commented about her child; "When she is able to understand, then if she was told to get a mitten and if she went and got it, and when she was told to bring it over to the person who sent her to get it and if she understood that, then we can know that she has learned language in that way today" (Crago, 1988, p. 207). Similarly, Inuit mourn the loss of Inuit language competence among the younger generation through comments such as "These children are losing their language. They don't *understand* [emphasis mine] what we ask them to do" (Crago, 1988, p. 209). Great emphasis on displays of comprehension is also characteristic of Japanese interactions with young children (Clancy, 1986). Mothers do not readily tolerate inappropriate responses of children and persistently repeat their utterances until a valid response is provided. Clancy suggests that insistence on the child's demonstration of comprehension socializes Japanese children to attend and empathize with others.

Displays of minimal grasp and guesses. In other situations, children may signal nonunderstanding through a minimal grasp (e.g., "huh?", "What?")

or expressed guess (e.g., "more?") type of request for clarification. In many communities, such requests are ubiquitous in interactions with young children. In other communities, children's requests for clarification may be rare. Scollon and Scollon (1981, p. 138) suggests this is the case for Athabaskan communities: "Where deference or respect for adults is valued, children must learn ways of gaining information without directly questioning adults." Similarly, Inuit women often comment, "We don't like our children to ask questions of adults" (Crago, 1988, p. 214). Native Hawaiian parents feel similarly and discourage children from asking questions. Boggs (1985, p. 55) notes: "In requesting information, children typically ask a question several times, reformulate it, and perhaps speculate, while waiting patiently for a reply. The parent typically does not reply right away, if replying at all." Goody (1978) reports that Gonja children of northern Liberia are also discouraged from asking questions.

Caregiver probes. In yet other cases,children's nonunderstanding may be revealed through some probing questions directed to the child relevant to prior talk. Much like in classroom discourse, caregivers and others may request that a small child show evidence that she or he has understood some piece of information expressed in the caregiver's or other's utterance. The requested piece of information is already known to the requester. What isn't known is whether the child knows the information. While such questions are characteristic of European middle-class households, they are rare in other communities, including Samoan (Ochs, 1988a), Kaluli (Schieffelin, 1990), Inuit (Crago, 1988), and Athabaskan (Scollon & Scollon, 1981).

Attempts to clear misunderstanding. Regardless of how children's nonunderstanding is signaled, others may subsequently utilize any one of the responses noted above, in sections discussing misunderstanding children's utterances and a priori unintelligibility. They may ignore the nonunderstanding, may tease the child, may insist that the child try again to produce a culturally acceptable response. They may simplify the misunderstood utterance or may repeat the earlier utterance, sustaining the same level of complexity.

Socializing Culture Through Misunderstanding

The discussion thus far has proposed that misunderstandings have a discourse organization that traverses languages and communities. That is, misunderstandings are almost universally characterized by similar verbal strategies for signaling and responding to perceived unintelligibility. In this sense, children the world over are exposed to and acquire a similar discourse structure of misunderstandings. It is this shared knowledge that facilitates communication among speakers who cross the boundaries of their speech communities. Speakers from all sorts of communities are able to coordinate their actions while engaged in the activity of misunderstanding because they share a partial understanding of how that activity is structured.

On the other hand, we have noted that children are socialized through the activity of misunderstanding into important local cultural structures of knowledge. The socialization of local knowledge takes place because the activity of misunderstanding has not only culturally universal properties—it is also organized in terms of culturally local preferences that are tied to the local social order and local theories of communication and understanding.

Communities of speakers display different preferences in their responses to children's unintelligible utterances, in how they expect children to respond to the unintelligible utterances of others, and in the extent to which others are expected to take into consideration children's limitations in designing their own utterances for children. As noted earlier, certain social groups (e.g., Inuit, Athabaskan) tend to ignore children's unintelligible utterances, particularly infants' vocalizations, whereas other groups orient caregivers toward the activity of trying to make sense out of such utterances. In attempting to make sense of children's utterances, some communities (e.g., mainstream American) prefer to express a guess, whereas in other communities (e.g., Kaluli, Samoan), this response is highly dispreferred. Similarly, some communities (e.g., Tamil, mainstream American) prefer to anticipate children's nonunderstanding of others' utterances by simplifying those utterances. In other communities (e.g., Kaluli, Samoan), simplification for children is less frequent and restricted to certain types of discourse simplification. And in some communities (e.g., mainstream American), children are encouraged to display their nonunderstanding by requesting clarification, whereas elsewhere such questions are highly inappropriate (e.g., Inuit, Athabaskan, Gonja, Native Hawaiian).

These differences are distributional and have been presented here in an altogether superficial manner. The preference for one strategy over another is constrained by further situational parameters, including age of child and gender of speaker. For example, simplified register in mainstream American households declines as children get older. Speech to infants less than one year old is more repetitive, grammatically abbreviated, and semantically restricted than speech to older infants and children. Further, within the same community of households, gender is an important consideration in that the preference for simplified register is more pronounced in mothers' speech than in fathers' speech to children (Gleason & Greif, 1983).

Misunderstanding and Social Order

These distributional patterns are important in that they reflect systematic expectations concerning how certain social personae are to behave. That one community prefers one set of misunderstanding responses over others is not arbitrary but rather rooted in social order. In the cases at hand, preferences are linked to local expectations concerning the social identities of child (at different developmental points) and caregiver (or other co-present party such as peer).

Let us consider, for example, the preference for explicit guessing as a response to a child's unintelligible utterance and the preference for simplifying one's own utterance in the presence of a child. As noted earlier, both of these preferences entail a cognitive orientation of high accommodation to the child (Ochs & Schieffelin, 1984). In the case of expressing a guess at a child's unintelligible utterance, the guesser accommodates by putting herself or himself in the position of some individual child at some particular moment and proposing a rendering of the proposition that individual child might at that moment be intending to convey. A good deal of cognitive reorientation may be entailed in formulating a guess. Guessing involves attempting to take the perspective of the other and where the other is an infant or young child, these attempts may include considerable detective work such as noting the direction of the child's gaze or gesture, objects in the child's environment, and recalling a prior action of the child.

Similarly, simplifying one's own utterances is an accommodation to what the speaker perceives to be the cognitive and social limitations of the infant or child. The speaker assumes the child to have a particular level of sociocognitive competence and then designs utterances to be understandable given that level of competence.

Societies that prefer simplification and guessing in misunderstandings involving children are those that nurture egocentricity and expect caregivers (e.g. mothers, sib caregivers, teachers) to be highly sociocentric in their communications with children (Ochs & Schieffelin, 1984). Simplifying and guessing are part of the expected role behaviors of caregivers. Thus, each activity of misunderstanding provides children with an opportunity for developing knowledge of this social role.

We have used simplifying and guessing to illustrate the socialization of social order but other verbal behaviors are equally powerful media for socializing this knowledge. For example, in societies where caregivers show a strong preference for (1) not exhibiting extensive simplication, (2) ignoring or (3) exhibiting only a minimal grasp of a child's unintelligible utterance, and (4) providing cultural glosses, caregivers display low cognitive accommodation to children. Where these preferences prevail, children are socialized into cognitively accommodating to caregivers and others in the situation at hand (cf. Ochs & Schieffelin, 1984) to a greater extent than where simplifying and guessing prevail. In contrast to simplifying and guessing, these responses to children's limited capacity to produce and understand demand that children attend closely to the utterances of others if they wish to understand them and that they repeat or reformulate their own utterances to meet the social and cognitive requirements of the situation at hand. The role of child in societies where these preferences prevail is thus somewhat different from the role of child where simplifying and guessing are preferred strategies in the activity of misunderstanding.

Misunderstandings in these ways socialize children into social statuses and social relationships. Through miscommunications, they come to understand what it means to be a child and a caregiver, for example. Similarly those who emigrate to different societies come to understand the status of "foreigner" through norms, preferences, and expectations that organize misunderstanding as a social activity. Misunderstandings in this sense constitute opportunity spaces for constituting and learning social order.

Misunderstanding and Theories of Knowledge

The activity of misunderstanding socializes not only social role expectations but also local theories of knowledge. When caregivers display preferences for one set of responses to unintelligibility over another, they may do so because they tacitly accept a particular set of assumptions concerning how knowledge is to be acquired, what kinds of knowledge can be acquired, and who can acquire (what kinds of) knowledge in what social situations.

For example, the strong preference for expressing a guess at a child's unintelligible utterance in American middle-class households is tied in part to a local theory that assumes that it is entirely appropriate to put oneself in the mind of another and to guess at the not-yet-intelligible psychological intentions of another (Ochs & Schieffelin, 1984). In this theoretical framework, one person's unclear psychological intentions constitute a culturally possible object of knowledge for another person.

In other societies, thoughts that are not evident through talk or gesture are generally off-limits as an object of knowledge for another person, or at least they are off-limits as an object of discursive knowledge. What another may be thinking is not a usual topic of verbal inquiry. This is the case for Kaluli (Schieffelin, 1990) and traditional Western Samoan communities (Duranti, 1988; Ochs, 1988a). For these speakers, verbally speculating what another is thinking is highly dispreferred. In Samoan communities, verbal guessing does occur but its object tends to be a reported account of some past event or a statement of some future event. Outside of Western organized social settings such as school, speakers tend not to speculate about another's thoughts in the form of riddles and test questions. Further, in court trials, litigants and jurors tend not to speculate concerning the intentions of a defendant. What the defendant may have been intending is not part of the case discussion, only the defendant's actions and the consequences of those actions. Hence children in these communities do not find their unintelligible vocalizations the object of explicit guessing. Such dispreferences socialize children into the bounds of the knowable, the bounds of instruments for knowing, and bounds of the knowing parties—that unclear thoughts are out of the speculative bounds for parties other than the experiences of those thoughts. Within this theoretical perspective, speakers prefer strategies that place the burden of clarification of unclear thoughts on the experiences of those thoughts (e.g., through expressing minimal grasp or ignoring unclear utterance).

Conclusion

In this chapter, misunderstandings are seen as activity loci for the socialization of linguistic and sociocultural knowledge. On a linguistic level, each instance of misunderstanding involving a young child socializes the child into the discourse structures that constitute recognition of and response to misunderstandings. I have put forward the notion that responses to misunderstanding are widespread (e.g., guessing, expressing minimal grasp, ignoring, simplifying, maintaining level of complexity, providing cultural gloss) and that hence children across many societies are acquiring similar knowledge of misunderstanding. It is this knowledge that allows human beings to coordinate their linguistic communication across communities and languages.

On the other hand, the chapter stresses that misunderstandings are more than language activities. They are social and cultural activities as well. Although misunderstandings are part of social life universally, and although members of all cultures have available to them similar discourse strategies for engaging in misunderstandings, local expectations concerning particular social identities and concerning the scope and path to knowledge organize when and to what extent particular strategies will be used. As such, the patterning of particular strategies indexes something about the immediate social situation (e.g., the social status of the speaker or addressee) and the cultural perspective on knowledge (e.g., that one can/cannot know the psychological states of another person).

From this point of view, misunderstandings are not loci in which social life breaks down. Rather, to the contrary, misunderstandings structure social life. Each misunderstanding is an opportunity space for instantiating local epistemology and for structuring social identities of interactants. Once we focus our ethnographic microscopes on misunderstandings, we can appreciate their extraordinary complexity and impact on human culture through the process of language socialization.

4

Uncovering the Human Spirit: Moving Beyond Disability and "Missed" Communications

Lerita M. Coleman
Bella M. DePaulo

> I could tell that at first the taxi driver didn't know that I was blind because for a while there he was quite a conversationalist. Then he asked me what these sticks were for (a collapsible cane). I told him it was a cane, and then he got so different . . . He didn't talk about the same things as he did at first. (Davis, 1977, p. 85)

Are interactions between *disabled* and *able-bodied* people characterized by miscommunications and problematic talk? The description above would suggest that they are. In most cultures, individuals who are disabled are also stigmatized. Usually stigmatization causes disabled and able-bodied people to interact "differently" (Ainlay, Becker, & Coleman, 1986; Farina, Allen, & Saul, 1968; Goffman, 1963b; Jones, Farina, Hastorf, Markus, Miller, & Scott, 1984). What differentiates the communication between disabled and able-bodied individuals from the communication between interactants who are more physically similar, and why? These and related questions will be the focus of our discussion.

AUTHORS' NOTE: The authors wish to thank the editors of this volume for their helpful comments on an earlier draft of this chapter.

Defining Communication, Miscommunication, and Problematic Talk

Miscommunications are difficult to define because of the lack of agreement about the definition of *communication*, from which the term is derived, and because of the complexities involved in applying the term to interactions between disabled and able-bodied individuals. Generally, communication is said to occur when the behavior of one individual affects the behavior of another (Buck, 1984; Miller, 1973). Other researchers, however, believe that communication only occurs in interactions among individuals with a shared signaling system (Wiener, Devoe, Rubinow, & Geller, 1972). By either system, though, displays of problematic talk in interactions between disabled and able-bodied individuals can occur at several levels. Highly salient modifications in speech are common, but miscommunications occur in other channels or modes as well (e.g., facial expressions, eye contact, kinesics, interpersonal distance). Puzzled looks or frowns, gaze aversion, tense body movements, and large interpersonal distances between disabled and able-bodied people are typical examples of miscommunications.

Both descriptions of communication are useful in understanding miscommunications between the disabled and able-bodied. One common example of a miscommunication is the selection of an inappropriate communicative register or style from the many available types. Able-bodied people, for example, may select a baby talk style or some components of such a style (e.g., higher pitch, slower rate of speaking) when interacting with a disabled person. That communicative behavior, in turn, affects the responses of the disabled person, which could range from anger or humiliation to amusement or friendliness. Another form of miscommunication may result from misperceptions or misunderstandings and represent *missed communication*; that is, the disabled and able-bodied interactants lack agreement about the meaning of communicative behaviors or about what constitutes appropriate communicative behavior. (This notion of miscommunication is similar to those included in certain sociolinguistic taxonomies of miscommunications [Gumperz & Tannen, 1979; Gumperz, Jupp, & Roberts, 1979; Milroy, 1984]). Miscommunication, then, can be a set of verbal and nonverbal behaviors that deviate from "normal" communication, or they can be communicative behaviors that are misperceived.

Although misperceptions can be hazardous, they do not always lead to a complete breakdown in communication. Communication can become increasingly problematic when one or more of the interactants perceives that something has gone wrong. Because of an incoherent communication, a lack of shared information, negative attitudes, stereotypes, or stigma, a disabled or able-bodied person may become frustrated or hostile and may even terminate the interaction (Sabsay & Platt, 1985). In fact, the disabling condition (e.g., blindness, deafness, mental retardation) may itself cause major disruptions to the flow or synchrony in communication. Thus, problematic talk may occur in interactions in which expectations are violated, or "the outcome is different from what the interactants expected or hoped for" (Grimshaw, 1980, p. 35).

Our argument is not that all interactions between disabled and able-bodied individuals are problematic, nor that all interactions involving only able-bodied individuals (or only disabled individuals) are nonproblematic. Whether or not any communication becomes problematic will depend on a wide array of factors, including (a) the accuracy of the expectations that the interaction partners have for each other, (b) the degree to which both people wish to be perceived in the ways in which they are perceived by each other (independent of the accuracy of those perceptions), (c) the communicative skills that each person brings to the interaction, and (d) the degree to which each person is committed to making the interaction work.

Historically, disabled people have often (though not always) been ostracized (e.g., Solomon, 1986). Even today, they continue to be socially and physically segregated from able-bodied people. This contributes to the development of negative attitudes, stigma, and stereotyping, which in turn guide and shape the process of communication. For example, able-bodied people may communicate in a way that is completely consistent with their expectations for their disabled interaction partner. However, to the extent that their expectations are inaccurate, their communicative behaviors are likely to be ill-suited to the disabled recipient. And although the disabled partner may respond reasonably competently to such communications, the response may be perceived as inappropriate by the able-bodied interactants, largely because it is inconsistent with their (inaccurate) expectations (e.g., Giles & Powesland, 1975).

Who Are Perceived to Be Disabled?

There are many categories of people who might be classified or who might classify themselves as disabled. However, in this chapter we restrict our observations of miscommunications and problematic talk to those involving physically disabled people. We have chosen to exclude from our discussion people with speech impairments (some of whom are discussed elsewhere in this volume). We will focus primarily on those individuals who are blind or hearing-impaired or who have a physically salient disability (e.g., paraplegics, quadriplegics, and people confined to wheelchairs). People with physical disabilities are of particular interest because they seem to experience problematic talk even though their physical limitations do not intrinsically interfere with their ability to talk.

Ethological studies indicate that the definition of a disability or handicap depends on the environment. A *defect* becomes a *handicap* when "the individual's environment requires significant use of the abnormal part" (Berkson, 1977, p. 190). For example, in nonhuman primates some deformities (e.g., fused or missing toes or fingers) do not inhibit sensory, motor, or social development, and so are not disabling with regard to those domains (Fedigan & Fedigan, 1977). As Berkson notes (1977, p. 190), "The concept of a handicap, therefore, is an ecological statement describing both the individual and the environment." Similar discussions about humans distinguish impairments (medical and pathological conditions) from disabilities (inability to adhere to physical, psychological, and social performance norms) and handicaps (the disadvantages that result from an impairment or disability) (Wood & Badley, 1980).

In human interactions, however, conditions that are not instrumentally disabling, such as facial scars, can still be psychologically disabling. This may be especially likely to occur in societies such as Western ones in which much value is placed on physical bodies and physical attractiveness. The value of stigma attached to a particular body part or function, then, can be an important determinant of whether or not a person who is in some way "different" is labeled as disabled.

The salience or visibility of a condition will also impact upon the labeling process. People whose special conditions are readily apparent to others are especially likely to be labeled as disabled (Conant & Budoff, 1983). External markers of a disability, such as the use of sign language by the deaf, canes and guide dogs by the blind, and wheelchairs by amputees and paraplegics, render those special conditions even more salient. However, even conditions that are almost completely invisible can be perceived as disabling and can engender miscommunications if they are known to others (e.g., Dunkel-Shetter & Wortman, 1982). For example, women who have recently had mastectomies may find themselves to be the objects of unusual visual regard in their initial interactions with others immediately following their surgery.

Even the prevailing economic conditions of the society are relevant to the definitional process. For example, when the rate of unemployment is extremely low and more persons need to be recruited into the work force, the threshold for classifying a person as disabled may creep upwards (cf. Jones et al., 1984).

Although special conditions that can potentially be perceived as disabilities are generally labeled in negative ways (some have even been regarded as sins or as punishments for sins), reactions that can be regarded as positive have also been documented. For example, in some communities, hallucinations and epileptic seizures have been (and in some cases still are) thought to be indicative of supernatural powers (Safilios-Rothschild, 1970). Scheer and Groce (1988), however, caution that the frequency with which this occurs has probably been exaggerated in the literature. From the point of view of the disabled people themselves, probably the most fruitful and engaging encounters with able-bodied people occur when the disability is *not* the focus of the interaction. Conditions that could be regarded as disabilities may be least likely labeled as such and to dominate interactions in small communities in which disabled persons interact with able-bodied people routinely, and in a variety of contexts and roles (Scheer & Groce, 1988; see also Becker & Arnold, 1986).

It is the lay conceptualization of a disability, rather than any official definition, that is likely to be most important in influencing the course of social interactions between disabled and able-bodied individuals. However, there are legal designations of disability, too (e.g., Asch, 1984), which may be underscored by official documents such as handicapped parking stickers. Explicit labels (e.g., signs designating special elevators and rest rooms, special entrances for wheelchairs) may further compound any differences in communicative styles that may have occurred even without the labels.

Persons at risk for being labeled as disabled also can contribute to the course and outcome of the definitional process. Some people choose to deny or to try to hide disabling or potentially disabling conditions, particularly if they highly value bodily competencies and physical attractiveness. This process of *deviance disavowal* (e.g., Davis, 1977) is the interpretation that is sometimes placed on concerted attempts to try to appear normal and to maintain the life-style that preceded the disability (Safilios-Rothschild, 1970). Other disabled people resist stigmatization by conveying their own alternative self-definition (Frank, 1988; Goffman, 1963b; Levitin, 1975; Voysey, 1972). Frequently, disabled people display these alternative self-definitions by engaging in normal social roles such as parent, teacher, or minister (even though surprising to or thwarted by able-bodied people), by ignoring negative social reactions (e.g., eye aversion, fearful facial expressions), and by initiating social interactions with the able-bodied. In some cases disabled people actively attempt to repair interactions that go awry as a result of stereotyping and stigmatization (Frank, 1988).

Origins of Miscommunication and Problematic Talk

Problematic talk is rooted in the attitudes and stereotypes that able-bodied and disabled persons have about each other, and in the stigmatization that can follow from these perceptions. Many miscommunications can be triggered by any labeled disability, regardless of its specific nature (cf. Thompson & Seibold, 1978). Beyond this basic categorization of a person as disabled or able-bodied, more precise discriminations within the wide range of people classified as disabled may govern the fine-tuning (or mistuning) of communications to particular disabled individuals. For example, the severity of the disability and the specific ways in which it interferes with the communicative process can affect the ways in which people miscommunicate (Chinn, Winn, & Walters, 1978). Fine-tuning also occurs with regard to differences across situations as well as persons. For instance, there are indications that disabled persons may be more accepted in work situations than in more interpersonally intimate situations such as dating or marriage (Bowman, 1987). The fine-tuning of miscommunications has also been described in an accommodation model proposed by Coupland, Coupland, Giles, and Henwood (1988) (see Coupland, Nussbaum, & Coupland, this volume). Although the model is based on communication with the elderly, it can be applied to interactions with disabled people. Both disabled and able-bodied people may over-accommodate (e.g., offer too much help or act in condescending ways), underaccommodate (e.g., avoid interacting or act in unhelpful ways) or contra-accommodate (act antagonistically or in ways actively to distance oneself).

The question of the degree to which able-bodied individuals differentiate among different categories of disabled individuals is an obvious one that has been addressed empirically (Altman, 1981; Bowman, 1987; Leyser & Abrams, 1982; Tringo, 1970). Less obvious, but no less important, is the question of the degree to which disabled persons differentiate among different categories of able-bodied people. For example, self-report studies of attitudes toward the disabled suggest that able-bodied women have more positive views of disabled people than do able-bodied men (Altman, 1981). Do these attitudinal differences translate into behavioral differences, and if so, are the behavioral differences sufficiently salient that disabled people can tell that women regard them more favorably than do men? What other kinds of discriminations might disabled individuals make? Might they, for instance, feel especially hostile toward those who are especially affluent, athletic, or attractive? Might they feel more positively toward others who, though physically intact, have been disadvantaged in their own way (such as by poverty or racism?) Or might they instead distance themselves from such persons or even derogate them so as to be able to enjoy the psychological benefits of a comparatively favorable (downward) social comparison (Wills, 1981)? In one of the only empirical investigations of these issues, Galanis and Jones (1986) found that blacks were more tolerant of a mentally ill person than were whites when victimization of blacks in other contexts was made salient, but were less tolerant when such reminders of stigmatization were absent.

In the following sections, we sometimes focus on the attitudes of able-bodied persons toward the disabled. This is not because we think that their attitudes are more important than are those of disabled individuals, but because the available research has so far had more to say about the perspective of the able-bodied. Future research should correct this bias, not by over-emphasizing the role of disabled persons in their interactions with able-bodied people, but by recognizing the mutual contributions of able-bodied and disabled people to the process of communicating.

Attitudes

Some studies have been conducted in an attempt to determine a hierarchy of disabilities based on the favorability of the attitudes about them as reported by able-bodied individuals. Such studies have found, for example, that people who are mentally retarded or who have cerebral palsy are less accepted by able-bodied individuals than are people who are blind, hearing-impaired, or wheelchair-bound (Altman, 1981). Perhaps more interesting, psychologically, than these ranking studies are those aimed at uncovering the determination of these attitudes and rankings. Without studies of the underlying psychological mechanisms, it will be difficult to know how to interpret the results of studies such as those showing that blind men are discriminated against more than are blind women (Gowman, 1957).

The positivity or negativity of attitudes toward disabled people is determined by some of the same factors that dictate whether the label of disabled will be applied in the first place, such as the salience or visibility of the condition. The degree to which the condition makes the person appear especially different in appearance or in patterns of movement is also important. People with skin disorders, body deformations, and cerebral palsy, for example, are less accepted by able-bodied people than are people who are deaf, blind, or paralysed. Among all types of visible disabilities, facial disfigurements seem to be the least liked, least tolerated, and the most likely to produce anxiety and aversion (Safilios-Rothschild, 1970). Another psychologically interesting factor influencing attitudes toward disabled people are able-bodied people's perceptions of the origin or etiology of the disorder. For example, people who are perceived as responsible for incurring or maintaining their condition are more likely to be rejected than are those who are seen as innocent victims (e.g., Brickman et al., 1982; Jones et al., 1984; see also Gibbons, 1986). Finally, the degree to which people with a particular disability are regarded as dangerous or unpredictable also predicts the degree to which they are derogated by others (e.g., Leyser & Abrahams, 1982). In some studies, contact with disabled individuals has been shown to lead to more favorable attitudes on the part of able-bodied people (e.g., Altman, 1981; Anthony, 1969); in other work, however, the effects of contact have been disappointing (e.g., Thompson, 1981, 1982a).

It may seem to require only a small leap of faith to suggest that the conditions that engender more favorable attitudes toward disabled people also engender more favorable behaviors. The conclusion warranted by perhaps hundreds of studies in social psychology, however, is that the link between attitudes and behaviors is often weak or qualified. Thus, we can surmise that people with more visible and less accepted disabilities are more likely to experience miscommunications and problematic talk than disabled people with concealable or more accepted disabilities, but much of the relevant research has yet to be conducted.

Stereotypes

The categorization of one set of people into a different group than another can have profound consequences, even when the categorization was based on an altogether trivial criterion, such as preferences for different works of art (Tajfel & Turner, 1979). Perceptions of differences between people within each group are minimized, and perceptions of differences between people who are from different groups are exaggerated. Once able-bodied people realize that a certain person is hearing-impaired, for instance, they might perceive that person as very similar to other hearing-impaired people and very different from unimpaired persons. The perceptions of outgroup members triggered by this process are generally negative ones, and they are not confined to dimensions relevant to the basis of the categorization. Hearing-impaired individuals, for example, are perceived as different not just in ways that are directly dictated by their impairment (such as the ease with which they can understand what is being said), but in many other ways as well. Able-bodied persons are essentially creating social and psychological distance between themselves and others who have been labeled as disabled. The kinds of differences that they "see" between themselves and disabled people are likely to be guided by their preconceptions about the disabled persons. An implication of the categorization perspective (worthy of further research) is that disabled people also see differences between themselves and able-bodied persons as a result of their membership in these different categories, and they too, will perceive the outgroup (in their case able-bodied people) more negatively than the ingroup (other disabled people).

There are many stereotypes that able-bodied people have of disabled people. For example, they often perceive them as dependent, socially introverted, emotionally unstable or depressed, hypersensitive, and easily offended, especially with regard to their disability. In addition, disabled people are often presumed to differ from able-bodied people in moral character, social skills, and political orientation (e.g., Emry & Wiseman, 1987). The process of perceiving others in accord with preconceptions can be a pernicious one in which even diametrically different behaviors can be seen in similar ways. For example, disabled people who ask for help may be seen as acting dependently, as expected; but those who do not seek help may be seen as denying their dependence (Deegan, 1977: Emry & Wiseman, 1987; Fine & Asch, 1988; Furnham & Lane, 1984). In either case, the disabled persons are perceived as acknowledging, either directly or indirectly, exactly what the able-bodied person already "knew" to be true of them – that they are dependent. Although most physically disabled people are *physically* dependent in some ways, the stereotype can become a self-fulfilling prophecy that needlessly exacerbates perceptions of dependency (Wiseman, Emry, Morgan, & Messamer, 1987). Stereotypes, which are very resistant to change, often determine what disabled and able-bodied people are likely to say as well as what they are likely to hear. For example, Giles and Powesland (1975) have shown that speakers sometimes continue to overaccommodate even when the listeners have responded in a normal way. Stereotypes can also influence whether or not an exchange is initiated, which of the special communication styles (e.g., baby talk) will be selected if the interaction does take place, and which topics will be discussed.

Stigma

Stigmatization is a process whereby people are discredited or discounted because they are different in some way (Goffman, 1963b; Jones et al., 1984; Katz, 1981). Individuals who are disabled are almost always stigmatized. For example, able-bodied people may think of all disabled people as childlike (dependent and helpless), and may therefore talk to them like children (cf. DePaulo & Coleman, 1986, 1987) and treat them like children. Disabled people, in turn, stigmatize able-bodied people in certain ways; for example, they may regard them as untrustworthy or as likely to mistreat others who are different from themselves.

Disabled people often remark that there is a tendency on the part of able-bodied individuals to center the interaction around the disability. It is as if the disability grows into a "master status" (Goffman, 1963b) through which all expectations, communications, and attributions are then filtered (Safilios-Rothschild, 1970; Thompson, 1982a; Wright, 1960). Thus, in many interactions, able-bodied people may restrict their conversations to certain topics or manage the interaction in ways that make the narrowest of their perceptions abundantly clear (Asch, 1984). A dramatically different, but perhaps equally galling strategy that nondisabled people sometimes adopt, is to avoid assiduously any mention of the disability. Because they are so focused on the other person's disability, able-bodied people are often surprised to discover that the disabled person is attractive, bright, or competent (Safilios-Rothschild, 1970), or has a family, job, or hobbies (Edelsky & Rosegrant, 1981).

The fear and anxiety that able-bodied people experience in interactions with disabled people might stem in part from a fear of acquiring a stigma (Coleman, 1986). Even if able-bodied people realize that the disability is not literally contagious, its salience in the interaction serves as a reminder to them of the possibilities and consequences of becoming stigmatized. This fear, although seemingly irrational, is not completely unfounded. Most people will become disabled or stigmatized at some point in life, especially if they live a long time (Safilios-Rothschild, 1970; Zola, 1979).

As noted above, the mere act of classifying one set of people (such as disabled people) into a different category from another (able-bodied people) can result in distorted perceptions. This sort of process can presumably take place completely out of awareness. But able-bodied people can also actively work to make themselves distinctive from disabled people, by purposefully exaggerating their differences and minimizing their similarities (e.g., Coupland, Coupland, Giles, & Henwood, 1988; Thakerar, Giles, & Cheshire, 1982). By making themselves seem very different from disabled people, they may be attempting to enhance their own feelings of self-worth (Crocker, Thompson, McGraw, & Ingerman, 1987). In competitive contexts, it seems to be especially important to able-bodied persons to outperform disabled persons, because they feel so superior to them. Failure to do so can be very esteem-threatening (Katz & Glass, 1979; Piner & Kahle, 1984; Safilios-Rothschild, 1970; see also Druian & DePaulo, 1977). If instead of risking threats to their self-esteem, they can avoid interacting with disabled people altogether, then they can continue to maintain their fragile sense of superiority based on fully functioning physical attributes.

Self-Stigmatization and Self-Assertion

That able-bodied individuals stereotype and stigmatize many people who are different does not go unnoticed by disabled persons. In fact, they may be the victims of these processes even at the hands of their own parents, who may be (at least initially) disappointed or angry about having a child who is not "normal" and who may lower their expectations disproportionately (Barbarin, 1986; Furnham & Lane, 1984; Kashyap, 1986). Although societal-level regulations prevent some of the most blatant exclusions (e.g., from schooling), at more informal levels exclusions and rejections are commonplace throughout the life span of a disabled individual. It is not surprising, then, that some disabled persons react to these repeated experiences of stigmatization by feeling angry, humiliated, or depressed. These are some of the feeling disabled people bring to their interactions with the able-bodied.

As Gordon Allport pointed out in his groundbreaking work on *The Nature of Prejudice* several decades ago (1954), however, self-hate is only one of a variety of responses that victims of prejudice display. Some of the other kinds of reactions are also negative ones, such as hypersensitivity to the evaluations made by able-bodied people and derogation of other disabled persons. But in addition, Allport noted that disabled persons sometimes react in more constructive ways. Contemporary theorists might describe the process as one of fashioning an alternative identity based upon strengths (cf. Schlenker, 1980; see also Chaiklin & Warfield, 1973; Cogswell, 1977; Frank, 1988). To many disabled persons, the disability is not central to their self-concept. Such disabled persons are capable of dealing with challenging situations by, for example, seeking help when that is appropriate, rather than feeling threatened by the need for help and foregoing the desired activity or plan (Nadler, Sheinberg, & Jaffe, 1981). It appears that after disabled people have had their disability for a number of years, the disability is indeed likely to become less central to their self-esteem and to their lives (cf. Schulz & Decker, 1985; see also Mest, 1988). Some disabled people actually engage in a resocialization process in order to combat stigmatization. In one study of paraplegics (Cogswell, 1977), a period of self-imposed isolation built greater competence and a stronger self-concept through the management of social interactions. In social exchanges with other paraplegics, these men and women learned to direct conversations so as to maximize the positive aspects of the self and minimize the negative aspects of the self and thus fostered the development of a new and more positive identity.

The Process of Miscommunication

Both able-bodied and disabled individuals contribute to miscommunication in their interactions with each other. The seeds of problematic talk are planted before the interaction has even begun, and they continue to bear their often poisonous fruit even after the interaction has drawn to a close. We construe the process as one in which both disabled and able-bodied people are joint contributors of attitudes and expectations, actual behaviors, and perceptions of each others' behaviors. We consider each of these factors in turn.

Contributions of Able-Bodied People in Miscommunications

Attitudes and Expectations

It was long recognized, before it was ever empirically documented, that able-bodied people often have negative attitudes about disabled people and pessimistic expectations regarding the likely course of their interactions with them. It is possible that able-bodied persons fear that the unappealing characteristics that they attribute to disabled people are psychologically contagious. Just as able-bodied men profit socially by associating with able-bodied and physically attractive women (Sigall & Landy, 1973), so too may able-bodied individuals fear that they will suffer interpersonally from their association with disabled people. Goffman (1963b) called this stigma by association a *courtesy stigma,* but its recipients are unlikely to regard it as a kindness. Problematic talk, therefore, may stem from a desire to avoid or minimize conversations with disabled people.

Able-bodied individuals may fear negative evaluations not only from other able-bodied persons who might notice them interacting with disabled individuals, but also by the disabled individuals themselves. They may expect disabled individuals to view them as bigoted and unfair, and as awkward and inept in their interactions with people who are different from themselves. In addition, they may expect to be resented for what they perceive to be their more fortunate lot in life.

Not all of the attitudes and expectations that contribute to problematic social interactions are negative ones, however. Sometimes able-bodied individuals simply do not know what to expect of their disabled interaction partners, and this uncertainty, too, can translate into irregular patterns of interaction (Crano & Meese, 1982; Davis, 1977; see also Thompson & Seibold,1978). Able-bodied persons might also be impressed by the courage, ingenuity, and fortitude of disabled persons, and these extremely positive impressions can also result in patterns of interaction that differ from those that occur in dealings with those perceived to be less extraordinary beings. Interestingly, however, this perception of disabled people as saintly is considered by disabled people to be a negative and patronizing attitude (Makas, 1988).

The attitudes and expectations that individuals hold can influence the way that they act toward the targets of those expectations even when (a) the targets are not physically present and (b) the expectations are totally wrong. Snyder, Tanke, and Berscheid (1977), for example, showed that men who believed they were speaking (via an intercom) with physically attractive women spoke to them in a warmer, more animated, and more interesting way than did men who believed that they were speaking with unattractive women, even though the women in fact were "of equal attractiveness" in the two instances. Snow (1972) documented differences in the ways that people spoke to children of different ages when no children were actually present and they were simply asked to speak into a tape recorder as they would if they really were addressing a child of a certain age. And DePaulo and Coleman (1986) demonstrated a wide variety of theoretically relevant differences in speech addressed to different categories of listeners, such as children, foreigners, and mentally retarded adults, even though the speakers were separated from their listeners by a one-way mirror and had no feedback whatsoever from those listeners. Thus, much of the contribution of able-bodied individuals to miscommunications with disabled individuals can occur independently of any behavior of the disabled persons.

Communicative Behaviors During Face-to-Face Interactions

When able-bodied people first perceive a disabled person, they may experience fear, surprise, repulsion, anxiety, and a variety of other affects and emotions that may become immediately apparent by their spontaneous nonverbal reactions (e.g., Buck, 1984). Among these reactions are facial expressions of fear and surprise and trembling voices. They also may experience ambivalence rather than completely negative or positive feelings (e.g., Gibbons, Stephan, Stephenson, & Petty, 1980; Katz, 1981; Katz

& Glass, 1979). These first reactions are frequently outside of one's conscious control.

A split-second later, however, the able-bodied individuals may make a valiant effort to suppress these spontaneous nonverbal reactions or to cover them over with more socially desirable expressions. When the initial emotional reaction is especially strong (and sometimes even when it is not), these attempts at disguise are unlikely to be completely successful (Ekman, 1985). Instead, traces of the underlying affects are likely to "leak" through the veneer.

The particular emotions experienced by able-bodied people while interacting with a disabled person will determine the precise characteristics of their communications. Thus, as those emotions change, so too will the corresponding communicative behaviors. Often, though, able-bodied people experience curiosity, which can result in staring (Langer, Taylor, Fiske, & Chanowitz, 1976), and discomfort, embarrassment, uncertainty, and anxiety, which are often manifest in faux pas, slips of the tongue (Davis, 1977), keeping one's distance (Goffman, 1963b), rigidity of verbal behavior (Kleck, Ono, & Hastorf, 1966), inhibition of nonverbal behavior (Barker et al., 1953; Kleck, 1968), and premature termination of the interaction (Mills, Belgrave, & Boyer, 1984; Snyder, Kleck, Strenta, & Mentzer, 1979; Thompson, 1982a).

The initial emotional reaction is the most spontaneous and least regulated communicative behavior that is likely to occur in the interaction. After it has subsided, it is likely to be replaced by deliberate attempts to convey a much more positive and "normal" impression (e.g., DePaulo, in press). Ironically, however, the more motivated people are to convey a particular impression that is not really sincere (e.g., that they feel very positively toward a person whom they actually fear or loathe), the less likely they are to succeed at so doing (DePaulo & Kirkendol, 1989; see also Makas, 1988). It is as if they are trying too hard to show how kind and tolerant they are, and their nonverbal behaviors betray the lie (DePaulo, Kirkendol, Tang, & O'Brien, 1988). One specific strategy that able-bodied people use in their interactions with disabled people is to distort their own attitudes so that they appear to be even more similar than they really are to the attitudes of the disabled target persons (Barker et al., 1953; Kleck, 1968). But these kinds of ingratiating lies are especially easy to detect (DePaulo, Stone, & Lassiter, 1985). It is possible that disabled persons, who have much experience as targets of such feigned positivity, are especially sensitive to the insincerity of these attempts (cf. DePaulo, Tang, & Stone, 1987).

Perceived Communicative Behaviors

Expectations color perceptions of other people's communicative behaviors. Thus, for example, if able-bodied individuals expect disabled persons to interact in anxious, hostile, dependent, or unskilled ways, they are likely to interpret the behaviors of disabled persons in this manner. For example, a disabled person's request for help might be construed as an indication of helplessness or incompetence (cf. DePaulo, Nadler, & Fisher, 1983), even when an able-bodied individual might also have requested help in the same situation. Misinterpretations may be especially likely to occur when the behaviors are ambiguous and therefore open to a variety of interpretations. When able-bodied people misperceive the reactions of their disabled partners as confirming their initial expectations, they might then proceed to act even more in line with those initial (and perhaps erroneous) expectations, thereby exacerbating the cycle of stigma.

Contributions of Disabled People to Miscommunications

Attitudes and Expectations

Disabled people can also contribute a dose of negativity in their own attitudes and expectations. Some disabled people may be bitter and resentful about their disability and may also feel negatively about themselves more generally. In addition, they are likely to expect to be perceived negatively by others. For example, blind people think that sighted persons perceive them as slightly retarded and hard of hearing (Coupland, Giles, & Benn, 1986; Scott, 1969). And people who really are hearing-impaired worry that others see them as neurotic and as "difficult" interpersonally (Furnham & Lane, 1984). Further, disabled individuals may harbor some negative feelings (such as resentment)toward able-bodied persons, and as an interaction unfolds, they may experience other aversive emotions, too, such as anger, frustration, or humiliation. These kinds of feelings can contribute to problematic talk.

Communicative Behaviors During Face-to-Face Interactions

Disabled people sometimes communicate differently than do able-bodied people as a direct result of their disability. Blind people, for example, are unable to make eye contact or to study other people's facial expressions (Rutter, 1984). Also, because they are deprived of visual feedback and stimulation, they sometimes develop "blindisms" such as facial manipulations and body tilts, ticks, and twitches (Carroll, 1961). Hearing-impaired people who try to read lips focus on the other person's mouth to an unusual degree. Even when they do thereby succeed in deciphering the words, they still will have missed out on the tone of voice with which the words were spoken, which could impair them in their efforts to interpret affects and intentions and act on them accordingly. Hearing-impaired persons also may enunciate poorly and make strange and distracting sounds of which they are unaware. Hearing-impairment, blindness, and a variety of other disabilities can also cause difficulties in turn-taking (Higgins, 1978; see also Buzolich & Wiemann, 1988), which could be particularly problematic because it is typically such a smooth and effortless process. Thus, disabilities involving sensory modes and responses may exert a more pronounced effect on social interactions than other types of disabilities (Berkson, 1977).

Other features that distinguish the communicative behaviors of disabled persons from those of able-bodied persons may be indirect effects of the disability. It is possible that disabled persons, as a consequence of their disability, engage in fewer social interactions (e.g., Thompson, 1981, 1982a), and that the interactions in which they do partake are not smooth (i.e., characterized by a synchrony of verbal and nonverbal behavior) nor as positively-toned as those experienced by able-bodied individuals in their interactions with each other. Disabled people may engage in self-protective accommodation or manage conversations so as to avoid topics that would lead to negative self-assessments (Coupland, Coupland, Giles, & Henwood, 1988). Thus, the communicative skills and strategies that they develop may differ from those of able-bodied interactants.

The discomfort and anxiety often experienced by able-bodied individuals in interactions with disabled persons are not unique to them; disabled people often feel the same. Their own verbal and nonverbal behaviors in many ways parallel those of their able-bodied partners. For example, they make less eye contact, smile less, are more inhibited in their bodily movements (e.g., gestures, posture, leg and feet movement) and terminate the interactions sooner when interacting with people who are different from themselves (able-bodied people) than when interacting with others who are disabled (Emry & Wiseman, 1987; Farina et al., 1968).

In addition, disabled children do not communicate better than able-bodied children to other disabled children (Thompson, 1982a). Perhaps disabled children have fewer social contacts than able-bodied children, and thereby have fewer opportunities to develop sophisticated listener adaptation (or perspective-taking) skills (Thompson, 1981). Other research demonstrates that some disabled people are passive responders; that is, they do not initiate new topics and they display a limited number of speech acts or interactional skills (Buzolich & Wiemann, 1988). Hence, disabled people may lack control in social exchanges and are often forced into a submissive role with able-bodied people. Both disabled and able-bodied people alike may feel uncomfortable with the forced role relationship (Emry & Wiseman, 1987). Moreover, life circumstances may be a prime factor influencing problematic talk (Coupland, Coupland, Giles, & Henwood, 1988). Living in a world of restricted physical mobility may create a world of restricted sociolingustic or psychological mobility for disabled people. Hence, if disabled people assume that an able-bodied person "has no idea what life is like for a disabled person," they may exclude topics and thereby create or contribute to problematic talk.

Problematic communication of this sort is not unique to disabled and able-bodied humans. Initially, able-bodied primates assist disabled primates. Disabled primates, however, rarely initiate interaction; they respond fearfully to interaction initiated by others; and they become increasingly subordinate and alienated from the group (Berkson, 1977; Fedigan & Fedigan, 1977). Just as able-bodied persons may try deliberately, when with disabled persons, to interact just like they do with able-bodied individuals, so, too, may disabled persons try deliberately to act as if they had no disability. In both instances, efforts to act "normally" may backfire, with the resulting performances appearing even more strained than they might ordinarily.

Perceived Communicative Behaviors

In part because they expect to be treated in certain ways, disabled people may sometimes misperceive or misinterpret the verbalizations or nonverbal behaviors of their able-bodied partners. For example, a smile expressing genuine friendliness may be misconstrued as an expression of pity. It is not necessary, though, to rely on anecdotes, impressions, and speculations in discussing the impact of expectations on impressions of other people's communicative behaviors. Relevant data have been gathered, and they speak clearly. In research conducted by Kleck and Strenta (1980), a grotesque scar was painted on the faces of half of the subjects. These women were given a mirror so they could see their new and unsightly disfigurement. Claiming to be applying moisturizing cream, the experimenter then—unbeknownst to the subject—wiped the scar from her face. The women, of course, continued to believe that the scar was present. Those women, who believed themselves to be physically deviant, became acutely sensitive about the ways in which their conversational partners looked at them, and they rated their partners as patronizing, tense, and distant. Detailed analyses of the videotapes of the interactions revealed no indications of unusual visual regard by the partners of the women who thought they looked disfigured. Feeling self-conscious about being different, though, can sometimes cause real differences in other people's behavior. For example, in one study participants were told that their partners believed that they were either homosexuals or ex-mental patients, or they were given no particular information about their partner's beliefs. Those participants who believed themselves to be stigmatized were spoken to less than were those who did not feel stigmatized (Farina et al., 1968).

Joint Contributions of Able-Bodied and Disabled People to Miscommunications

Both the disabled person and the able-bodied person are likely to feel and appear awkward and anxious while interacting with each other. Their conflicting emotions (e.g., Katz & Glass, 1979), their attempts to cover their spontaneous expression of negativity with more dutiful displays, and their uncertainties about how best to proceed in such difficult situations can all lead to the communication of discrepant verbal and nonverbal cues. In addition to the inter- and intrachannel discrepancies that might characterize the communications of each party to the interaction, the two together may communicate in dyssynchronous ways. More specifically, as one or more of the interactants "misaccommodates" (overaccommodates, underaccommodates, or contra-accommodates), their joint behavior becomes less coordinated and more problematic. When two people disagree in their views of each other and of how the interaction should proceed, and when each is perhaps misaccommodating and misreading the other person's signals, the likelihood of establishing a coordinated and synchronized style of interaction is slim.

Perhaps what is absent in problematic exchanges between disabled and able-bodied people is interaction management, a vital aspect of communicative competence (Wiemann, 1977). A competent communicator is other-oriented, affiliative, supportive, empathetic, flexible behaviorally, and relaxed in social interactions. Rarely, in the innumerable anecdotal descriptions and empirical observations of the exchanges between disabled and able-bodied individuals can we claim that either or both parties act with the kind of communicative competence described in Wiemann's model.

Effects of Miscommunications on Disabled and Able-Bodied People

Effects on Disabled People

What are the effects on disabled persons of being the targets of anxious and avoidant communicative behaviors in their interactions with able-bodied individuals? Intuitively, it would seem that the effects would be undermining of their competence and their dignity. Some suggestive evidence from outside the realm of physical disabilities is available. One of the most compelling examples comes from the domain of interracial interactions. In the first of a two-part study, whites interviewed black and white applicants for a job. When interviewing the blacks, the interviewers made more speech errors, sat farther away, and terminated the interview more quickly than they did when interviewing whites. The second part of the study was designed to address the question of how whites might behave if they were treated like blacks. Therefore, in part two, all participants were white, but the interviewers were trained to act either like the part-one interviewers of the white applicants, or like the interviewers of the blacks. The part-two applicants who were treated like the black applicants of part one thought that their interviewers were less friendly. These applicants were also judged by observers (who knew nothing of the fact that the interviewers had been coached to act more avoidantly) to be less qualified for the job than were the applicants that were treated like the part-one whites (Word, Zanna, & Cooper, 1974). This study suggests that being treated like a member of a stigmatized group can have deleterious effects on affect and on task performance in important contexts. Thus, it is not surprising that stigmatized or disabled people may be perceived as, and sometimes may even become, more reserved, alienated, introverted, and defensive than nonstigmatized people (Thompson & Siebold, 1978).

That targets of expectancies often come to act in line with those expectancies is, of course, the lesson of decades of research on the self-fulfilling prophecy (e.g., Rosenthal & Rubin, 1978). Frequently, disabled people internalize the labels that able-bodied people assign and their self-concepts reflect these labels (Curra, 1975; Scheff, 1974). There is another sad lesson in the literature on expectancy effects, and that is that there can be negative consequences even for those who resist the erroneous expectation. In their classic study of teacher expectations for the disadvantaged, Rosenthal and Jacobson (1968) found that students who were not expected to "bloom" intellectually, but who did blossom anyway, were derogated by their teachers.

Even very subtly negative behaviors can have consequences for important life decisions. An example of this comes from research on tone of voice cues. Doctors who had treated alcoholic patients were interviewed about their experiences with those patients. Audiotapes of the interview were content-filtered so that only the tone of voice, and not the words, could be deciphered. Judges listened to the tapes and rated the degree of anger that seemed to be communicated by the tone of voice. Those physicians whose voices sounded more angry were less successful in referring their alcoholic patients for treatment (Milmoe, Rosenthal, Blane, Chafetz, & Wolf, 1967). It is unlikely that either the doctors or the alcoholic patients consciously realized during their interactions with each other that some of the doctors may have been conveying negative affect with their voices, yet the alcoholics who were paired with such doctors were markedly less likely to heed their advice.

Even the communication of well-meaning affects, such as sympathy (nurturing tone of voice often accompanied by touching), can have deleterious effects. Although able-bodied people may feel that they are being kind-hearted when they convey sympathy for people they regard as less fortunate than themselves, the targets of such expressions are rarely grateful (e.g., Ladieu, Hanfmann, & Dembo, 1947; see also Makas, 1988). And in a study in which the communication of sympathy was experimentally manipulated in a teaching context, the children who failed a test and were subsequently the targets of their teacher's sympathy felt less intelligent and less sanguine about their future prospects for success than children who had also failed but to whom no sympathy was conveyed (Graham, 1984).

It is too simplistic to assume, however, that all modifications made in the interactions with "special" categories of people will have harmful effects. For example, a study of the use of baby talk among staff members to address the elderly residents of a nursing home uncovered the surprising result that not all elderly persons resented this mode of communication; elderly persons who were less successful at functioning independently reacted more positively to the baby talk register than did elderly persons who were more competent (Caporael, Lukaszewski, & Culbertson, 1983; see also Coupland, Nussbaum, & Giles, this volume). This study, of course, does not show that severely disabled persons will not mind being treated like babies; however, it does suggest that the relevant data should be collected before even the most intuitively compelling hypotheses are accepted.

Effects on Able-Bodied People

Although the effects of miscommunications are likely to be most pernicious for the disabled parties to interactions between able-bodied and disabled individuals, able-bodied persons are not unaffected. To the extent that the interaction failed to proceed smoothly, able-bodied people may feel ashamed of their own inability to interact effectively with people who are different from themselves. They also may worry (perhaps appropriately) that they may have offended the disabled person. If they feel incapable of doing better in future interactions with disabled persons, they may try to avoid such interactions completely.

Rendering Problematic Talk Less Problematic

Interactions between disabled and able-bodied individuals are not the only ones in which problematic talk can be observed. Many interactions between able-bodied individuals, especially those who are strangers to each other, are also fraught with hesitations, false starts, and awkward moments of silence. As two able-bodied individuals learn more about each other, they are able to establish commonalities which help to erase the difficulty, uncertainty, and perplexity that characterizes the talk between unfamiliar or dissimilar people.

Likewise, able-bodied adults who have had more contact with disabled adults often evidence more favorable attitudes toward them (Altman, 1981; Anthony, 1969; Makas, 1988; but see also Thompson, 1981, 1982a). Research suggests, for example, that people with more contact with hearing-impaired individuals see them as more normal than do people who have less frequent contact with them. The type of contact may also be important, though. For example, in helping contexts, such as psychotherapy (not necessarily involving disabled people), it has been amply documented that professionals often develop negative perceptions of their clients (Wills, 1981). Perhaps in helping contexts involving disabled persons (e.g., physical therapy), though, the positive effects of contact are more important than the negative effects of the processes that work against favorable perceptions of help-recipients. It is difficult to determine, however, whether miscommunications and problematic talk vary with the length and type of interpersonal relationship that disabled and able-bodied people may have. In some circumstances, attitudes change and interactions become less characterized by miscommunications as disabled and able-bodied people become more familiar with each other. Other empirically documented scenarios, however, are less hopeful. For example, some mentally retarded people show little awareness of others, have a limited topic repertoire and often omit essential information in their conversations (Sabsay & Platt, 1985). Contact with such people is likely only to exacerbate the inclination of nonretarded people to avoid retarded people.

Social psychological research suggests ways in which situations can be arranged so as to facilitate effective and respectful patterns of communication. Cooperative contexts in which the contributions of all individuals (i.e., both able-bodied and disabled) are valued and in fact indispensable, have just such salutary effects (e.g., Lucker, Rosenfield, Sikes, & Aronson, 1976; Slavin, 1980). In these situations, the unique strengths of each individual are underlined, and their disabilities are irrelevant (e.g., Nolan, 1981, 1987). The disability becomes *ground* instead of *figure* (Yamamoto, 1977).

It is also possible, though the relevant data have not yet been collected, that changes in labels could facilitate communicative effectiveness. It has been argued, for example (Longmore, 1985), that terms such as handicapped, the disabled, and the blind, imply that the person is socially incapacitated in ways that transcend any physical restrictions imposed by disability. To combat the objectification of disabled individuals, civil rights activists proffer other labels such as "dis-ABLE", "handicapable" or "physically challenged".

Even simpler strategies than widespread societal changes in labeling practices may also prove useful. For example, there is evidence to suggest that able-bodied people would rather work and socialize with disabled people who acknowledge their disability than with those who do not acknowledge it (Belgrave & Mills, 1981; Hastorf, Wildfogel, & Cassman, 1979). Although acknowledgment of the disability on the part of the disabled person does not always lead to acceptance (Thompson & Seibold, 1978), it does reduce uncertainty and tension and enhances the attractiveness of the disabled person. Interactions proceed less problematically when a disabled person "appropriately" self-discloses about the disability (Thompson, 1982b). One way that self-disclosures might ease tension is by assuring others that a disabled person is not hypersensitive about the disability. And in fact, research has shown that self-disclosures do enhance interactions when it appears that the disabled person is coping with the disability; however, they may actually hinder exchanges when it appears that a disabled person is *not* coping effectively with the disability (Bazakas, 1979). More positive interactions may also occur when both able-bodied and disabled people express interest in other aspects of each other's lives. Having more information about each interactant than that which is provided by social categories or sociological roles makes the interpersonal communication more personal and individual (Miller & Steinberg, 1975).

Finally, perhaps disabled people can contribute to the education of able-bodied people and to the smoothness of social interactions by explicitly communicating their own preferences and expectations for how they should be treated. There is now evidence indicating that able-bodied people with little experience with disabled people are unlikely to figure out for themselves how to interact effectively with them (see also Dunkel-Shetter & Wortman's [1982] analysis of interactions between physically healthy people and cancer patients). When urged to be as positive as possible toward disabled people, they often act in ways that disabled people find irritating and condescending. For example, they give disabled people more chances or "breaks" in games and other competitions and they describe extraordinarily positive attitudes toward them (Makas, 1988; see also Weitz, 1972). In general, it is likely that the most important contributions to effective social interactions between able-bodied and disabled individuals are made by disabled people, especially those who have had the disability for a long time. Over the course of repeated experiences, they have probably learned successful strategies for facilitating social interactions, such as those used to put fretting able-bodied persons at ease, in a matter-of-fact manner.

Conclusion

We can learn a great deal about communication when it is incomplete, when it breaks down, or when interactants attempt to repair it. A host of revealing affective responses, such as amusement, apprehension, anger, contempt, curiosity, embarrassment, frustration, exasperation, self-doubt, and sympathy, spill forth in such situations, and provide intriguing clues as to the ways in which these difficult interactions are experienced by the participants.

Miscommunications between disabled and able-bodied people seem to stem from attitudes, stereotypes, and stigmatization. One common type of miscommunication is the selection of a distinctive (and perhaps inappropriate) communication style, such as baby talk, or some of the components of such a style. Another form of miscommunication may result from the misinterpretation of verbal and nonverbal behaviors. In other situations, the disability itself (e.g., blindness, deafness, mental retardation) can impede communication.

Sometimes one person's misperceptions go unnoticed by the other person (Milroy, 1984). Other times, one or more of the interactants may intentionally ignore the miscommunications as a way to "save face" for the other or as a way to maintain the conversation (Milroy, 1984; Sabsay & Platt, 1985). Although many people opt to leave an interaction puzzled, others attempt to repair miscommunication (Drummond & Hopper, this volume; Gass & Varonis, this volume) especially if they believe the repair is vital to maintaining an interaction and a relationship. These repairs may take the form of repetitions, questions of clarification, topic switches and other communicative devices used to encourage a smooth flow of exchange. The degree of communicative skill on the part of disabled and able-bodied people may be a major determinant of whether or not these attempts at repairs are successful.

It is our hope that by studying the communicative process, we can learn how to prevent many miscommunications and the hurt feelings that they can engender. For as Safilios-Rothschild notes, "Unless modern societies are successful in altering social and affective prejudices in such a way that the disabled are accepted as 'people with a disability' in the same way that people with green eyes or blond hair are accepted, we will not have moved very far from the prejudices and discriminatory practices of the Middle Ages" (1970, p. 11). We must also find more ways to sensitize disabled people to the ways in which they contribute to miscommunications and problematic talk. Otherwise, we will continue to *miss* much of the human spirit if our distorted and stereotyped perceptions of ability and disability continue to serve as the basis for communication.

5

The Reproduction of Aging and Agism in Intergenerational Talk

Justine Coupland
Jon F. Nussbaum
Nikolas Coupland

Two commonplace rationales[1] for addressing gerontological concerns in social science are (a) that elderly people are often all but invisible in many existing research traditions, which have over-invested in young adults as an implicit developmental norm; and (b) that the postretirement sector of Western societies is rapidly expanding as a proportion of the population. These factors are an important backdrop to our own discussion too, not least since it seems that a fundamental dimension of gerontological "miscommunication" is the way the language and communication sciences have been conspicuously slow to contribute to our understanding of social aging. At the same time, recognizing the demographic trend toward a "graying" Western world is not in itself a wholly appropriate starting point. To construe older people as a new and pernicious social force risks perpetuating the climate of social alienation and devaluation that is endemic to the miscommunicative processes we want to highlight in this chapter. Old people are only a problem for society to the extent that we assume they are peripheral rather than constitutive of mainstream society itself.

AUTHORS' NOTE: This chapter was prepared while the authors were Visiting Professors at the University of California, Santa Barbara during the 1989-1990 academic session. We gratefully acknowledge the support of the Department of Communication at UCSB and input from faculty and graduate students there.

In what follows, we want to overview linguistic and communicative research that has begun to explore the elderly as a unique (though highly differentiated) subgroup of the general population, and how they must constantly adapt to a world that too often confronts them with stereotyped perceptions and ultimately miscommunication. For analytic convenience, as a way of organizing a selective and still-developing literature (for more detailed reviews, see Coupland, Coupland, & Giles, in press; Nussbaum, Thompson, & Robinson, 1989; Ryan, in press), we focus on two broad groups of processes that interact to constitute miscommunication: *social attitudes and agism* and *interaction.* Studies under the attitudes rubric have been concerned with stereotyping processes, prejudicial beliefs about aging and elderly people, and the case that many Western societies sustain a broadly "agist" orientation. Although the literatures on attitudes and agism have developed independently of interactional considerations, we assume social interaction is the hub of miscommunicative processes, where attitudes are molded, consolidated, or modified. So, for example, research relating to health and medical settings has traced the problematical consequences of misunderstandings and in other respects poor alignment between doctors and elderly patients. We overview three different approaches to interaction and aging: talk to the elderly, research in the accommodation theory tradition, and recent discourse analytic work which explores the development of age-identities in cross-generation talk. We suggest that much more extensive research of this general kind should be able to offer an integrated statement of the social construction of *intergenerational miscommunication,* and even of social aging itself.

Social Attitudes and Agism

Few would argue with the fact that human beings form preferences and attitudes which, to some degree, reflect predispositions to behave (Bennett & Eckman, 1973) and, again to some extent, reflect the social, political, and economic world within which an individual exists. Attitudes formed about the aging process or about elderly individuals have often been said to influence the lives of older people. Palmore (1982) writes that "many, if not most, of the 'problems of aging' stem from or are exacerbated by prejudice and discrimination against the aged" (p. 333).

Slater (1964) suggests that two contradictory traditions of thought have produced mixed attitudes toward the process of aging. The ancient Greek tradition stresses the fortune of youth and the great misfortune of the old. Within this ideology, it is better to die than to suffer the indignities of old age. On the other hand, the Middle Eastern view of aging is more positive;

it is principally through aging that status and prestige are to be accomplished. Old age is a blessing; those who die young are the wicked. Palmore (1982) holds that these dichotomous construals of aging have a modern parallel in the differences between attitudes in industrialized and agricultural societies. Broadly speaking, within industrialized societies, production is paramount and the most productive people have traditionally been thought of as the young generation. Agricultural societies seem to place more emphasis on worldly experience as a resource for coping.

An extensive literature has reported on all aspects of the attitudes (of younger and older people) toward the aging process, since the pioneering work of Dinkel (1944). Several excellent reviews are available: for example, Bennett and Ekman, 1973; Botwick, 1984; Kastenbaum, 1964; Palmore, 1982. Kite and Johnson (1988) give a meta-analysis of 43 studies (published before 1985) that compared attitudes to differing age-groups. Although mixed results do exist (due to measurement differences, effect size differences, specification of a target individual, etc.), one cannot help but conclude that attitudes toward the aging process and toward elderly individuals are relatively negative, at least in U.S. and U.K. cultures. Palmore (1982) summarizes the major conclusions of this research as follows: (1) relative to ratings of other age categories, ratings of old age tend to be more negative; (2) most people have mixed feelings about various aspects of old age and tend to rate old age positively on some dimensions and negatively on others; (3) there are more stereotypes associated with old age than with younger ages; (4) many negative stereotypes are held by a majority of persons; (5) knowledge about aging can be improved and misconceptions can be reduced by training in gerontology, although attitudes are more resistant to change (pp. 340-341).

Research in the social evaluative paradigm has also considered age-discriminatory responses to *vocal* stimuli. These are audio-recordings of either genuine or (most often) imitated vocal styles that differ along specific controlled dimensions—the so called *matched guise* technique. Stewart and Ryan (1982), for example, found that younger adults can be rated more positively than older adults in competence-stressing situations (see also Rubin & Brown, 1975). Research findings have not been entirely consistent. Crockett, Press, and Osterkamp (1979) found relatively favorable reactions to older speakers, and attributed the finding to the effects of judges' negative stereotypical expectations of elderly speakers being disconfirmed. In Ryan and Johnston's (1987) study, the variable *effective* versus *ineffective message* was the only significant factor for competence ratings across younger and older speakers, with no main effects emerging for age itself. Giles, Coupland, Henwood, and Coupland (1989) again found that, in a matched-guise design, speech-rate was a more potent variable than either accent (standard versus nonstandard voice) or age (older versus younger speaking guise). There was also some evidence, though, that an elderly voice in conjunction with nonstandard accent and a low speaking rate conspire to produce very high ratings of perceived "vulnerability". In an open-ended phase of the investigation, respondents invoked age- and class stereotypes to rationalize the evaluative decisions they had made cross all conditions of the study. For example, while the nonstandard speaking guises called up images of a homely, provincial speaker, the elderly vocal guises were associated with incompetence, forgetfulness, and disaffection. Austin (1985) presents evidence that attitudes toward aging have improved significantly since the 1970s. Levin (1988) and Sanders and Pittman (1988), however, show that negative attitudes remain well ingrained in our society. Both studies conclude that the more information we have about a target individual, the less negative the attitude held; however, when only general information is available, age becomes a very salient variable and negative age stereotyping emerges.

The existence of negative attitudes toward the aging process and the elderly becomes important when those attitudes are manifested in some form of discriminatory behavior. Butler (1969) coined the term *agism* to connote wholesale discrimination against all elderly individuals, "a deep-seated uneasiness on the part of the young and middle-aged—a personal revulsion to and distaste for growing older" (p. 243). Atchley (1980) writes that "age discrimination occurs when human beings are avoided or excluded in everyday activities because they are the 'wrong age' " (p. 261). Levin and Levin (1980) also recognize a specific condition they term *gerontophobia*, fear of one's own aging, of the elderly, and of association with death (p. 94; see also Bunzel, 1972). Several studies have in fact indicated that younger individuals would be less willing to interact with an elderly individual even if that elderly person was similar in all respects to a younger individual other than age (Golde & Kagan, 1959; Levin & Levin, 1981; Long, Ziller, & Thompson, 1966).

In a youth-oriented society, institutionalized agism is not difficult to document, from the workplace that forces retirement at age 65 rather than according to level of competence, to the media that either underrepresent the elderly or portray them as dependent and weak (see Robinson, 1989). A critical manifestation of gerontophobia is to be found in the caring professions, where, according to Norman (1987),

> the poor image of old age inevitably rubs off on those who are working in this field. Work with old people is not a prestigious occupation and there is a vicious circle in that jobs with low prestige tend to attract unambitious or less-skilled workers. (p. 9)

In addition, Nussbaum, Thompson, and Robinson (1989) and Nuessel (1982) discuss the way our society places the elderly into age-segregated ghettos which separate the main stream of daily activity from those who live in retirement communities or nursing homes built on the fringe of town. For Levin and Levin (1980) agism shows up as a propensity to "blame the [elderly] victim" to blame "biology or the ravages of time" for the states and conditions of old age, rather than focus on "the social forces that make old age a difficult, even dreaded stage of life" (p. 35). Age-prejudicial forces have been documented across very many domains including literature (Berman & Sobkowska-Ashcroft, 1986), humor (Palmore, 1971), magazine fiction (Martel, 1968), and television drama and commercials (Kubey, 1980).

Experimental research has often been able to demonstrate ageist effects. For example, Carver and de la Garza (1984) showed how, following a supposed road accident, further information is requested from younger and older drivers in stereotype-consistent ways. Drivers labeled "elderly" were asked to supply information to do with their physical, mental, and sensory adequacies; "young" drivers tended to be asked whether they had been speeding or had drunk alcohol. In an extension study, Franklyn-Stokes, Harriman, Giles, and Coupland (1988) found similar patterns of differential questioning, but this time distributed incrementally across ages 22, 54, 64, 74, and 84 years (the ages given for the supposed addressee). Health and physical condition were increasingly considered relevant to subsequent questioning as the age of the supposed subject increased. To this extent, information-seeking can be seen to be agist across the adult life span, with agist attributions made of people as young as 54.

In this climate, it is perhaps not surprising that research on aging has—*itself*—sometimes endorsed generally agist assumptions in "problematizing" the elderly. According to Levin and Levin (1980), "the literature in gerontology is shot through both with the assumption of decline with age and, perhaps partly as a result of this assumption, with the findings of physical, psychological and sociological deterioration in aging individuals" (p. 2). This would also appear to be the case in the research questions predominantly pursued in the language and communication literatures (Coupland & Coupland, 1990). Here, language and communication in normal aging are most often characterized through an appraisal of *residual* competence, with research focusing on precisely those dimensions of language use that are known potentially to show, or are suspected of showing, decrement. As a result, language use in normal aging tends to be represented by providing evidence of group's non-impaired competence in some respect, or sometimes their achieving a higher score on some index than an impaired group achieves. Sometimes, the "normal" elderly will themselves be shown to have declined on some psycholinguistic measure in relation to a younger group (taken to represent the central norm).

Very many facets of speech production, linguistic knowledge, and processing have been investigated from these perspectives over more than three decades, producing complex and sometimes inconsistent results (for reviews, again see Coupland & Coupland, 1990; also Ryan, in press). For example, Gold, Andres, Arbuckle, and Schwartzman (1988) identify so-called *off-target verbosity* among elderly speakers, a phenomenon they recognize when speech "quickly becomes a prolonged series of loosely associated recollections increasingly remote from, relatively unconstrained by, and irrelevant to the present external contextual stimuli" (p. 27). The authors find no direct association between such talk and age itself, but suggest that it "becomes manifest in older people who are extroverted, socially active, not concerned with others' impressions of them, undergoing more stress and experiencing declining performance in nonverbal cognitive functioning" (p. 32). Although Gold et al. are not able to commit themselves to a single interpretation of their findings, they consider cognitive impairment a candidate explanation for behavioral characteristics of elderly talk.

Similarly, from a series of formal tests of sentence comprehension and manipulation (including many varying in syntactic complexity), Emery (1986) reports that in morphological respects and on every measure of syntactic function, she repeatedly finds significantly lower levels of performance among the normal elderly (aged 75-93) than among the pre-middle-aged (30-42). Kynette and Kemper (1986) also report that subjects in their 70s and 80s produced more syntactic errors and used less complex syntactic structures (which impose lower memory demands) in interview responses than people in their 50s and 60s. Kemper (1986) reports that elderly adults (70-89) were less able to imitate complex syntactic constructions than young adults (30-49). Nebes and Andrews-Kulis (1976), on the other hand, report no decremental age-effects in subjects' construction of grammatical strings. But Emery (1986) concludes from her study that "diminished linguistic processing appears to be a concomitant of normal aging" (p. 60).

In ways that are reminiscent of early and problematical studies in the language and social class domain, the paradigm throws up results that are highly difficult to interpret in any socially sensitive frame. There is generally no consideration of motivational factors that might mediate different levels of performance (why do older people respond more slowly in some experimental conditions?); or of contextual factors (in what range of circumstances do older people use less complex syntax or underachieve on tests of receptive ability?); or of real-life implications (do measured differences have any contrastive or *emic* significance to everyday people in everyday settings outside of the test situation?); or of semiotic impact (which elderly characteristics in fact connote "elderliness", to whom, and with what evaluative weighing?). This research tradition also needs to explore the possibilities of elderly people outperforming younger communicators, when more positively construed elderly communicative characteristics have been looked for. For example, Smith, Reinheimer, and Gabbard-Alley (1981) found that elderly women (mean age 70.8) coped better with the demands of crowded and close communication environments than young women (mean age 20.4). Overall, it seems appropriate to remind ourselves of "the pitfalls of the health/wholeness archetype" (Guggenbuhl-Craig, 1980, p. 21), the blinkered concern with perfect competence and with individuals' deviations from it to which Western society is arguably prone.

Some studies have set out to demonstrate the ways in which parts of the language system itself play a part in the reproduction of agist attitudes. Covey (1988) traces the changing meanings of terms relating to old age. The etymology of the word *old* itself, for example, associates it with the meaning *to nourish*, and it has for a long time carried connotations of experience, skill, and wisdom (p. 293). More recently, it has variably been associated with meanings of endearment ("old friend", "Old Bright"), but also conservatism ("old guard"); it has been used in references to the Devil ("Old Harry", "Old Nick") and very often in derogative terms ("old hag", "old fogey", "dirty old man"). Covey claims that "contemporary older people do not like to use the word old in describing themselves or their membership groups" (p. 293), and concludes generally that terminology in this area reflects "a decline in the status of the elderly and the increased focus on the debilitative effects of aging" (p. 297).

Nuessel (1984) likewise argues that there is a vast lexicon of agist language in everyday usage, within which most terms are used to describe or refer to the elderly in a pejorative way, or at least carry negative overtones. Instances relating to females (often prefixed by "old") include: "biddy", "crone", "bag", and "battle-ax"; and referring to males: "gaffer" and "geezer". Attributives often used to describe the elderly show the same process of pejoration: cantankerous, crotchety, fussy, garrulous, grumpy, rambling, and wrinkly. Studying elderly labels in the United States, using experimental methods, Barbato and Feezel (1987) asked groups of people in three different age categories (17-44, 45-64, 65+) for their evaluations of the connotative meanings of ten words referring to an older person. Some terms (including *mature American*, *senior citizen*, and *retired person*) were positively rated on the scale "active", "strong", "good", "progressive," and "happy". On the other hand, *aged*, *elderly*, and nouns using *old* were more negatively evaluated. Interestingly, few evaluative differences between the responses of the different age-groups were found.

Intergenerational Interaction

The value of an interactional perspective on miscommunication is partly that it is able to contextualize particular instances of the macro-level social forces we discussed up to this point in the chapter. In so doing, it can give us access to the socially constructive and *variable* processes through and in which age-prejudicial orientations are culturally reproduced or modified. For some theorists, discourse analysis is in fact the *only* adequate research methodology for investigating social attitudes and prejudices (e.g., Potter & Wetherell, 1986). In this section, we discuss available studies of cross-generation interaction, themselves still quite diverse methodologically, under three subcategories: *talk to the elderly*, studies in the *accommodation theory* paradigm; and those addressing the construction of *age-identities in discourse*.

Talk to the Elderly

Styles of talk used in addressing the elderly have been the subject of some of the most sustained research to date, mostly driven by concern for what is, in context, the proper treatment of older people as conversational recipients. Ashburn and Gordon (1981) compared specific formal and functional characteristics of care-givers' and volunteers' speech among themselves and to elderly residents in a nursing home. They found more questions and repetitions being used by staff and volunteers to elderly residents than among their peers, and that staff used more questions to nonalert than to alert residents. Rubin and Brown (1975) found that students used significantly shorter utterances, and hence arguably simpler syntax, to explain the rules of a game to older adults (who they assessed to have lower intellectual abilities) than young adults.

There is a need for more contextual sensitivity in work of this sort, and contrastive quantitative designs may well tend to obscure the dynamic processes relevant to specific contexts. For instance, Greene, Adelman, Charon, and Hoffman (1986) found no differences in the frequencies of questions, compliments, or negative remarks made by physicians to older (over 65) and younger (under 45) patients in medical interviews. But their more qualitative assessments led them to conclude that "it was more difficult for elderly patients than for young patients to get their agendas addressed"; also that "physicians were less respectful, less patient, less engaged and less egalitarian with their old than with their young patients" (p. 121). The authors take these differences of approach by physicians as evidence of agist professional practices in medical encounters (see above; also Adelman, Greene, & Charon, in press).

The focus of Caporael and colleagues' research (Caporael, 1981; Caporael & Culbertson, 1986; Caporael, Lucaszewski, & Culbertson, 1983; Culbertson & Caporael, 1983) has been the use of *secondary baby talk* (or *BT*) by caregivers to the institutionalized elderly. In the 1981 study, BT (defined as a specific set of prosodic configurations including high and variable pitch) was found to be frequent in care-givers' talk to residents (up to 20%), and to be indistinguishable when content-filtered from primary BT (that is, talk actually addressed to children). As Caporael's term "BT" shows, the research aligns itself at a general level with other sociolinguistic traditions investigating simplified addressee-registers, not only *baby talk* (or *motherese*, see Snow & Ferguson, 1977) but also *foreigner talk* (Ferguson, 1981). Although overlaps in manifest language and communication styles to these diverse groups are of course interesting, and although there might be implications in these similarities for a universal theory of linguistic complexity/simplification, each demographic context subsumes its own unique clusters of considerations of social motivation, evaluation, and consequence. For example, Brown (1977) considers a possible pedagogic intent behind using simplified registers to children; descriptively similar styles to nonnative speakers may conceivably be intended to suppress linguistic and cultural integration (Valdman, 1981); simplified talk to the visually handicapped may be demeaning because it overgeneralizes from a particular sensory handicap (Coupland, Giles, & Benn, 1986). An approach that glosses "talk to the elderly" as one of a family of speech registers will inevitably obscure key sociopsychological processes.

Indeed Caporael and colleagues' important research clearly demonstrates the value of probing further with a very precisely contextualized, multilevel analysis. What emerges from this series of studies is a rather complex evaluative pattern of responses to BT styles. Even within one physical setting, goals, attributions, and evaluations of sociolinguistic styles proved to be highly differentiated. The Caporael et al. (1983) study found that care-givers predicted that residents with low functional ability would *like* to be spoken to with BT, and felt that *non*-BT speech would be ineffective for interacting with them. Also, it emerges that BT is indeed variously evaluated as demeaning or *nurturing* by different categories of institutionalized elderly people. Dependent elderly were more likely to hear BT as nurturing, and prosodically defined BT was also found to be associated with a high frequency of "encouraging comments". Other dimensions of *elderspeak* also may be facilitative in some instances. Cohen and Faulkner (1986), for example, report positive effects for speech-styles with exaggerated primary word-stress on elderly recipients' comprehension and recall. Findings such as these show that opposition to sociolinguistically discriminative language use, and the assumption that negative stereotypes of aging constrain communicative choices to the detriment of elderly recipients, may not always be appropriate ideological positions. They also show that a variety of research methods is ultimately needed for sociolinguistic explanation, and that interpretations will at many points need to reflect how talk is embedded within multiple layers of textual, as well as social and psychological *con*textual considerations.

Accommodation Theory

It was in response to this need for better integrated theoretical modeling of communication in aging that Coupland, Coupland, Giles, and Henwood's (1988) extension of *Communication Accommodation Theory* (CAT) to gerontological contexts was proposed. The accommodation model (see Giles, 1973; Giles, Coupland, & Coupland, in press) draws together motivational, attitudinal, evaluative, and behavioral (sociolinguistic) factors in trying to explain the relational processes that operate in specific contexts of talk. In the 1988 formulation, CAT is specifically geared to modeling potential *mis*matches between speakers' discourse strategies and hearers' needs and wishes for interaction—hence the modeling of miscommunication.

The central insight on which CAT is premised is that, during interaction, conversational styles show variable degrees of *attuning* to each other, along multiple simultaneous dimensions, and that interactants may strategically modify their accommodative stances in pursuing relational and identity goals. Typically (though very many caveats have been empirically established in the literature—see Giles, Mulac, Bradac, & Johnston [1987] for a detailed review), relatively high levels of interpersonal attuning will correspond with positive relational goals such as desiring social approval and establishing affinity. Lower levels of attuning (including the maintenance of one's habitual style) will often reflect dissociative intents, such as the desire to establish a group-identity that is different from the interlocutor's. Attuning possibilities will span at least the following four dimensions:

(1) *approximation strategies* through which a speaker may converge toward or diverge away from selected features or qualities of her or his partner's style (e.g., in terms of speech-rate, nonverbal style, accent/dialect);
(2) *interpretability strategies* through which a speaker will modify the complexity/clarity/explicitness of her or his talk (e.g., in terms of vocal amplitude, syntax, or lexical familiarity);
(3) *discourse management strategies* which can variably facilitate or impede a conversation partner's own participation in ongoing discourse, for example in terms of "field" characteristics (such as topic selection), "mode" (e.g., patterns of turn-allocation) and "tenor" (e.g., signaling degrees of agreement or support in back-channeling)[2]; and
(4) *interpersonal control strategies* by means of which a speaker may modify the other's freedom to assume particular conversational roles and personas (e.g., through interruption or the use of power-implicated address forms).

With the above conceptual apparatus, CAT can identify constellations of "over-" and "underaccommodative" talk that may lie at the heart of intergenerational conflicts and problems. For example, patterns of demeaning, deindividuating talk to the elderly are represented as categories of overaccommdation, talk that transcends perceptually ideal levels of interpersonal adaptation. Underaccommodation to the elderly may on the other hand take the form of excessively regulative talk. Correspondingly, younger people's perceptions of elderly speech-styles as inappropriate or "difficult" can be specified in these terms. Although space constraints do not allow us to discuss specific strategic possibilities and the contextual complexities associated with them, Table 5.1 (from Coupland, Coupland, Giles, & Henwood, 1988) summarizes particular *young-to-elderly* and *elderly-to-young* patterns that have surfaced in case-studies and pilot-work to date. At this stage, the table can serve only as a heuristic for more systematic research on cross-generational discourse still to be conducted.

Studies of doctor-elderly patient interaction, however, have already suggested several respects in which care-providers may underaccommodate to their elderly care-recipients. Many older people express dissatisfaction with the interaction they experience (Nussbaum, Thompson, & Robinson, 1989). Patients report being unhappy because of the doctor's unfriendly manner (Daly & Hulka, 1975; Korsch, Gozzi, & Francis, 1968), and because doctors baffle patients with technical language (Korsch & Negrete, 1972). Further problems emerge because patients often feel as if the doctor is too busy or that a large cultural/socioeconomic difference exists between care-providers and patient (Skipper, 1965b; Walker, 1973).

Relatedly, Greene, Adelman, Charon, and Friedmann (1989) investigated what they termed *interactional concordance* between doctors and

Table 5.1 Summary of the Sociopsychological Contexts and Sociolinguistic Instantiation of Ten Processes of Intergenerational Miscommunication (from Coupland, Coupland, Giles, & Henwood, 1988)

	Sender				*Receiver*	
	Social/ sociopsychological trigger	*Interactional goals(s)*	*Addressee focus*	*Sociolinguistic strategies activated*	*Judged Strategies*	*Speaker performance labeled*
Young-to-elderly language strategies[a]						
1. Sensory over-accommodation	Assumption of physical/sensory handicap (e.g., hearing loss)	Promote communication efficiency	Other's interpretive competence	Interpretability (e.g., much increased amplitude)	Overcompensation	Overcompensation
2. Dependency overaccommodation	Perception of social/institutional roles	Confirm/exert own control	Other's social role	Interpersonal control (regulative talk)	Authoritarianism	Underaccommodative/Overaccommodative
3. Intergroup divergence	Threatened identity (e.g., elder seen as superior)	Promote intergroup distinctiveness	Other's productive performance	Approximation (divergence)	Dissociation	Contra-accommodative
4. Intergroup over accommodation	Perception of social stereotype (e.g., of "aged communicator")	Promote social attractiveness/ communication efficiency/ nurturance	Other's conversational needs/interpretive competence	Discourse management; interpretability (e.g., simplification, etc.)	Depersonalization	Overaccommodative
5. Intergroup under-accommodation	Life circumstances	Presumably positive	Weak (egocentric focus)	Discourse management (lowly attuned)	Disinterest	Underaccommodative

Elderly-to-young language strategies

6. Intergroup underaccommodation	Life circumstances (probably little intergenerational contact)	Presumably positive	Weak (egocentric focus)	Discourse management (lowly attuned)	Passivity/overassertion/high self-disclosure/egocentricity	Underaccommodative
7. Self-protecting	Threatened identity (e.g., actual/anticipated negative interindividual comparisons)	Exert control/guardedly positive/defensive	Other's productive performance	Interpersonal control (indirect); Discourse management (field: topic deflection)	As in 6	Underaccommodative
8. Self-handicapping	Threatened identity (e.g., anticipating poor performance)	Promote positive face	Other's attributions and subsequent productive performance	Discourse management (field: accounts/excuses; tenor: negative face)	Apologizing/over compensating	? Over-accommodative
9. Self-stereotyping	Perception of social stereotyping (e.g., of "aged communication")	Presumably positive	Weak (group-centered focus)	Discourse management (lowly attuned)	Stereotypically elderly	Underaccommodative
10. Intergroup divergence	Threatened identity (e.g., young seen as illegitimately superior)	Promote intergroup distinctiveness	Other's productive performance (e.g., "hip"/colloquialisms)	Approximation (divergence)	Dissociation	Contra-accommodative

NOTE: a. cf. Ryan et al. (1986).

both their older and younger patients. Concordance was operationalized in this study as "whether physicians and patients agreed about the main goals for the visit, the primary medical problems dealt with, and the major topics discussed during the visit" (Greene et al., 1989, p. 810). Previous research suggested that greater doctor-patient concordance results in higher patient satisfaction (Korsch, Gozzi, & Francis, 1968), also in improved patient compliance (Korsch, Freeman, & Negrete, 1971), a highly problematical issue with elderly patients (Nussbaum et al., 1989). Greene et al. (1989) videotaped 30 doctor-older patient (65+ years) and 30 doctor-younger patients (up to 45 years) medical encounters in a general medical outpatient area of a major urban teaching hospital; in addition to coded analyses of the tape-recorded data, post-visit interviews with patients and doctors were available. Results indicate that although both older and younger patient-physician encounters produced low levels of concordance, the older patient-physician medical encounters were significantly lower: "Based on the findings from this study, older patients and their physicians may be more at risk for misunderstanding about the main goals and the topics of the visit, especially regarding medical topics, than younger patients and their physicians" (Greene et al., 1989, p. 811). Possible explanations include agist attitudes held by physicians, that physicians are less engaged and less willing to share decision making with their elderly patients, and that older patients are less assertive and less likely to be good information-givers than younger patients (Greene et al. 1989).

Age-Identities in Discourse

Taxonomic and contrastive approaches to cross-generation interaction are needed to organize data and find possible generalizations, although they also risk *over*generalizing and being insensitive to the local sequencing of conversation. Appreciating what Maynard (1988) has called the *interaction order* is paramount if we are to explore how speaking partners *jointly* facilitate and constrain each other's roles and identities as their conversations proceed. In a series of recent studies (see Coupland, Coupland, & Giles [in press] for an integrated overview of this work), we have attempted to trace the identity loading of cross-generation talk generally in qualitative terms and working with relatively small data sets. We have explored the possibility that particular recurring and even ritualistic sequences of cross-generation self-disclosure are involved in the construction of *age-identities* for older people. From this perspective, it is the interplay of strategies and moves, and their cumulative effect in particular exchanges, that is of greatest significance. These studies give a more subtle perspective on miscommunication than those we have considered up to this point. Miscommunication is characterized here as the incremental construction of stereotyped "elderly" identities for older people through the apparently benign and certainly well-intentioned initiatives of younger adults conversing with them.

In investigations of *Painful Self-Disclosure* (PSD) and age-telling strategies (Coupland, Coupland, Giles, & Wiemann, 1988; Coupland, Coupland, & Giles, 1989; Coupland, Coupland, Giles, Henwood, & Wiemann, 1988), we have examined data from 40 video-taped first-acquaintance interactions between women aged 70-87 and women in their 30s. The elderly women, most with (grossly characterized) upper-working-class backgrounds, are members of two Day Centres (nonresidential social centers) in Cardiff, Wales; most live alone and are widowed. The young women are mostly lower-middle-class and married, and were recruited through an advertisement in a local newspaper. Twenty of the dyads are, at least in terms of the study's design, intergenerational (young-old); 10 are peer-young and 10 peer-elderly. Each participating speaker takes part in two interactions, one within-and one across-generation.

PSD designates the revelation of a cluster of categories of personal and often intimate information on ill-health, bereavement, immobility, loneliness, and so on. We developed an initial template of the interactional possibilities available to disclosures and recipients (of PSD) to introduce, encode, respond to, and close PSD sequences. This was then available to document how PSD is in fact managed in the 40-interaction corpus as a whole. Older speakers in the data behave significantly more "disclosively" than the younger women by the gross index of the frequency of PSD in their talk. This is also true in the sense that, as qualitative analyses show, they determine their own disclosing (rather than disclosures being directly or indirectly elicited, for example) in approximately half of the documented instances; they also take little responsibility (relative to younger speakers in the data) for the closing of such sequences. The emerging patterns suggest a range of *positive* functions for highly disclosive behavior by older speakers, despite the apparent counter-normativity of its intimacy in first-acquaintance settings. PSD brings the benefits of engagement and newsworthiness; it may also earn credit for older speakers as having coped with arrays of difficult life-circumstances. There is evidence in the studies to suggest that, for at least some elderly people, locating oneself in relation to past experience, to one's own state of health, to chronological age, and perhaps to projectable future decrement and death, is functional at a more profound level. Discourse can enact a negotiative process, centering on life-position and life-prospects, that may have immediate consequences for boosting or lowering morale and, quite plausibly, psychological well-being.

But, crucially, it emerges that "elderly" identities are often manufactured for older people through choices made by their younger conversation-partners. It is highly significant, for example, that younger participants in the interactive study *elicit* PSD from their elderly interlocutors to a considerable extent, contrasting with older speakers who elicit it far less from their peers. We take this to be evidence of young speakers sharing responsibility for the engendering of elderly PSD. The two processes (elderly disclosure and young elicitation) are of course not in competition. Young people's eliciting role will require particular disclosive acts, but will more generally legitimize elderly disclosive behavior; conversely, elderly disclosure will establish interactional norms that legitimize eliciting behavior.

The data contain instances of young women's eliciting behaviors that presuppose interrogatory rights they would presumably not have in peer-young conversations (and which may not, of course, be endorsed by particular elderly conversationalists either). On one occasion, a young speaker asks, "is your husband still alive?" (in a context where there is no on-going PSD talk). Another asks, "*do you sleep alright when you get to bed?*" when previous talk has been on the general theme of reading habits. These are surely intrusive questions in first-encounter conversations and impose obligations upon elderly interlocutors either to disclose or to prevaricate. Also, the younger women as recipients of older speakers' PSD tend to signal interest and engagement, and thereby often sustain particular PSD sequences and that general mode of talk. In just the same way, younger speakers endorse age-disclosure by elderly people, expressing surprise and admiration (though in quite formulaic ways: "*well I'd never have thought it*"; "*gosh you don't look it!*"; etc.) Overall, the various contributions we find younger participants making in these data justify labeling them as facilitators, particularly of older speakers' PSD and age-telling strategies. The findings more generally demonstrate that older people do assume age-related roles and stances in response to interactional opportunities; which in turn suggests that *elderliness* itself is in fact a *variable* social attribution and at least in part contextually constructed during interaction. To the extent that the emergent age-identities are stereotypic, assuming older speakers are incapable, isolated, depressed, and so on, and adopting nurturing orientations (as is often the case in our own data), the process is fundamentally miscommunicative. The routine progression of everyday conversation across the generations, no less than the social institutions and some academic research, proves to be able to problematize elderly people.[3]

Overview

Outside of clinical and psycholinguistic traditions, language and communication research on aging, and particularly socially grounded studies, are still relatively few. Correspondingly, our knowledge of the particular means by which older adults come to be disenfranchised and alienated from mainstream social life remains very limited. Inexplicably, aging and older people have not yet become a staple subject of sociolinguistics or discourse studies in the way that, say, gender- or ethnic groups have been for a considerable time.

Nevertheless, studies we have reviewed in this chapter have demonstrated diverse associations between language/communication and generalized negative societal beliefs about elderly people. Cues to the identity of speakers as "elderly" have been shown to result in downgraded evaluations of individuals' attributed competence, and to cause people to act in discriminatory ways toward them. We have considered sporadic claims that even the language system itself might have come to reify society's agist assumptions in its lexicon. There is growing evidence of elderly groups being spoken to in characteristic styles, and some suggestions that these styles can be unwarranted and demeaning. In medical encounters, age-differentiated patterns of patient management could have the most profound implications for the success of health care delivery (Kreps, 1986). It is not surprising that a major current growth area in social gerontology is the impact of close relationships (Rook & Pietromonaco, 1987) and social support processes (Krause, 1986) as buffers against stress in the promotion of elderly health and well-being (Nussbaum, 1985).

In the accommodation theory framework we introduced in the middle of the chapter, there exists a model (see also Williams, Giles, & Coupland, 1990) that could appropriately be used for future multidisciplinary studies of the social attitudes, interactional strategies, social situations, and outcomes that we have suggested conspire to constitute intergenerational miscommunication. One important challenge for future research will be to reflect the contextual range of this model while respecting the fine detail of conversational sequence and strategy through which interactional "problems" come to be. The discourse analytic approach invites an analysis of how social actors make sense of their social circumstances, and not least of themselves, through communicative practices. It is for these reasons that discourse theorists over a considerable period (cf. Berger & Luckmann, 1967; Potter, 1988; Shotter & Gergen, 1989) have resisted deterministic assumptions about the constitution of social categories and their effects upon linguistic performance. Therefore, perhaps the greatest challenge for studies of communication and later life is to explore how themes of aging, agism (and indeed anti-agism) arise in social discourse generally. An interactional focus is essential if we assume, as independent research suggests (Bengston, Reedy, & Gordon, 1985), that elderly people are prone to assimilate society's devalued appraisals of their own social group, and so lower their self-esteem. It may well prove to be true that the miscommunicative cycle we have begun to trace in this chapter becomes established in the early years of life, and without "the elderly" themselves coming directly into question as an explicit topic of talk or as interacting participants. Agism may prove to be a social force that is ingrained in, and reproduced through, commonplace discourses of health, of change, of individual competence and achievement *throughout* the life-course. If so, the appropriate starting point for an improved understanding of miscommunication and older people will be studies of life-span communication, not merely of the elderly themselves.

Notes

1. We are grateful to Carl Carmichael for his important contributions to the conceptual framing of this chapter.

2. This three-way categorization of discourse dimensions is a familiar one in systemic linguistics; see, for example, Halliday, 1978.

3. Coupland, Coupland, and Grainger (in press) offer a contrastive case study, from the same interactive data set, showing the range of possible formulations of age-identity in two conversations involving the same older woman (with an elderly peer, then with a young adult).

6

Intercultural Encounters and Miscommunication

Stephen P. Banks
Gao Ge
Joyce Baker

It is ironic that a chapter about miscommunication, such as this one, is itself susceptible to the charge of exemplifying miscommunication. One reason for this susceptibility is, as Carbaugh (1989) points out, that labels for genres of talk are themselves culturally conditioned. For example, to St. Vincentians "talking sense" identifies conversations where "decorous and deferential" speech is evident, and "chanting" for the Kuna is a form of ceremonial dialogue whose purpose is to persuade an audience (Carbaugh, 1989, pp. 99-100). Consider by comparison how differently Western European and North American English speakers might view talking sense and chanting. In view of the cultural conditioning of terms for talk, then, any analysis of miscommunication should be understood as framed by the cultural milieu of the analyst.

Two other sorts of problems present obstacles to a useful discussion of miscommunication in intercultural encounters: First, what is meant by "miscommunication" is often unclear and varies among intercultural studies; and second, what constitutes the realm of intercultural encounters is not universally agreed upon. In this chapter, then, we begin by confronting those two preliminary problems for foundations for a critical overview of

AUTHORS' NOTE: We thank Nikolas Coupland, Howard Giles, and John M. Wiemann for their helpful comments on earlier drafts of this chapter.

research and the development of a model for miscommunication in intercultural encounters. Our model takes into consideration the cultural conditioning of the researcher and research activity themselves.

We note at the outset that although almost all of the work we discuss here conceives of encounters as face-to-face interaction, the principles and issues broadly apply to communication through various other media as well. Because the sheer bulk of intercultural communication literature that might be considered relevant to modeling miscommunication is too extensive to cover exhaustively, our overview is necessarily selective.

Varieties of Miscommunication and Encounters

In our view miscommunication is a label for an interpretation by one or more persons, either observing or participating in interaction. It is a decision about the meaning of another person's communication behavior and its consequences for the persons involved in the interaction. As such miscommunication in our view is a retrospective recognition that one person's intentions have not been "read" accurately by another participant, and that future actions or opinions of the participant will be predicated on the inaccurate reading.

The following discussion of diverse, often implicit, views of miscommunication found in the intercultural communication literature provides a rationale for our perspective. With rare exceptions (e.g., Erickson, 1979; Tafoya, 1983; Varonis & Gass, 1985a), miscommunication is not invoked in the literature as a technical term but as a representative of a genre of interaction outcomes that are undesirable. Popular synonyms for miscommunication include such terms as *misunderstanding* (Carroll, 1988), *error* (Hall & Hall, 1987), *trouble* (Hinnenkamp, 1987), *problem* (Smith, 1987), and *breakdown* (Gudykunst & Ting-Toomey, 1990). These terms belie certain assumptions about both the nature and conditions of miscommunication in intercultural settings. Accordingly, we first examine different views on the nature of miscommunication and then discuss the range of its possible conditions as a way of identifying the varieties of miscommunication that have been deemed relevant to intercultural encounters.

The Nature of Miscommunication

To conceive of miscommunication as instances of error is, in our view, to make effects identical with their causes. Speech performance errors, such as slips of the tongue (Cutler, 1982), omissions, substitutions, and dysfluencies, are problems in the first place only to the extent that they interfere with the smooth ongoingness of interaction. If participants in the communicative encounter understand each other's contributions in spite of these kinds of errors, or if they recognize the errors and repair them within the ambit of the encounter (see Varonis & Gass [1985a] for a scheme of possible reactions by participants; also Gass & Varonis, this volume), miscommunication as a result of an episode of interaction has been mooted. Similarly, errors of judgment about hearers' language ability or about cultural presuppositions can lead to difficulties, but their implications for miscommunication remain only potentialities until they are manifested in some form of problematic discourse.

Problematic discourse/talk (as well as *troubled discourse/talk* and *communication breakdown*) undoubtedly encompasses miscommunication. In our approach to miscommunication, the issue with troubled talk and related terms is that they encompass more interactional phenomena than just miscommunication. Many forms and instances of trouble talk or problematic discourse are profoundly communicative. For example, troubled talk is a hallmark of international negotiations for the release of terrorists' hostages and for the extradition of suspected drug-runners; moreover, these genres of discourse occasionally degenerate into a total cessation of constructive efforts at communication and can culminate in military action.

Hinnenkamp (1987) takes a narrower view of "trouble." He focuses on "critical moments of talk exchange that need treatment in order to enable 'the normal flow of talk' to be continued smoothly and which, as a matter of fact, are repaired in one way or another" (p. 139). Trouble in this sense is akin to errors—both are channel disturbances that are relevant to miscommunication only insofar as they disrupt talk and are not repaired as they occur. A key sense of miscommunication, however, regardless of one's theoretical orientation, is something gone awry communicatively that has social consequences for the interactants; without social consequences, the phenomenon would be of trivial interest. By social consequences, we refer generally to misattribution of motives, unwarranted actions, changes in patterns of interaction, and similar responses to encounters that might over time debilitate relationships. Consequently, for miscommunication to have impact, it is not likely to be a perturbation of smooth performance that is repaired in the current interaction.

If miscommunication is not errors or troubles in these senses, what is its essential nature? Nearly all discussions of miscommunication appeal in some ways to misunderstanding (see White, 1989, p.70); when misunderstanding is expressly identified as problematic, it typically is left to stand as an intuitively transparent concept, a state that simply happens. Misunderstandings in actual discourse, however, do not occur as agentless mysteries: One or more participants and their circumstances of interaction are ultimately accountable for misunderstandings. Although a growing tradition of research in conversation analysis (e.g., Atkinson & Heritage, 1984; Button & Lee, 1987) demonstrates that talk is a jointly and contingently created event, misunderstanding is *experienced* as either a misstatement (the problem is initiated by the speaker/writer, see Rehbein, 1987) or a misinterpretation (the problem is initiated by the hearer/reader's failure to understand, see White, 1989), or both.

Two other issues need to be raised because they demonstrate how miscommunication in the perspective we advocate is not coterminous with misspeaking or misunderstanding. First, it is not a case of miscommunication if the failure of one participant to understand the interaction at hand results from the other's intentional efforts to baffle, confuse, or manipulate. In other words, miscommunication is not a matter of intentionally caused misunderstanding: When discovered, this sort of misunderstanding is usually called deception. Moreover, miscommunication in our view is not tacit. Many cases of misunderstanding can go unnoticed or unremarked, either by speakers or hearers: So long as a misunderstanding has no consequences for further interaction, miscommunication is not an issue. Countless romantic farces and sitcoms depend for their integrity on this difference between misunderstanding and miscommunication, and they derive their essential dramatic force from that moment of enlightenment at the transition from naive misunderstanding to the realization and acknowledgment of miscommunication.

Thus, miscommunication in our view is a label for a particular kind of misunderstanding, one that is unintended yet is recognized as a problem by one or more of the persons involved. It can but does not necessarily lead to dissatisfaction or a breakdown of interaction. It is a form of troubled or problematic talk (or, conceivably, of other kinds of readings), but it is not simply a matter of difficulty because of dysfluencies and speech errors. This view, of course, does not address possible motives or conditions of miscommunication; to grasp its domain in intercultural encounters requires a brief consideration of how intercultural miscommunication can take place.

The Conditions of Miscommunication

The two most basic conditions for miscommunication in intercultural encounters are: (a) the precipitating events are fundamentally the same as those that precipitate miscommunication in *intra*cultural encounters; and (b) the precipitating events are uniquely attributable to differences of culture of participants. As to the first of these basic conditions, instances or patterns of miscommunication that are unrelated to cultural differences are not addressed by intercultural communication research and theory. Only those instances of miscommunication qualify for attention whose causes are the same as those in intercultural settings but are exacerbated by cultural differences. An example is provided by Price's (1989) description of his efforts to discuss with a native informant the historical distribution of the Brazilian Nambiquara Indians. Price tried to co-orient his informant and himself to a map by establishing agreement on the names of major rivers; but Americo, his Nambiquara friend, would only say "big water." Price became more and more discouraged as Americo would agree the rivers had names but would not enter discussion about them, as if "he didn't seem to understand what rivers I was referring to" (p. 105). Price eventually managed to convey to Americo that he wanted to name the rivers because he wanted to know where the Nambiquara ancestors had lived, and with that key account, Americo commenced informing him more fully about where people had lived in relation to landmarks. Price learned that the Nambiquara do not share information without sensing a practical and personal purpose to the other's knowing it. While myriad similar communication problems associated with interactional cooperativeness occur in intracultural settings, in this example the problem was made salient by the cultural differences of the participants.

The second condition involves miscommunication that is deeply sedimented in abstract cultural norms. This condition exhibits not difficulties of expressive techniques but difficulties of incompatible cultural concepts that underlie expression. Scollon and Scollon (1981), for example, describe how Athabaskans come to see English speakers as egocentric while native English speakers see Athabaskans as uncreative, and both views are based primarily on differences of cultural preference for length of speaking turns.

In sum, then, the relevant sorts of misunderstandings addressed as miscommunication emerge from cultural differences, either exclusively or partially, in intercultural encounters. Since intercultural communication scholars often struggle with the terms culture and intercultural encounters (Kim, 1986; Knapp & Knapp-Potthoff, 1987), a brief clarification is in order.

Culture and Encounters

Most intercultural communication studies implicitly or, more rarely, explicitly take culture to be shared knowledge of how to behave and recipes for understanding experience in specific ways (e.g., Barnett & Kincaid, 1983; Tafoya, 1984). Knapp and Knapp-Potthoff (1987) claim that what is interesting about culture are "those properties of the shared knowledge of a social group which, because of their distinctiveness, cause or may cause trouble in interaction with members of another group" (p. 5). Tautologically, in this definition the notion of culture itself defines what constitutes intercultural miscommunication and vice versa. Surely this is not helpful for understanding what aspects of group differences contribute to miscommunication, nor does it facilitate an improved understanding of culture. The many perspectives on culture should be dealt with head-on by investigators of intercultural miscommunication. Our view is that culture must embrace a group's logic of expression that members accept as natural and foundational to the group's way of being. This approach places participants' meanings and motives at the center of intercultural miscommunication.

As to types of encounters, Kim (1986, pp. 10-11) has explored the definitional problems of such labels as interethnic, international, interracial, intergroup, and intercultural. She envisions interethnic studies to be subsumed under intercultural communication because ethnicity is only one of several possible domains of culture. Insofar as ethnicity is taken to be grounded in ascribed or perceived group membership based on symbolic markers of race, color, national origin, religion, or language, it indeed could be analyzed as cultural. On the other hand, little agreement exists on the meaning of ethnicity (Edwards, 1985; Knapp & Knapp-Potthoff, 1987); moreover, just as cultural differences do not totally determine individuals' communication, so culture does not totally define racial, national, or other group differences. Nonetheless, multiple races, nations, and so on tend to reflect different cultural attributes; consequently, we believe these categories are partially included within one another, and we advocate treating the terminological differences as marking different foci and emphases in intergroup studies that all potentially have cultural implications. Cross-cultural studies traditionally are comparative research aligning culture with national or regional boundaries (Gudykunst & Kim, 1984; Smith, 1987).

A Selective Overview of Research

As the foregoing implies, the theoretical underpinnings and methodological approaches taken to the relevant issues reflect the multidisciplinary nature of the field. Consequently, *intercultural encounters* functions more as a convenient aggregating category than as a disciplinary label. The variation of approaches adopted, however, permits us to schematize research roughly along the lines of general views of miscommunication and their associated disciplinary origins.

We find four major areas of interest which, although mutually informing and overlapping, reflect concerns for differing aspects of intercultural encounters and miscommunication:

- first is a line of research that investigates miscommunication as problems of assessing others' norms, based on generic culture types;
- second is studies of miscommunication as inadequate linguistic performances;
- third is miscommunication as failed pragmatics, by which we refer to sociolinguistic norms that link action, meanings, and social contexts; and
- fourth is miscommunication taken as the misattribution of group traits, motives, and other features grounded in group identity.

We discuss these separately, and we conclude by developing a model of miscommunication that is oriented specifically toward intercultural encounters.

Miscommunication as Culture Difference

Hall (1976) proposed the concept of *High Context* (HC) and *Low Context* (LC) communication, based on the information theory notion that some communication processes assume much shared background information and thus code and transmit little information, while other communication assumes little background information in common and codes and transmits much information. Hall asserted that cultures are characterized by their tendencies toward HC or LC communication, and this concept has been borrowed by numerous intercultural communication theorists. Ehrenhaus (1983), for example, used the HC/LC concept as the basis for advancing hypotheses about the relation between culture and the attribution process. Not surprisingly, Ehrenhaus concluded that persons in intercultural encounters seek attributional cues about others in ways that are consistent with their cultural HC/LC orientation and might experience miscommunication as a result of incompatibilities in making attributions.

Ehrenhaus's assumptions have been partially put to the test in Cohen's (1987) historical study of "missed opportunities" in diplomatic relations between Egypt and the United States. Cohen operationalized HC/LC as expressive directness/indirectness and exaggeration/understatement. In the records of diplomatic communication, Cohen found evidence of "missed opportunities or miscalculation" based on manifest incompatibilities. For example, relations between Egypt and the United States were damaged for half a decade because of President Lyndon Johnson's interpretation of statements by Prime Minister Nasser. Upon hearing that U.S. Ambassador Lucius Battle had advised his Egyptian counterpart not to press President Johnson to conclude a wheat deal, Nasser gave a scorching speech in which he characterized the diplomatic move as "gangsterism by cowboys" (p. 35). Johnson was infuriated by the speech, which he considered a personal insult. When later asked about the speech, Nasser's account was "I was only talking to my own people" (p. 37), an expectable response from a member of a HC culture where hyperbolic attacks on outsiders are normative. In a more qualitative application, Yousef (1978) used the HC/LC scheme to analyze three cases of intercultural relationships that ended in frustration because of misattribution of motives based on HC/LC orientations in nonverbal expression. In one case, a U.S. middle-class couple gave a new-baby gift to their Lebanese neighbors. The neighbors thanked the American couple for the gift, but put it away during their visit and never opened the gift in their presence. The American couple regarded the Lebanese response as irritating and rude. Yousef's analysis shows that the Lebanese couple were acting on an HC cultural norm of gift-giving in the guest-host relationship, and they were attempting to be tactful. On the other hand, the Americans expected a more explicit demonstration of the uniqueness of their largess; they applied an LC cultural norm of expecting behavior in such situations to be elaborately spelled out, and they interpreted their neighbors' response from that perspective.

Much recent work aligns HC/LC culture with another set of generic cultural variables—individualism/collectivism (Hofstede, 1980). Gudykunst (1989b) calls this difference "the major dimension of cultural variability isolated by theorists across disciplines" (p. 226). Individualistic cultures emphasize individual goals and careers, universalistic value standards, and multiple specific ingroups; collectivistic cultures tend to emphasize group goals, different value standards for ingroups versus those for outgroups, and fewer but deeper ingroup relationships. Associations have been proposed between individualism/collectivism and moral development (Westin, 1985), conflict style (Ting-Toomey, 1988), and ethnolinguistic identity (Gudykunst, 1989b). Triandis, Brislin, and Hui (1988) have pointed out some of the implications for miscommunication of the individualistic/collectivistic differences among cultures. For example, the group-centeredness and ingroup orientation of collectivistic cultures can lead members of individualistic cultures to misattribute group exclusivity as hostility; likewise, individualistic cultures' tendency to allocate culpability and praise to individuals might be taken by members of collectivistic cultures as efforts to embarrass or sabotage.

In addition to exploring generic differences that categorize all cultures, some studies have investigated cultural differences that are unique to one group or another. For example, Barnlund (1975) examined the implications of interaction between Japanese and U.S. speakers on the basis of their differences in willingness to disclose information about the self. Since Japanese are more reluctant to report feelings and personal information than their U.S. counterparts, the U.S. participants interpreted the Japanese speakers' actions as "unfriendly," despite the Japanese speakers' expressed intentions to appear just the opposite. Relatedly, Barnlund and Araki (1985) extended this line of work by demonstrating how differences in Japanese and American ways of managing compliments can result in intended compliments being read as embarrassing personal disclosures (Japanese hearing American compliments) or as politeness being read as denials (Americans reading Japanese responses to compliments).

Studies of culture variability treat culture differences as the pivotal influence determining the outcomes of communication attempts. They generally do not account or control for differences in members' linguistic competence, social knowledge, or salience of individual and group identity. Moreover, members of cultural groups tend to be viewed as cultural automata whose salient behavior is programmed and shared across the group. Similarly, much work on intercultural encounters that focuses on language treats language differences as the sine qua non of culture and miscommunication and view linguistic performance as systematically predictable.

Miscommunication as Linguistic Failures

A great deal of work in linguistics, such as research on phonology, morphosyntactics, and semantics, even when situated in intercultural contexts, is only marginally related to our interest in miscommunication because failed communication is rarely made a central issue. Language contact and second language learning situations, however, offer fruitful contexts for identifying linguistic implications of miscommunication as we have conceived it (cf. Gass & Varonis, this volume): interaction between native and non-native speakers readily displays how the lack of shared linguistic systems can result in miscommunication, which typically is the impetus for efforts to understand how L2s are learned. Most researchers go beyond the taken-for-granted assumption that interactants must share basic lexical meanings and explore more subtle linguistic codes that are culturally differentiated (Smith, 1987).

White (1989), for example, quantitatively examined the differences between U.S. speakers' frequency and purposes of backchannel utterances and those of Japanese speakers. In experimental conditions, she identified significant differences in how the Japanese confirmatory backchannel code, called *aizuchi,* is perceived and how often it is evident in conversation compared to the routine backchanneling of U.S. subjects. White, however, found no evidence that American speakers interpreted Japanese speakers' more frequent backchannel utterances as troublesome or as signs of incomprehension or impatience. LoCastro (1987), in contrast, used an ethnographic approach to examine the role of *aizuchi* in intercultural Japanese conversations. LoCastro concluded that *aizuchi* makes a critical contribution to Japanese language conversations, and non-native speakers' competency with *aizuchi* helps avoid conversational misunderstandings.

Miscommunication as Failed Pragmatics

Neither studies based on differences in culture variables nor those based on differences in linguistic competence envision interactants as choice-making agents with respect to these factors. However, as Ting-Toomey (1989b) points out, many studies of language use in intercultural settings do account for events as outcomes of individuals' choices. In such instances, research aims to discover how contexts and culturally conditioned pragmatics contribute to choices that result in miscommunication. Pragmatics covers a wide stretch of territory (Leech, 1983; Levinson, 1983; Stalker, 1989); however, from the viewpoint of intercultural encounters, what is particularly relevant to miscommunication is the link pragmatics makes between the ways that communicative behavior is performed and the ongoing understandings of people in interaction. Pragmatics thus directs attention to both the cultural premises for performing interaction and the cultural knowledge that enables persons to make sense of behavior.

Hansell and Ajirotutu's (1982) analysis of conversations between white American adults and Afro-American teenagers demonstrates how such Black English prosodic features as dialect pronunciation, rising intonation, stress, and speech rate contribute meaningful cues to interaction. For example, when the white researcher asked the teens to pick a subject for discussion, "any old subject," one teen replied, "any old thang [i.e., thing]" (p. 87). Throughout the rest of the conversation the teen said "thing" only in the standard dialect phonology; the authors point out that the invocation of the Black English dialect "thang" initially "can be seen as a metaphoric switch, indicating to the others his willingness and ability to lead the researchers astray" (p. 89), which he proceeds to do. Moreover, "use of these Black variables is more than simply a marker of ethnic identity. It serves clear communicative ends and the researcher's failure to perceive this significantly affects the success of the interview" (p. 89).

Gumperz, a dominant figure in the study of sociolinguistics and interethnic communication, employed two key concepts that are relevant here.

Contextualization conventions are those conversational cues, "constellations of surface features of message form," that tell hearers how to interpret utterances and to relate them to what preceded or follows (1982a, p. 131). Contextualization conventions that precipitate miscommunication form the basis of Gumperz's (1978) study of British white teachers and Indian and Pakistani immigrant trainees. A careful analysis of such prosodic features as tonal contour, segmenting of utterance units, and stress patterns revealed precisely how miscommunication depends on incompatible systems of linking contextualization cues and meaning; more importantly, Gumperz illustrated that neither party is "right" or mistaken in relation to the pragmatic failure: Both participants are contributors to miscommunication, but because one code, one way of interpreting, is institutionally sanctioned in the context of that investigation, the immigrant became the victim of the miscommunication.

The second key concept invoked by Gumperz is the notion of sociocultural knowledge, the extralinguistic knowledge of culture and the world that often is revealed in discourse behavior. For example, Gumperz (1982a, p. 168-171) analyzed the response of a West Indian bus driver in London to passengers who crowded in without the exact change required by the bus company. The driver's statement, "Exact change, please," was interpreted by some passengers as rude and threatening, even though it was a formulaic statement commonly used by all London bus drivers. Gumperz's analysis showed how the driver's utterance resulted in misattribution of motive because he applied the West Indian prosodic conventions and placed stress on the last syllable, "please." Hearers interpreted the prosody as a contextualization cue, then applied what they knew of expectable discourse in the given circumstances to interpret the utterance. As Gumperz described the process, people "listen to speech, form a hypothesis about what routine is being enacted, and then rely on social background knowledge and co-occurrence expectations to evaluate what is intended and what attitudes are conveyed" (p. 171).

Sociocultural knowledge, however, is not manifested solely in displays or interpretations of paralinguistic phenomena. Trosborg's (1987) study of native and non-native speakers' use of apology formulas illustrated that limitations in sociocultural knowledge can be apparent in both content and structure of discourse, and that choices of communicative behavior can be influenced by linguistic competence. Danish learners of English were asked to respond to a range of complaint situations. In certain situations the learners displayed apology formulas, such as rejecting the complaint, that were inappropriate in the U.S. culture. Trosborg found that the culturally unwarranted response was linked in part to low linguistic competency for creating explanations coupled with low sociocultural knowledge about how responses to complaints are acceptably formulated. Her findings suggest that differential knowledge of culturally appropriate ways of responding can lead to loss of face and a failure to "convey . . . intended communicative acts" (p. 147).

Miscommunication as Problems of Identity

A major stream of research and theory that parallels the sociolinguistic tradition flows primarily from work in the social psychology of individual and group identity (Edwards, 1985; Giles & Johnson, 1981; Tajfel, 1982). Gudykunst and Ting-Toomey (1990) provide a concise description of the scholarship that explores the relationships between ethnicity and language and between ethnolinguistic identity and communication "breakdown"; therefore, we will not review those issues here. The thrust of this approach, however, is to account for members' communication behavior, including their choices of linguistic codes and interactional strategies, as aspects of individual and group identity maintenance. Giles and associates (e.g., Giles, 1977; Giles & Johnson, 1987; Hewstone & Brown, 1986) have developed theory and considerable confirming research that suggests speakers will modify their behavior depending on such situational and personal factors as perceived threats to ethnic identity (Bourhis & Giles, 1977) and need for social approval or desire to associate or dissociate with others (Street & Giles, 1982). An expanding list of social and cognitive factors has been posited as influencing language behavior and, implicitly, miscommunication as we have described it.

Recently scholars in this area have explicitly identified social and psychological bases for miscommunication in intergroup interaction by proposing theoretical models of miscommunication (Hewstone & Giles, 1986; Gudykunst & Ting-Toomey, 1990). In Hewstone and Giles' model, miscommunication is framed as the result of inaccurate negative stereotyping, usually the dissolution of group relationships. Stereotyping is conceived as the attribution of characteristics to groups and their members; individuals' communicative behaviors are deemed to be predicated on that cognitive phenomenon. Stereotypes are thought to be activated and group-related patterns of discourse used when members are in intergroup situations, and the nature of the stereotyping and speech behavior depends on the salience of ethnolinguistic identity in the given context. The authors acknowledge that the relation between stereotyping and behavior is not yet clear, and they do not address problems that might arise from erroneous positive stereotyping. They do, however, link the cognitive predispositions of participants in communication with the sociostructural context of the interaction. Gudykunst and Ting-Toomey's (1990) theoretical model similarly takes members to be strategic, consciously motivated representatives of groups whose ethnolinguistic identities and language behavior are influenced by members' assessment of the situation. Instead of focusing on stereotyping,Gudykunst and Ting-Toomey apply models of language and uncertainty reduction to Giles and Johnson's (1987) propositions of ethnolinguistic identity theory. In any ingroup situation, social categorizations determine perceived similarity, which leads to perceptions of uncertainty; the degree of uncertainty influences the likelihood of breakdowns and influences the nature and salience of uncertainty reduction attempts. Gudykunst and Ting-Toomey describe miscommunication this way: "Inaccurate attributions or mistypifications [of the nature of the other group] . . . will result in an increase of uncertainty. If such episodes are repeated over time, communication breakdown is the most likely result" (p. 322).

A Critique of Models and Research

These two models initiate a significant move toward understanding aspects of intercultural miscommunication, even when the concepts are diversely or only implicitly presented. More broadly, the four streams of research and theory described here sensitize us to the complexity of people communicating, regardless of their cultural origins. And therein lies the rub: In the later three streams, culture is backgrounded while language, group identity, sociolinguistic phenomena, and social-psychological principles are foregrounded. Although culture is foregrounded in the first stream, it is operationalized as a set of member attributes that can be observed objectively and measured. The only relevant area to work extensively with first-hand, in vivo communication behavior is the sociolinguistic contribution to pragmatics. In such instances, however, culture is a backdrop for sociocultural knowledge, and what is highlighted are the ways members as representatives of socially situated groups manage interactions—they instruct us less about culture than about group patterns of language behavior.

In all four interrelated paradigms, attributes are treated as variables composed of group characteristics and behaviors and members' perceptions of group characteristics and behaviors; much of the theory is a concatenation of such variables in the abstract, often developed as causal and rule-like propositions; and research consists of testing the propositions by examining the experience of speakers, typically by asking speakers about their experience relative to the variables, or by eliciting behaviors and asking speakers about their elicited experience relative to the variables. Finally, studies in intercultural communication implicitly ask the fundamental question: What can be learned about communication from what is known about culture(s)? (Sarbaugh, 1984). By and large they do not attempt to increase our understanding of particular cultures or of a concept of culture. In designing research explorations that begin with representatives of multiple cultures, assumptions about the differences among those representatives have already been made, and culture becomes the presuppositional frame for studying communication behavior. But any examination of work dealing expressly with culture reveals how little is settled about culture (e.g., Geertz, 1986; Ortner, 1984). It would seem prudent, then, for any theory of intercultural communication (or miscommunication) to address issues of what can be learned about culture from what is known about communication.

What is needed, consequently, is a model of miscommunication in intercultural encounters that addresses these lacunae in the tradition. Such a model must foreground culture as a knowledge objective, and it should take into consideration the idea of culture held by the discipline most involved with culture – anthropology. Such a model should build on theories already proposed (Deetz, 1982), but the nature of (mis)communication in the model must not be inconsistent with its conceptualization of culture. In the following section, we propose a modest theory that responds to these issues, a starting point for a culture-centered model of miscommunication in intercultural encounters.

Toward a Culture-Centered Model of Miscommunication

First, culture is to be understood in the way of symbolic-interpretive anthropology (e.g., Boon, 1986; Carroll, 1988; Rosaldo, 1989), that is, as unconscious acceptance of a logic of signification within a group's ways of being. Because of its grounding in symbolism and individuals' symbolic behavior, this view of culture is preeminently hospitable to communication research and theory. Culture in this sense is knowable through members' appeals to common sense for accounts of their experience, through the advent of unique genres of situation that members take as normal and routine, and through uniquely symbolic systems that members take differentially as normal and routine.

The model presented here departs radically from other theory proposals because it installs the nature of the research activity as a basic feature of the theory. Models of social phenomena heretofore have attempted to lay out conceptually and graphically the antecedents, covariates, consequences, and other influences related to the phenomenon, without accounting for the cultural practice of the researcher. Social events have been treated as *in res* phenomena, as if their nature is knowable without knowers or knowledge procedures. We propose that recognition be given to the epistemological insight that our knowledge and understanding are dependent on what we ask and what techniques we apply to obtain answers.

The features of the model thus do not include culture per se. A concept of culture is explicitly inscribed in the nature of the research activity applied to the social phenomena under examination. Thus, the first feature of the model (see Figure 6.1) is the *research activity* generated by a cultural problematic that forms the basis for inquiry. The research activity is further described below when emergent situation is discussed.

Of the other five principal features of the model, *communicators* refers to the necessary but not sufficient requirement for the participation of heterogeneous speakers/writers and hearers/readers. What must be known about communicators has been elucidated in earlier social psychological and sociolinguistic theories—goals, expectations, linguistic competence, sociocultural competence, individual and group identity, subjective ethnolinguistic vitality (Bourhis, Giles, & Rosenthal, 1981), and so forth. We would also include communicators' affective states, such as mood, arousal level, and similar personal conditions.

We identify two types of situation: Situation$_S$, which represents the sociostructural aspects of context, and Situation$_E$, which denotes the emergent situation. *Situation$_S$* encompasses the institutional relationships among communicators, their ethnolinguistic vitality (Giles, Bourhis, & Taylor, 1977), their perceived demographic identities and stereotyped characteristics, and the perceived genre of communication event (e.g., small talk, contract negotiations, asking for a date, etc.).

Situation$_E$ includes the place and time ecology of the interaction's occurrence. More crucially, it takes cognizance of the by now unarguable observation that "Anything ever said is said by someone, to someone, at a particular moment of some specific socially organized and culturally informed occasion" (Moerman, 1988, p. x). Ethnomethodology has taught that account must be taken of individuals' communication actions in vivo. It is doubtful that any ethnomethodologist would claim all human action is knowable only as the contingently produced, sequential responses to emergent events; however, Cicourel's (1980) idea of *practical action* and Garfinkel's (1967) notion of *accomplishment* express the critical importance of everyday life of action motivated by tacit, routine competencies that are below consciousness. Thus, if culture is assumed to be the unconscious acceptance of signification and routine practices of everyday life that are particular to a group, the clearest inroad to understanding culture is to examine those very routines that are unconscious but systematic cultural accomplishments.

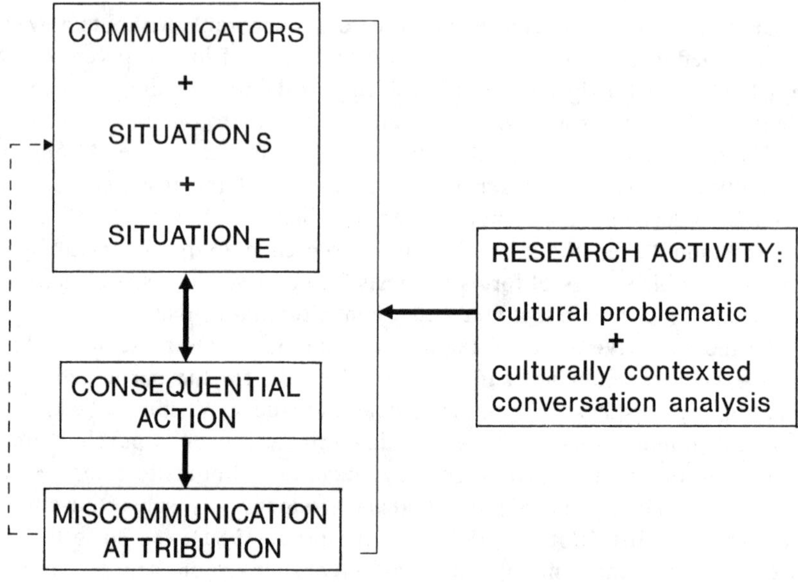

Figure 6.1 A Model of Miscommunication in Intercultural Encounters

To do so, researchers must ask not what the content of communicative interaction is (Sarbaugh, 1984) but what is cultural about the techniques by which interaction is conducted in the first place. A superb illustration of work that engages in this kind of inquiry is Michael Moerman's extended project to blend conversation analysis and ethnography (Moerman, 1988). Moerman attends to "natural events in the real world" by generating a "culturally contexted conversation analysis" (p. 11). He uses the techniques of conversation analysts (see, e.g., Hopper, Koch, & Mandelbaum, 1986) to identify discourse commonalities, which serve as contrast media for the discovery of cultural differences in interaction. The questioning of a lawyer and the testimony of the defendant in a Thai murder trial, for example, reveal culturally specific strategies of adequately accounting for the defendant's actions and motives and the subtle conversational techniques for eliciting those strategies. The implications for miscommunication studies are profound if we consider the plight of non-native defendants in courtrooms where they might be tried for crimes.

This work relies on the principle that the experienced world of members is partially comprised of their doing, their "calling into being" of social life, and the orderliness of social life is revealed in their micro-level management of interaction. A truly cultural interpretation of Situation_E

would apply what can be known about communicators and about Situation$_S$; what can be known about communicators and their sociostructural context is reflexively informed by interpretations of their in vivo interaction. Because communicators, structural situation, and emergent situation in any instance of miscommunication are not sequentially time-ordered, we show them in the model as co-present aspects.

Consequential action, as the next feature of our model, then, refers to noticeable subsequent action that elucidates any stretch of discourse under study. Such actions might be further turns of talk, metacommunicative comments, silences, leavings, laughter, or physical confrontation. The meanings of interaction can only be inferred by experiencing real histories with participants and knowing the real-world contingencies and consequences of their communicative behavior. To the extent that communicators are changed by learning from consequences of their actions, this element feeds back into the nature of communicators, represented in the model by the double arrow.

Finally, the model must include an event component expressing the idea that miscommunication occurs only when a participant (including possibly a researcher) recognizes and acts on his or her interpretation of interaction as such, regardless of whether or not the interpretation is so labeled by participants. Attempts in intercultural settings to address injured feelings, to metacommunicate about misattributions of motives, to correct misinterpretations of intent, and so on (cf. Drummond & Hopper, this volume) are clues that miscommunication might have occurred. Even in the absence of such evidence, a researcher might infer that miscommunication as we have defined it has occurred without participants' awareness. Such a judgment would be based on the researcher's interpretation of discourse and observation that clearly deviant or unwanted behavior ensued. For this reason, we show a restricted feedback loop between miscommunication and the situational elements of the model. In either case, a culturally contexted conversation analysis would reveal if the occasion for miscommunication were influenced by cultural differences.

This model advocates amalgamating conceptual approaches to understanding intergroup encounters while centering culture as the analytic focus and a class of misunderstandings as the practical concern. Adopting this model would thus demand of researchers that they innovate with multiple theories and methods. In particular, studies based on this model would require that researchers and their readers focus attention on actual talk (or use of other communicative media) by persons from diverse cultures in natural settings. Moreover, accepting a concept of miscommunication as a decision about the meaning of interaction's consequences places researchers in the often delicate position of being both interpreter of others' intentions and interpretations and rationalizer of one's own reportage. On balance, application of this model will provide a fuller picture of the dynamics of intercultural encounters and a deeper understanding of the cultural issues implicated in miscommunication. Most important, it will focus the research lens more sharply on the sometimes tragic consequences of unintentional misunderstanding in intercultural encounters.

7

Miscommunication in Nonnative Speaker Discourse

Susan M. Gass
Evangeline M. Varonis

In the Philippines, the names of Saints are often bestowed on infants. After World War II, one child was named Ababis, supposedly the name of the patron saint of the United States. The child's father had repeatedly heard American soldiers, in moments of emotional stress, call on the saint: San Ababis. (Hockett, 1958, p. 404)

Introduction

Examples of miscommunication abound in interactions involving native (NS) and nonnative speakers (NNS) of a language. To explain why, investigators must go beyond an analysis of the purely linguistic features of the interaction (phonology, morphology, syntax, and prosody), and consider as well its pragmatic and sociocultural dimensions. No natural speech utterance is ever made in a linguistic vacuum. Each is enriched and empowered by a social history that considers the relationships of class, status, power, and solidarity, and a linguistic history that includes culturally specific rules of discourse (Labov & Fanshel, 1977), politeness (Brown & Levinson, 1978), conversational maxims (Grice, 1975; Keenan, 1976), conversational inference (Gumperz & Tannen, 1979), and patterns of interpretation (Tannen, 1981a). In discussing the meaning of an illocutionary act, speech act theorist John Searle (1969) specified:

AUTHORS' NOTE: We are grateful to the editors of this volume for extremely helpful comments on an earlier draft of this chapter. Any errors or inconsistencies are, of course, our own.

> On the speaker's side, saying something and meaning it are closely connected with intending to produce certain effects on the hearer. On the hearer's side, understanding the speaker's utterance is closely connected with recognizing his intentions. In the case of literal utterances the bridge between the speaker's side and the hearer's side is provided by their common language. (1969, p. 48)

When the interaction involves NSs and NNSs, however, the bridge is unstable if not downright shaky. When interlocutors do not share the same native language or the same sociocultural rules of discourse, the possibility for miscommunication is profound.

Gumperz and Tannen (1979) have argued that the more participants in a conversation know about each other, the less the likelihood of significant instances of miscommunication. Conversely, when participants have little shared background (be it cultural, linguistic, or personal), the conversation is likely to be peppered with interruptions for clarification of content or language form. In conversations involving NNSs, this becomes readily apparent. Varonis and Gass (1985b) showed that even in conversation between two NNSs, the degree to which the interaction proceeds without interruption is dependent on the amount of shared background; in the case of that study, this includes language background as well as similarity in language proficiency.

Before beginning our discussion on NNS communication and the problems related to it, we need to make clear what we are excluding in our discussion. We are not considering those conversational interactions in which the exchange of turns, the exchange of information, and the exchange of ideas occur relatively smoothly, as in the initial portion of the telephone call in extract 1.

Extract 1

Stanley: Hello
Stephanie: Hi! Oh, I hope I didn't wake you.
Stanley: No, I've been up for hours.
Stephanie: Good, I wanted to get you before you left town — to clear up some last minute details.
Stanley: Yeah, I sent you a copy of a memo I sent to Janice and she's supposed to get in touch with you when she has an answer.
Stephanie: That's fine and what about the money from Jenkins and Co?

In this excerpt from a telephone conversation between two NSs, each participant takes his or her turn in full understanding of the preceding utterance (as well as preceding conversations) and where his or her own utterance fits within the context of this particular conversation. In conversation in which there is shared background, the turn-taking sequence proceeds smoothly with each speaker responding appropriately to the preceding utterance.[1] Thus, we are eliminating any discussion of speech events in which the speaker's and hearer's semantic interpretations of an utterance are initially congruous (see also Milroy, 1984).

Problematic communication with specific reference to NNSs covers a wide range of phenomena. In Figure 7.1, we schematize the most prevalent types and below we attempt to distinguish among them. First, it is important to note the inherent terminological difficulties in dealing with aspects of problematic communication. As discussions of miscommunication in recent years have become common in the second language acquisition literature, the terminology to describe the phenomenon has similarly flourished. Unfortunately there is little consistency between and even within authors concerning such terms as "miscommunication," "misunderstanding," and "communication breakdown." For example, what Tannen (1975) refers to as "communication mix-up," Gumperz and Tannen (1979) refer to variously as "misunderstanding" or "miscommunication," Thomas (1983) as "pragmalinguistic failure," and Milroy (1984) as "communicative breakdown,170. Varonis and Gass (1985a) discuss a hearer's interpretation or misinterpretation of a speaker's utterance without confidence, while in the present chapter, we use the term "negotiated communication". Similarly, Thomas's "pragmatic failure" is akin to Milroy's "miscommunication" and Clyne's (1977) "communicative breakdown." Thus, this literature is particularly difficult to interpret because different researchers are using different terms for the same phenomenon, on the one hand, and the same term for different phenomena, on the other. We hope in the following sections to make our terminological position clear.

Initially, we see problematic communication as being made up of two broad types: nonengagement (or talk avoidance) and miscommunication. In the former, no communicative event takes place although given the social constraints (e.g., the physical proximity of two people who know each other or who need to transact business together), one would be expected. In the latter, an attempt is made to carry out either an interactional or a transactional conversation (cf. Brown & Yule, 1983), yet problems arise in the transmission and/or reception of a message.

Nonengagement

There is at least two types of nonengagement: (1) noncommunication and (2) communication breakoff.

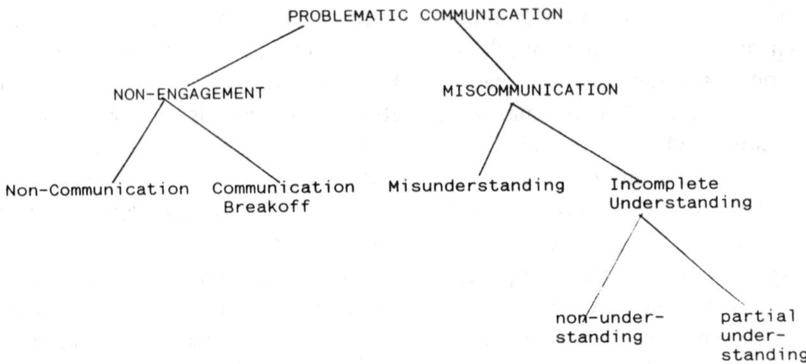

Figure 7.1 Problematic Communication Types

Noncommunication can only be illustrated anecdotally. An American university student once told us that if she were walking down the street and saw her NNS conversation partner[2] when she was particularly tired, she would turn around and walk the other ways so as not to engage in what would undoubtedly be a difficult and stressful conversation. Similarly, an Easterner traveling in San Francisco once reported to us an instance in which he needed to accomplish a difficult bank transaction. He avoided any teller who appeared to be a NNS of English because he feared communicative difficulty. In this one instance, he chose a NS teller as "the path of least resistance." Such avoidance of communication may result when the perceived loss of energy necessary for communication outweighs the perceived benefit (social or otherwise) to be gained.[3] The second type of nonengagement (communication breakoff) occurs when a conversational interaction is abruptly terminated when one person or the other realizes that continuing the conversation is not in his or her best interest. An extreme example of this is the case of a woman who, taking advantage of the fact that conversation with a NNS is often problematic, upon responding to an obscene telephone call, immediately feigns a "thick" foreign accent which inevitably causes the caller to immediately hang up the phone.

Miscommunication

Our second main category is miscommunication, which we have also divided into two subcategories: (1) misunderstanding and (2) incomplete understanding.

In broad terms, miscommunication occurs when other than the intended message is understood, in other words, when there is a mismatch between the speaker's intention and the hearer's interpretation (Milroy, 1984, p. 8). This may also be described in the language of artificial intelligence as an incongruity between the belief spaces of the participants (Marlos, 1981).

Following Milroy, we distinguish between *misunderstanding* which involves "simple disparity between the speaker's and hearer's semantic analysis of a given utterance" (Milroy, 1984, p. 15), and *incomplete understanding* (akin to her communicative breakdown), wherein "one or more participants perceive that something has gone wrong" (1984, p. 15). A major differentiating factor between these two types is whether or not the participants overtly recognize a problem and manifest a subsequent attempt at remediation. In the former case they do not, in the latter they do.

To illustrate a misunderstanding, consider the example in extract 2 which comes from a conversation between a South Africa woman (English NS) and a French woman. They had both left London early in the morning, had taken a train to Dover and had an unusually long delay in Dover before being able to cross the English Channel to Calais on their way to Paris. The conversation occurred immediately after they had boarded a train in Calais bound for Paris and had settled into their seats facing each other. Prior to this conversation they did not know each other, having only met on this journey.

Extract 2

NS: When I get to Paris, I'm going to sleep for one whole day. I'm so tired.
NNS: What?
NS: I'm going to sleep for one whole day.
NNS: One hour a day?
NS: Yes.
NNS: Why?
NS: Because I'm so tired.

(data from Selinker & Gass, 1984)

At this point the conversation terminated, with each lapsing into silence, presumably thinking the other somewhat odd. This type of misunderstanding can also occur cross-dialectally. An example is offered by Milroy (1984) in her discussion of the Hiberno-English dialect spoken in Belfast. The temporal conjunctions "whenever" and "when" do not contrast in that dialect, and thus "whenever" may be used to indicate the simple past. Milroy explains that the utterance *whenever he came he hit me* was misinterpreted by a standard English speaker (Milroy herself) as "referring to several different occasions" (1984, p. 19) although the speaker intended it to refer to one specific event.

Finally, we present an example of the most common type of communicative situation involving NNSs, that is when there is overt recognition that part (or all) of the desired message has not been received. The excerpt in extract 3 comes from an interview that an NNS conducted about food and nutrition.

Extract 3

NNS: There has been a lot of talk lately about additives and preservatives in food. How –
NS: – a a a lot, a lot of talk about what?
NNS: uh. There has been a lot of talk lately about additives and preservatives in food.
NS: Now just a minute. I can hear you – everything except the important words. You say there's been a lot of talk lately about what [inaudible]
NNS: – additive, additive, and preservative, in food –
NS: Could you spell one of those words for me, please
NNS: A D D I T I V E
NS: Just a minute. This is strange to me
NNS: h h
NS: -uh-
NNS: 'n other word is P R E S E R V A
NS: – oh
NNS: preservatives and additive
NS: -preservatives, yes, okay. And what was that –
-what was that first word I didn't understand?
NNS: OKAY in –
NS: – additives?
NNS: OKAY.
NS: – additives and preservatives
NNS: yes
NS: ooh right . . .

(data from Gass & Varonis, 1985b)

In this example, there is eventually a congruity between what the NNS was asking and what the NS understood. This "happy ending" does not always obtain in talk involving NNSs, as the example in extract 4 illustrates. At the end of the exchange, there was till only partial understanding.

Extract 4

NS: Who is the best player in Colombia?
NNS: Colombia?
NS: Does uh...who is *the* Colombian player?
NNS: Me?

NS: No, in Colombia
NNS: In Colombia plays. Yah.
NS: No, on your team. On the Millionarios.
NNS: Ah yah, Millionarios
NS: No, on the Millionarios team
NNS: Millionarios play in Colombia. In Sud America. In Europa.
NS: Do, do they have someone like Pele in Colombia?
NNS: Pele? In Colombia? Pele?
NS: In Colombia? Who is, who is "Pele" in Colombia? Do you have someone?
NNS: In Bogota?
NS: Yeah, who is the best player?
NNS: In Santo de Brazil?
NS: OK (gives up) and are you center forward?

(from Butterworth, 1978, as cited in Hatch, 1983)

What we have been discussing up until this point has to do with the outcome of a communicative encounter. That is, in dealing with miscommunication, we have been referring to whether or not there was symmetry in message transmission and reception and whether or not the participants recognized the asymmetry, when it existed. The next question we need to ask is: How do the problems get resolved? We deal with this more extensively below, but for now it is necessary to introduce the concept of negotiated communication. By this we mean those exchanges in which participants in a conversation focus their attention on straightening out problems once they have occurred (cf. Drummond & Hopper, this volume). Negotiated communication can be a complex matter (see Varonis & Gass, 1985b for a lengthy discussion of negotiation of meaning) yet a highly frequent occurrence with regard to NNS discourse. It includes routines or exchanges that involve indications of nonunderstandings and subsequent negotiations of meaning. Such negotiation may ultimately result in transmission of the intended message or may instead result in a lack of understanding. We saw extensive examples of negotiated exchanges in 3 and 4 above. Negotiated communication is thus the process by which speakers attempt to resolve difficulties.

Modeling Miscommunication Types

Before dealing specifically with NNS communication, we present a model of miscommunication. We begin by noting that a precondition to a communicative act involving two people[4] begins with the mutual recognition of self-involvement in the conversation. Thus, if one party speaks to another, but the second person does not recognize that he or she is being spoken to, we do not have a communicative act. Both parties need to be aware of the involvement. Clearly, there are many reasons why this precondition may not be met, ranging from lack of opportunity to communicate, to lack of desire to communicate, or even to hearing loss. In Figure 7.2 we model various ways in which incipient miscommunication takes place once the precondition of recognition of mutual involvement is met.

The first path that a conversation can follow, labeled 1a, is that which ultimately results in what we have termed a misunderstanding. In this case conversation proceeds with no overt evidence of interruptions for clarification. Yet, it results in a semantic mismatch, or in Milroy's terms a difference in the semantic analysis of message transmission and reception. On the other hand in path 1b, there is a recognition of a problem. When there is a recognition of difficulty, there are essentially three resolutions: (1) to terminate the thread of the conversation indicated by path 2a (this may involve an abrupt topic shift); (2) to negotiate that which is unclear (path 2b)—this, of course, is a recursive function, as is indicated by path 3a which returns to the point at which there is another recognition of difficulty; and (3) to ignore the difficulty and proceed with the conversation (path 4 → 1b). Once a negotiated exchange has taken place, another decision has to be made and here there appear to be two options: (1) recognize again that there is still a problem (path 3a → 1b) (this then results in a subsequent choice: to negotiate [2b]; to terminate the conversation [2a]; or to ignore [4]; and (2) return to the main thread of the conversation (3b). Once an interlocutor has determined which of these paths to follow, there are essentially three possible outcomes: that in which there is a match in message transmission/reception (5c); that in which there is still incomplete understanding (5b); or that in which there is a mismatch (misunderstanding) (5a).

Once a communicative act has terminated, imagine an objective interpreter of the true state of the world that can determine the congruity between the intended message and the received message. In the case of congruity, by definition communication has been successful provided the speakers recognize such congruity; in the case of incongruity, there is misunderstanding or incomplete understanding. Below we deal with various ways in which incongruity is recognized.

Cross-Cultural Differences

We turn now to a discussion of the sources of NNS problematic discourse. Here we focus on two areas: (1) the ways in which conversation is perceived, including the indirectness/politeness continuum (Tannen,

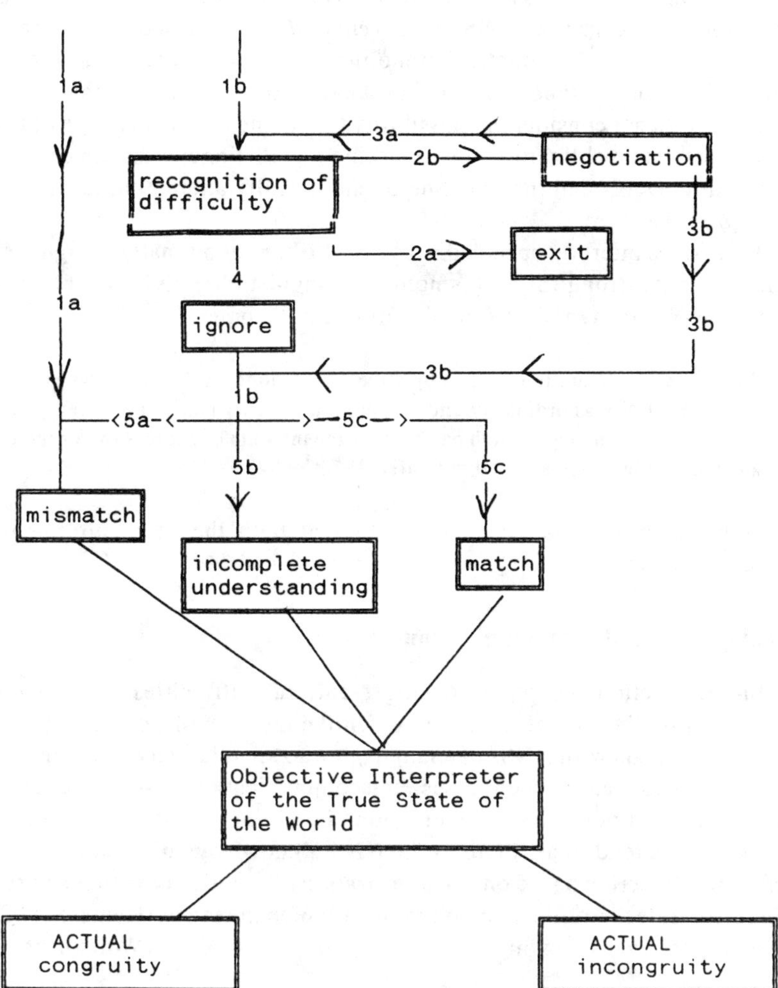

Figure 7.2 Model of NNS Miscommunication

1975); and (2) the *grammar* of the language, including such aspects of language as phonology, the lexicon, and word order. The first can be viewed as subjective, related to the sociocultural ways in which language is interpreted; the second is objective, related to the grammatical facts of the language.

To understand the nature of cross-cultural miscommunication, let us assume a monolingual speaker engaged in conversation with an NNS. The NS most likely interprets the speech of the NNS according to first language (L1) norms. That is, if an NNS says *I went to the store,* it seems reasonable to assume that our hypothetical monolingual NS interprets that as though the NNS intends to report on some past event. In all likelihood that native speaker does not consider the possibility that in the native language of that NNS, there is no obligatory tense marking that distinguishes between past and future events and that what he or she is really attempting to say is: *I will go to the store.*

That is, we interpret speech through the "filter" of our native language[5]/ culture. In its strong form, this notion of linguistic relativity is known as the Sapir-Whorf hypothesis. Sapir, for example, notes:

> Human beings do not live in the objective world alone, nor alone in the world of social activity as ordinarily understood, but are very much at the mercy of that particular language which has become the medium of expression for their society. (Sapir, 1929, as cited in Hoijer, 1954, p. 92)

This has implications for interpretation at both the sociocultural and grammatical level.

Sociocultural Miscommunication

In this section we report on cross-cultural difficulties, focusing in particular on the role of inferencing. Unlike the bulk of this chapter, this discussion deals with NNSs of a language who are relatively fluent in their second language. In such cases, miscommunication assumes a social weight it does not carry in interactions involving learners, because NS interlocutors tend to attribute to the NNS a knowledge of sociolinguistic rules of interaction based on a demonstration of familiarity with the purely linguistic rules. A failure in communicative competence (Hymes, 1972), then, is perceived as an intentional act and not a mistake. As Wolfson notes,

> Since linguistic competence is an aspect of communicative competence, people who have one are expected to have the other and are therefore held responsible for sociolinguistic violations in a way which those with less ability to communicate would not be. (1989, p. 149)

Takahashi and Beebe (1987) further point out that, in contrast to Taylor's (1974) finding that there is less *linguistic* transfer from the native language to the target language as a function of increased proficiency, there is more *sociolinguistic* or *pragmatic* transfer because with greater proficiency, there are more opportunities for error.

Tannen (1975, 1981a) deals with communication difficulties between husbands and wives of different native language backgrounds, reporting on miscommunication resulting from differing interpretations of indirectness in speech. One example from her 1975 paper is given in extract 5:

Extract 5

NS (wife):	Bob's having a party. Wanna go?
NNS (husband):	OK
NS:	(later) Are you sure you want to go?
NNS:	OK, let's not go, I'm tired anyway.

Although, as Tannen explains, the interlocutors obey Grice's (1975) conversational maxims, the end result of the conversation was what she terms a communication mix-up, or what we term a misunderstanding. In this case the wife employs a fairly direct strategy, questioning her husband's willingness to attend the party (line 3), so as not to force it on him. He, however, interprets her question as being an indirect way of communicating that she really doesn't want to go, and in order to please her he responds as at line 4. By being direct, the wife is displaying camaraderie with her husband; by perceiving her (misunderstood) indirectness, the husband is displaying camaraderie with his wife.

This type of communicative event, which fits our category of miscommunication, is more frequent in conversations with relatively fluent second language speakers than in those with second language learners. It is furthermore the case that miscommunication resulting from NS perceptions of relatively proficient NNS language use as opposed to learner's with low-level comprehension and productive skills is often the more serious in terms of interpersonal relations because the source of the difficulty is attributed to a defect in a person (or a culture) (e.g., Americans are insincere, Israelis are rude, Japanese are indirect) rather than an inability to map the correct linguistic form onto pragmatic intentions. As Gumperz and Tannen (1979, p. 315) point out, because the interlocutors "assume that they understand each other, they are less likely to question interpretations." This is precisely the communicative situation that Varonis and Gass (1985a) label the most "dangerous". Without shared background, in terms of linguistic system and specific beliefs, "when on interlocutor confidently [but inacurately] interprets another's utterance, it is likely that participants will run into immediate problems because they do not share a common discourse space" (Varonis & Gass, 1985a, p. 342).

Further examples of sociocultural miscommunication are presented in the research of Blum-Kulka (1983, 1987), Cohen and Olshtain (1981), Olshtain (1983), Olshtain and Cohen (1983, 1987) involving speakers of Hebrew and English. A summary of much of this research, termed *pragmatic transfer*, appears in Wolfson (1989). According to these authors, differences in the rules of *politeness* between Hebrew and English result in appropriate communicative acts on the part of a NNS, specifically in terms of apologies and requests. Hebrew speakers "apologize considerably less" (Olshtain & Cohen, 1983, p. 28) and are far more direct in their requests (Blum-Kulka, 1983) than their English-speaking counterparts. Such differences can have at least two effects: (1) the NNS of Hebrew may be unable to effectively communicate her intent in English, as the illocutionary force of, for example, a request is misinterpreted; and (2) the NS of Hebrew will be perceived as being rude by an NNS. As Wolfson notes, "since it is also very likely that this direct style of speech is transferred by Hebrew speakers learning English, it may also account for the well-known fact that Israelis are often stereotyped as being rude and abrupt when they are interacting in English-speaking communities" (Wolfson, 1989, p. 152).

Similar findings are presented in Beebe, Takahashi, and Uliss-Weltz (1990) and Beebe and Takahashi (1989a, 1989b) on Japanese learners of English. They found pragmatic transfer of Japanese norms of discourse when learners were asked to perform (on a pencil and paper task) face-threatening speech acts, specifically refusals, chastisement, disagreement, and embarrassing announcements. They consistently found pragmatic differences between the behaviors of the learners and native speakers of English, especially with respect to the greater sensitivity of the Japanese to interlocutor social status. The authors attribute these differences to transfer from native language norms. Beebe et al. (1990, p. 68) note: "We accept that incomplete knowledge of target language sociolinguistic patterns is one impetus for transfer. However, we also believe that deeply held cultural values are not easily given up."

With early stage second language learners, such interpretation of speech events is less likely to occur because incongruities between a person's speech and the speech of the target language community is more often seen as a linguistic deficit rather than a reflection of a personality or a cultural characteristic.

Such examples point out that "the locus of a miscommunication may be specifically 'pragmatic' rather than 'structural' " (Milroy 1984, p. 24), located in the disparity between inferences participants draw rather than in their respective linguistic systems. Research in this area owes much to the pioneering work of Gumperz (1976, 1977) and Gumperz and Tannen

(1979) on conversational inferences. Consider, for example, the conversation in extract 6.

Extract 6

NNS (male): I was surprised to see you with that boy.
NS (female): horrified silence

In this case, the NNS, a native speaker of Farsi, was transferring his cultural attitudes about boyhood and manhood in choosing a lexical item in English to convey his sentiment. The "boy" under consideration was a medical doctor in his late twenties known to both of them. The NS interpreted the statement as an insult to the man she had been having dinner with, and also as an affront to her own judgment. In fact, as the NNS later explained, in his culture, the Farsi equivalent of "boy" would be used until the male was married and even had a family of his own. As the interlocutors did not share an understanding of the semantic scope of the word "boy," the conversation quickly ran aground. It was not until much later that the misunderstanding was negotiated and resolved.

Labov and Fanshel (1977) build on the work of Sacks, Schegloff (1979), and others to establish a hierarchy of *rules of discourse* that apply to conversation, thus furthering the work of Austin (1985), Searle (1969), and others on speech acts in isolation. More recently, Tannen (1981b) argues for *patterns of interpretation* that would take into account "context, individual and social differences and interpersonal dynamics" (Tannen, 1981b, p. 484). A clearer understanding of the rules, norms, and inferences involved in conversation assumes greater importance in cross-cultural communication because, as Gumperz has repeatedly pointed out, miscommunication in such a context may contribute to *hostile stereotyping* (Milroy, 1984, p. 26), or what Clyne (1977) terms *communication conflict*.

Grammatical Miscommunication

A second major type of miscommunication is that whose source can be found in the differences between the grammars of the interlocutors, with grammar being loosely defined to include the phonological, morphological, syntactic, and prosodic systems. An interesting example of miscommunication (with disturbing ramifications) with a grammatical basis is given by Naylor (1979), reporting on a court case in which two Filipino nurses were on trial for murder. It happened that during one summer there were an unusually large number of cases of respiratory arrest at the Veterans Administration Hospital in Ann Arbor, Michigan, where these two women worked. It was, furthermore, determined that one or the other (or both) were on duty during the time of each of these suspicious deaths. They were accused of injecting intravenously into each of the patients a muscle-relaxant drug (Pavulon). The motivation, it was claimed, was to draw attention to the hospital and the difficult conditions under which they worked. The evidence presented was only circumstantial. Why then did the jury arrive at a guilty verdict?

In newspaper reports published after the trial, it appeared that the nurses' credibility was severely damaged by discrepancies and inconsistencies between reports of witnesses and nurses' own reports. Naylor, in a very interesting and informative report, argues that the difficulty was largely linguistic. She set out to see what factors were responsible for the lack of credibility of these two nurses.

Naylor attributes the specific difficulty to tense/aspect distinctions in the native language compared to those in the target language. In Tagalog, the native language of these two women, there is a rich system of aspect with tense not being marked on the verb. For example, "is eating" and "was eating" are expressed by a single form. A major distinction that is made in Tagalog is between an action that has begun and one that has not begun, as can be seen below.

kakain	"will eat" — an action that has not yet begun	
kumakain	"eats/is eating/was eating"	These two are actions that have begun. They are distinguished by whether or not the action has terminated.
kumain	"ate/has eaten/had eaten"	

We can consider in particular how the use of English by these two women was likely to have been misinterpreted by native speakers of English.

Extract 7

Q: Would you say that the two of you were close friends during that period of time?

A: I would say we *are* good friend, but we are really not that close because I *don't know* her and we *don't know* each other that much (p. 5000 of transcripts)

(from Naylor, 1979)

What she intended to say was that they were not good friends before they were accused, but that having gone through the experience of the trial, they had since become close. Yet, she chose only the present tense, which makes this statement appear internally contradictory, as well as contradictory to her prior testimony in which she had stated that they had become close friends during the trial.

Evidence for the fact that the Filipino nurses were using their native language aspectual system as a basis for interpreting and hence producing the English system is given in extract 8:

Extract 8

1. **Q:** Weren't you a relief supervisor for about six, seven months?
2. **A:** I think I started in December of '74.
3. **Q:** '74 until about June of '75?
4. **A:** Yes.
5. **Q:** So, are you saying that some time during that time you learned about Pavulon?
6. **A:** Yes.
7. **Q:** And what else did you learn abut Pavulon, other than it was given at surgery?

→ 8. **A:** Are you asking me about what I know about Pavulon in the summer of '75 or what I know about Pavulon at the present time, after hearing all these experts?

9. **Q:** What you knew abut Pavulon at the time.

→ 10. **A:** I know a little about Pavulon.

11. **Q:** What did you know about it?

→ 12. **A:** I know it's used in anesthesia.

13. **Q:** Why? Or, what else do you know about it?

→ 14: **A:** When I work in ICU, I learn that it's used to a patient to relax. It's a muscle relaxant. The patient should be on a respirator and it should be ordered by a doctor.

(from Naylor, 1979, pp. 5106-5107, transcripts)

There is obviously some confusion on the defendant's part as to the time frame which is being asked about (see line 8). Even after this is explained and it is clear to her that the prosecutor is asking about the time during which the deaths occurred, she continues to use the present tense form to talk about past actions (lines 10,12,14). This is so despite the prior "model" of a past tense form in line 9. As Naylor says, "she appears to read 'did you learn' as *have you learned*, thus missing the tense cue for the narrative discourse and failing to contextualize correctly into the discourse set established by the preceding dialogue" (1979, p. 9).

As Naylor points out, a listener (i.e. the jury) hearing the testimony in English is unlikely to realize that there is a linguistic problem. Rather, he or she hears the responses as inconsistencies, at best, or contradictions or lies, at worse. A linguistic mismatch frequently goes unrecognized as such and in this case resulted in the tragic conclusion that these women were guilty[6] (see also Aronsson, this volume).

Within the framework we established earlier, this reflects a 'Path 1a' communicative event with the objective interpreter (in this case, Naylor) recognizing the incongruity. The message that was intended was not received (by the prosecuting attorney, the jury, etc.). Sapir (1929, as cited in Hoijer, 1954) would claim that the Filipino nurses on trial and the American jurors were bound by the conventions of their respective languages: the nurses as they sought to express and the jurors as they sought to interpret.

The Nature and Function of L2 Conversation

In this section we briefly describe typical patterns of L2 conversation. In Varonis and Gass (1985b) we discussed in greater detail the nature of conversations involving NNSs. We pointed out that a major characteristic of NNS conversation is that it is filled with interruptions. In conversation between interlocutors who share a common background and language, turn-taking generally proceeds smoothly, with each speaker responding to the previous utterance of the other. On the other hand, in conversation involving NNSs, there are numerous interruptions in the flow of meaning. As Gumperz and Tannen (1979) comment, "While different rhetorical strategies can lead to misunderstandings, cross-cultural, which consist of more generalized discrepancies in use of prosody and paralinguistic cues, can lead to the disruption of conversational rhythm and thematic progression" (1979, p. 317). NNS interlocutors are much more likely to lose their "footing" in the conversation and often spend much of the conversational time in figuring out the scope of the discourse. Thus, there is significant negotiation of meaning in NNS discourse, negotiation which is essential to its success. We argued that these routines function to "help interlocutors regain their places in a conversation after one or both have 'slipped' " (Gumperz & Tannen, 1985a, p. 73).

There are a number of external variables that shape the structure of NNS talk (e.g., task type, status of interlocutors, topic knowledge, ethnic background, gender). Each of these variables impacts on the degree to which there is an attempt to resolve partial or complete lack of understanding (i.e., negotiated communication). For example, the results of studies of task types (Duff, 1986; Gass & Varonis, 1985a; Pica, 1987) show that the greater the opportunity for the information flow to be bidirectional, the more learners will negotiate meaning. In such conversations there is a greater frequency of questions asked and hence a large number of meaning clarifications at all levels (phonology, syntax, semantics, pragmatics).

Furthermore, in talks in which the information exchange is required, negotiation is more extensive (Pica, 1987; Gass & Varonis, 1985a).

In a recent study by Takahashi (1989) in which she considered NS/NNS interethnic (Spanish and Japanese) talk, the author found that in interethnic dyads there is a greater amount of meaning negotiation than in dyads in which the interlocutors share a native language. Takahashi, in interviews with her subjects, found that although in dyads composed of speakers who shared a native language there was less need for negotiation due to the greater shared background, there was, however, a greater feeling of discomfort in speaking the second language (see also Varonis & Gass, 1985a).

Yet another example of external variables impinging on meaning negotiations is one that treats gender in NNS communication (Gass & Varonis, (1986). We found clear sex-linked differences in conversation. Similar results can also be found in Pica, Holliday, Lewis, and Morgenthaler (1989) although their study was not designed to deal specifically with gender. Although it is clear that the degree to which incomplete understanding occurs in discourse is in part determined by variables relating to the task of conversation and to the participants themselves, it remains to be seen what effect this might have on actual learning.

Much of the emphasis in the recent second language literature involving conversations is predicated on the notions of input (Krashen, 1980), interaction (Long, 1980) and output (Swain, 1985). Krashen has argued that the *sine qua non* of acquisition is input. In his view, learners must receive comprehensible input in order for acquisition to proceed. Input that is not comprehensive is of no value for acquisition. Comprehensive input can, of course, be obtained in a number of ways, for example, through speech modification on the part of one's interlocutor or through negotiation of meaning, an outcome of miscommunication.

Another dimension to consider is the notion of comprehensible output developed by Swain (1985). She argues that more than comprehensible input is necessary. Comprehensible output, or the productive use of language plays a central role in acquisition because it provides learners with a forum for testing out hypotheses and refining the knowledge of the target language. It is often possible to understand the meaning of an L2 utterance without detailed analysis of that utterance. It is not possible, however, to participate in discourse, that is produce language, without imposing some grammatical structure on the L2. Thus, output, and in particular within this context comprehensible output, forces learners to impose structure on their second language. Interaction in which learners are forced to make output comprehensible is claimed to have importance for language development.

Taking into account the notions of comprehensible input and comprehensible output, it is clear that an important forum in which to obtain both is conversation itself. Long (1980, 1983, 1985), Pica (1987), Scarcella and Higa (1981), and Varonis and Gass (1985b) have argued that negotiation of meaning is a major driving force of acquisition: It is through negotiation that meaning becomes clarified. By negotiating, learners work hard to get the linguistic information that is necessary to maintain conversational footing. It is this *linguistic work* that makes the negotiated input meaningful and hence available for intake.

On a practical level, how can we determine that what is negotiated is retained? That is, how can we truly determine that participation is truly linguistically beneficial to a learner? Schachter (1986) argued that it is necessary to present evidence of the effect of L2 input on the process of learning in order to counter the proposal that input serves only to *trigger* the acquisition faculty, a faculty that is innate. The argument that we have put forth in this chapter, and that Schachter also makes, is that negative evidence (information that indicates to a learner that his or her utterance is deviant in some way) provides learners with metalinguistic information about the target language. The negotiation routines that often follow give learners an opportunity to test their hypotheses about the second language in their follow-up turn.

Gass and Varonis (1989) present evidence for the direct positive effect of conversational interaction on second language acquisition. The data, involving NS/NNS interactions, reveal numerous instances of self-correction by a NNS following extended instances of negotiated communication. Many of these self-corrections occurred some time after the actual negotiation. In a second study devoted to this issue, Gass and Varonis (1988) set up NS/NNS dyads in which the NS described to the NNS where to place objects on a picture board. In half of the dyads the NNS participant was allowed to negotiate unclear parts of the discourse, while in the other half no conversational interaction was allowed. Following this task, the NNSs described to the NS interlocutors where to place objects on a similar board. Descriptions by those NNSs who had been allowed to clarify meaning on the first trial were more effective than those in which no negotiation was allowed.

It therefore appears from these preliminary investigations that negative evidence and negotiation play a significant role in the internalization of linguistic information. Whether this is a necessary condition of second language acquisition awaits further research.

Recognizing Incongruities

Up until this point we have discussed instances of miscommunication that occur in NNS discourse. In concluding, we turn to a discussion of how and when communication problems are recognized[7]. (Note that our model given in Figure 7.2 only deals with (a) and (b) – those situations covering the actual communicative event; it does not address the issue of what happens when an instance of miscommunication is recognized later.) Briefly, there are seven possible outcomes (see also Varonis & Gass, 1985a):

(a) Immediate recognition of the problem but no comment (path 1b→4)
(b) Immediate recognition of problem and makes comment, i.e., negotiates (path 1b→2b)
(c) Later recognition of problem but doesn't comment
(d) Later recognition of problem and makes comment
(e) Recognition after conversation but doesn't comment
(f) Recognition after conversation and makes comment
(g) No recognition of the problem

(c) through (g) above are all, at least initially, instances of misunderstanding, whereas (b) represents incomplete understanding mediated by negotiated communication. Outcome (a)may result in successful communication or misunderstanding depending on whether the hearer correctly interprets the speaker's intention regardless of the "noise" in the transmission of the message. Below are examples of each of these 7 types.

Example of (a)
A teacher of a low-level ESL class was presented with an assortment of Valentine's Day cards from her class. One particularly well-meaning student gave her a card and waited proudly as she opened it. On the cover was a beautiful bouquet of flowers with the touching sentiment: 'With Deepest Sympathy'

The teacher was amused at the student's obviously unintentional mistake, but deemed it better not to comment in order not to hurt his feelings. In a worst-case scenario, failure to comment may result in the hearer's misunderstanding of the intended message, although with the Valentine example, this as not the case.

Extract 9
Example of (b)

NNS: and they have the chwach there
NS: the what?
NNS: the chwach . . . I know someone that . . .
NS: what does it mean?
NNS: like um like American people they always go there every Sunday, you know . . . every morning that
NS: yes?
NNS: there pr-that -the American people get dressed up to go to um chwach
NS: oh to church..I see

(data from Pica, 1988)

Here, the problem is recognized immediately and a resolution is attempted, resulting in this case in successful communication.

With the third possibility, there is an after the fact recognition of the problem with no overt indication that any sort of faulty communication had taken place:

Extract 10
Example of (c)

Luis: I want to ask you about somethin'
NS: [female teacher] Yes, Luis, what is it?
Luis: I don't understand about urinals.
NS: What is it you don't understand about them?
Luis: I don't understand what you're supposed to do with them.

(data from Varonis & Gass, 1985a)

In this conversation, the teacher (much to her relief) realized well into the conversation that he in fact was not talking about urinals, but about the *journal* assignment that she had made.

The fourth possibility is to realize the problem later in the conversation (as in Extract 9), but is differentiated from the third possibility by the fact that a comment is made which straightens out the misunderstanding:

Extract 11
Example of (d)

Waiting for salesman to return; phone is ringing for extended period
José: Should we get those rings?
Rachel: Would we be able to give them any information?
José: [long pause] I meant the napkin rings.

(data from Varonis, 1981)

In this case Rachel, familiar with the sometimes idiosyncratic speech of José, an NNS of English, attributed to him a proposition even more idiosyncratic than usual despite the fact that his comment is meaningful and well-formed. This is because she uses inappropriate contextualization cues (Gumperz, 1977; Gumperz & Tannen, 1979)—namely the persistent ringing of the phone. It also differs from possibility (c) by the fact that in this case the interlocutor has committed herself to the wrong interpretation. Hence, only an overt comment will suffice to straighten the matter out.

The fifth possibility is one in which an interlocutor realizes the problem after the conversation has occurred, but does not make a comment. In many instances an interlocutor may be embarrassed to make the correction:

Example of (e)

An American undergraduate on a summer research scholarship in Scotland at the home of an English professor and his wife. At dinner one evening, a piece of lettuce lands on her lap and the oil stains her clothing. She comments: 'Oh no, I got my pants dirty'.

She notes that the couple respond with concealed surprise to her comment and surmises it is not appropriate to discuss soiled clothing at the table. Many weeks later, however, she notices at a dry cleaner that a price list includes both 'pants' and 'trousers' and finally realizes that 'pants' refers, in British English, to an undergarment. Amused at her mistake, she nevertheless is too embarrassed to reinvoke the topic for comment.

In the sixth possibility the problem is overtly commented on after the conversation. The example below illustrates a miscommunication that took a year to resolve:

Extract 12
Example of (f)

Rajid (NNS): What do you want your future husband to be like?
Linda (NS): Tall, dark and handsome.

Rajid was asking a serious question which Linda did not feel like answering. She hedged, responding with a cliché that might be termed "formulaic." Unfortunately, as an NNS, Rajid did not recognize the expression as formulaic, and found himself surprised and disappointed by the seeming shallowness of Linda's response. The misunderstanding was not resolved until over a year later, when through letters they were able to resolve the problem they had not discussed face-to-face. Gumperz and Tannen (1979) note that "formulaic use of language is always a problem for non-native speakers or visitors to a foreign country" because the NNS may be familiar with neither the utterance nor the contextualization cues that might "alert the listener to the possibility of a formulaic interpretation" (1979, p. 315).

Finally, in the seventh possibility, neither participant is aware of the incongruity between the message intended and the message received. In such cases, the misunderstanding may be obvious only to a third-party observer, or becomes obvious to participants through protocol analysis such as that described in Hawkins (1985).

Conclusion

We have drawn upon research in the fields of speech act theory, sociolinguistics, artificial intelligence, discourse analysis, and second language acquisition in order to describe how interlocutors who do not share a native language may be particularly susceptible to miscommunication. We argue that this is the case for at least two reasons: (1) because of the grammatical differences between their languages, they may not share an understanding of the referential meaning of individual utterances; and (2) because of sociocultural differences, speakers may share a referential meaning but not conversational inferences, thus misinterpreting each other's intent.

Following Milroy (1984) we distinguish between two types of miscommunication: *misunderstanding*, in which it is not immediately obvious that the message received is not the one that was intended, and *incomplete understanding*, in which interlocutors recognize a problem and thus seek to negotiate meaning before returning to the main topic of discourse. It is misunderstandings that are particularly dangerous to interethnic or intercultural relations: When miscommunication is not recognized, the result is most often that the minority group member, in this case the NNS, is judged negatively by the majority group, leading to hostile stereotyping and the increasing feeling of powerlessness (Gumperz, 1978). Negotiated communication, on the other hand, offers the hope of social and linguistic reconciliation. The amount of difficulty interlocutors may face seems to be affected by social and situational factors, such as task, status, knowledge of topic, and ethnicity and gender; the greater the difficulty, the more the negotiation required for conversation to proceed. Such negotiation has implications for intercultural communication in general and for language learning in particular: The more opportunity NNSs have to negotiate meaning and produce comprehensible output, the more they may advance their own language learning. Thus, the important issue is not whether NNSs have the opportunity to *converse,* but whether they receive the same message their interlocutors are sending and conversely send the same message their interlocutors receive.

We hope to have made clear in this chapter that NNS discourse is a fertile area for the investigation of problematic discourse, because much of NNS discourse (at least that of early stage learning) results in some sort of difficulty. What is less obvious is to what extent our modeling of miscommunication is in fact an adequate account of NNS conversation. Furthermore, it remains to be seen whether or not NNS discourse is qualitatively different from problematic discourse occurring between two NSs of a language. That is, are differences only a matter of degree or are they truly a matter of kind? We suspect that the answer is both. Miscommunication of the type we have discussed under cross-cultural differences (above) is unlikely to occur in anything but cross-cultural communication. On the other hand, misunderstandings stemming from noise in the channel misunderstood, partially, or non-understood lexical items may occur in NS discourse, albeit less frequently than in NNS discourse. What differentiates the two discourse situations is the complexity of the resultant negotiation needed to resolve the difficulty as well as the likelihood of a recognition of the problem. In other words, in NNS discourse the problem is more likely to go unrecognized or, if it is recognized, is likely to be resolved in a relatively straightforward manner. For example, in an NS-NNS conversation reported in Varonis and Gass (1985a), a NNS speaker called what he thought was a TV sales store, but which in actuality was a TV repair store. The conversation began in the following manner:

Extract 13

NS: Hello
NNS: Hello could you tell me about the price and size of Sylvania Color TV
NS: Pardon?
NNS: Could you tell me about price and size of Sylvania TV color
PAUSE
NS: What did you want? A service call?
NNS: uh 17 inch huh?
NS: What did you want a service call? or how much to repair a TV?
NNS: yeah TV color
NS: 17 inch
NNS: OK

When two NSs made the same phone call, the problem was resolved within two exchanges (as opposed to more than two minutes coupled with complex negotiation, as was the case in the NS-NNS conversation).

We conclude with one final example. The conversation in extract 14 is between the same NNS husband and NS wife that miscommunicated seven years earlier in extract 11 above.

Extract 14

NNS: Didn't we say once we were going to make a [wiəl]?
NS: A what?
NNS: A [wiəl]
NS: What kind of wheel, you mean a tire?
NNS: A [wiəl]. W I L L, a [wiəl]
NS: Oh, a will

In this case rather than reply prematurely on the basis of a misunderstanding about the referent of [wiəl], as she did about the referent of "rings", the wife twice initiates negotiation subroutines that finally make clear to her the referent of her husband's speech: Not a tire for the children to swing on, but a will to insure their future. Their bridge may still be shaky, but they have learned to step a little more carefully.

Notes

1. It is important to note that this is an idealized approach to "smooth conversation." It by no means implies that overlaps do not occur or that speakers do not have their own personal agendas of conversational direction. We are aware of the inadequacies of attempting such a definition, particularly because there are so many possible variations of this notion. We only present this example to give the reader a sense of what it is we are eliminating in our discussion of problematic communication.

2. For purposes of language practice, at many universities an American student is paired with an international student. They arrange schedules to meet and agree on how many hours per week they will speak and in what language.

3. There is yet another type of noncommunication event, which is nonetheless communicative. Consider Person A, angry with Person B. One way of communicating that anger is to deliberately snub Person B, by making noncommunication obvious. Although this is noncommunication, it differs from our examples here in that Person A, by means of talk avoidance, communicates a message. This, of course, is beyond the scope of this chapter.

4. For the sake of simplicity, we limit our discussion to communication that occurs between only two people. We further limit our discussion to verbal communication.

5. This is of course an idealized situation which would be immediately complicated with a speaker who knows other languages and has had experience with other cultures (see Gass & Varonis, 1984).

6. The nurses were eventually acquitted after the judge "granted the motion for a new trial, essentially on grounds of prosecutorial misconduct" (Naylor, 1979, p. 5).

7. The issue of incongruity by necessity has been simplified for the purposes of this chapter. Giles (personal communication) rightly suggests that incongruity may be intentionally fostered to anger, to "stir up the waters" or even to be humorous.

8

Openness, Uncertainty, and Intimacy: An Epistemological Reformulation

Julie R. Brown
L. Edna Rogers

All that is needed is a sufficient lack of disagreement about one another for each to proceed in some degree with his [or her] own plans of action. (McCall & Simmons, 1978, p. 123)

At first glance, McCall and Simmons' description of the conditions enabling human action appears ingenuous, if not altogether obvious: planned action may proceed until impediments are encountered. The presentational simplicity of the statement, however, belies a potent set of assumptions concerning the nature of humans and their social connections. Most fundamentally, McCall and Simmons remind us of the socially embedded nature of individuals and their actions. However "personal" or "private" our plans may seem, the ability to both formulate and execute them requires more than individual will or skill alone. With others we find the context and conditions within which we exercise will and out of which we acquire skill.

What then, is the nature of our inescapable social bond? For McCall and Simmons, sociality is based, not in the hard substances of certain knowledge, complete agreement, or finely tuned coordination, but in the shifting sands of "rough and ready working consensus" (p. 123). Action depends upon the absence of debilitating opposition rather than on the elimination of opposition, uncertainty, or disagreement. McCall and Simmons' conceptualization of a *working consensus* (p. 139) is based on the acceptance of the problematic nature of talk. A consensus *works* when interactants' cognitive processes do not grossly contradict their outward expressions (cf. Wiemann & Kelly, 1981, for a related observation). From this viewpoint, working relationships demand neither continual harmony nor discord. To relate successfully is to satisfactorily manage *both* polarities. This position implies that relationships are dialectical propositions. As such, partners must negotiate competing tensions, rather than eliminate differences or subsume one position in another. A dialectical view forces attention to relational *processes;* to the mutually negotiated patterning of relational constraints in contrast to arbitrarily selected moments taken to be relational states.

Working from these and related philosophical positions, we devote this chapter to a reexamination of the epistemological premises underlying much extant research on personal relationships. More specifically, we examine literature concerning *open* communication and the development of relational knowledge. We argue that, in the main, these literatures rest on problematic epistemological premises and binary, nonprocessual logics. We offer a critique of these literatures aimed at the level of epistemology and metatheory, positing a reformulation which, we believe, holds greater potential for uncovering the nuances of relational trajectories. From this reformulated vantage point, we argue that events otherwise construed as *miscommunications* in interpersonal relationships emerge as something altogether different. They emerge as necessary, unavoidable moments in ongoing patterns of relational tension management. They constitute iterations in the larger cycle of forging, modifying, recreating, and dissolving a working consensus enabling relational members' activities, both joint and individual.

To illustrate the kind of working consensus we envision, imagine a married couple in which the spouses hold firm, but opposing, political commitments. Their efforts to discuss politics produce argument after argument and mutual resentment begins to build. Imagine, then, that the partners "agree to disagree" about politics. They acknowledge that no conversions are likely but express continued commitment to the relationship. They allow differences to exist in their political conversations and agree, perhaps, to discuss politics less or to understand that when the disagreements arise, they can be voiced without either party fearing dire consequences (e.g., the ending of the relationship). It may well be that subsequent discussions produce changes in the partners' positions. It may be that such discussions become less frequent, or are entered into with more humor. In any case, the "agreeing to disagree" consensus, for however long it lasts, allows the spouses to function politically with more ease. The consensus may also allow the couple to maintain their togetherness without abandoning their principles. Most importantly, the couple need not suppress conflict or "be of one mind" to progress in a mutually satisfying fashion.

In the next section, we offer a brief exposition of the philosophical position introduced above, contrasting it with the more traditional position undergirding much of the research we discuss. We elaborate our position more fully as we move to the reviews themselves. Finally, we sketch the implications of our critiques for future study in the area.

From an "Epistemology of Objects" to an "Epistemology of Pattern"

Notions concerning our inescapable sociality and the dialectics of relational process have, to some degree, penetrated the study of intimate relations (see for instance, Altman, Vinsel, & Brown, 1981; Baxter, 1988; Hawes, 1989; Millar & Rogers, 1976, 1987; Penman, 1980; Rawlins, 1983a, 1983b, 1989; Rogers & Millar, 1988; Rogers, Millar, & Bavelas, 1984). Nevertheless, much of the literature in the area continues to focus on *objects.* The self, for instance, is frequently construed as some-*thing* to be revealed to or concealed from others. Similarly, relationships are often assumed to be syntheses of self/objects animated by the pursuit of some unified goal such as the realization of transcendent oneness, uninterrupted harmony, or unabridged knowledge of one's self and one's partner. On this view, moments of differentiation, conflict, or uncertainty become problems, errors, disruptions, or miscommunications.

Such an approach is further propagated by the commonly held *conduit metaphor* of communication; a visualization of messages as *packets* of information that transport the sender's meaning to the receiver (Reddy, 1979). Thus, messages either contain or fail to contain, communicate or miscommunicate, the information necessary for a successful transfer. Communication failures (miscommunications) are seen to rest most fully on the sender. Receivers, however, if not skilled in *total listening* (Villard & Whipple, 1976), may also err and contribute to the mechanistic notion of communication breakdown (Fisher, 1978).

From inside this set of epistemologies (what we call the *epistemology of objects*) the message, or more importantly for the argument made here, the individual-qua-individual becomes the analytic focus. The self, then, is analyzed as a substantial, more or less privatized entity that reveals or conceals, acts or reacts. Relationships become matters of bridging the differences and idiosyncrasies thought to characterize selves in order to create the sense of empathic communality necessary for sustained intimacy. Moreover, these traditional epistemologies tend to gather around the assumption (tacit or explicit) that relationships too are substantial quantities composed of ever-increasing stores of knowledge concerning the other. Such a view allows relationships to be differentiated and categorized (e.g., intimate relationships are those in which self possesses more knowledge of other than is available for, say, acquaintances). In addition, behavioral strategies associated with relationship types are identified and opposed (e.g., *open* versus *deceptive* communication). Often, this move to dichotomize comes with a move to privilege one polarity over its opposite (e.g., open communication is more desirable between intimates than is deception) (Bochner, 1982).

By contrast, our critiques and reformulations come out of an *epistemology of pattern* wherein the emphasis on the individual per se, notions concerning the linear accumulation of relational knowledge, and binary theorizing are eschewed in favor of the following positions.

First, we see social life as a *process of interrelating* in which "self" becomes a nodal point on a continually shifting relational circuitry. Here, relational recursivity is foregrounded and as the relational pathways reconfigure, so does the "self." We take the existence of "self" to be predicated on the existence of "other." The way in which a person connects to another (e.g., as friend, enemy, spouse, parent, etc.) influences who that person *is* and how he or she will behave in the relationship. As a relationship changes (and all relationships do), so do the "selves" comprising it. The self, from such a position, is forever under construction; selves, like relationships, are processes and not essences.

Second, we take the process of relating to be inherently problematic and fraught with contradiction. Rather than building steadily, ongoing relationships bob and weave in a jagged pattern as negotiations and renegotiations occur. Any given moment or behavior draws its significance from other moments or behaviors and, as such, no given behavior-moment-state can be deemed *inherently* more healthy, more functional, more desirable, or more miscommunicative than any other.

Our argument here is that behaviors take on meaning as a consequence of interpretation and we look to the context surrounding behavior for interpretive cues. What, for instance, does it mean when one person opposes another? Is the "opposer" mean-spirited? Is he or she frustrated? Is he or she righteously indignant or presenting a challenge? And who is making the interpretation? Might the person receiving the opposition hold a different view than the person delivering it? Might an observer hold another view altogether? And might not these different interpretations serve different functions? Would we not make a different assessment of opposition born of frustration than opposition born of mean-spiritedness? The point is that behaviors "mean" for someone(s) and for some purpose(s).

Interpretations of motivation and function derive from the relational context(s) in which the behavior, and its interpretation, occur (see Ellis, 1982).

The instrumentalities of behaviors, then, can only be discovered by contextualizing. Often, sequentially ordered behavioral patterns allow for the interpretation of any isolated behavior (Fisher, 1985; McNamee, 1988).

As may now be obvious, the view we propose makes the task of grouping behaviors into distinct classes problematic. Taxonomies often serve to cut behavior lose from its contextual and relational moorings, making it difficult to anchor an interpretation. Consequently, we orient the following discussions not toward the precise definition of a class of behaviors labeled *miscommunications,* but toward a demonstration of the problems and ambiguities such an approach engenders. In so doing, we also suggest how the concept *miscommunication* may change shape and function when viewed from inside a different set of epistemological assumptions.

Let us turn now to literature focused on the self-other relationship. We use this review as the basis for our critiques of prevailing ideologies woven through much of the study of interpersonal relationships.

Understanding Self, Understanding Other, and Intimacy: Review and Critique

As Parks (1982) notes, concerns with the self and its availability to or concealment from others has dominated study in interpersonal communication for several decades. The rationale for such a focus has been that *interpersonal* relations are best distinguished from other classes of social relations (e.g., *public* or *institutional* relations) by the degree to which information about one's self is known to (an) other(s) (Miller & Steinberg, 1975). Interpersonal relations proper are those in which one's partner has greater access to the unique aspects of one's self than is available by examining one's public behavior alone; interpersonal relationships are relatively idiosyncratic or intimate as opposed to institutional or role-based (Bochner, 1983; Fitzpatrick, 1987; Hinde, 1978). This belief about the distinguishing features of interpersonal relations undergirds social penetration theory (Altman & Taylor, 1973) which has, in turn, spurred much of the voluminous literature on self-disclosure. Insofar as self-disclosure has been seen as the mechanism by which relationships become personal and intimate, it has received a great deal of attention from psychologists and communication researchers alike. As Parks (1982, p. 80) observes, self-disclosure has long stood as virtually "*the* variable" of interest in interpersonal communication scholars.

Drawing on classical psychoanalysis and personality theory, self-disclosure is typically defined as an intentional revelation of information about one's self that would be unavailable to others by alternative means of discovery (DeVito, 1983; Jourard, 1971a, 1971b; Pearce & Sharp, 1973).[1] One of the pioneers of self-disclosure research, Sidney Jourard (1971b) described self-disclosure as a crucial index of psychological health:

> Self-disclosure is a symptom of personality health *and* a means of ultimately achieving healthy personality. . . . I mean a person who displays many other characteristics that betoken a healthy personality *will also display the ability to make him* [or her] *self fully known to at least one other significant human being.* (p. 32)

The implications of this statement (and of Jourard's program in general) for subsequent study are several. First, Jourard assumes that individuals are fully known to themselves while remaining "opaque" to others (Jourard, 1971b). Second, the opacity of ourselves to others can be altered through revelation of self. Third, it is through self-revealing acts that we achieve meaningful bonds. Fourth, the ideal, maximally "healthy" social bond is one based on intimacy. Intimacy, defined as partners' full knowledge of each other, becomes the privileged relational state.

These beliefs have been both expanded and challenged in research on self-disclosure. Self-disclosure has, for instance, been construed as a personality or individual difference variable (Chelune, 1975; Davis & Franzoni, 1987; Goodstein & Reinecker, 1974; Jourard, 1959; Miller, Berg, & Archer, 1983; Pederson & Higbee, 1969; Tuckman, 1966). Interestingly, the evidence linking propensity to self-disclose with mental health is mixed (Cozby, 1973; Stokes, 1987) and the consistently produced findings connecting self-disclosure to personality traits include a link only to "sociability," "extroversion," and private self-consciousness (Cozby, 1973; Davis & Franzoni, 1987; Stokes, 1987). High self-disclosers tend to be highly sociable, extroverted, and concerned with their internal states or past experiences.

Jourard (1971b, pp. 34-41) also claims that men tend to disclose less than women and are, therefore, less psychologically and physically healthy. Tests of this hypothesis have again yielded mixed results. Women have been found to disclose more in general (Grigsby & Weatherly,1983; Jourard & Lasakow, 1958; Petronio, Martin, & Littlefield, 1984), to disclose about different topics than men (Hacker, 1981; Rubin, Hill, Peplau, & Dunkel-Schetter, 1980), to disclose more to other women than to men (Brooks, 1974), and to receive disclosures from others more often than men (Caldwell & Peplau, 1982; Komarovsky, 1974). Petronio, Martin, and Littlefield (1984) also found that women tend to be more concerned than men with the characteristics of their disclosure target. On the other hand, Wheeless, Zakahi, and Chan (1988) suggest that:

> Seeing one as male or female is not as important to the disclosure process as are the perceived qualities of the individual. Regardless of the target's sex, feminine . . . characteristics tempered by some masculine qualities . . . are important when disclosing personal information. (p. 118)

Recently, more attention has been given to the function of disclosure in developing and long-term relationships than to the personality or demographic features of disclosers and targets. Miller and Read (1987), for example, although still maintaining an interest in personality traits, propose that such traits are related to strategic social goals and that high disclosures frequently use disclosure as a means of accomplishing such goals. Various researchers have found that self-disclosure, particularly positive self-disclosure (Gilbert & Hornstein, 1975), leads to liking or attraction in initial encounters (see, for instance, Worthy, Gary, & Kahn, 1969), but that a linear relationship between amount of disclosure and liking does not exist (Cozby, 1972). Disclosure tends to reduce uncertainty in initial interactions (Berger & Bradac, 1982) and open up the possibility for longer term relationships (Gilbert & Whiteneck, 1976; Wheeless, Zakahi, & Chan, 1988). Disclosure patterns change in marriages (Fitzpatrick, 1987; Mayer, 1967) and in phases of relational dissolution (Baxter, 1979, 1987; Tolstedt & Stokes, 1984).

The relationship of self-disclosure to intimacy is particularly intriguing in its counterintuitive complexity. Contrary to what Parks (1982) calls the *ideology of intimacy* that characterizes a number of theories of communication, long-term, presumably intimate relationships (e.g., marriage) are not, in all cases, characterized by spirals of increasingly frequent, intimate disclosures. Bochner (1982, p. 121), for instance, cites data from two major investigations of couples' communication (Gottman, 1979; Rausch, Barry, Hertel, & Swain, 1974) which suggest that "direct examination of feelings" and open talk does not occur continuously among satisfied couples. Current research continues to suggest that couples speak in indirect, circuitous ways and partake in "illusions about the other, exaggerations of similarity, expectations of goodness, and less than full disclosure" (Fitzpatrick, 1987, p. 137). In her studies of married couples, Fitzpatrick (1984, 1987) has identified various types of couples who differ in their levels of interdependence, their beliefs concerning the importance of tradition and change, and their approaches to conflict. She argues persuasively that, "enormous differences emerge in the degree to which couples engage in and value self-disclosure" (Fitzpatrick, 1987, p. 132) and finds no evidence to suggest that more restrained disclosure is associated with marital satisfaction.

In their research on marital communication patterns, Rogers and Millar (1988) found a subtle but noticeable difference between couples differentiated by level of marital satisfaction. In conversations with one another, both satisfied and less satisfied couples avoided expressing disagreement and nonsupport, but differed in their expression of support. In contrast to satisfied couples who frequently offered supportive messages to one another, less satisfied couples, although avoiding nonsupportive statements, withheld supportive messages as well. Rather than putting relational harmony at risk by actively pursuing disagreement and difference (Simmel, 1955), martial couples seem to focus on maintaining a neutral or positive tone. Relational maintenance appears to "turn on somewhat misguided and misleading premises" (McCall & Simmons, 1978, p. 193).

Sillars, Pike, Jones, and Murphy (1984) also challenge the prevailing belief that "understanding" between married couples necessarily produces satisfying marriage. They claim that past studies have confounded agreement and "stereotypical perception" with understanding, thus allowing what could be simply projections or cultural expectations to pass as particularized understandings (pp. 318-319). They also question the extent to which explicit, verbal disclosures alone affect understanding and the extent to which understanding necessarily facilitates relational harmony (pp. 319-320). Their own findings include: (a) that information that is "immediate" or concrete influences understanding the most and that, in their study, "the most immediate source of information about the spouse's feelings was the subject's own feelings" (p. 341); (b) that verbal information had little effect on understanding; and (c) that understanding was negatively correlated with marital satisfaction. In relation to the latter finding in particular, Sillars et al. (1984) note that understanding is as likely to produce conflict and the recognition of difference as it is the converse. In a subsequent study, Sillars, Weisberg, Burggraf, and Zietlow (1988) reported that agreement, rather than understanding, was more highly associated with satisfaction.

The work of Sillars et al. bears an interesting relationship to recent work on verbal *disqualification* (Bavelas, 1983, 1985; Bavelas & Chovil, 1986; Bavelas & Smith, 1982). Disqualified messages are those that avoid direct identification of one or more of the following elements of a statement: speaker, message, receiver, or context. Bavelas and Chovil (1986, p. 71) claim that, "even in hypothetical situations that might be said to favor 'good' communication, disqualified messages were chosen far too often to be due to individual differences in communicative ability or pathology." Instead, disqualified messages are selected in *avoidance-avoidance* situations. Such situations demand speech but promise negative consequences for direct speech.

Although Bavelas and her colleagues have not focused on marriage per se, given Sillars et al.'s observation concerning the potentially polarizing effects of understanding and Rausch et al.'s (1974) observation concerning indirect speech between otherwise well-adjusted couples, it may well be that disqualification is used as a strategy by which couples manage the ideological pressure to reveal one's self honestly and deflect the uncomfortably differentiating consequences that could result from such revelations. This suggestion is in line with McCall and Simmons' (1978) discussion of the overly simplistic notion that with complete communication relational problems would vanish in an "orgy of understanding." They insist that whether "ethically distasteful or not, some kind of secrecy and deception are vital parts of human life" (1978, p. 192).

The numerous inconsistencies in findings concerning self-disclosure and related concepts lead us to follow Bochner (1982) and Parks (1982) in their critiques of established conceptualizations of openness and its relation to intimacy. The more restrained disclosure patterns between satisfied couples, the lack of direct associations between self-disclosure and interpersonal understanding, and the not uncommon occurrence of disqualified speech suggests that viewing intimacy as predicated on continually spiraling frank, self-revelations may be a gross oversimplification of a subtle and contradictory process.

As such European critics as Volosinov (1973) and Althusser (1971) remind us, we cannot operate outside of (an) ideology. Furthermore, scholars (try though we might) can never completely escape the cultural parameters in which they operate. The perspective on intimacy we challenge is probably as much a function of prevailing cultural predispositions surrounding research as it is a function of the practice of research itself.[2] We share many cultural commonplaces with those we study. Nevertheless, one of the important contributions that we have to make is to challenge dominant ideologies—common sense—by exposing their contradictions and reframing social practices on more enabling (potentially) ideological terrain.

In the case of the literature reviewed here, one fundamental contradiction is evident. The ideology of intimacy prescribes relational "oneness," brought about by clear, candid self-revelation, as the goal of interpersonal relationships. Ironically, as various researchers point out, candid self-revelation often produces differentiation, undermining a sense of oneness, although strategies that violate the demand for complete candor may temporarily normalize or eliminate the disruption brought on by differentiation. In sum, the ideology of intimacy demands that we: be open, be different, and be "one" simultaneously. Such a demand simply cannot be satisfied.

Rausch et al. (1974), Gottman (1979), and Fitzpatrick (1987) all note that intimate partners "overestimate" their similarities and actively gloss any number of problems and differences. This evidence leads us to wonder whether intimacy is not as much a *negotiated collusion* as it is a state of "true oneness." That is, in order for relationships to be sustained, couples may collaborate on how to relate and on what issues are central; couples may agree to ignore certain bits of information and focus on others. The process of being intimate, then, may well be a matter of forging a working consensus concerning what is to be discussed and what is not; what is to be believed about each other and what is not; what is open to disagreement and what is not; and how much "understanding" is allowed and what will simply be projected. To explore this possibility, relationships must be seen as dialectical in nature and as capable of accommodating various levels of "honest" talk.

In citing the work of Komarovsky (1967) on blue-collar marriage, Fitzpatrick (1987) hints at another sort of ideological infusion into theory and research on openness and intimacy. So-called blue-collar couples are different in their degree of openness to each other, suggesting that prescriptions of frank disclosure may be attempts to generalize primarily white, middle-class values. "Lack" of openness, then, rather than being a matter of miscommunication, may in fact be ethnic or class variation. Identifying such variation as a problem may bespeak the socioeconomic biases of the observer and say very little about the *inherent* functionality or dysfunctionality of the observed. In any case, we argue that *relationships themselves* (dyadic, sociocultural, and so forth) provide the basis for judgments of "lack" or "sufficiency," that we need to respect others' relationships on their own terms, and that we need to be circumspect in our judgments and prescriptions.

In addition to the criticisms mentioned above, the literature on self-disclosure reinforces a problematic conception of the nature of the self. Research on self-disclosure frequently assumes the self to be a collection of relatively stable characteristics that are consciously available to their owners. The self, in this view, is an essence or a substance that can be reduced to its composite parts for analytic purposes and that is "there" to be disclosed or not. This view ignores the continual *process* by which self is formed and modified as well as the role of discursive activity in both its construction and revelation. We posit that the "self" is a *discursive production* fashioned out of interaction with others.[3] We cannot know ourselves as distinct from others or disclose ourselves to others outside of social action, primarily symbolic or discursive in nature. The interpretations and descriptions of "self" we produce occur within the codes governing language-use. Language is not, from this perspective, a transparent, expressionary medium in which speakers can unproblematically encode their thoughts or feelings (Belsey, 1980). Rather, language is a *constitutive* force that predates individual speakers, prescribes positions from which they may speak, and is inextricably connected to the sociohistorical context in which it is spoken. As a result, self-disclosure is not an *im*-mediate, mimetic *re*-presentation of some underlying entity (self/personality), but a mediated, presentational, discursive construction. This is not to suggest that self-disclosures are somehow false or distorted. On the contrary, judgments of truth/falsity or fidelity/distortion become indeterminable, if not beside the point, from this perspective. What comes into focus is discursive convention and its role in structuring the "self."

Along related lines, "self," construed as "personality" or transcendent essence is an *idealist* notion. By idealist, we mean *im*-material; somehow above, outside, or prior to social practice. Besides being fundamentally unfalsifiable, idealist constructs obscure their ideologically driven origins and functions. Idealist notions of self function to bolster the ideology of individualism (Althusser, 1971; Wilden, 1980) and draw attention away from issues associated with the collective roots of human action. If "selves," for instance, are social products (created in and out of shared discursive codes) then we need to foreground collective or relational phenomena in order to understand "selves" as opposed to the other way about. Such a focus means that attributions about the behavior or characteristics of "selves" immediately implicates the relational systems out of which such attributional conclusions are drawn.

Less abstractly, as Sillars et al. (1984) also note, the literature on self-disclosure often presupposes the innocence of self-disclosing statements. That is, very little attention is paid to the functionality (with or without speaker intention) of self-disclosure beyond the assumed desire to know and be known. It seems reasonable to wonder whether self-revelation does not accomplish any number of social tasks, especially those related to "face" management (Goffman, 1959) and maintenance of or resistance to relations of power (see Coupland, Nussbaum & Coupland's discussion, in this volume, of face-considerations in elderly self-disclosure). Is it possible that demands for openness about one's self in one's talk do not apply equally for all persons in all settings? Is it possible that self-revelations may function to increase one's vulnerability while decreasing one's partner's? Could not a single disclosure have a number of functions? And what is the functionality of strategically withholding a disclosure? Exploring these questions again involves turning to relationships and the interpretive clues they offer. These questions may also pose a challenge to conventional theories of interpersonal communication that would assume a clear separation of the personal and the institutional. We are always operating from within (an) institutional context(s) (be it marriage, work, religion, government, or the like). Institutional contexts and their tacit or explicit codes of conduct may well provide insights into variations in the occurrence and instrumentality of disclosure.

Our review and critique suggest several related conclusions concerning the connection of openness and miscommunication. Most obviously, miscommunications in personal relationships emerge as those acts that violate the presumed norms of unrestricted self-disclosure and direct speech. We have argued that, from an alternative perspective, these presumptions may be arguable ones insofar as they maintain problematic views of what the self is and how it relates to others. When the roles of language, relationship, and speaking context are considered, "non-disclosure," lack of "openness," and ambiguous speech may not *necessarily* be communicative *mis*-haps or threats to relational stability. They may instead be inevitabilities; endemic, predictable behaviors in the construction (versus destruction) of relational realities.

Bearing in mind the foregoing review and critique of prevailing conceptions of the self and its relationship to others, we now turn to extant theoretical perspectives focused more directly on developing relationships themselves. Perhaps the most prevalent such perspective is that associated with uncertainty reduction theory. Our review and commentary, therefore, centers on this theory and its applications.

Relational Development and Uncertainty Reduction: Review and Critique

Sunnafrank (1986, p. 3) observes that uncertainty reduction theory "proposes that a key element in relational development is individuals' uncertainty level concerning knowledge and understanding of selves and others." The general proposition of uncertainty reduction theory, then, is that the process of forming and deepening relationships is a matter of increasing one's knowledge of (and, hence, the predictability surrounding) others' beliefs and likely actions. Berger (1986, p. 35) adds that "coping with uncertainty is a central issue in any face-to-face encounter, whether interactants are conscious of this fact or not." He goes on to claim that high levels of uncertainty disrupt interactions and that, as a result, uncertainty reduction is essential to maintaining smooth-flowing relationships.

Berger and Calabrese's (1975) original work on uncertainty reduction and relationships defines a series of behaviors and affective states related to initial interactions and links these variables with uncertainty reduction. Although they state a number of variable relations, the following are most relevant to our discussion. First, verbal exchange relates to uncertainty in a circular, spiraling manner: Verbal exchange reduces uncertainty which, in turn, leads to more verbal exchange. Second, high levels of uncertainty "cause" interactants to seek information about each other. As the information about one's partner stockpiles, information-seeking activity decreases. Third, the more uncertain partners are about one another, the less intimate is their talk. As uncertainty declines, intimate talk increases.

Berger and Calabrese's model (and extensions of it) are primarily cognitive in nature (Sunnafrank, 1986). The model rests on the assumption that uncertainty is a cognitive condition, the affective correlate of which is anxiety. Moreover, knowledge, achieved through and accumulated within individuals' cognitive apparati, allows for relational growth. Behavioral correlates of uncertainty and its reduction, although acknowledged (Berger, 1979; Berger & Bradac, 1982), are thought to be influenced by or the outgrowth of cognitive mediation.

Elaborations and specifications of uncertainty reduction theory have centered on two general types of issues. The first set of issues concerns information-gathering strategies and their consequences. Berger and Bradac identify passive, active, and interactive information-gathering techniques. These techniques refer to observation of partner, observation of or inquiries made to partners' associates, and direct questioning of partner, respectively. Berger and Douglas (1981) and Berger and Perkins (1978) found that persons often prefer passive strategies; at least when dealing with relative strangers. Berger and Kellermann (1983) and Calabrese (1975) observe that, when anticipating future interactions with a partner, individuals indicate a greater desire and tendency to seek information from their partners. Yet, contrary to what uncertainty reduction suggests, Kellermann (1986) found that anticipation of future interaction does not increase initial uncertainty and has little effect on information exchange. Studies of direct questioning (Berger, Gardner, Clatterbuck, & Schulman, 1976) suggest a fairly stable sequencing of informational topics exchanged; topics graduate in levels of intimacy and willingness to exchange more intimate information varies with partners' educational level and age.

A second strain of uncertainty reduction research focuses on extending uncertainty reduction principles into more established relationships. Parks and Adelman (1983) examined changes in uncertainty levels in romantic relationships at two different times over a three-month period. They studied levels of communication between partners as well as between one member of a couple and his or her partner's network of family and friends. Increased communication with partner's associates was found to decrease uncertainty but this connection was strongest for those who experienced the highest levels of uncertainty at the first measurement. Most interestingly, Parks and Adelman "failed to find strong evidence of temporal connection between communication with a partner's network and uncertainty" (p. 27). Moreover, amount of communication between partners was "modestly" related to uncertainty at the first measurement, but not significantly related to uncertainty at the second measurement. Although Parks and Adelman point to methodological issues that may have led to the equivocal findings, they also note that uncertainty reduction theory is challenged by the lack of a clear relationship between amount of partners' talk and uncertainty reduction in developed relationships.

Baxter and Wilmot (1984) argue that uncertainty reduction research has focused exclusively on information exchanged about individual members and that very little research examines the presumed extension of uncertainty reduction principles into interactions beyond initial encounters. They write that, in addition to member-centered information, persons in "nonstranger relationships acquire information about the state of the relationship" (p. 173). Focusing on cross-sex friendships and cross-sex friendships in the process of becoming romantic, Baxter and Wilmot explored the extent to which information-gaining strategies used by strangers appear in the repertoires of cross-sex friends as they attempt to discover the state of their relationships, whether females use more or different sorts of strategies than do males, and whether more information-seeking occurs between friends making the transition to romance. They discovered that partners administer a number of "secret tests" to their partners that involve elements of passive, active, and interactive information-gathering strategies. Partners tended not to test the relationship per se, but focused their tests on individual attitudes and feelings. Females performed more tests than males and transitional couples test more than their platonic counterparts. In sum, Baxter and Wilmot find support for extending uncertainty reduction principles into established relationships while also noting a particular relational phase—the transition into romantic intimacy—in which uncertainty re-emerges following the relative certainty achieved in platonic friendship.

With an eye for the resurgence of uncertainty in established relationships, Planalp and Honeycutt (1985) and Planalp, Rutherford, and Honeycutt (1988) investigated particular types of occurrences that promote uncertainty. In an interesting twist on the conventional wisdom associated with uncertainty reduction theory, Planalp and Honeycutt claim: "It is possible, however, for communication to increase uncertainty if new information is so inconsistent with established knowledge that the knowledge itself is undermined" (p. 593). They speculate that uncertainty in established relationships could well affect partners' beliefs, emotions, and communication habits, as well as the future of the relationship itself. Questionnaire responses revealed that subjects could recall uncertainty provoking events (e.g., sexual transgressions, lies, betrayals of confidences) and that these events altered levels of trust between partners, generated "negative" emotions, and stimulated both engagement in *and* avoidance of communication. Interestingly, Planalp and Honeycutt's findings suggested that relationships ended, became less close, and had no change in closeness with approximately equal frequency as a result of the inciting incident. Planalp and Honeycutt comment that "uncertainty increase does not necessarily have [a] negative impact on relationships" (p. 600).

In order to refine the results of the first study, Planalp et al. (1988) asked a new group of subjects to track the occurrence of uncertainty increasing events in their own relationships over a twelve-week period. When such events occurred, subjects were to fill out questionnaires concerning the nature of the event and its consequences for relational certainty, beliefs, communication, and methods of coping. The questionnaire yielded similar classes of uncertainty increasing events. In addition, subjects reported more positive events, that increases in uncertainty following the noted events were only temporary, that the uncertainty sparked relatively undramatic emotional reactions, and that they often talked to friends as a means of interpreting, understanding, and coping with unsettling events. Planalp et al. conclude by commenting that uncertainty appears to alter, but not to wholly disrupt, relationships and that uncertainty increasing events often stimulate reflection on the accuracy of knowledge held with some certainty prior to the event. They write: "Thus it seems that knowledge of relationships and the certainty with which it is held are to some extent separable concerns" (pp. 543-544).

Parks and Adelman (1983) and Baxter and Wilmot (1984) observe that notions concerning degrees of certainty about the other permeate many treatments of relational development and maintenance. In most treatments, however, certainty, or at least stable stores of knowledge, are centered while uncertainty is taken as less desirable, or as something in need of reduction. Uncertainty is construed as a glitch (a *mis*communication) in what could or should be a relational teleology. Early work in uncertainty reduction theory implied that the ultimate end-state of relationships—intimacy—is predicated on knowing the other fully and being able to predict his or her attitudes and actions with a high degree of accuracy. Although recent work (Baxter & Wilmot, 1984; Gudykunst, 1989b; Planalp & Honeycutt, 1985; Planalp et al., 1988) has found "uncertainty" to be a fairly common condition at particular times in relationships and, perhaps, to be dialectically related to "certainty," the assumption that certainty is somehow more advantageous, comfortable, or *frequent* persists. Uncertainty remains the deviant condition. We find these views troublesome on several grounds.

Most obviously, perhaps, teleological perspectives on relationships are problematic in that they have difficulty accounting for novel, unforeseen circumstances or for changes in the environment that impact relationships. To view relationships teleologically is to remain within a causal frame, to see relationships as invariantly predictable rather than as open systems (Watzlawick et al., 1967; Wilden, 1980). Open systems, by contrast, are fluctuating, adaptive, and multifinal. Insofar as neither relationships nor individuals exist in sociohistoric vacuums divorced from sources of learning or change, the open systems model appears to us as a more compelling, communication-based approach for understanding relational processes.

Traditional versions of uncertainty reduction theory are also laced with linear, *progress*-ive assumptions (Bochner, 1978). These assumptions may be most noticeable in the depiction of relationships as fundamentally knowledge-based. The notion of *relational knowledge*—and the word *knowledge* itself—is steeped in connotations of progress, referentiality, ahistoricality, and reification. Knowledge accumulates (we know more now than we did, say, last year) knowledge refers to some identifiable content (we know *about* some referent), knowledge holds across time and place (what we knew last year we still know today and what we know in one context we still know in another), and knowledge has a solid form (we know some-*thing*). Such connotations distract us from the uneven, constitutive, sociohistoric, political, and interpretive character of relationships and what we think about them. That is, what we claim to *know* at any moment is a *temporally specific* accomplishment rooted in (conventional) modes of *interpretation.* As such, knowledge is influenced by social history and the network of political-ideological-discursive forces marking the context in which we know. What we know today is based on extant social categories that are open to revision.

Over time, "revisionist histories" of a relationship may be "written" that expose earlier knowledge as exclusionary, unfair, troublesome, biased, and the like. For example, a person may have known their spouse to be insecure and dependent when it comes to financial matters. Over the years, the spouse's insecurity may diminish as he or she makes successful financial decisions. He or she might then reinterpret the past behavior as "inexperience" rather than insecurity. He or she might claim that his or her partner helped to create the insecure image as a means of maintaining control over family finances. Such revisionist relational histories may be asserted as "knowledge" ("I did not know myself before, but now I do") and serve to stimulate relational change. It is not that previous knowledge (insecurity) was wrong or even immature. It was simply an historically bound construction evoked to accomplish ends relevant to the context in which it was created; a context that now may no longer exist.

Our point, then, is that knowledge and the very things we claim to know about are not givens and do not stay stationary. The most seemingly certain may be quite fragile and fleeting, the most obvious "facts," categories, and judgments may soon become perplexing or irrelevant, and the most predictable of events may often become the most unlikely. As Planalp and her colleagues suggest, uncertainty increasing events occur rather frequently and with varying degrees of intensity. These events may well serve as a reminder of the time-boundedness of knowledge and its utility.

Uncertainty reduction theory assumes uncertainty to be an uncomfortable state holding the potential to erode social interaction. Again, the binary logic woven into elements of this theory emerges: certainty/comfort facilitates continued social interaction, uncertainty/discomfort threatens its survival. We argue that neither state in isolation facilitates social interaction. Without "uncertainty" many of the vitalizing forces in relationships—surprise, novelty, excitement, and change—are crippled. By the same token, without a certain degree of predictability (however short-lived), relationships become unduly effortful. The question is again one of *continually negotiated balance*, of managing the dialectical tension created by the simultaneous presence of both certainty and uncertainty, and of struggling to create relationships capable of accommodating satisfactory levels of both forces.

Uncertainty reduction theory also paints a picture of relationships as summative entities. Relational development is construed as both partners accumulating individually held storehouses of knowledge. From the perspective we advance, a relationship cannot be reduced to the "sum of its parts" (Watzlawick et al., 1967). Relational knowledge, to the extent that it is an important construct at all, belongs to the relationship itself; it exists *between* partners rather than *within* individuals. Harkening back to our earlier discussion of the self and its relation to others, we can neither be nor know in isolation. Being and knowing are both relational processes draped with *social* content.

Once again, events that appeared to be miscommunications from one angle, become predictable and productive activities from another. Uncertainty, from our vantage point, is not something that necessarily requires immediate reduction nor is its occurrence necessarily anomalous or inherently problematic. The value and functionality of uncertainty must be examined in the full context of patterned communication within relationships.

Conclusions

The study of interpersonal relations and the underlying communicative processes out of which relationships emerge and take shape is not a trivial nor small undertaking. A central challenge for communication research is how to conceptualize and investigate the process of interrelating so that its human, social, and formative qualities are retained. Toward this effort, the present chapter offers an alternative view to the prevailing, and we suggest problematic, research practices evident in much interpersonal literature.

Traditionally, the study of relationships has been steeped in the logics of reductionism and linearity, in which primacy is given to monadic units over relational levels of analysis. Substance has been privileged over form and causal thinking has been privileged over recursive, stochastic thinking. Given these priorities, particularly when coupled with the ideology of openness and unequivocality, a phenomenon such as miscommunication can be identified and construed as a mis-doing, as off-target, as an error to be corrected. But with a paradigmatic shift to a set of assumptions that emphasize the dialectic between process and form, the notion of miscommunication becomes reformulated as a movement in time, combined and embedded within other such movements, and, thus, is radically redefined from a mis-hap to a happening.

When relationships are conceptualized as codefined, ecological structurings, emphasis is placed on the interactive cycles produced and reproduced as relational members move toward, around, against, and away from one another via their distance-regulating, communicative behaviors. Within this perspective the phenomenon of miscommunication merges into the temporal flow and evolving form of the interactional "dance." Single events are not relabeled as facilitative or harmful, but become part of a larger negotiated pattern of system regulation which, over time and within different contexts, may or may not be empirically judged as relationally functional or dysfunctional.

Clearly, our view poses a challenge to some conventional methods of empirical investigation. If the epistemological premises we sketched are to be put into practice, analytic techniques requiring interactional sequences to be severed so that discrete acts can be identified, categorized, and studied outside of the sequence in which they occurred might well be deemed inappropriate. Our point is not to suggest a wholesale dismissal of quantification by any means, but to make a case for process sensitive methods. Such methods may include the *interpretive* as well as the *statistical.*

Yet insofar as methodological choices are predicated on conceptual ones, the position we have advanced in this chapter demands that we attend to our conceptualizations of self, other, and relationship in future empirical study. Most germane to the theme of this volume may be the conceptualization of behavior itself. We have argued throughout this chapter that, from our vantage point, it is patterns, rather than messages, that should draw our attention. If our concern is with communication or relationships found to be problematic or unsatisfying (and, as we have claimed, the labeling of communication as problematic may itself raise a number of issues concerning who is labeling and to what ends), then we need to focus on "problematic" *sequences.* What, for instance, are the behavioral cycles that couples enact that may account for dissatisfaction? Answering this sort of question requires that we look at extended sequences of interaction in order for redundancies to be identified. It may also require that we focus more on the historical and contextual particularities of the cases we select.

Finally, we may need to rethink or modify views of communication and relationships that would mark "problematic talk" or "problematic relationships" as special cases. The epistemological premises we have discussed would have us see all relational communication as, in some sense, problematic. That is, relationships are effortful—they must be produced and negotiated—and we can never know in advance what consequences a single message or behavior will bring about. In this way, a relationship can be likened to a jigsaw puzzle, the shape of which is constantly changing. One partner fits a piece, the other partner fits one as well, and, in the way the fittings combine, the parameters of the puzzle itself may shift, requiring the partners to search for new pieces and new combinations. In terms of empirical investigation, this view directs our attention to the range and flexibility of interactional routines, to the processes by which interactional obstacles are identified or ignored, and to the cycles by which couples' "combinations" move together and apart.

We end this chapter as we began by suggesting that the notions captured in McCall and Simmons' (1978) conceptualization of a *working consensus* underscore the interwoven cycles of viable, close relationships. As Simmel (1950) observes, the very processes that build up relationships may function to tear them down: The "strain toward totality" holds the seeds of both commitment and alienation. The bonds of intimacy rest precariously on the delicate balance of separateness and connectedness, on partners being free to move in and out of closeness. The lack of distancing between self and other may be the very process that unravels the relational promise of totality. In the temporal unfolding of relationships, the ideology of being "one with other" may cycle toward the potential for stagnation and triviality (Simmel, 1950). By the same token, the acceptance, perhaps even the encouragement, of the "stranger in other" may lie at the heart of sustaining intimacy. Moreover, we concur with George Bernard Shaw who observed: "The danger in communication is the illusion that it has been accomplished."

Notes

1. See Bochner (1982) and Petronio, Martin, and Littlefield (1984) for a discussion of disagreements and confusions among researchers on the definition of *self-disclosure.*
2. Ting-Toomey (1989a) observes that the ideology of intimacy is indeed a Western bias.
3. See Brown (1988) for a full discussion of this position on the self as well as for a full discussion of the philosophical/theoretical literature out of which it emerges.

9

Miscommunication in Medicine

Candace West
Richard M. Frankel

Introduction

Miscommunication is a threat to any form of interaction, be it casual conversation or formal ceremony. In purely social settings, its costs can be calculated in relation to the value of an interaction and the selves of the participants involved in it (Goffman, 1967, pp. 97-113). In those settings in which business is conducted through interaction, the costs are even higher—including instrumental losses as well as social ones (Schegloff, 1982). Given that the ultimate goals of interaction in medical settings are the restoration of health and preservation of life, the stakes involved in "good" communication are very high indeed.

Research on communication problems in medical settings has a rich tradition in both clinical and social sciences. Among the recurring themes in the literature are the limiting consequences of using specialized technical vocabulary, cultural differences between providers and patients, and institutional constraints on the forms of interaction that occur in medical milieux. In many empirical studies, *communication* is operationally defined in relation to the business of medical management. Technical jargon, cultural differences, and external constraints are variously conceived in the service of tasks such as enhancing patient satisfaction, achieving patient compliance, and ensuring provider control.

AUTHORS' NOTE: For their helpful comments on an earlier draft of these ideas, we thank Howard Beckman, William Gronfein, Aida Hurtado, and the editors of this volume. This project was supported by the Academic Senate Committee on Research at the University of California, Santa Cruz, and by the Department of Health and Human Services Residency Training Grant in Primary Care Internal Medicine No. PE 1562-05

The results of this research are impressive, documenting important consequences of problems in communication for providers and recipients of health care. And yet, many of the fundamental concepts underlying these results remain to be explicated. What *is* "miscommunication" in the context of a medical setting, and where does it originate? How can cases of miscommunication be recognized and what—if anything—can be done to avoid them? Perhaps most important, what are the implications of answers to these questions for the quality of health care?

Our aim in this chapter is to address these questions through a broad but selective overview of research on communication problems in medical settings. Through a history of work on this topic, we identify theoretical assumptions that have guided research and examine the consequences of those assumptions for our understanding of communication breakdowns. We specify methods that have been used to evaluate various forms of medical communication and assess their utility for health care recipients and providers. Clearly, a comprehensive overview of the literature on communication in medical settings is beyond the scope of this chapter. Here, we attempt to illustrate the range of approaches that have been used to investigate the topic and to synthesize from these a new understanding of what "miscommunication" might consist of.

An Applied Beginning

Interest in the relationship between communication and medical care can be traced as far back as Hippocrates (1923). It was not until the 1960s, however, that *miscommunication* in medical settings became the object of sustained empirical attention. Concern for the topic was fueled by the growing realization that problems in communication were implicated in two of the most pressing practical problems in medicine: patient dissatisfaction and patient failure to follow medical advice.

In the 1960s, studies of satisfaction found that many patients were unhappy with the flow of information between themselves and their providers; some rated this as the least satisfactory aspect of their care. Such studies (e.g., Cartwright, 1964; Hugh-Jones, Tanser, & Whitby, 1964; Raphael, 1969; Spelman, Ley, & Jones, 1966) originated in British hospital settings, but subsequent research in the United States (e.g., Korsch, Gozzi, & Francis, 1968) and on general practice patients in the United Kingdom (Kincey, Bradshaw, & Ley, 1975; Ley, 1980) revealed the breadth and depth of the problem (Ley, 1983). As Korsch and Negrete (1972, p. 66) put it: "The quality of medical care depends in the last analysis on the interaction of the patient and the doctor, and there is abundant evidence that . . . this interaction all too often is disappointing to both parties." Korsch and Negrete found ample grounds for patient dissatisfaction in their investigation of a walk-in emergency clinic in Los Angeles. In more than half of the 800 pediatric visits in their sample, physicians used specialized technical terminology that was "Greek" to their patients; in fewer than 5% of the visits were physicians' comments of a friendly or sociable nature; and in more than 25%, the chief concerns of those initiating the visit were never mentioned, as physicians afforded them no opportunity to do so.

Similar problems with communication were implicated in research on patients' nonadherence to medical advice (Berkowitz, Malone, Klein, & Eaton, 1963; Davis, 1966, 1968; Elling, Whittemore, & Green, 1960; Francis, Korsch, & Morris, 1969; Freemon, Negrete, Davis, & Korsch, 1971; Korsch et al., 1968; Ley & Spelman, 1965). Francis et al.'s (1969) pediatric data indicated that non-adherence was more common when parents failed to receive explanations of the cause of their child's illness. Davis (1968) reported that for patients at a general medical clinic, nonadherence was more likely when physicians took time to collect information from patients but failed to provide them with feedback. According to Davis (1968, p. 284), an implicit issue in any discussion of nonadherence is the matter of controlling patient behavior: "The doctor must rely on his ability to establish good rapport in order to inculcate in his patient a positive orientation and commitment to the relationship so that ultimately the patient will follow his advice." Such practical suggestions were more than welcome in light of the severity of the problem. Recent estimates indicate that 20% to 80% of patients do not follow their physicians' recommendations (DiMatteo & DiNicola, 1982; Sackett & Snow, 1979) and that on average, one patient in two does not do so (Ley, 1983). Insofar as most medical advice is offered in the interests of patients' health, one can see why high rates of nonadherence would be profoundly disturbing to health care professionals in general and physicians, in particular. In short, serious interest in miscommunication in medical settings began when research demonstrated its relationship to practical problems in medicine. As a result, much early work on the topic consisted of a search for factors that would contribute to better practical outcomes (e.g., enhanced patient satisfaction or improved patient compliance).

A Search for Better Outcomes

One of the first, and subsequently one of the most widely documented factors identified in the search for better outcomes was the *amount* of information patients received in interactions with their physicians. Spelman et al. (1966) found that patients were discontented with how little they were told about virtually every aspect of their care (including diagnosis, treatment, and prognosis). Cartwright (1964) reported that "obtaining information" was the most difficult task patients faced in the hospital; Houston and Pasanen (1972) demonstrated that patients' satisfaction was directly related to the amount of information they obtained. Others (Ley & Spelman, 1967; Pratt, Seligmann, & Reader, 1957; Skipper, 1965) confirmed that most patients wanted much more information than they were given. Thus, one of the first conceptualizations of miscommunication was a quantitative understanding: Patients are dissatisfied with medical information because they do not get enough of it.

Applications of this understanding soon revealed its inadequacy. For example, Korsch and Negrete (1972) expected that visit time would be positively correlated with patient satisfaction, inasmuch as patients would be more satisfied when physicians spent more time communicating with them. But they found no significant relationship between these factors: Neither patient satisfaction nor clarity of physicians' information improved in longer patient visits. Indeed, longer visits were often indicative of communication "failures"—which took extra time to resolve. Cartwright, Lucas, and O'Brien (1974) found that physicians were less satisfied with longer visits, particularly when these resulted from their patients talking more. Such contradictory results led researchers to take a closer look at *what* patients were told.

Analyses of the content of medical dialogues revealed one of the most prevalent complaints about medical settings: that providers often employ specialized "jargon" that is not readily understood by their patients (Boyle, 1970; Korsch & Negrete, 1972; Ley & Spelman, 1967; McKinlay, 1975; Redlich, 1945; Seligmann, McGrath, & Pratt, 1957; Silver, 1979). Korsch and Negrete (1972) found that physicians used highly technical terms (such as "nares," "peristalsis," and "Coombs titre") that were virtually unintelligible to those they cared for. One mother, told that her child would require a "lumbar puncture," expected that surgery would be performed to drain her child's lungs. Another, whose child was to be "admitted for a work up," had no idea this meant he would have to be hospitalized.

Highly technical terms were not the only ones that were misinterpreted. Ley and Spelman's (1967) study at a general hospital in Liverpool demonstrated that even the names of common illnesses (such as "arthritis," "diabetes," and "stomach ulcer") often meant something different to patients than they did to providers. Forty percent of patients in their sample believed that an attack of *asthma* could be helped by an injection of penicillin; 40% or more thought that *chronic bronchitis* and lung cancer were usually cured by treatment.

Emergent in these studies was a relatively straightforward model of communication: a transmission of information from "sender" to "receiver." From this perspective, jargon was decried for its negative effects on receivers – preventing them from understanding the transmission that was sent. Thus, miscommunication (that is, bad or wrong communication) was seen to result from the lack of a common code.

A Bias Toward "Clear" Communication

Implicit in the model we have so far described is the assumption that good communication is *clear* communication: a transmission of information that is readily understood by its receiver. Yet the evidence for this assumption was equivocal. For example, even though the majority of patients in Korsch and Negrete's (1972) study admitted that physicians' terminology often mystified them, this did not necessarily mean they were dissatisfied. Some patients found the use of such terminology impressive, and some, even flattering. And although many studies found a relationship between physicians' transmission of information and patients' satisfaction (see DiMatteo & DiNicola, 1982, pp. 58-61; Ley, 1983), not all of them did (cf. Freemon, Negrete, Davis, & Korsch, 1971; Kupst, Dresser, Schulman, & Paul, 1975).

The most serious challenge to the "good equals clear" hypothesis came from research on communication with cancer patients. McIntosh's (1974) review of this literature concluded that even though most patients (including those with incurable cancer) wanted to know their diagnosis, most physicians preferred to avoid telling them. In one sample of U.S. physicians (Fitts & Ravdin, 1953), 69% of physicians indicated that they always or usually refrained from telling patients; in another (Oken, 1961), nearly 90% said they refrained from doing so.[1] Comparable proportions were reported for France, where it was estimated that fewer than 10% of oncologists' patients were aware that they had cancer (Sontag, 1977).

Why would physicians withhold such important information from their patients? McIntosh (1974) argued that uncertainty was a primary explanatory factor in this form of miscommunication. Studies of providers' interactions with polio patients (Davis, 1960) tuberculosis patients (Roth, 1963a, 1963b), and those who were terminally ill (Glaser & Strauss, 1965) indicated that physicians were loath to deliver bad medical news when they themselves were unsure of its implications. Many cited patients' inability to cope with such news (Fitts & Ravdin, 1953; Louis Harris & Associates, 1982; President's Commission for the Study of Ethical

Problems in Medicine and Biomedical and Behavioral Research, 1982). Others contended that patients truly did not want to hear it (Ley & Spelman, 1967), that patients should be told only what they asked for (Shands, Finesinger, Cobb, & Abrams, 1951), or that patients should be given only as much information as is needed to ensure their adherence to medical advice (Bard, 1970).

Obviously, providers' beliefs about what patients want and need to know may be in error, but they are more than real in their consequences. Believing that patients will suffer from clear communication about their condition, physicians may phrase diagnoses in general rather than specific terms and thus, obscure patients' understanding of their prognoses (Quint, 1965). Their answers to questions may be put in "such hedging, evasive or unintelligibly technical terms" as to lead patients to anticipate a more favorable prognosis than is warranted by the facts then known (Davis, 1960, p. 44). And they may well employ a language of euphemism (Oken, 1961), substituting terms such as "lump" and "growth" for "cancer" and "malignancy," thereby avoiding patients' ready comprehension of their diagnosis. In practice, then, physicians do not always operate on the assumption that clear communication is good for their patients.

Characteristics of Senders and Receivers

A second assumption implicit in the sender-receiver model was that cases of miscommunication could be explained as a function of the individuals involved in them. The search for better practical outcomes prompted an examination of those characteristics and behaviors that made for better "senders" and "receivers."

Where physicians were concerned, the initial approach was largely psychological—as Innes (1977, p. 636) described it, "to attempt to select the 'right man' for the job and to train him for it." Tests of intelligence, aptitude, and personality were employed to this end, as were revisions of the curriculum and approach of medical schools (Gough & Hall, 1975; Hickson & Thomas, 1969; Walton, Drewery, & Phillip, 1964). Like practitioners in many other fields that were reexamined in the 1960s, physicians were the target of efforts to promote humanism, sensitivity, and interpersonal skills (cf. Pelligrino, 1974).

Patients, of course, posed a different problem, inasmuch as one could not "select out" those whose interpersonal skills facilitated their treatment. A number of studies, however, yielded information about the "kinds of patients" most likely to be involved in medical misunderstandings. Among those "problem patients" (Lorber, 1975) first identified were alienated patients, whose sense of powerlessness was associated with their lack of knowledge about their condition (Seeman & Evans, 1962; Skipper, 1965), and diffident patients, whose lack of confidence prevented them from acquiring information about their care (Cartwright, 1964; Ley & Spelman, 1967).

Sociodemographic factors were also scrutinized for their contributions to miscommunication. Studies of patients' social class and educational backgrounds suggested that lower-class and less educated patients were less knowledgeable about preventive health care (Coope & Metcalfe, 1979), less familiar with medical terminology (Samora, Saunders & Larson, 1961) and less likely to listen to their physicians (Bochner, 1983; Pendleton & Bochner, 1980). Researchers also found that patients' interpretations of their symptoms differed by ethnic group (Croog, 1961; Stoeckle, Zola, & Davidson, 1964; Zborowski, 1958; Zola, 1963, 1966), age, and gender (Banks & Keller, 1971; Coburn & Pope, 1974; Hetherington & Hopkins, 1969).

Despite the promise of such findings, most researchers were hard-pressed to explain the mechanisms involved. For example, if there were a direct positive relationship between education and understanding of medical information, one would expect better educated patients would understand more of what physicians told them. But Plaja, Cohen, and Samora (1968) found no significant relationship between these variables—nor between age, gender, or ethnicity and understanding. Korsch and Negrete (1972, p. 72) noted that satisfaction with physicians' communication "was not significantly higher among college-educated mothers than it was among those with less education"; Steele and McBroom (1972) suggested that the relationship between patients' socioeconomic status and their health-related behaviors might well be spurious (see also Moody & Gray, 1972; Suchman, 1972).

The most promising insights into this problem came from Davis (1963) and Roth (1963a). Davis observed that physicians' *perceptions* of patients' socioeconomic status (and related attributes) helped to determine what they were told, while Roth reported that the ways patients *presented themselves* on the ward influenced the kinds of information they received. Such findings implied that providers' images of the kinds of patients they were dealing with mattered at least as much as—if not more than—patients' actual characteristics.

This explanation helped reconcile many inconsistencies within the literature (cf. McIntosh, 1974; Pratt et al., 1957). However, it also undermined one of the fundamental assumptions of the model; namely, that miscommunication could be traced to characteristics of senders and receivers as individuals.

A "Telephone-Booth" Bias

A third defect of the sender-receiver model of communication was its limited view of the participants involved. As Goffman (1967) observed in the case of psychiatry, the tendency for most consultations to occur on a one-to-one basis led to a very restricted understanding of who had an impact on them. As a result, psychiatrists labored under the view that their patients' behaviors were a tortured form of communication to clinicians, "the problem being that the line was busy, the connection defective, the party at the other end shy, cagey, afraid to talk or insistent that a code be used" (Goffman, 1967, p. 139). However, psychiatric symptoms are often public in nature and thus potential concerns to anyone in a patient's presence. As Goffman observes, a "telephone-booth bias" blinded psychiatrists to the fact that most people who come to their attention have in effect been referred by their lay associates. In the case of medicine more generally, it soon became apparent that relations between communication and practical outcomes involved more than the individual physician and patient. Numerous studies indicated that close friends and family members were likely to influence whether a person's symptoms were even seen as illness, and thus, whether they would ever come to the attention of a physician (Freidson, 1960, 1961; Knapp, Knapp, & Engle, 1966; McKinlay, 1973). One study (Osterweis, Bush, & Zuckerman, 1979) reported that families often established their own rules for using medication; another (Suchman, 1972) found that people's health habits followed the norms of their community, rather than the medical advice they received.

Although such research offered clues to the impact of friends and relatives on medical communications, evidence from the literature on patients with cancer was far more direct. As McIntosh (1974, p. 176) put it, the relatives of cancer patients were more likely to be told about patients' conditions than were patients themselves. Quint (1965) demonstrated that although breast cancer patients were usually kept guessing about their prognoses, their family members received detailed explanations of their condition. Others (e.g., Fitts & Ravdin, 1953) showed that physicians who generally withheld patients' cancer diagnoses from them nonetheless agreed that the patients' relatives should be told. Most striking, perhaps, was the growing evidence of physicians' and relatives' cooperation in withholding information from patients (Glaser & Strauss, 1965; McIntosh, 1974; Quint, 1964; and more recently, the President's Commission for the Study of Ethical Problems in Medicine and Biomedical and Behavioral Research, 1982; Schoene-Seifert & Childress, 1986).

Such evidence suggested that physicians were not alone in conveying partial or misleading information to patients.

Further proof came from analyses of nurses' roles in the process (e.g., Coser, 1962; Davis, 1963; Freidson, 1970; Glaser & Strauss, 1965; Quint, 1965). To be sure, physicians' licensed authority to apprise patients of their condition prevents nurses from legally dispensing such information on their own (Glaser & Strauss, 1965; Quint, 1965). What is more, physicians do not always share their diagnoses with nurses in the early stages of patient care (Glaser & Strauss, 1965). However, as Quint (1965) pointed out, nurses *can* help patients cope with the information they receive by allowing them to talk about it. Her results indicated that nurses generally avoided this function. Faced with anxieties of breast cancer patients, many nurses moved through their shifts in an obviously "busy" manner that discouraged patients from speaking about their concerns. Some nurses made small talk the sole focus of their conversations with patients; others refocused discussions on specific procedures when patients veered too close to diagnostic or prognostic topics. The structural organization of patient care facilitated these strategies through rotating shifts and assignments that made sustained contact with patients virtually impossible (cf. Coser, 1958; Seeman & Evans, 1961; Zola, 1963). Quint (1965) concluded that such avoidance practices constituted *institutionalized* means of information control that tended to heighten (rather than alleviate) patients' anxieties. If so, it would explain why many studies (Coser, 1962; Davis, 1963; Fox, 1959; Roth, 1963b) found patients turning to other patients, rather than to health professionals, for clues about their condition. Their findings indicated that the sources of medical misunderstandings were far more diverse than the sender-receiver model could account for.

Advanced "Factor Analyses"

By the mid 1970s, it was clear that miscommunication in medical settings was a far more complicated problem than was initially supposed. As a consequence, the search for better outcomes turned to more sophisticated explanations of the factors involved.

In some cases, this has led to a reduced emphasis on communication per se. For example, the study of patient compliance has been heavily influenced by psychological theories that seek explanations for health-related behaviors in patients' perceptions. Elaborations of the Health Belief Model (Becker, 1974; Becker & Maiman, 1975; Maiman & Becker, 1974; Rosenstock, 1974) have focused on patients' health motivations and attitudes toward interaction with their providers as well as their perceptions of susceptibility, severity, cost, and benefit. Application of the concept of *locus of control* (Becker et al., 1977; Kirscht & Rosenstock, 1977; Strickland, 1978) has proven more helpful in predicting patients' adherence to medical advice than global personality variables studied earlier (King, 1983; Pendleton, 1983). Social psychological theory has also been useful in accounting for misunderstandings that can arise from physicians' and patients' differing attributions of health and illness (Eiser, Sutton, & Wober, 1978; Rodin, 1978). But by and large, intricate models of these *antecedents* to medical communication have not contributed much to our understanding of communicative behaviors. As Pendleton (1983, p. 17) observes, the specification of differences among patients in antecedents to the consultation "requires the investigation of related consultation processes."

By contrast, a number of studies that examine actual communicative behaviors have shown significant relationships between consultation processes and outcomes (e.g., Greenfield, Kaplan, & Ware, 1985; Roter, 1977; Stiles, Putnam, Wolf, & James, 1979; Waitzkin, 1983; Waitzkin & Stoeckle, 1976; Wallen, Waitzkin, & Stoeckle, 1979). Such studies represent a major advance in our understanding, by moving from purely descriptive toward explanatory goals (Inui & Carter, 1985). Detailed analyses of specific components of communication processes make it possible to ask when, and under what conditions, particular improvements might be made (Beckman, Kaplan, & Frankel, 1989).

But the results of these analyses are not always consistent (see DiMatteo & DiNicola, 1982; Inui & Carter, 1989; Pendleton, 1983; and Tuckett & Williams, 1984 for excellent overviews). For example, Waitzkin and his colleagues (Waitzkin, 1983; Waitzkin & Stoeckle, 1976; Wallen et al., 1979) compared physicians' estimates of the amount of time spent providing patients with information (assessed through a post-visit questionnaire) with the actual time spent doing so (recorded on audiotape). They found that physicians overestimated the time they spent giving information "by a factor of nine." Moreover, although patients' desires for information did not vary systematically with their educational level or social class, college-educated and upper-middle-class patients received more information than those with less education or lower-middle-class and lower-class backgrounds. Waitzkin (1983, p. 2442) concluded that: "Lower-class patients tend to be diffident; that is, they usually ask fewer questions. Partly as a result, doctors tend to misperceive these patients' desire for information and generally believe that they want or could use less information."

To be sure, patients' diffidence and their failures to ask questions in general were well documented in earlier studies of physician-patient communication (see Cartwright, 1964; Ley & Spelman, 1967; McIntosh,

1974). But Roter (1977) was the first to demonstrate their effects through an experimental intervention. She assigned patients in an experimental group to a health counselor, who trained them to formulate their concerns as direct questions; patients in a control group received no such advance training. Not only did those in the experimental group ask significantly more questions during their consultations with physicians, but they were also significantly more compliant (measured by subsequent appointment keeping). Surprisingly, patients in the experimental group were also less satisfied and displayed more negative affect (e.g., anger and anxiety) than those in the control group.

Further surprising findings emerged from Greenfield et al.'s (1985) randomized control trials of patients' involvement in care. Greenfield and his colleagues sought to increase assertiveness among diabetic patients by encouraging them to ask questions, identify logical steps in medical decision making, and negotiate those steps with their physicians. Patients who received such assertiveness training had better blood sugar levels and functional status at follow-up than patients in the control group, showing that the intervention had a valuable impact on their health. Moreover, they displayed more affect, shared their opinions more often, and were more active in their interactions with physicians (measured by numbers of patient utterances per minute, numbers of controlling utterances by patients and ratios of patient utterances to physician utterances). However, they did not ask significantly more questions—nor were they significantly more satisfied—than patients in the control group.

Contradictions such as these have illuminated major gaps in our knowledge of what miscommunication really means. For example, if patients' failures of understanding are products of their failures to ask questions (Ley, 1983; Waitzkin, 1983), why don't increased patient questions lead to increased levels of patient satisfaction? If patients' reluctance to ask questions is a function of their lack of assertiveness, why doesn't provision of special training produce a significant increase in the numbers of questions patients ask? And if good communication is characterized by large numbers of patient questions, why do some patients react to it with anger and anxiety? At issue here are fundamental questions about method and measurement.

Stiles (1989, p. 213) observes that one major problem with such correlational studies is their reliance on statistical association to assess the relationships that are hypothesized:

> According to the correlational approach, if a process component contributes causally to an outcome, then a greater amount (percentage, frequency, intensity) of the process should lead to a better outcome, whereas a lesser amount should lead to a worse outcome. . . . Conversely, failure to find a significant

> correlation (i.e., a null result) is taken to indicate that the process component does not contribute causally to outcome.

As he notes, this approach assumes that patients' needs, wants, resources, and abilities are at least randomly distributed—if not constant—with respect to the process components in question. Herein lies the problem: If patients require different "amounts" of some process component, then it is only logical for them to seek different amounts. And to the extent that physicians perceive differences in patients' requirements, it is only logical for them to respond to patients differentially. In the extreme case, where physicians perceive differences correctly and respond to them appropriately, "the expected correlation would be zero, insofar as no outcome variance would be accounted for by inadequate levels of the process component" (Stiles, 1989).

A second problem with correlational studies is their insensitivity to the context of communication. For example, although patients may come to medical settings with different requirements for information (Stiles, 1989), their individual requirements may also vary across the course of their care—and even across the course of a particular encounter. Sheer numbers of patient questions may offer an indirect measure of patients' abilities to express their concerns, but they cannot locate specific communication problems in the context of their occurrence.

A third problem with studies of this kind is their lack of attention to questions of interpretation. Investigations of the relationship between process and outcome variables have gained access to participants' perceptions in post-visit interviews and questionnaires. Thus, relative levels of patient satisfaction have only been determined after the fact. In the course of daily provision of health care, providers have no way of assessing patients' interpretations of the information they provide other than by observing patients' responses to it then and there. Retrospective measures of problems in interpretation are not much use in the course of actual practice.

A fourth and final problem worth noting here is the inability of the "variable approach" to come to terms with the sequential organization of communication. Aggregate numbers of patient questions can only tell us how often patients seek further information from their providers. They cannot tell us what prompted those questions or what became of them once they were asked. In order to treat such requests for information as exemplars of good communication, one would need to know how they were responded to—and how they emerged from a given sequence of interaction in the first instance.

In short, although studies of the relationship between process and outcome variables have been useful in identifying the basic parameters of communication problems, they have not been as useful in explaining or interpreting their results, even where the results are positive. Their focus on isolated variables has led to a general neglect of issues of context, sequence, and interpretation. Moreover, their reliance on correlation coefficients has raised initially problematic measurement procedures to an even higher level of abstraction. The most fruitful alternative to the variable approach is research that focuses on miscommunication in the context of its occurrence.

Miscommunication in Context

A growing number of studies approach problems of communication in medicine by focusing on the social and linguistic contexts of medical discourse. These studies share the same theoretical emphasis on the relationship between language and social interaction. They also share a methodological concern to represent the actual speaking practices of those involved in medical encounters via verbatim transcripts of audio and videotape recordings. One overall difference between discourse-based studies and those we have reviewed thus far is the display of raw data that accompanies their theorizing. Another difference is that their evidence of communication difficulties is directly observable. Still another difference is that their recordings and transcriptions of communication difficulties may be compared within or across different contexts.

Tannen and Wallat (1982, 1983), for example, examine physicians' use of linguistic and paralinguistic cues to segment patient participation during pediatric visits. They find that physicians use different linguistic registers (i.e., forms of talk characterized by distinctive uses of pitch, pace, and intensity) to enhance, limit, and exclude patients' participation over the course of medical encounters. In the excerpt just below, they offer a verbatim transcript of a pediatrician's interaction with a mother about the arteriovenous malformations (i.e., abnormal blood vessel connections) in her child's brain:[2]

Mother: I've often wondered about how
Physician: mhm
Mother: dangerous they are to her right now.

Physician: We:ll (1.5) um (1.5) the only danger would be from bleeding (2.0) From them. If there was any rupture or anything like that which can happen (2.0) um (1.5) that would be the danger (2.0) for that. But they're
Mother: mhm
(1.5)
Physician: mm (1.5) not going to be something that will get worse as time goes on.
Mother: Oh I see.
Physician: But they're just there. Okay? ((returns to exam))
(Tannen & Wallat, 1983, pp. 214-215)

As Tannen and Wallat observe, this pediatrician downplays the significance of the child's ailment to the mother through her use of "only" in relation to the dangers involved. Moreover, her response to the mother's query is replete with conditional tenses and paraphrases that mitigate the seriousness of the information she delivers.

Contrast the excerpt just above with the pediatrician's comments about this case at a meeting of the medical staff:

Physician: . . . uh I'm not sure about how much counseling has been done, (1.5) with these parents, (1.5) around (1.0) the issue (1.5) of the a-v malformation ((4 lines deleted)) and I think that this is uh (1.5) uh (1.5) an important point. Because I don't know whether (1.5) the possibility of sudden death, intracranial hemorrhage, if any of this has ever been discussed with these parents.
(Tannen & Wallat, 1983, p. 216)

Here, Tannen and Wallat note the pediatrician's use of "sudden death" and "intercranial hemorrhage"—terms that were never used in her description to the mother. They also note that the pediatrician's speech to the staff is less conditional (addressing "the possibility of" danger rather than what the danger "would be"), revealing a deeper concern than she showed to the mother.

Tannen and Wallat's conclusions echo those of many studies reviewed earlier, namely, that physicians may deliberately choose to limit the kinds of information patients receive. What distinguishes their findings are their explicit comparisons of *how* the physician's speech style changes in different clinical contexts. By observing differences in language behavior across contexts, Tannen and Wallat are able to demonstrate the limiting effects of the physician's communication style on the mother's understanding of her child's problem.

So, although Tannen and Wallat's work also rests on a quantitative model of communication—conceptualizing miscommunication in relation to the amount of information patients receive—it represents a theoretical advance over earlier studies by identifying the specific linguistic behaviors that limit patients' understanding and participation in the context in which these occur. Moreover, by expanding the scope of analysis to include comparative evidence, it provides additional insights regarding the division of communicative labor and responsibilities for full disclosure. When the pediatrician states "I'm not sure how much counseling has been done with the parent," she acknowledges that the task of informing may, and in this case does, fall to others in addition to herself—an assumption that has not been factored into many earlier studies of miscommunication (see our discussion of the telephone-booth bias above).

Shuy (1976) also provides specific linguistic evidence of miscommunication in his analysis of adult patients' encounters with physicians. He begins with the familiar observation that patients' failures to understand their physicians stem largely from physicians' use of "doctor talk":

(1)

Physician: Have you ever had a history of cardiac arrest in your family?
→ **Patient:** We never had no trouble with the police

* * *

(2)

Physician: How about varicose veins?
Patient: Well, I have veins, but I don't know if they're close or not

* * *

(3)

Physician: What's your name?
Patient: Betty Groff
Physician: How do you spell that?
→ **Patient:** B-E-T-T-Y

(Shuy, 1976, p. 376)

In excerpt 1, for example, the physician's query about "a history of cardiac arrest" leads the patient to disclaim any "trouble with the police." In excerpt 2, the physician's question about "varicose veins" stimulates the patient to wonder just how "closely" their veins are situated. However, in excerpt 3, the physician's request for information regarding the proper spelling of "that" (meaning "Groff") prompts the patient to itemize the letters in "Betty" (her first name).

Shuy's (1976) detailed comparisons of such data yield at least two important findings. First, he shows that miscommunication in medical encounters can arise from talk that is nontechnical as well as technical in nature, as we see in excerpt 3. This is an important fact to remember in light of the heavy emphasis on technical jargon in many earlier studies of the subject. Second, he shows how problems with medical communication are contextually located. Confusions such as "varicose" with "very close" arise at specific points of interaction between particular speakers and hearers, and may actually represent problems of hearing rather than understanding (cf. Grimshaw, 1980). Shuy's (1976) focus on specific linguistic behaviors in actual medical encounters permits him to make distinctions between such types of miscommunication and to generate preliminary rules for their classification. By contrast to the "variable approach" we discussed above, Shuy's categories are generated from the data themselves, which is a distinct advantage when addressing the range, complexity, and seriousness of communication failures.

Cicourel's (1975, 1983) analyses of how physicians transform patients' verbal descriptions into written medical records offers yet another perspective on the problem. In his investigations of this process, Cicourel shows how the medical encounter creates competing frames of reference that may lead to subsequent misunderstandings. He moves between the physician's progress notes in a patient's medical record and the discourse reflected by the notes, comparing the two as forms of literacy (bureaucratic problem solving on the one hand, and commonsense reasoning on the other).

Below, for example, is an excerpt from his case study of a medical encounter:

Physician: What can I do for you?

Patient: Well, uh, I was concerned about, uh . . . last summer, I guess, I-I was having a problem in the uh . . . uh, I guess w-what you call the bulk of the outer uh part of the organ. There's like, paper thin uh cuts, just a little bleeding. And finally when I went to have my checkup, which was uh . . . about 3 months ago, my internist asked me if I'd had a paps, test and I hadn't so he took one and he said uh my uterus was kind of spongy, and also I had uh, very low, I was very low in hormones and he-uh-the estrogen

Physician: mh

Patient: the count was so low he said I didn't get it so he put me on hu . . . oh, uh on the estrogen pills. Now, about four years ago when I went through Phipps, uh, they had cut me down to a half and I still was getting alot of uh swel-swelling and soreness in my breasts and they took a mameograph that time and they told me to get one about every six months, but, I sort of took myself off the estrogen and found that I didn't have any of that feeling, so I've been off of it, and uh that's what-I didn't realize when first my husband died nine months ago, but still, anybody'd just look at me and you know I'd just be . . . be uh the bereavement. I don't know, I uh never used to be like that . . .

(Cicourel, 1983, p. 224)

And below is an excerpt from the physician's written note about this encounter:

Widowed 9 mos. - depressed. Saw internist 4 mos. ago because of vulva irritation - started 1.25 mg. Premarin → breast soreness, so stopped EST.

(Cicourel, 1983, p. 223)

Detailed inspection of the written note and transcript allows a comparative analysis of conflicting interpretations between them. Cicourel notes that although the patient said she visited her internist "about 3 months ago," the physician's notes indicate that she did so "4 mos. ago." Moreover, the physician's notation, "started 1.25 mg. Premarin" could later be read as an action taken during the patient's visit, rather than as part of her past history with the internist.

Another problem, says Cicourel, is the physician's notation of "depression" in the medical record—his *interpretation* of the patient's rambling and emotional style. This interpretation is not based on any direct statement by the patient (who in fact spoke of her bereavement in specific relation to her husband's death). Nor is there any objective evidence, according to Cicourel, that the patient is impaired or unable to conduct her daily affairs. Cicourel argues that the recording of disembodied inferences like "depression" into a medical record potentially transforms the physician's own understanding of the patient's problems. He concludes that there is an inherent tension between bureaucratic and individual forms of expression in the medical encounter that makes misinterpretation and misunderstanding inevitable. By focusing on the contexts in which discrepancies in communication occur, he pinpoints those discrepancies and illuminates their potential consequences for the parties involved.

Theoretically, Cicourel's study illuminates another complexity that has been overlooked in many earlier investigations of communication in medicine, namely, the accuracy with which physicians' written records reflect patients' verbal concerns. By comparing interview transcripts with written records of care, Cicourel demonstrates that the transformation of discourse into text is itself an influence, if not a bias, on what counts as accurate reporting or description. This question of interpretation has not been addressed by studies of the relationship between process and outcome variables.

Mishler (1984) focuses on an even more fundamental problem in research on miscommunication in medicine—the uncritical acceptance of the values of medicine over the life-world experiences of patients. To demonstrate how previous research ignores the question of values, Mishler analyses transcripts of physician-patient encounters that show how the structure of the interview constrains patients' abilities to tell their stories coherently. Below is an excerpt from one transcript, dealing with a patient's use of alcohol:

Physician: . . . when do you get that? [heartburn]
(0.8)
Patient: Wel:l when I eat something wrong
Physician: How- how soon after you eat it?
(2.5)
Patient: Wel:l (1.0) probably an hour (0.4) maybe [less.
Physician: [About an hour?
Patient: Maybe less (1.2) I've cheated and I've been drinking which I shouldn't have done.
(0.9)
Physician: Does drinking make it worse?
Patient: Ho ho uh ooh yes (1.0) Especially the carbonation and the alcohol.
(0.8)
Physician: Hm hm (0.8) How much do you drink?

(Mishler, 1984, p. 84)

Reviewing this excerpt, Mishler suggests that the interpretation of the patient's introduction of her drinking problem in "tag" comment form ("I've cheated and I've been drinking") depends upon one's frame of reference. Within the medical frame, which Mishler terms "the voice of medicine," the physician treats the patient's drinking as just one of several activities that make her heartburn worse (only later does he pursue it as a problem in its own right). Mishler contends that within this frame (and without reference to the larger structures of meaning that stand behind the patient's utterance), it is easy to see the physician's questions and the patient's answers as providing a normative order and coherence to their encounter. From this perspective, the patient's tag comment about her drinking intervenes in the logical flow of the physician's questions.

But Mishler offers a contrasting perspective through patient narratives, which he compiles from the serial fragments of information patients provide. Below is an excerpt from the patient narrative he compiled, in part, from the transcript just above:

> My symptoms occur after eating and particularly after drinking. Although I know I should not drink, alcohol helps me with some problems that have developed since my marriage four years ago, such as tension and sleeplessness. For these purposes, alcohol works better for me than pills that have been prescribed. (Mishler, 1984, p. 101)

Adopting the patient's narrative, "the voice of the life world," as an alternative frame of reference, Mishler shows how the physician's questions actually disrupt and redirect the patient's attempts to tell her story. He thereby shows how communication difficulties can arise from speaking practices that reinforce the values of one perspective over another. Mishler's approach highlights the ways in which researchers often unwittingly adopt the physician's perspective in defining what counts as good communication. Such one-sided definitions may overlook significant sources of patient dissatisfaction and mask a range of attempts to articulate them.

Taken together, discourse-based studies offer several useful correctives to the advanced factor analyses discussed above. Their focus on language and social interaction in the context of actual medical encounters allows researchers to pinpoint communication difficulties as they occur, rather than relying on indirect methods of measurement. This not only affords a more detailed understanding of the types of problems that can arise (e.g., mishearings, misunderstandings, or cases of deliberate deception); it also permits those problems to be tracked and their impact assessed over the course of the encounter. Moreover, expanding the scope of investigation to include variations in communication style across social contexts provides for questions about the complexity of role relations in bureaucratic settings (such as hospitals and health maintenance organizations) and their effect on the clarity, consistency, and completeness of communication between individual physicians and patients. Finally, discourse-based studies reveal some of the presuppositions other researchers have relied on regarding the accuracy and neutrality of data for analysis. In both cases, unexamined assumptions about the nature of record keeping and interaction process are shown systematically to influence communication outcomes.

The results of discourse-based studies are tantalizing and suggest that linguistic, paralinguistic, and sequential features of talk play an important part in determining the quality and success of communication between physicians and patients. But these studies are limited to analyses of single or small numbers of cases; in addition, they do not attend to larger practice patterns and outcomes. A more specific set of linkages between problems in communication and medical care outcomes comes from conversation analysis – in which miscommunication is defined as the *violation of specific discourse rules.*

Miscommunication as Rule Violation

Conversation analysis was originally developed as a means of understanding the temporal and sequential organization of utterances in dialogue (see Sacks, Schegloff, & Jefferson, 1974). Research to date has shown that conversations acquire their orderliness, describable by procedural rules, through the organized practices and systematic efforts of speakers and hearers. Among practices that have proven consequential for the analysis of miscommunication in medical settings are those involved in the organization of turn-taking (Sacks et al., 1974: see also Wilson, Wiemann, & Zimmerman, 1984), questions and answers (Sacks, 1972; Schegloff & Sacks, 1973), and conversational repair (Schegloff, Jefferson & Sacks, 1977).

Turn-Taking

Whatever participants in a medical encounter do or do not communicate occurs largely through the exchange of turns at talk. But despite longstanding complaints regarding patients' lack of opportunities to express their concerns (cf. Francis et al., 1969; Korsch & Negrete, 1972; Wallen et al., 1979), researchers have been hard-pressed to explain the mechanisms involved. Analyses of the organization of turn-taking in medical encounters afford an understanding of how patients' abilities to express their concerns are constrained in and through the transition of turns between speakers.

For example, Sacks et al. (1974) advance a model of turn-taking for conversation that accounts for the orderly transition of speaker turns with little gap (or silence) and little simultaneous speech. Through an ordered set of rules, speakers achieve a preferred order of interaction in which at least one but not more than one party talks at a time. The operation of the rule-set affords a means of distinguishing between various types of simultaneous speech (such as errors in transition timing and displays of active listening), including *interruptions*—violations of the rules for turn-taking (West & Zimmerman, 1977, 1983; Zimmerman & West, 1975).

Building on this work, West (1984b, 1984c) analyzed the organization of turn-taking in encounters between physicians and patients. In the majority of encounters she examined (in which the physicians were white men), she noted a striking and asymmetrical pattern: physicians interrupted patients far more often than the reverse. Of further interest here are the effects of this pattern on the exchange of information between physician and patient. For example:

Patient: When I'm sitting upright. Y'know=
Physician: =More so than it was even before?
Patient: Yay::es=
Physician: =Swelling 'r anything like that thet chew've no:ticed?
(.)
Patient: Nuh:o, not th[et I've nodi-]
Physician: [TEN:::DER duh the tou]ch? press:ing any?
Patient: No::, jus' when it's- si::tting.
Physician: Okay:=
Patient: =Er lying on it.
Physician: Even ly:ing. Stan:ding up? walking aroun:d? ((singsong))
Patient: No: [jis-]
Physician: [Not] so mu:ch. Jis'- ly:ing on it. Si:tting on it. Jis' then.

(West, 1984b, pp. 61-62)

As West (1984b) observes, each of this physician's intrusions into the patient's turns at talk is seemingly reasonable and warranted by the external constraints of medical examination and treatment. Asking where a patient is feeling pain, how often, when, and under what conditions is all justified by (if not required for) diagnosis of the problem. But when these inquiries cut off the patient's utterance-in-progress, particularly when that utterance-in-progress is the presumed necessary response to a prior necessary question, then the physician is not only violating the patient's rights to speak, but is also systematically cutting off potentially valuable information that is necessary to achieve a diagnosis (cf. Frankel, 1983).

Although earlier studies (e.g., Davis, 1968) tended to equate physicians' control over patients with the ability to treat them, West (1984b) concludes that this form of control may hinder rather than help clinical work. Patients may consult physicians because they do not know what ails them or what to do about it, but physicians must *listen* to patients to find out what brings them in for treatment. Thus, she suggests that physicians—as well as patients—have much to lose when turn-taking rules are violated and patients are unable to "get a word in edgewise."

Beckman and Frankel (1984) offer explicit support for this suggestion in their analysis of the opening segments of medical interviews. They note that it is in the turn-by-turn development of patients' concerns that physicians influence how much patients will tell them. On the one hand, physicians can encourage patients' full expression of their chief complaints by providing ongoing displays of acknowledgment as those complaints unfold:

Physician: How you been doing?
Patient: Oh, well, I been doing okay, except for Saturday, Sunday night. You know I been kinda nervous off and on but I had a little incident at my house Saturday and it kinda shook me up a little bit.
→ **Physician:** Okay.
Patient: And my ulcer, it's been burning me off and on like when I eat something if it don't agree, then I'll find out about it.
→ **Physician:** Right, okay.
Patient: But lately I've been getting this funny, like I'll lay down on my back, and my heart'll go "brrr" you know like that. Like its skipping a beat or something, and then it'll just start on back off beating like when I get upset it'll just start beating boom-boom-boom and it'll just go back to its normal beat.
→ **Physician:** Okay.
Patient: Is that normal?
Physician: That's- that's a lot of things. Anything else that's bothering you
Patient: No

(Beckman and Frankel, 1984, pp. 692-693)

Here, for example, the physician offers turn-by-turn acknowledgment of the patient's emergent troubles ("Okay," "Right") as they develop.

On the other hand, physicians can discourage patients from expressing their concerns by actively intervening in them and prematurely focusing on the first stated concern:

Physician: What brings you here today?
Patient: My head is killing me.
Physician: Have you had headaches before?
Patient: No.

(Beckman and Frankel, 1984, p. 693)

Here the physician employs a close-ended question following the patient's first turn at talk, thereby narrowing the focus of the encounter from the outset.

Beckman and Frankel (1984) report that in over two-thirds of the medical encounters they examined, physicians intruded on patient's initial statements and redirected talk toward specific concerns. In only 1 of 52 opening segments did patients who were intruded upon offer additional concerns, and on the average, physicians made their first interventions within 18 seconds of the encounter's start. Moreover, Beckman and Frankel's (1985) follow-up to this study indicates that patients whose initial statements are cut short are significantly more likely to raise additional concerns later in the visit. These results lead to the conclusion that "over directed interviewing at the beginning of the visit [may obscure] the very concerns that the initial segment of the visit is designed to capture" (Beckman & Frankel, 1984, p. 695). They also show how a seemingly unrelated occurrence—such as a patient's initiation of concerns at the end of the encounter—can be traced to the violation of a specific discourse rule governing the elicitation of problems and concerns at the beginning of the encounter.

Questions and Answers

A rule-based approach to medical discourse affords a means of reconceptualizing another recurring complaint in the existing literature; namely, patients' failures to ask questions (cf. Cartwright, 1964; Ley, 1983; McIntosh, 1974; Waitzkin, 1983). For example, questions and answers belong to a class of sequences known as *adjacency pairs* (Sacks, 1972; Schegloff & Sacks, 1973). The rules that govern the organization of these pairs dictate that the second part of a pair is conditionally relevant on the occurrence of a first, and that the design of the first sets the stage for what will count as a second. In casual conversation among peers, types of adjacency pairs and control over their initiation vary freely. But in more restricted forms of speech exchange, control over who initiates and who responds may be relatively fixed—by formal arrangement (as in a court of law), or by tradition and informal negotiation (as in most medical encounters). In either case, limitations on the distribution of initiation options create the potential for the initiating party to control the form, substance, and appropriateness of subsequent talk. As we have seen (Beckman & Frankel, 1984; West, 1984b), physicians' repeated violations of turn-taking rules lead to a type of control that can inhibit or actually prevent the flow of clinically relevant information. Specification of the conversational rules that link questions and answers to one another and to larger sequential structures sheds additional light on how patients may be constrained or hesitate to ask questions.

Analyses of the distribution of questions in medical encounters suggest that in terms of sheer proportions, physicians initiate between 91% (West, 1983, 1984b) and 99% (Frankel, in press) of the total questions asked. Frankel (in press) reports that physicians often begin gathering information about a particular organ system or problem using a complete question, following up with a list or string of related question particles:

Physician: Does anybody have tuberculosis?
Patient: No, not that I know of
Physician: Heart disease
Patient: No

(Frankel, in press)

Such formulations may limit patients' options for responses over a series of turns at talk and lead patients to refrain from asking questions of their own. For example, when he looked at how patients introduce new topics and information onto the floor, Frankel found that they most often used the tag response, similar to that presented by Mishler (1984):

Physician: How- how soon after you eat it?
(2.5)
Patient: Wel:l (1.0) probably an hour (0.4) maybe [less
Physician: [About an hour?
→ **Patient:** Maybe less (1.2) I've cheated and I've been drinking which I shouldn't have done.

(Mishler, 1984, p. 84)

He notes that use of the tag response yields sequential control over the option to question and thus, control over the flow of information to the physician—who may choose to ignore the additional information or only investigate some of its dimensions. Frankel found no cases in which patients expressed their additional concerns as direct questions, leading him to conclude that such concerns are often missed because they are introduced indirectly.

West (1983, 1984b) observes that physicians, who are asked far fewer questions by their patients, also answer fewer of those they are asked. In addition, patients' questions are often marked by some form of speech disturbance:

Patient: Ah me:an i::s it *ri:ll* serious? Iz- izzit somethin' that could-

* * *

Patient: Wull that- Is that nor:mul? I mean is that:t oka::y?

(West, 1983, p. 96)

The existence of such hitches and stutters in the queries of otherwise articulate patients indicates that patients may also treat self-initiated questions as somehow problematic.

Findings such as these suggest that patient-initiated questions are *dispreferred* in the context of medical encounters (Frankel, in press; West, 1983, 1984b). In this light, patients' fewer questions can be seen not as a function of their diffidence but as products of an achieved order of interaction: one in which physicians ask the questions and patients respond to them. Conversation analytic studies make it clear that communication difficulties such as patients' failures to ask questions can be usefully reframed in terms of sequencing rules and the consequences that follow when these are violated or ignored.

Conversational Repair

To this point, we have described rule violations that limit or interrupt the communication process. But Schegloff et al.'s (1977) work on conversational "repair" (see also Hopper & Drummond, this volume) indicates what may well be the most promising direction for research – the analysis of speakers' procedures for redressing identified cases of miscommunication in the context of their occurrence. This work affords an alternative to retrospective interviews and questionnaires through the detailed study of speakers' practices for ensuring that they are heard and understood.

Schegloff et al. (1977) identify a variety of means through which a speaker can initiate a *request for repair* of another party's prior turn at talk. For example, a speaker may use an interrogative query (such as "what?" or "Hunh?") to elicit repetition of the prior turn:

Patient:	Bo:y, that thing (is) col::e.
	(0.6)
→ **Physician:**	*Whut?* ((pulling stethoscope away from one ear))
	(0.2)
Patient:	That- THAT STETHOSCOPE IS COL::E!
Physician:	AH'M SORRY.

(West, 1984a, p. 112)

A speaker may also initiate a request for repair by partially repeating some prior turn (with an interrogative intonation), thereby specifying the source of the trouble:

Physician:	Any (mo:ss) in yer (0.2) bladder? 'r [°bowel problum-]
→ **Patient:**	[Mo:::ss?]
	Nuho, my bladder's fi:ne=
Physician:	=Uh kay

(West, 1984a, p. 112)

Still another means of initiating repair is tying "Y'mean . . . " to some candidate understanding of the prior turn:

Patient:	An' ah cun take thi:s hand an' li:ft it, an' it duh'unt hurt.
→ **Physician:**	Yuh mean, when yuh *lif'* the ar:m up, using yer other han:d?=
Patient:	=Uh huh

(West, 1984a, p. 113)

Though their forms may vary, all of these requests for repair pose queries about another party's prior turn to talk, thereby locating the source of mishearing or misunderstanding in the context in which it occurs.

West (1984a) identifies a further class of queries that serves a related end. *Requests for confirmation* involve the pairing of otherwise declarative utterances with "Y'know . . . ?, " "Okay?," "Like . . . ?" and "Right?" in pseudo-question form:

Physician:	.h Alri:ght I think you've jus' got some- (.) bur*si::dus* there Oka:y?
Patient:	.hh hhh Ah've ha:d- *had* bursi:dus in muh shoul:der buhfo:re (0.4) Bud I never had anything (0.6) (*much*) like this,

(West, 1984a, p. 127)

Here, the physician's request ("Okay?") provides an opportunity for the patient to confirm her understanding of his diagnosis ("You've jus' got some bur*sidus* there.") Simultaneously, he gives the patient the opportunity to confirm her understanding of his diagnostic terminology ("Ah've *had* bursidus before.")

Meehan (1981) demonstrates the utility of this approach to miscommunication in medicine through his analysis of the sequential consequences of repair. His findings show that what counts as a mishearing, misunderstanding, or failure to communicate often resurfaces subsequently in participants' attempts at repair. So, what might be coded as a communication failure at one point in time may be resolved at another. Previous studies of aggregate jargon use have failed to take this broader context of the medical interview into account and as a result, are insensitive to its outcomes. By contrast, conversation analysis affords a means of identifying instances of miscommunication as they are oriented to by the participants involved.

Although the application of conversation analysis to communication problems in medical setting is still relatively new (cf. Frankel, 1983, 1984; Maynard, in press; Steele, Jackson, & Gutmann, 1985; Treichler, Frankel, Kramarae, Zoppi, & Beckman, 1984), it has already proved useful in the pursuit of applied concerns we identified earlier. For example, Maynard (in press) observes that patients' acceptance of bad medical news is largely dependent on the local context in which such news is delivered. Steele et al. (1985) report that patients' compliance is directly related to the form and specificity of physicians' questions. And Frankel and Beckman (1989, February) are finding that over 90% of patients' formal complaints about their care stem from the ways that medical staff members communicate with them. Results such as these suggest that "the search for better outcomes" will be substantially advanced by conversation analytic principles.

Conclusions

In this chapter, we have attempted to provide an overview of research on miscommunication in medicine through a history of work on the topic. We began by noting that interest in this subject evolved from a concern with improving the outcomes of patient care. Thus, early work consisted primarily of a search for better outcomes, attempting to identify characteristics of communication that would enhance patients' satisfaction and compliance. The results of this search were impressive, implicating communication breakdowns in some of the most practical concerns facing medicine. As in the case of many applied research problems, however, initial attempts to resolve them did not fully articulate the scope and the complexity of the issues involved. Early studies of communication problems in medical settings were largely descriptive, resting on commonsense understandings of what good communication might consist of. These included the belief that good communication is clear communication, the assumption that senders' and receivers' traits determine the quality of transmissions, and a focus on individual physicians and patients as constituting the relevant parties involved.

Subsequent research on the topic has yielded many important developments, including theoretical models of antecedents to the medical consultation and sophisticated empirical demonstrations of relations between various features of medical discourse and particular outcomes of patient care. Descriptive goals have given way to explanatory ones as researchers attempt to show when and how specific communication problems might be remedied. But a focus on isolated variables has led to findings that are often contradictory, in the absence of a clear conceptual model of how medical discourse is organized in the first instance. So, while studies of the relationship between process and outcome variables have illuminated the problems with earlier understandings (e.g., the equation of good with clear communication), they have also posed problems of their own. Among these are their assumption that patients' needs, resources, and abilities are constant with respect to various components of the communication process, and their general inability to address issues of context, sequence, and interpretation.

Recent discourse-based studies have illuminated the most promising directions for resolution of these problems, through the analysis of the elementary forms of participation that underlie more abstract assumptions about process and outcome. In particular, conversation analysis provides a systematic approach to the very organization of speech exchange through direct observation of the contexts in which participants succeed or fail to communicate. An understanding of the basic structures of participation in medical encounters—such as those regulating turn-taking, questions and answers, and conversational repair—offers a theoretically grounded way of identifying cases of miscommunication in the course of their production. It also offers a means of asserting their impact *on* medical encounters in the course of their management.

As we learn more about the basic properties of speech exchange and the ways in which these relate to problems of communication in the medical encounter, we will be forging new links in the relationship between social theory and practice. In 1977, Engel proposed a biopsychosocial model of medical care as a challenge to the traditional biomedical model of disease.

Engel's singular contribution in this regard was to claim that the standards of medical practice under the assumptions of the biomedical model were simply too restrictive and reductionistic. Echoing Sir William Osler's suggestion at the turn of the twentieth century, namely, that it is not so much a question of what disease the patient has but the sort of patient that has it, Engel revitalized the idea that patients have social and emotional needs that should not be divorced from the central goal of medicine—which is not simply to treat disease, but to treat illness; not simply to cure, but to heal.

As we look forward to the twenty-first century, one of the certain challenges we will face is to understand the relationship between communication, social structure, and healing. For example, in the United States, people are already healthier and more free of disease than at any time in history; yet they continue to seek medical attention at a record pace. Nearly 11% of the U.S. gross national product is spent on health care, and of that amount, 40% is spent on the last month of life. Unraveling the keys to effective communication in medical encounters goes beyond the traditional conception of "good bedside manner." It involves deeply rooted questions about the nature of society and the meaning of reality. To address these questions in a context of humane medical care it will be necessary to expand our knowledge about the interplay between various forms of communication and their effects on the experience and course of disease and illness. Since talk is the major medium of exchange in many medical settings, analysis of the "routine complications" of speech exchange (West, 1984b) promises to advance our understanding of how miscommunication interferes with health and healing.

Notes

1. More recent research (e.g., Louis Harris & Associates, 1982; Novack et al., 1979; President's Commission on Ethical Problems in Medicine and Biomedical and Behavioral Research, 1982) suggests that among U.S. physicians, attitudes toward informing the cancer patients have changed dramatically. Whereas in 1961, 88% of physicians favored not telling patients their diagnosis (Oken, 1961), in 1977, only 6% favored this policy (Novack et al., 1979). Novack et al. attribute much of the shift in physicians' attitudes to advances in therapy for many forms of cancer, increased understanding of issues associated with death and dying, and mounting concerns for patients' rights.

2. Transcribing conventions employed in many of the discourse extracts appear in the Appendix to this book.

10

Miscommunication in Clinical Contexts: The Speech Therapy Interview

Michael F. McTear
Florence King

Introduction

The purpose of this chapter is to examine miscommunication in clinical contexts. Broadly speaking, the term *clinical contexts* encompasses professional encounters between an individual, often called the patient, who presents with some medically defined problem, and the professional who is competent to deal with that problem. Thus clinical contexts include encounters between doctors and patients, nurses and patients, clinical psychologists and their clients, psychiatrists and patients, as well as encounters involving speech therapists, physiotherapists, occupational therapists, and many more.

It would not be possible within this chapter to exemplify miscommunication in all these types of clinical context. Rather, what we will attempt to do is to examine miscommunication in one context—dialogues between speech therapists and their child patients—and suggest how our findings could be generalized to the other contexts that we have mentioned.

It could be argued that dialogues between psychiatrists and their patients would provide more striking exemplification of miscommunication, especially because some types of psychiatric disorder are defined in terms that predict miscommunication—such as thought-disordered schizophrenia, Alzheimer's disease, and senile dementia. However, we have chosen speech therapy interviews because they illustrate the main point that we wish to make about miscommunication: that it derives primarily from discrepancies between the mental states of the dialogue participants—that is, what they believe and what they believe their interlocutor believes—rather than from some problem in the linguistic channel arising out of the communicative disability of one of the participants, that is, the patient.

It will be important to stress this point, because it is normally assumed that patients undergoing speech therapy have a communication disorder that involves problems with encoding or decoding utterances. Indeed, a communication disorder of this type will be the reason why the patient was referred for treatment in the first place. The patient's problems may occur at one or more linguistic levels of language—such as phonology, syntax, semantics, and discourse/pragmatics—and may involve either language production or comprehension (or both). Thus a patient may display a disorder of articulation, be unable to produce grammatically correct sentences, have difficulties in finding the correct word, and so on.

It is not too difficult to imagine that communication with a patient suffering from one or more of these complaints might be fraught with difficulty and that miscommunication might frequently ensue. Indeed it could be argued that it might be possible to predict the degree of miscommunication that would be associated with the type and severity of the patient's disorder. It is not necessarily the case that linguistic impairments lead to miscommunication, however. Connolly (1986) has provided a useful overview of how the loss of functional distinctions available in language may impair communication, by making utterances less intelligible, ambiguous, or simply illusive (i.e., when it is impossible to determine exactly what an utterance means). Nevertheless, it is not too difficult to find cases in which miscommunication does not arise in an interactive situation involving a patient suffering from a language disorder, because the patient's partner has somehow been able to make sense of what was said. This point was demonstrated recently in a study that contrasted the ability of professionals and the patient's family to interpret the impaired expressive language of a young head injury victim (Davies & Mehan, 1988). Although the patient's language was virtually incomprehensible to the professionals, her family were able to interpret her utterances under "blind" conditions in verifiable ways, thus suggesting that communicative success does not depend on the fidelity of the communication channel so much as on the sense-making capacities of interlocutors. In turn, patients often devise strategies to make themselves more easily understood in spite of their handicap. In other words, communication has to be viewed as a two-way process in which both participants attempt to reach some degree of interpersonal agreement, using whatever methods are available to them, for example, gestures or circumlocutions.

Taking an interpersonal rather than an intrapersonal view will affect how we define miscommunication. It will also have a bearing on how we might view the nature of clinical encounters involving language-disordered patients. Traditionally, the view is that the patient presents with a problem and the aim of the therapy is to eradicate the problem, or at least alleviate it to the extent that the patient's communicative ability might be enhanced. In order to achieve this aim, however, it is essential to define what is meant by successful communication, and this in turn will involve an exploration of definitions of miscommunication. It will also be important to stress that therapy occurs in a communicative context and that a critical examination of what is happening in this context will provide a useful basis for evaluating the success or otherwise of the therapy. Thus by looking at examples of miscommunication in clinical contexts we can achieve two goals—we can arrive at a more appropriate conceptualization of what is meant by miscommunication, and we may also contribute some useful insights to the therapeutic process.

This chapter is structured as follows. In the next section we will explore in greater detail what we mean by miscommunication. Following this, we will introduce a particular type of language disorder—commonly referred to as *semantic-pragmatic disability*—which frequently gives rise to situations involving miscommunication. We will then present a detailed analysis of part of an interview between a child, whose problems appear to be largely in the areas of discourse and pragmatics, and his speech therapist. We will conclude by exploring the implications of our findings for a more general view of miscommunication in clinical contexts.

The Nature of Miscommunication

Communication has been traditionally viewed in terms of a sender, a receiver, and a transmission channel. The sender and the receiver are assumed to have compatible encoding and decoding devices that allow them to send and receive messages. According to this view of communication, which Reddy (1979) has referred to as *the conduit metaphor*, miscommunication arises if there is 'noise'—for example, problems of articulation, lexical choice, syntactic form—in the channel which results in message distortion. As was pointed out in the introductory section, however, such distortions do not necessarily result in miscommunication and can certainly not be considered as explanatory factors in a theory of miscommunication.

An alternative view of communication that Reddy proposed envisages a system in which people located in slightly different environments exchange information. The different environments represent the notion of *radical subjectivity*, that is, the idea that each person's view of the world is unique and different from that of other people. Communication is possible because there is sufficient common ground, but miscommunication is inevitable because the perspectives of each person are not totally identical. Moreover, in this view, the essential process of communication is not explained in terms of the transmission of messages but in terms of the attempt by a recipient of a message to reconstruct its intended meaning. This view of communication corresponds to what Sperber and Wilson (1985) have called the *inferential model* of communication. According to this view, each person will interpret messages in terms of their own view of the world, which will not be entirely compatible with that of the sender. From the viewpoint of this paradigm, miscommunication is not aberrant; rather it is the norm.

The theoretical foundations of the inferential paradigm are to be found in Grice's definition of intentional communication, or, as Grice (1957) called it, *non-natural meaning*. Under this definition, for a communication to be successful two things must occur:

(1) the sender must intend by uttering something to cause the hearer to believe or to do something;
(2) the sender intends that (1) should be achieved simply by the hearer recognizing that intention.

In other words, communication is defined as a complex kind of intention that is achieved just by being recognized. In this process the sender's communicative intention becomes mutual knowledge to both sender and receiver. It follows from this definition of what is required for successful communication that discrepancies between the beliefs of the sender and the receiver about the communicative intentions behind the utterance will result in miscommunication. That is, the sender will believe that, by uttering X, proposition P has been communicated, and further that the hearer recognizes that it was the sender's intention to communicate P. However, the hearer might instead believe that the sender intended to communicate Q. In this case, miscommunication will have occurred, because sender and hearer hold discrepant beliefs about the communicative intentions behind X.

A second important foundation for our discussion is also to be found in the work of Grice. Conversation has been considered as a goal-directed activity in which goals and actions of each participant contribute to the overall success of the conversation. Grice (1975) described some basic maxims of conversation underlying the co-operative use of language in terms of the following general cooperative principle: "Make your contribution such as is required, at the stage at which it occurs, by the accepted purpose or direction of the talk exchange in which you are engaged." Grice's view of communication as a cooperative activity forms the basis of attempts to relate the planning mechanisms developed in artificial intelligence to the analysis of goal-directed behavior in conversation (Hobbs & Agar, 1985; Hobbs & Evans, 1980). In this view participants in conversation are guided by the overall goals that they hope to achieve. Furthermore, in order to participate cooperatively in a conversation, the participants must attempt to work out their partner's goals and beliefs – in other words, their mental states.

Turning now to the question of miscommunication in clinical situations, if we adopt Reddy's (1979) view we can treat communication between a clinician and a patient as an attempt on the part of each participant to achieve goals against a background of beliefs – that is, as communication between mental states. Miscommunication can arise because of incompatibility between mental states, either because the participants have obviously discrepant goals or beliefs or, more elusively, because their goals or beliefs are discrepant without one or the other being aware of this discrepancy. We will discuss examples of both types of discrepancy presently.

Semantic-Pragmatic Disability

The term *semantic-pragmatic disability* (SPD) was coined by Rapin and Allen (1983) to describe a childhood language disorder in which the primary impairment is in the use of language in everyday conversation and in the comprehension of connected discourse. The following are some commonly reported features in speech of SPD children (Bishop & Rosenbloom, 1987):

(1) the content of their speech is odd and their remarks are often tangential or inappropriate;
(2) their speech is literal and they pay undue attention to surface meanings rather than underlying meanings;
(3) they exhibit odd associations and reasoning;
(4) they have problems in organizing their ideas and in making generalizations;
(5) their social behavior is odd and inept;
(6) they have problems in comprehension to the extent that they can usually cope well with standard picture description tasks involving single words or isolated sentences, but they have difficulty in understanding sequences of everyday events which are related temporally or causally.

There are several reports of case studies of children with disabilities such as these (see, for example, Conti-Ramsden & Gunn, 1986; McTear, 1985b, 1989). There have also been a few larger scale studies providing comparisons with children suffering from a variety of other language disorders (Prutting & Kirchner, 1987). We can imagine that conversations with a child who has a language disorder of this nature would likely be fraught with problems of miscommunication. We will explore the degree and nature of such miscommunication in the next section.

An Example of Miscommunication in a Speech Therapy Interview

We will base our discussion on the following extract from an interview between a speech therapist (the second author) and a young boy J, aged 5;11 (5 years, 11 months), who was attending a school for children with moderate learning difficulty. The extract was transcribed from an audio recording of the interview, the purpose of the recording being the provision of data to enable various assessments to be made of J's language ability.

Extract 1

1. **T:** Right (.) you ready?
2. **J:** Play time.
3. **T:** It's not play time. We're going to have a star.
4. **J:** Play play play play (.) play with D.
5. **T:** Play with D. Who's going to play with D?
6. **J:** Have R.
7. **T:** Have R. I'm going to play with 'you (.) but we're // not going to *
8. **J:** // play * with you R.
9. **T:** I'm going to play with 'you J.
10. **J:** Play with 'you R.
11. **T:** I'm not R.
    (1.5)
12. **J:** R.
13. **T:** Am I R?
14. **J:** Yeh.
15. **T:** R who?
16. **J:** R Ramsay.
17. **T:** R. Ramsay
    (J laughs)

18. **T:** Who's R Ramsay?
19. **J:** This is.
20. **T:** This is (.) who.
21. **J:** No no don't know.
22. **T:** Don't know. I don't know either. Y' going to see if you can get a star for each picture.
23. **J:** Yeh.
24. **T:** OK. Tell me about that one.
25. **J:** It's writing pencil.
26. **T:** It's colored with a writing pencil. Can you see under the writing pencil (.) Can you see the picture of the boy?
    (2.0)
27. **T:** What's the boy doing?
    (2.5)
28. **T:** The boy (.) is
29. **J:** Digging.
30. **T:** L Well done J (.) and you can get a star. I want you to stay on your chair (.) and tel;l me about the next one
    (2.5)
    (J looks through stars in their container and chooses a red one. He stays on his chair).
31. **T:** Oh you'll get another red star.
32. **J:** That's a round table.
33. **T:** Which is a round table?
34. **J:** Here.
35. **T:** This one here?
36. **J:** Yeh.
37. **T:** This one is not. This one is a rectangle shape.
38. **J:** Rectangle (spoken to self in low voice)
39. **T:** Rectangle (1.0) OK (1.0) What about this picture here?

*
*
*

61. **T:** Could you get a red star for one of these?
62. **J:** Tangle tangle.
63. **T:** Now which one are you going to tell me about?
    (1.0)
    (J points)
64. **T:** This one.
65. **J:** Tangle.
66. **T:** Tangle. Which where what's tangled?
67. **J:** A Bike (.) that's a writing pencil.
68. **T:** It's all scribbled over with a writing pencil.
69. **J:** Not that one.

70. **T:** What's the man // doing *
71. **J:** // but it's * not it's not scribbling
72. **T:** No that's not scribbling that's nice coloring.
73. **J:** Is this one scribb.
74. And this scribbling.
75. **T:** That's a little bit scribbly isn't it?
76. **J:** Scribbling (spoken in low voice)
77. **T:** What about this one?
78. **J:** Scribble (spoken in low voice)
(1.0)
79. **T:** Is it scribbled?
80. **J:** No
81. **T:** No

*
*
*

242. **T:** Oh there's mine. How many did I catch?
(0.5)
243. **T:** One, two, three.
244. **J:** // go now.
245. **T:** // can we count yours.
246. yes count yours and then you can go now.

First a few words about this particular case. J had known the therapist for 2 months. His difficulty had already been assessed as being largely a discourse or pragmatic problem. In particular, he seemed to have problems in using language appropriately to interact with another speaker. Furthermore, these difficulties were beyond those normally experienced by children of the same age who were not communicatively impaired (for a detailed account of conversational development in children, see McTear, 1985a). This difficulty in the use of language gave rise to a further problem, because it was not possible to conduct formal assessments of his language understanding abilities due to his behavioral and communicative difficulties. On the basis of informal assessments it was estimated that his comprehensive ability was at least at a 3;6 to 4;0 level, although his expressive language showed use of syntax up to about the level of a normally developing child aged between 2;6 and 3;0. He understood and used a wide and varied vocabulary.

Part of J's therapy at one time involved making appropriate responses to pictures in a simple description task, and the extract to be discussed here is taken from one such therapy session. The transcripts were subjected to a wide range of analyses, involving several discourse analytic constructs such as turn-taking, response contingency, repairs, topic organization, and exchange structure. By and large there were no problems with fairly surface levels of dialogue, such as turn-taking and making self-repairs to his own utterances. The major difficulties arose with respect to responses to the therapist's questions (adjacency pairs) and to the negotiation and maintenance of conversational topics.

One of the main points that will emerge from the analysis of the samples of therapist-child dialogue is that there is a discrepancy between the goals of the therapist and the child and that this discrepancy in goals gives rise to miscommunication. A simple case of goal conflict, which is not included in Extract 1, occurred when J attempted to put away a game before he and the therapist had begun to play it. The therapist had planned to use the game as part of her therapy program, but J insisted that they had played the game the previous week. Over a series of turns the therapist managed to persuade him to play the game and thus to fit in with her overall plan for that part of the therapy session. Obviously such discrepancies between what the dialogue partners wish to do can give rise to miscommunication, which may or may not be resolved satisfactorily from the point of view of either or both participants. For the purposes of the remainder of our discussion, however, the term *goal* will be interpreted in a broader sense to include the beliefs of the participants about what is going on in the interaction – for example, what they believe the goals and beliefs of their conversational partner to be. How these mental states interact with instances of miscommunication will become clearer as the analysis proceeds. We will begin by looking at adjacency pair structure to examine the degree of contingency in the responses of the therapist and the child to each other's utterances. Then we will examine the ways in which conversational topics were introduced and maintained. This surface level analysis provides a way of quantifying aspects of the data although they do not provide an explanation for miscommunication. Accordingly, we will extend our analysis by examining the role of goals and beliefs in the dialogue and by showing how miscommunication arose because of the participants' discrepant goals and beliefs.

Adjacency Pairs

Adjacency pairs are sequences of two utterances produced by different speakers, typical examples being question-answer, greeting-greeting, and offer-acceptance (Schegloff & Sacks, 1973). It is useful to be able to quantify the extent to which J and the therapist were able to maintain a coherent conversation in terms of the adjacency pairs they produced. To do this, we have adopted a procedure developed by Blank, Gessner, Esposito (1979). Essentially this procedure involves the construction of a matrix in which each participant has two roles: speaker-initiator and speaker-responder. Each speaker-initiator utterance is evaluated as to whether it contains an explicit demand for the listener to respond (oblige), or does not contain such an explicit response demand (comment). The speaker-responder's contributions are evaluated as being one of the following:

(a) adequate (i.e., it meets, extends or appropriately elaborates on the speaker-initiator's utterance);
(b) inadequate (i.e., the response is invalid, irrelevant, or insufficient as a response to the speaker-initiator);
(c) no response;
(d) other (i.e., unintelligible, unclear, or ambiguous).

Each utterance was coded in terms of these categories and an inter-observer reliability procedure was administered which resulted in virtually full agreement on the coding (differences were resolved as a result of discussions). The most important results from our perspective are those concerning J's responses to *obliges,* that is whether he failed to respond, and the nature of his responses to both obliges and *comments.* that is whether the responses were adequate. Although comments do not require a response and nonresponse is thus not to be penalized in the terms of our analysis, any responses that did occur can still be evaluated as to their adequacy. The results are presented in Table 10.1.

As can be seen from Table 10.1, there was only one instance in the data of the therapist not responding to J. This was a "comment" utterance by J and it occurred when J and the therapist were competing to establish topics. When J was the responder, however, the picture was very different. Almost a third of his responses to comments and almost a quarter of his responses to obliges were inadequate. Furthermore, he failed to respond to 14.3% of the utterances addressed to him that required a response. Because almost one third of his total responses were inappropriate in some way, it comes as no surprise that communication with J during this interview was perceived by his speech therapist as difficult.

Some simple examples of odd responses are to be found in lines 1-2 and 61-62 of Extract 1. In the first example J knew it was not playtime, but instead of answering the therapist's question—whether he was ready to do some work—he suggested playtime. J does not produce the expected second pair part and does not indicate why it is absent by using a marker of displaced topic. In the second example J begins to talk about something else—in fact, as the therapist later discovered, the picture had been

Table 10.1 Matrix of Initiations and Responses in Therapist-Child Interview

	J as speaker-initiator			
	Comments		*Obliges*	
Therapist as speaker-responder	*No*	*Percentage*	*No*	*Percentage*
Adequate	18	94.7	3	100
Inadequate	0	0.0	0	0.0
No response	1	5.3	0	0.0
Other	0	0.0	0	0.0
	Therapist as speaker-initiator			
	Comments		*Obliges*	
J as speaker-responder	*No*	*Percentage*	*No*	*Percentage*
Adequate	12	46.2	42	54.5
Inadequate	8	30.8	19	24.7
No response	3	11.5	11	14.3
Other	3	11.5	5	6.5

scribbled over and so J seems to have been referring to the fact that the scribbles look like a tangle.

These and similar examples suggest a level of miscommunication between J and the therapist. Instead of responding appropriately to the therapist's initiations, J either suggests an alternative course of action (without giving due attention to the therapist's expressed goal) or talks about something that has caught his attention, in apparent disregard of what the therapist had just said to him. As can be imagined, frequent occurrences of such behaviors would be likely to give rise to miscommunication. We can see these responses in a clearer light, however, when we examine the ways in which topics were introduced, maintained, and closed in the sample transcripts.

Negotiation of Conversational Topic

Participants in a conversation collaborate to adhere to a topic, close a topic down, and introduce new topics. In clinical discourse, topic selection tends to be under the control of the therapist and the topic is often made more concrete for the child by the use of materials that the therapist believes will promote discussion. We can examine how topics were negotiated in the session between J and the therapist by looking in some detail at examples from Extract 1. We can begin with a fairly informal, qualitative description of the progress of the therapy session. In the next section we will attempt to relate this analysis to a view of conversation as planned behavior.

At the beginning of the interaction, the topic has not been negotiated, although the therapist has a plan in mind—to carry out a therapy session with the aim of remediating some aspect of J's language disorder, while J has an alternative plan—to play (lines 1 and 2). In line 3 the therapist rejects J's suggestion and restates her own—trying to get J on to the remedial topic. J persists, and when in line 5 the therapist diverts and follows up J's topic, J changes the topic again, suggesting that R should come to the therapy room. J persists with his plans for "playing" and "R" and the therapist responds until they both reach a point at which the topic can go no further (lines 18-22). By now the therapist has reintroduced the remedial topic and this time it is successful. It is interesting to note that J's topic had to be followed through and brought to a complete collaborative ending, and that the therapist temporarily gave up her topic. In other words, for this part of the interaction at least topic selection was under the child's control. Indeed, J introduced three topics in this first part of the interaction. At line 2, he introduced "play", at line 6 "R Ramsay". It is not easy to discern the relationship between these topics, although their disruptive effect on the therapist's plan is obvious.

A second example (lines 24-27) further illustrates this issue. The therapist starts her remedial topic in line 24 but J introduces something different in line 25. This time J's topic is "touched off" by the fact that the therapy materials for the lesson have been colored with a writing pencil. J's response is only tangentially related to what is expected of him. Again the therapist takes up J's topic, makes his contribution appear appropriate and through it reintroduces the remedial topic (lines 26-27).

A similar situation arises in lines 31-39 and 61-82. In lines 61-82 there was a great deal of competition for the choice of topic. The therapist made three unsuccessful attempts to get a response to her topic and had to give in to J until he appeared to be satisfied that his suggestion had been carried through. Finally, in lines 244-246, there was again a brief disagreement about topics. J suggested going back to the classroom, but the therapist had just introduced the topic of counting the fish. The therapist incorporated both topics in her next utterance and the topic of counting was allowed to continue.

As has emerged in this qualitative analysis of the samples, J was able to impose his will on the interaction as far as topic selection was concerned. Although the therapist tried several times to initiate the topic, she was persuaded to follow J's lead—in fact, it was only by remaining cooperative that she was able to reconcile the conflict between maintaining some degree of conversational spontaneity while at the same time not losing complete control over the dialogue. Thus the therapist was able to compensate to some extent for J's ineffectiveness as a conversational partner and to give to the dialogue the appearance of successful communication resulting from collaboration in the selection of topics. If we probe deeper, however, we will find that there is miscommunication at a deeper level. In order to do this, we need to consider the mental states of the participants as they engage in this interaction.

Beliefs and Plans in Dialogue

The analysis in the previous section could have given rise to the conclusion that J was simply unwilling to contribute to a topic of someone else's choosing. This would not be dissimilar to many classroom situations when pupils are unwilling to comply with the teacher's agenda. Indeed, the ability to evade unwelcome topics is often seen as the mark of an astute politician in televised interviews. In J's case, however, it is not clear whether he has clearly defined goals in this sense, because he occasionally makes inappropriate responses in exchanges where he has chosen the topic (for example, lines 18-19), so that his problem seems to be more than a simple case of being determined to pursue his own goals regardless of his conversational partner. In order to pursue this point in greater depth, we will examine the dialogue from two viewpoints—first in terms of the therapist's goals and beliefs and then in terms of the child's perspective.

The Therapist's Goals

We can begin with the assumption that a person planning to engage in a conversation has some high-level goals to achieve which provide the motivation for engaging in the conversation in the first place. Examples of such goals could be: to find out some information, to get someone else to carry out a desired action, or, as in the case of much casual conversation, to be sociable or simply to pass the time. In the case of a more structured interaction such as a clinician-patient interview, we can assume that the clinician has goals such as remediating the patient's language disorder, which will first require a diagnoise of the disorder. Typically the diagnosis as well as the remediation will be effected by engaging the patient in conversation, either to elicit samples of talk for analysis or to provide opportunities for practice. These are very basic assumptions that underlie speech-therapeutic discourse. A major property of this type of discourse, which is shared by other discourse types such as teacher-pupil talk in second-language classrooms (see McTear, 1978) is that the purpose of the talk is to focus on the talk itself, not to achieve some external goal such as the general conversational goals described earlier.

These then are the high-level goals that will determine how the therapist plans the details of the therapy session. During the actual session he or she is likely to be guided by these global goals, even if temporarily distracted from them as happens in this example. In this case, in order to operationalize these goals the therapist has chosen some pictures that she wishes to use as a means of eliciting talk with J. More specifically, she will plan to introduce each picture, get J to say something about it, respond to what he says, and then move on to the next picture, and so on through the remainder of the pictures. In so doing she may use various discourse strategies, such as frames and focusing moves (Sinclair & Coulthard, 1975) to direct J's attention to the discourse topic she has in mind (line 1), and she may also attempt to provide links between the topics represented in the pictures as well as generalizing the topic to some aspect of J's experience. The therapist's plan at the beginning of the session can thus be represented in a tree-like structure as in Figure 10.1.

Although this structure provides a representation at a simple level of the therapist's plan for how the session might be ideally conducted, as in all conversational encounters planning has to be opportunistic—that is it has to be able to deal with input from a changing and unpredictable world, in particular, with the responses and reactions of other conversational participants. Even thought the therapist has some degree of control over the therapy session, she is unlikely to be able to conduct the session without compromising her goals to fit with the behaviors of the patient. At a micro level this might involve spending more time on an item that is causing local difficulty, such as the articulation of a particular word or the clarification of a message. At a higher level it might involve negotiation of the topic, as happens in the examples quoted here. In principle, discussion could also focus on the highest level goals—for example, the purpose of the therapy, why the therapist has chosen to conduct the session in this way—though this would appear to be rare, certainly as far as therapy sessions with young children are concerned.

Thus, from the therapist's perspective, a therapy session is a planned course of action to achieve predetermined goals. For the plan to proceed successfully, the patient should be prepared to adopt the therapist's goals and to cooperate with them. Whether such behavior is likely to enhance remediation of the patient's language problem is beyond the scope of the questions being addressed here.

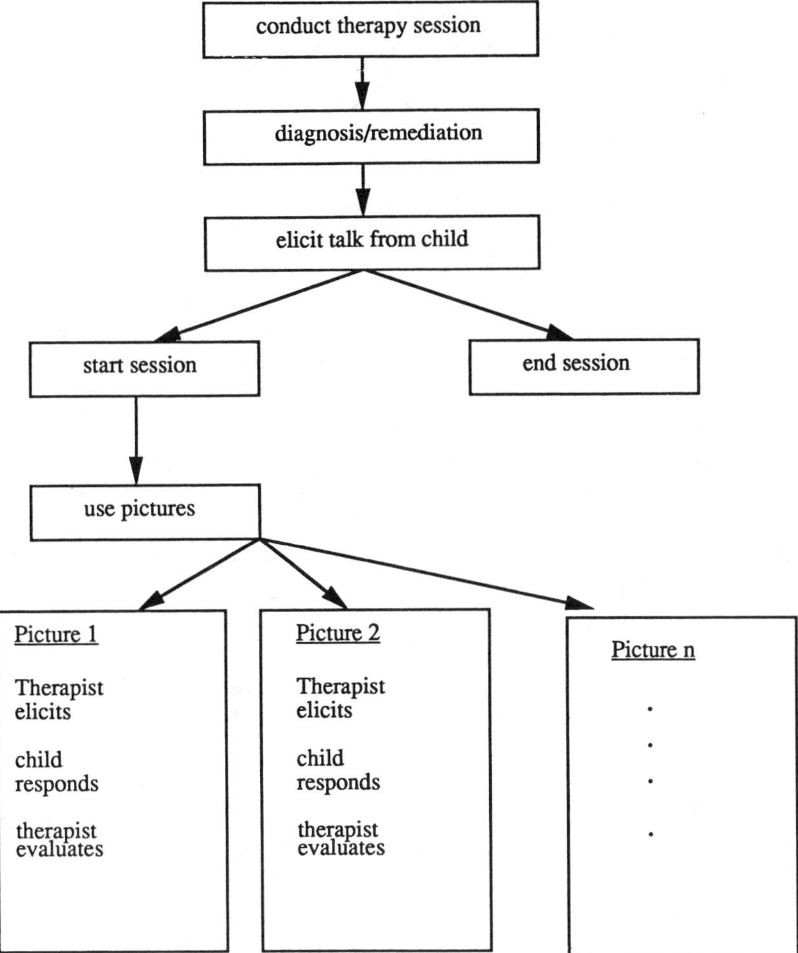

Figure 10.1 The Therapist's Ideal Plan for the Session

Looking at the Conversation from J's Perspective

Let us now look at the conversation from J's perspective. At this point we should indicate that our analysis is only suggestive, because we have no direct access to J's perspective and must base our analysis on an interpretation of the data available to us – how J behaves in the interview. Although recognizing the difficulty – indeed the impossibility – of accessing J's perspective accurately, we would argue that some attempt to consider what his goals in the interview might be, based on the most principled data available, is a necessary step in the explanation of miscommunication in terms of discrepant mental states.

In the case of J it is less easy to propose a set of high-level goals similar to those of the speech therapist. As far as a child of J's age is concerned, it is unlikely that he would view the encounter in the same way as the therapist—that is as an opportunity to diagnose or remediate his language disorder. Indeed, it might be an implicit goal of the therapist to conceal the fact that the purpose of the session is to focus on his language, because knowledge of such a goal might impede his language performance during the session. (With adults the situation is different, although even here it is an interesting question whether patients are aware of the extent to which their performance in interviews with therapists is treated as a basis for analysis rather than as a means of communication.)

Assuming then that J is unaware of the therapist's highest level goals, we can ask to what extent this might affect his awareness of her lower level plans. For example: When she introduces the pictures, or when she asks a question about a particular picture, what does J believe about the therapist's goals? In particular, what does he believe that she wants him to do, assuming for the moment that he has a desire to be cooperative? Again, we stress that we cannot answer this question directly, because we do not have access to J's mind, although we can make suggestions based on what J says. For example: In the first part of the transcript (lines 1-21) J is mainly concerned with opting out of the therapist's plan to discuss the pictures, by suggesting an alternative plan—play. The exact nature of J's plan is unclear, however, as the subsequent discourse indicates. He suggests playing with D, then introduces R, apparently suggesting that R should come to the therapy room. The dialogue becomes confused to the extent that, on the surface, it looks as if J believes that the therapist is called R (lines 10-21). A likely interpretation can be found, however, if we examine line 10. Here J responds to the therapist's assertion "I'm going to play with 'you J' (stress on *you*), with 'play with 'you R', to which the therapist responds 'I'm not R'. This gives rise to a confused sequence in which J seems to confirm that he believes that the therapist is called R. However, a different interpretation for line 109, and one that is consonant with a potential plan of opting out of the therapy session at this point, is that he wants the therapist to play with R. Once this suggestion has been misinterpreted, J is unable to break out of the misunderstanding and simply reacts to the therapist's questions by providing responses that attend to local coherence but do not attend to external reality nor to the more global goals of the conversation. To clarify: To a *yes/no* question, J provides the answer *yeh* (lines 13-14), and to a *who* question he provides a name (lines

15-16). Taken as isolated exchanges these responses are correct, yet in the context of the session as a whole and of external reality they are inappropriate. What this suggests is that J's behavior is mainly reactive and locally driven. He responds to the therapist, but often only at the local level of her utterance, rather than in terms of her more global plans. This strategy means that he will be able to cope effectively with more superficial aspects of conversation, such as taking his turn or making minor self repairs. It also means that, once he adopts the therapist's goal of discussing the pictures, his responses will tend to be more appropriate, as was the case for longer stretches of the discourse.

J, however, was not always cooperative in this sense and, as was pointed out in the previous section, there were several more cases of topic conflict. These examples show a similar pattern to the one analyzed here, in that J introduces a topic unrelated to the therapist's current goal and conversation ensues that is coherent only at a local level (e.g., discussion about the table in lines 32-39). A striking example occurs in lines 61-82 in which for some of the time the therapist is confused as to what J is talking about so that she is not even able at first to go along with his topic with the aim of eventually leading him back to her own topic.

Conclusions

We are now in a position to summarize the main points of this chapter and then to draw some more general conclusions concerning miscommunication in clinical contexts.

We have taken the view that conversation can be viewed as planned behavior in which the participants have high-level goals that they implement in terms of lower level plans. For example: In a therapy interview the therapist has high-level goals such as remediation and attempts to achieve these by creating situations in which the patient produces talk. At the lowest level this will involve the therapist in asking and responding to what the patient says. The patient is faced with these low-level actions, but in order to respond to them appropriately he or she might need to know what lies behind the therapist's questions. This would enable the patient, for example, to understand that an apparently unmotivated question might have the goal of eliciting a verbal response rather than the more usual goal of attempting to elicit information. However, as can be seen from the analysis presented in the previous sections, miscommunication can occur at various levels. At the lower levels, miscommunication is likely to be easier to resolve. In the case examined here, problems seemed to occur not only at the higher levels—the inability of the patient to discern the therapist's more global goals — but also at interactions between the levels, that is, an inability to see how the therapist's individual actions were motivated by higher-level goals. Thus the miscommunication that has been described in this sample of clinician-child discourse can be seen in terms of a more general view of conversation as planned behavior.

The situations that we have described here can arise in any communicative situation, so that miscommunication can be predicted at any point where it is possible for the mental states of the participant — that is their goals and beliefs — to diverge. It would be helpful, however, to be able to characterize what clinical situations have in common and how they differ from other communicative contexts.

We begin with the observation that, for successful communication to be possible, there has to be some common ground. This common ground includes the assumption of shared perspectives with respect to general world knowledge, of similar processes of commonsense reasoning, and of a shared linguistic system in which to encode messages. If there are problems with this common ground, then miscommunication is likely. Once again, such situations may arise in nonpathological situations. For example: Two people may have different perspectives on some piece of general world knowledge or they may apply different processes of reasoning (see Johnson-Laird, 1983 for some discussion of these issues). Similarly, people may have different linguistic systems which give rise to miscommunication (see Milroy, 1984). Various degrees of miscommunication may thus arise because of these incompatibilities.

If we turn to pathological cases, however, as in speech therapy or psychiatric interviews, then we encounter situations in which one of the participants presents with communicative problems that are recognized as abnormal. In the case of children with semantic-pragmatic disorders, the problems appear to be in the domains of unusually inadequate world knowledge or deficient reasoning processes. Abnormal reasoning processes and odd associations also characterize the communication of patients in psychiatric interviews, although not necessarily for the same reasons. In contrast, in the case of children with syntactic and phonological disorders and of adults with disorders such as aphasia, the problems are mainly at the linguistic level. Communication with the former groups (i.e., children with semantic-pragmatic disability and patients with psychiatric disorders) is problematic because the mental states of the patients, in terms of their goals for the conversation and their beliefs which underlie what they say and how they interpret their interlocutor's utterances, are not easily reconcilable with the mental states of more normal communicators. With the latter group (children with language impairment at the syntactic or phonological levels, or adults with similar difficulties), it is usually the case that the patients are willing to communicate and that they have a clear idea of the content of their communication, but that their difficulties are at the stages of encoding and/or decoding. Miscommunication can arise in both cases, but it is more easily resolved in the case of strict linguistic disorders because there is common ground at a higher level. In contrast, communication with pragmatically disordered children and psychiatric patients is more difficult because there is less common ground. Thus even when the message is linguistically well formed and fluently articulated, the therapist is less likely to be able to arrive at an interpretation of the message because there is too wide a discrepancy between the mental state of the therapist and that of the patient.

In conclusion, we have seen that miscommunication can be viewed in terms of a hierarchy. At the highest level we are concerned with interaction between the mental states—that is, the goals, plans, and beliefs—of the participants. These mental states are dynamic structures that change as a result of events such as actions in the world or utterances in a dialogue—events that are subjected to interpretation by each of the participants in terms of their own unique perspective (current mental state). This situation will often give rise to miscommunication, given discrepancies between mental states. A further potentially contributory factor is the nature of the transmission channel—whether the message is distorted in some way, although, as we have seen, such distortion is not sufficient to predict miscommunication.

Taking this view of communication in terms of mental states we can make predictions about the extent to which miscommunication might arise in clinical situations as a function of the type of disorder the patient presents. At the same time we can locate such miscommunication within a continuum stretching from largely successful through to grossly pathological communicative encounters, thus providing a basis for a more functional approach to the diagnosis and treatment of communicative disorders. Furthermore, by adopting an interpretative view of communication as an interactionally negotiated achievement, we can explain the disparity between the extent of well-formedness of a message and the degree of miscommunication that arises in a communicative situation.

We hope that, through our analysis of Extract 1 as well as our informal presentation of a model of communication, we have been able to shed some light on the nature of miscommunication. Clinical contexts provide a useful basis for the study of miscommunication because the difficulties that arise are more obvious and more frequent. This does not necessarily mean that they are more amenable to analysis, however. For example: In studies of miscommunication between adults, Gumperz and Tannen (1979) used the technique of interviewing the participants afterwards to discover their views on the miscommunication. Although such retrospective analysis of communication is itself fraught with reliability problems, it is impossible to implement in the clinical cases we have been describing. Given that the mental states of the patients are so out of touch with normal expectations, any attempt to elicit their reflections on miscommunications arising from discrepancies between their own and others' mental states would lead to infinite regress.

We see two ways forward. On the one hand, there is a need for a formal model of communication that defines the structures and processes of communication in terms of mental states. The origins of such a model are to be found in the work of philosophers of language such as Grice, and have been developed in theories of communication such as Sperber and Wilson's (1985) relevance theory. Work in artificial intelligence also contributes to such formal models of communication (see, for example, papers in Reilly, 1987; Reilly, this volume). At the same time there is also a need for more empirical analysis of miscommunication in the types of context we have described, showing how clinical contexts are different from, as well as sharing features with, other communicative contexts. The empirically based approach of the conversation analysts seems to provide a principled methodology for this research (see Levinson, 1983 for a clear discussion). What is missing so far, however, is an attempt to integrate the formal and the empirical approaches, largely because they are perceived by proponents of each side to be incompatible. What we would argue is that formal models are necessary to provide an explicit account of communication and a firm theoretical basis for empirical enquiry, and empirical studies are necessary both to validate the formal models and to suggest where they require modification. Thus future work that integrates formal and empirical approaches will contribute to the understanding of miscommunication in clinical and other contexts and will provide both theoretical and practical benefits for all who are interested in the dynamics of interpersonal communication.

11

Social Interaction and the Recycling of Legal Evidence

Karin Aronsson

Miscommunication in Legal Settings

The legal process bridges the gulf between the disorder of lived disputes and the order of the written law. In judicial settings, this tension between order and disorder manifests itself in various types of problematic talk. Much is at stake in legal settings and the problematicity of verbal discourse is often more evident than in everyday interaction.

Legal processes vary in different cultures (Andenaes, 1968; Bohannon, 1967; Danet, 1980b). Presently, I will focus on some features of legal setting interactions that may generate miscommunication. Cultural variation itself, though, falls beyond the scope of the present chapter (see Banks, Gudykunst, Ge, & Baker, this volume). Yet, much of the present discussion will be relevant to many legal systems in that I will emphasize the underlying orality of legal documents such as sentences, trial records, police reports, and so on. The principle of oral examination is a central one in most legal systems. Thus, in trials, "what happened" has to be reconstrued through "what is said". Legal systems tend to have more or less strict procedural rules excluding the use of hearsay evidence. It can be argued that the oral testimonies of trials are, nevertheless, pregnant with traces of ongoing and past dialogues. Courtroom evidence does not exist

---

AUTHORS' NOTE: Nikolas Coupland, Howard Giles, Per Linell, and Ragnar Rommetveit have provided helpful comments on a preliminary draft of this chapter. Thanks are also extended to Per Linell, Viveka Adelswärd, Linda Jönsson, and Claes Nilholm, and to the Swedish District Court, which has been most helpful in our examination of courtroom discourse.

in vacuo. Within an interactional perspective, legal evidence must be interpreted in terms of its "social history". Hence, the testimony that is delivered in court must be understood in terms of the questions that have been posed in court, as well as the questions that have been posed during previous interrogations (police interrogations, probation officers' questioning, etc.) My present point of departure is that the social history is to a great extent the history of past dialogue, including the way questions have been formulated and time-ordered.

In the legal process, evidence is deeply embedded in language use (interrogations, reports) and in stereotypes and conflicting framings of discourse. By compiling findings from conversation analysis, sociolinguistics, and witness psychology, it can be shown how "truth" is at best evasive. It is obvious that witnesses may at times deliberately hide the truth. This will not be dealt with here. Discrediting rhetoric and various strategic uses (and misuses) of legal discourse are not defined here as miscommunication; talk may thus be misleading or problematic without entailing miscommunication. In the present context, I will talk about miscommunication exclusively when the different parties mishear or misconstrue evidence in nondeliberate ways—that is, in the case of genuine misunderstandings and misrepresentations (including mishearings, misquotes, etc.).

In the legal arena, Danet (1980b) has emphasized coercive aspects of courtroom questioning. In contrast, Atkinson and Drew (1979) have emphasized the bureaucratic rationality of courtroom dialogues; how multiparty and other turn-taking requirements shape institutional "coerciveness." Following the critique of Rommetveit (1989) and Rorty (1979), I would argue that traditional speech act models of conversation are often linked to somewhat mechanistic notions of causality. Hence intentions are inferred from utterance types in quite a unidirectional fashion, and discourse style is primarily seen as the product of speaker intentions. Thus a credible testimony style is analyzed as the outward manifestation of honesty or lawful intentions. From the perspective of a more interactional philosophy of language, credibility or control could also be studied as the *products* of social interaction.

My present focus will in fact be on how "truth" is generated and negotiated in different types of legal encounters. I will not discuss whether legal interrogations are "objectively" coercive or not. Instead, I will try to show how legal evidence is partly generated with (problematic) social encounters, and how "truth" (and misrepresentations) are grounded in social negotiations, rather than in speaker intentions alone. First, I will focus on specific processes that explain some types of misrepresentations: the transliteration of oral events into the written register, social attribution in legal settings, and linguistic influences on memory processes. Second, I will offer a time-ordered analysis of legal process interactions that may generate misrepresentations and misunderstandings. Last, I will analyze how legal setting interactions can be construed and misconstrued from different perspectives.

The Bureaucratic Format and the Written Register

The legal trial is circumscribed by written documents, the written law, the summons, the final judgment, as well as the verbatim trial record. Hence, interrogations are intimately linked to written documents, both in police interrogations and in the courtroom. Ultimately, a complex, multi-faceted reality should fit into the strict categories of the written law. Therefore, legal discourse is restricted with respect to topic selection. The legal interrogation is the prime device for bridging the gulf between the precise technical language of the law, and the vagueness and multi-perspectivity of life as lived. Normally, examinations are conducted by professionals who master the rule system, and who can pose the appropriate questions that make "what happened" fit into the strict and precise categories of the law.

Quotes and Misquotes

There are several legal events that highlight the problematic interface between written and oral practices. One such situation is that of reported speech. When speech is reported during interrogations, statements are reconstructed within a new framing. This in itself presents several referential problems for the reporter. In quotes, statements are generally presented in isolation, whereas real-life talk emerges in dialogues.

In a study of police interrogations, Jönsson (1988a, 1988b) has compared written police reports with interview transcriptions showing how police officers quite often recycle disconnected pieces of information into coherent narratives. One device in police narratives is a relatively frequent use of more or less ambiguous quotes. For instance, citation verbs are used in a somewhat misleading fashion. It is said that the suspect "said", or "reported" something when it is often the case that he or she merely confirmed or disconfirmed the policeman's prior statement (and ultimately, the policeman's implicit narrative), for example:

Extract 1a
(Police report on suspect's testimony)

. . . Åberg had nothing against this, but he simultaneously reports that "then I understood that it was all over"

(translated into English from Jönsson, 1988b, p. 701)

The above "quotation" has been derived from a prior police interrogation (Extract 1b).

Extract 1b
(Police interrogation of suspect)

Q: And you were not against it? ((coming along with the police))
A: No.
Q: But then you understood that now it was all over?
A: Well, yes.

(translated into English from Jönsson, 1988b, p. 70)

As can be seen, the suspect merely confirmed the policeman's interrogative statement (whether he was willing to come along with the police). Yet, the ensuing police report (Extract 1a) implies a spontaneous narrative on the part of the suspect. This, in turn would presumably cast the suspect as somewhat more remorseful, which may have a favorable effect on the court.

Jönsson demonstrates how the police at times use quotation marks in another ambiguous ways, for example:

Extract 2
(Police report on alleged theft)

. . . Klasson mentioned that he could "borrow" the car that belonged to Berggren.

(Jönsson, 1988b, p. 69)

In this extract, the police officer does not quote the suspect. He apparently wished to bracket his own (police report) use of jargon. The quotation marks thus set off colloquialisms or jargon from institutional language or the written register. In these cases (Extracts 1a; 1b, and 2), policemen's misquotes can be seen as part of a police rhetoric which may ultimately serve to produce more coherent and more convincing or more lively narratives. There are no indications in Jönsson's study (1988a, 1988b) that the police deliberately try to use ambiguity in an intentionally deceitful fashion. Rather, ambiguous quotation practices form part of routine transliterations of oral events into written language.

Misleading use of quotes can also be found in other courtroom contexts. Quotes bear the hallmark of literal concreteness and "authenticity". Moreover, quotes in court have rhetorical (at times dramatic) qualities, possibly signaling not only the wordings but also the attitudes of the original speaker (see also Liebes-Plesner, 1984). In a case study of reported speech in an adversarial U.S. legal context, Philips (1985) has documented how an indirect courtroom testimony is recycled into "quotes". The two opposing parties both transformed a police witness's reported speech into direct but somewhat different "quotes". Yet, the defense lawyer conserved the essential features of the indirect reported speech, whereas the prosecutor produced quotes that misrepresented the order of events in a way that carried negative implications for the defendant (Philips, 1985). Obviously, the misleading exactness of false quotes (misquotes) may be employed more or less deceitfully and more or less successfully in the service of adversary rhetoric.

Courtroom Interpreting and the Misrepresentation of Testimony Style

Literal truth is important in the legal process. In real life it may, however, be difficult to trace if statements are recycled into less literal ones. When the court employs interpreters, testimonies are necessarily transformed. Yet, translations may, of course, be more or less literal. In a pioneering investigation, Berk-Seligson (1987) analyzed more than two thousand question-answer sequences from North American criminal trials, comparing the English translations with their Spanish originals. In general, it could be shown that the interpreters changed the responses into lengthier ones. This, in turn, produced a greater relative frequency of hypercorrections, hedges, polite forms, meaningless particles, and so on. In many cases, quite assertive responses were transformed into more polite, more hesitant, less definitive testimonies. Thus, the Spanish "un promedio de veintiuno" was, for instance, transformed into "uh probably an average of twenty-one people". The interpreter's transformation of testimony styles could also be seen in the very opening of the examination. For instance, a question about country of citizenship was answered quite briefly in Spanish as "Mexico", but rendered as "I am a citizen of Mexico" in English; that is, a more formal style, more like that of written than spoken language. It can thus be seen how testimonies subtly shift into a different testimony style than that which the witness employs in his or her native language. As has been argued in the conversational analysis of courtroom discourse, style is intimately linked to assessments of evasiveness versus sincerity, credibility, and so on (e.g., Atkinson & Drew, 1979;

Brannigan & Lynch, 1987; O'Barr, 1982), which, in turn, means that style shifts may change the court's assessment of the witness's credibility.

Language Use and Speaker Evaluations

Testimony Style and Credibility Estimates

In some recent work Berk-Seligson (1988, 1989) has employed a speech evaluation design with a matched-guise technique investigating listeners' evaluations of nonnative speakers. The nonnative witness's testimony has been kept constant, varying only the interpreter's use of politeness markers such as "sir" (Berk-Seligson, 1988) or the interpreter's use of hyperformal language (Berk-Seligson, 1989). In the evaluation studies, Berk-Seligson found that jurors consistently evaluated the formal style as more credible ("trustworthy", or "competent", "intelligent") than an informal style. That is, polite or hyper-formal styles were more successful in the courtroom setting than less polite or less formal registers (Berk-Seligson, 1988; 1989). On the other hand, Berk-Seligson (1989) points out that the hyperformal style is more smooth, more narrative-like (less fragmented) than the informal style. Similarly, politeness markers may mitigate very brief yes/no responses which may otherwise give a somewhat rude or noncooperative impression. Thus, Berk-Seligson's results need not necessarily contradict some of O'Barr's (1982) reasoning on the negative evaluations of politeness and hyper-formal indicators within a "powerless" testimony style.

In any case, Berk-Seligson's evaluation studies have produced conclusive evidence that court interpreters may (unwittingly) recycle testimonies in such ways that mock jurors judge the same nonnative witness as significantly more or significantly less credible. A second major finding is that this general effect holds also in those cases where the mock juror knows some Spanish him- or herself. That is, a juror is affected by the interpreter's stylistic variations—and not only by those of the witness—even in those cases where the juror is indeed able to understand the language of delivery in the original testimony. Such a result illuminates the intrinsically variable constitution of "truth" in a multiparty setting with different testimony styles and with speakers wittingly or unwittingly up- and down-grading the good standing of participants.

Berk-Seligson's speech evaluation design is related to that of O'Barr (1982) who has investigated standard versus nonstandard varieties of testimony styles in relation to speaker evaluations. In a series of experiments, Conley, Lind and O'Barr with collaborators have shown how different testimony styles condition jury perceptions of credibility (Lind & O'Barr, 1979; O'Barr, 1982). Drawing on ethnographic insights and authentic trial transcripts, the researchers have edited tapes in such a way that it has been possible to compare the original (nonstandard style) with a standard style. The experimental videotapes contrast three sets of styles: powerless versus powerful style, hypercorrect versus formal style, and fragmented versus narrative style.

Powerless style refers to a relatively prominent use of hedges (e.g., "sort of"), hesitation forms (e.g., pause fillers "uh"), meaningless forms ("well"), intensifiers (e.g., "very", "surely"), and polite speech ("sir"). Powerless male and female witnesses were assessed as less credible than powerful witnesses (less convincing, less trustworthy, less intelligent, etc.). For a methodological critique, see Bradac and Mulac (1984). *Hypercorrect style* is defined in terms of overly formal language (cf. O'Barr's example " . . . But I, I relapsed into a comatose state, and I, I can't remember anything after that for the next 72 hours or so": O'Barr, 1982, p. 84). Theoretically, this style may appear overly anxious or ingratiating. This expectation was borne out in the results as mock jurors evaluated hypercorrect witnesses as less convincing and less competent than witnesses speaking in a less formal style (O'Barr, 1982).

Similarly, the *fragmented style* was not highly evaluated by mock jurors (O'Barr, 1982). Witnesses who employ this style offer information in a piecemeal fashion. O'Barr exemplifies with two excerpts from the experimental tapes. In both cases, the judge has posed a WH-question about time. The narrative style response is "Well, I was working from, uh, 7 a.m. to 3 p.m. I arrived at the store at 6:30 and opened the store at 7." This can be compared to the authentic much briefer fragmented style response "Well, I was working from 7 a.m. to 3 p.m." (Extract 3):

Extract 3
(Lawyer questioning witness)

Q: Now, calling your attention to the twenty-first day of November, a Saturday, what were your working hours that day?
A: Well, I was working from 7 to 3.
Q: Was that 7 a.m.?
A: Yes
Q. At what time that day did you arrive at the store?
A: 6:30
Q: 6:30. And did, uh, you open the store at 7 o'clock?
A: Yes, it has to be opened by then.

(O'Barr, 1982, pp. 76-77)

In the case of a fragmented testimony style (Extract 3, above), it thus takes three more questions from the judge to extract the same amount of information that the narrative style witness produced spontaneously in one single Q-A sequence. The fragmented testimony style had somewhat different effects on different groups of jurors, but on the whole, testimonies in the fragmented style lead to lower credibility estimates.

These experimental findings tie in with observations in authentic legal settings. Drawing on observations of Austrian traffic court trials, Wodak (1980) maintains that working class defendants tend to produce fragmented responses, which are less well received than more narrative speech. Of course, nonstandard language can not per se be seen as a type of miscommunication. Yet, nonstandard style may generate miscommunication if the witness unintentionally produces a misrepresentative self-presentation, less credible, less competent than what could be inferred from the facts in the particular case. Hence, misrepresentations can be identified from an observer perspective in cases where neither speaker not listener need be aware of any miscommunication.

Nonnative Speakers and Misrepresentations

In Berk-Seligson's (1987) courtroom observations, interpreters were employed. In real life, trials with nonnative speakers often proceed without the assistance of interpreters. Often the witness may (rightly or wrongly) give the impression that he or she is indeed quite fluent and comfortable in his or her second language.

In a case study of a perjury case, Gumperz (1982b) shows how the responses of the nonnative defendant (of Philippine origin) were probably misunderstood by his Anglo North American interrogators. A close analysis of the hearing transcripts reveals that this highly educated nonnative, a medical doctor, does not always mean what he appears to at first glance. In this specific case, the result is that the doctor seems to assert that he had seen a particular photograph (important evidence) which he had actually not seen before the first hearing, and so on. Similarly, he appears to say that he had indeed noted sunken eyes (signs of child abuse) which he had previously denied seeing:

Extract 4
(U.S. Navy hearing of defendant (Dr. A) in perjury case).

Q: What steps did you take to determine that? ((dehydration)) If it was there or absent?

A: When the child came, I initially examined the patient and I noted the moistness of the tongue, sunken eyes, the skin color, and everything was okay.
Q: Are you suggesting that there were no sunken eyes?
A: No
Q: I think we better slow down a little bit more and make sure the record. . . did you observe sunken eyes?

(Gumperz, 1982b, p. 176).

In this analysis of this sequence in a lengthier transcript, Gumperz (1982b) demonstrates how Dr. A seems to contradict himself. On the one hand, he "noted sunken eyes" and, on the other "everything was okay". Moreover, Dr. A's first "no" is ambiguous. In this sequence, it eventually takes two more questions to disambiguate Dr. A's initial ambiguous reply. Gumperz (1982b) convincingly demonstrates how Dr. A often uses language in a way that may appear inconsistent or evasive, and how ensuing misunderstandings between Dr. A and the interrogators may well explain part of the initial perjury charge (which was, in fact, ultimately dismissed by the jurors).

As a complement to the Dr. A case, it is instructive to analyze some findings by Lane (1985), who studied nine nonnative witnesses (of Samoan, Cook Island, and Nivean origin) who all spoke fluently and in quite well-formed sentences. Counsel and judges evidently felt that these nonnative speakers coped adequately without interpreters. Yet, a close reading of the trial transcripts reveals that the witnesses, in fact, do not seem to grasp some of the questions during the cross-examinations. Evidently, cross-examinations may exacerbate language difficulties in such a way that nonnative witnesses do not fully understand the legal professionals' questioning. These communication difficulties, in turn, produced inconsistent and evasive responses on the part of the nonnative witnesses. It can thus be seen how nonnative speakers may become involved in misunderstandings because of defective comprehension (Lane, 1985) or because of nonnative ways of speaking (Gumperz, [1982b], and Gass & Varonis, this volume) or any combination thereof. Beach (1985) has documented part of the cognitive background in demonstrating how legal interrogations tend to involve substantial time-traveling; references to the alleged crime as well as references to past crimes or other events of the distant past, interfoliated with references to the immediate past (e.g., prior statements during the same trial). Criminal events also tend to involve sets of personages and pronoun references that can at times be ambiguous (Shuy, 1986). Such time-traveling seriously taxes witnesses' language competence and it is, obviously, even more demanding for nonnative speakers who do not always master important nuances that entail such phenomena as facticity or choice of verb tense. To quite a high extent, examinations tend to involve both problematic sequential implications and problematic reference (see Schegloff, 1987b, on misunderstandings).

Nonstandard Dialects and Guilt Attributions

In general, standard varieties of speech are more favorably evaluated than nonstandard varieties. Hence, standard varieties are associated with competence (e.g., credibility, intelligence, ambition), whereas nonstandard varieties are less favorably evaluated – even by nonstandard speakers themselves (Giles, Hewstone, Ryan, & Johnson, 1987). In the foregoing, I have primarily discussed referential problems related to interactions where a nonnative speaker is assumed (mistakenly) to be fully competent in the majority language. Moreover, different nonnative accents may of course be related to stereotypical evaluations of different social or ethnic groups. Through use of the matched-guise technique, it has been shown that listeners in legal settings may evaluate different accents differently. For instance, Received Pronunciation of English (R.P.) and broad Australian accents are associated with different attributions of guilt (Seggie, 1983) in that the Australian accent was significantly associated with crimes of violence (versus the crime of embezzlement in the case of R.P. English).

Silence as Evidence

As I emphasized at the outset, legal evidence is deeply embedded in social interaction and hence in social evaluations (and stereotypes). In legal settings, any act can take on legal significance, and any act can be interpreted from conflicting perspectives. This means that any communicative act is pregnant with multiple meanings and can, in consequence, embody a type of miscommunication (from the viewpoint of one or another of the opposing parties or from an observer's perspective).

A witness may remain silent for large portions of the examination or respond reluctantly (after some delay). Yet, there is no way that he or she can escape the legal professionals' and the lay judges' evaluations. Silence can take on alternative meanings, though, as in the following conflicting reports of the prosecutor's witness's testimony in a rape case:

Extract 5
(Conflicting interpretations of prosecutor's witness)

Prosecutor:
This experience of being here in court was a most difficult experience for this young woman. You saw her embarrassment as you heard her describe how she was raped. Think of how difficult it was to go to the police in the first place. Think of what it must have been like when. . . How would you react if you were in her place?

Defense lawyers:
You saw how slow the prosecution witness was to testify. Was it perhaps because she didn't know the answers or the questions she was asked? Was it because it didn't happen the way she says? Or, perhaps, because it didn't happen at all?

(O'Barr, 1982, pp. 109-110)

In the above extract, what is unsaid can be interpreted in terms of embarrassment (prosecution) or evasiveness (defense). These two interpretations of silence are mutually exclusive. Either one of the opponent readings is, of course, highly relevant as evidence. Silence can also be interpreted as a pause for thought, that is as a response to referential complexity. As discussed, trials tend to entail complex sequential implicatures, and problematic reference. Walker (1985) has studied pausing by witnesses during pretrial dispositions and the effects of pausing on lawyers' interpretations. Her data show how lawyers may read silence as a pause for thought (same side witness) or as a pause for concealment (witness for the other side). She also documents how witnesses may be at risk if they violate the standing rules of legal proceedings at any point (e.g., if they interrupt the legal professionals). Negative attributions of one factor tend to lead to misattribution about others. In general, silent pauses are more likely to lead to judgments of concealment or hesitancy, whereas filled pauses do not. Yet, if lawyers detect signs of "bad attitude" in a witness they tend to misattribute hesitancy to this witness even when the "objective" pausing behavior does not warrant any such attribution.

Objective "facts" and subjective attributions are necessarily difficult to disentangle in trials. Within interrogations, much of what is said can be interpreted as blame pre-sequences (Atkinson & Drew, 1979). Silence must be read in terms of the sequential implications of questions within this blaming context of the trial process. Superficially innocuous questions may be understood/misunderstood as blamings. In fine-grained analyses of pauses and delays in courtroom responses, Atkinson and Drew (1979) demonstrate how minute delays on the part of the interrogator can (rightly or wrongly) be interpreted as impatience or disbelief by the witness (Extract 6).

Extract 6
(Counsel interrogating witness in rape trial.)

Q: Now wasn't it true whooah (1.5) Miss Le Brette that uh (2.5) the area where that car stopped isuh (2.5) some distance from any house (0.5) isn't that so?
(2.5)

A: Yeh

(drawn from Atkinson & Drew, 1979, pp. 200-201)

In the above extract, the first two pauses can be seen as part of the counsel's speech planning. On the other hand, the second pause (2.5) and the ensuing tag can be interpreted by the witness as bullying and impatience on the part of the counsel. Rightly or wrongly, silence can thus be attributed to discrediting intent on the part of the opponent lawyer or to concealment on the part of the witness (see also Drew, in press).

Language Use and the Recycling of Evidence

Labeling and Misrepresentations

According to procedural rules, leading questions are allowed in cross-examinations (more adversarial contexts) but not in direct examinations. Through the use of leading questions, evidence can be retrieved from forgetful, reluctant, or inarticulate witnesses and displayed to the court. By the same token, "facts" may be fabricated or distorted, and witnesses may express viewpoints that are not their own.

Psychologists have paid attention to leading questions for quite a long time. Muscio (1915) showed how the interrogator's use of the definite article influenced subjects' testimonies. Similar results have been obtained more recently by Loftus and Zanni (1975) who showed that the definite article (e.g., "Did you see *THE* truck?" rather than "Did you see *A* truck?" produces a greater number of false recognitions. Loftus (1976) has also shown how the tag question (the prototypical leading question) works more suggestively than the direct question with inverted word order. Thus, subjects would more often confirm the false presence of specific objects after being asked "You did see a bicycle, didn't you?" than after being asked "Did you see a bicycle?"

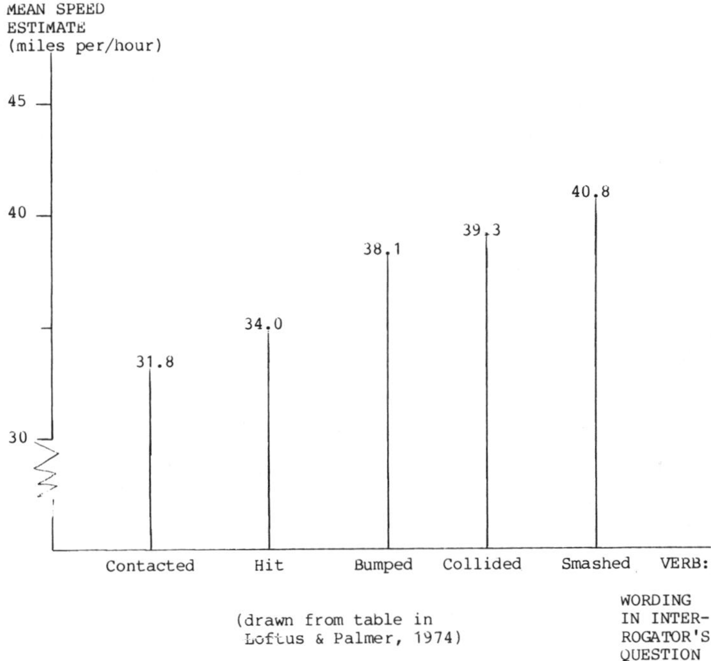

Figure 11.1 Interrogator's Wordings and Recycling of Speed Testimonies

Blatantly suggestive questioning tends to be ruled out in court. Yet, suggestive labelings work also when they are more subtle. It has, for instance, been shown that length estimates can be affected by small differences in interrogators' wordings, such as "How tall/short was the basketball player?" or "How long/short was the movie?" (Harris, 1973). In both cases, those subjects who were asked questions in the marked form ("short") also offered significantly smaller estimates. In a classic experiment, Loftus and Palmer (1974) exposed their subjects to the same film, and then posed different questions to different subjects, varying only the verb in the target questions. The experiment demonstrated how witnesses offer systematically different speed estimates depending on the interrogator's choice of words in the question "How fast did the cars go when they contacted/hit/bumped/collided/smashed into each other?" (see Figure 11.1).

As Figure 11.1 shows, the mean speed estimates vary with the interrogator's choice of verb. Yet, all subjects have seen the same cars, moving at the same speed. The interrogator's wordings may thus shape—and recycle—subjects' initial perceptions of the evidence. Some subjects are more easily influenced than others, and some linguistic choices may have a stronger effect than others. The most important point, in the present context, is that misrepresentations can be traced to labeling in the interview situation. Recycling is thus interactionally grounded.

In a related memory experiment, it has been shown how listeners make little difference between implicit statements on the one hand, and assertions on the other; for instance, the implicit statement "He RAN up to the burglar alarm"was at times remembered as an assertion, that is "He RANG the burglar alarm" (Harris, Teske, & Ginns, 1975). Listening is a constructive affair, and implications may be remembered as assertions.

These findings, like those of Loftus, demonstrate how memory works selectively and creatively, forming coherent stories out of disconnected questions, implications, and perceived "facts". Thus, memory works constructively without necessarily differentiating sharply between past events and wordings in questioning (Loftus, 1975) or between assertions and implications (Harris et al., 1975). Likewise, contextual implications may at times be as suggestive as syntax-based or labeling type implications. Theoretically, this makes good sense in terms of constructivist models of memory (Bartlett, 1932; Neisser, 1982) or story framework models of courtroom discourse (Bennet, 1978; Bennet & Feldman, 1981; Caesar-Wolf, 1984). The experimental constructivist findings are also congruent with case study reports of authentic criminal cases (Trankell, 1972, 1982).

Misrepresentations and Past Dialogues

Legal questioning and answering is related to latent or manifest implications concerning crucial events. These implications can also be grounded in *past* dialogues. In a further series of studies, Loftus and her collaborators have shown how witnesses are unwittingly influenced by the implications of questioning in prior interviews. In the Loftus and Palmer study (1974), no question was initially asked about broken glass (nor did the filmed scenes include any broken glass). Yet, the "smashed"-condition group subjects would significantly more often report the presence of broken glass than the subjects in the "hit" group. In a related experiment, subjects were asked whether they had "noticed the demonstrators GESTURING/THREATENING?" (after seeing a film about demonstrations). Again, the more emotive verb resulted in stronger assessments (Loftus, Altman, & Geballe, 1975).

In several experiments on the effects of postevent information, Loftus (1975) has introduced novel (fraudulent) information into her questioning, suggesting the presence of objects or persons that were in fact not present in the original event. In one experiment, a group of 7 was referred to as a group of 12 or 4. For instance, the question "Was the leader of the 12 a male?" would significantly increase group size estimates in future interrogations. In a parallel experiment, the interrogator referred to a stop sign that did not exist in the target event. Again, some subjects introduced this type of novel postevent information into their responses, referring to the "stop sign" in their future testimonies. Loftus has also varied the question format. Again, embedded false implications affected subjects' later retrieval more than direct questioning (see the summary of findings in Table 11.1).

Loftus primarily discusses leading versus nonleading questions in her summing up of these experiments, focusing on how postevent information is integrated into later recollections. Yet, a closer scrutiny of the above results reveals that there is also a primacy effect for "nonleading" (direct) questions (when compared to the "no question" control group). As can be seen, twice as many subjects report false objects if they have previously been asked about this object, even when the question had been asked in a "nonleading" form (confirmations of the false presence of a bus, a truck, or a barn; first two questions and the last question in Table 11.1). I would argue that this finding is an important one. Evidently, the very act of questioning subjects about specific objects may affect their later recollections—even when the question is formulated as an innocuous nonleading one. If we analyze questions contextually, any question in an interrogative situation will be likely to alert the subject to its possible truth value (and later on, this type of information will not always be distinguished from factual events). By merely being exposed to questions, subjects' recollections may thus become contaminated. It can thus be seen how evidence is construed and recycled against a background of prior social interactions. Evidence is affected by past dialogues, as well as by ongoing dialogues, and it is thus meaningful to try to reconstrue the social history of specific testimonies.

Negotiations in Legal Settings: Truth and Equivocations as Interactional Accomplishments

In the foregoing, I have primarily discussed misrepresentations grounded in the less-than-perfect processing of information (memory distortions, misattributions, etc.; see the two preceding sections). Obviously, such misrepresentations could occur even if all parties concerned were neutral or disinterested. Yet, legal processes do not take place in a moral vacuum. Trials are multiparty events with conflicting interests.

Table 11.1 Different Types of Initial Interview Questions and Percentage Later Confirmations of Nonpresent Objects (School Bus, Truck, etc.). (Figures drawn from Loftus, 1975, p. 568)

Initial condition (question in initial postfilm interview):		Percentage of yes-responses to direct question asked 1 week after the film in relation to initial interview condition:			X^2	p
(D)	*(F)*	*C*	D	*F*		
Did you see a school bus in the film?	Did you see the children getting on the school bus?	6	12	26	8.44	.025
Did you see a truck in the beginning of the film?	At the beginning of the film, was the truck parked beside the car?	0	8	22	26.01	.01
Did you see a center line on the country road?	Did another car cross the center line on the country road?	8	14	26	6.26	.05
Did you see a woman pushing the carriage?	Did the woman who was pushing the carriage cross into the road?	26	36	54	8.52	.025
Did you see a barn in the film?	Did you see a station wagon parked in front of the barn?	2	8	18	7.66	.05
	Means:	8.4	15.6	29.2		

NOTES: Control condition; no question (C). Direct question (D). Leading question; false presupposition (F)

Thus, any statement must be understood in its interactional embeddedness (at the very least in relation to the immediately preceding questioning and in relation to prior questioning).

Woodbury (1984) has suggested that we think of trials as "story-telling contests" in which each lawyer (prosecution/defense) needs to convince the third party (the jury) that his or her side's story is the most plausible one. Yet, he or she must not tell the story him- or herself. This raises strategic problems on the part of the lawyers, who must elicit the story from witnesses (and demolish the opponent's story)—through questioning—and in an unobtrusive manner so that the story does not lose its coherence and apparent spontaneity.

Obviously, opponent interests are at stake from the very beginning of any legal process. Ultimately, the police represent prosecution (or defense) interests. The police report is not useful unless "what happened" can be made to fit official categories of criminality (and noncriminality). Similarly, probation officers and other agents in legal processes are likely to promote one of the two competing stories. Most actors are well aware of the adversarial aspects of legal processing. What is less well known is how this affects social interaction beyond the cross-examination as such or in what ways court reporters, interpreters, social workers, and other agents may wittingly or unwittingly promote one of the two competing stories.

Police Interrogations and the Social Construction of "Remorse"

The police report is, at times, the product of extensive conversational inferencing on the part of the police (see above). Yet, police interrogation talk is, of course, not constructed by one party alone. The suspect may contribute to a greater or lesser extent, depending on social and criminal background.

In a classic investigation, Cicourel (1968) presents detailed analyses of how youths are labeled (or not labeled) as "criminals". Cicourel draws on a series of well documented cases in which he has specified the relationship between unofficial and official negotiations, and between ongoing talk on the one hand, and official reports on the other (sentences, police reports, probation officer reports, school reports, etc.). He carefully maps the various contingencies for a punishment versus a treatment frame of interrogation. Within a treatment framework, a great number of acts such as probation violations, can be defined as "pranks" or as the outward manifestation of family problems (divorce, illness). In contrast, similar actions would be defined as the products of defective moral character within a punishment frame.

To quite some extent, treatment frames are associated with *trust relationships* (Cicourel, 1968). If the juvenile expresses "remorse" or "sincerity" police officers and/or probation officers often tend to view past events in terms of treatment frameworks (Cicourel, 1968). In the interrogations, police officers and probation officers reinterpret past events, indirectly telling the juvenile "what happened" (Extract 7).

Extract 7
(Police officer interrogating juvenile)

Q: When were you born? (the police officer then begins filling out an arrest report with factsheet type of information). Well, what about this?
A: What you mean about it?
Q: Well. . . . .
A: I took a tool case from a guy's place and put it back in the bushes (a quick exchange then occurred during which time the officer sought to establish the sequence of events that led to the theft)
Q: Now, he's out a tool kit, right?
A: Yah
Q: Would you like to be out something like that?
A: No
Q: Now, right is right! If you do something wrong you ought to pay for it. I think that your folks should get $5.00 out of your hide one way or another. . .

(Cicourel, 1968, p. 123)

Evidently, the police officer tries to elicit remorse and is not quite satisfied with the somewhat noncommittal "yah". On the other hand, the juvenile's assertive "no" evidently amends his first more noncommittal responses. This can be inferred from the fact that the police officer does not probe further; in any case, she evidently terminates the moral negotiation part of this particular encounter. In other cases, Cicourel documents how police officers or probation officers protract the moral lesson/investigation, eliciting statements about church-going practices and so on. Evidently, in these cases, sincerity and remorse are to quite some extent the joint accomplishment of the professionals' questions and the juvenile's willingness/reluctance to go along with the professionals' representations of reality.

Pretrial Negotiations and Social "Facts"

Pretrial negotiations take place in multiparty contexts with several different actors (prosecution, defense, police, social workers, etc.). The multiparty character of the legal process is dramatized in the case of the juvenile delinquent in which parents may also enter as intermediaries between the delinquent and the legal professionals. This also means the parents' education and bureaucratic competence may influence the pretrial process. In his work on punishment and treatment frames, Cicourel (1968) has documented how type of frame may be closely linked to family resources. Hence, middle-income parents may mobilize influential neighbors, friends, acquaintances (e.g., school principals, psychiatrists, and others) who formulate "what happened" in terms of treatment frames (rather than punishment frames).

In his comparative analyses of a series of cases, Cicourel (1968) demonstrates how social class seems to be important in forming teachers', probation officers', and police officers' attributions of "bad attitude" (punishment frame) versus "depressed state" (treatment frame). In one such case, the case of Robert Bean, Cicourel (1968) thus shows how this white middle-class youth is offered a second chance again and again. For instance, the recent divorce of this boy's parents is interpreted in terms of temporary upset (that is, in terms of treatment rather than punishment thinking). In contrast, similar "facts" are read quite differently in the case of a black youth from a lower-income family, the case of Smithfield Elston. Thus, the recent divorce of Smithfield's parents is read as yet one more sign of "moral disorder" in the boy's family. In this latter case, the parental divorce indicates a placement outside the home, and there is a notable absence of treatment interpretations of social "facts".

In Cicourel's material (1968), punishment framing is thus more often employed in cases where white officials encounter black ethnic youngsters. It can thus be seen how some young persons are systematically misunderstood (Smithfield) or how others are understood and given a second chance a third, fourth, or fifth time by parents and other intermediaries. This, in turn, is often accomplished through strategic reframings and indirect (dialogue) instruction by the different intermediaries (see remarks above on the social construction of "remorse").

In a related case study analysis, Darrough (1984) has shown how a probation officer negotiates with parents of a juvenile delinquent in order to secure a probation placement (rather than incarceration). This negotiation involves quite subtle conversational compromises in that the probation officer wishes to discredit the youth sufficiently to establish the "necessity" of placement, but without alienating the parents (Darrough, 1984).

Pretrial negotiations are, of course, quite dependent on the suspect's (or suspect's parents') awareness of the different legal framings of such things as specific attitudes. Spencer (1983) demonstrates how probation officers elicit various statements from the suspect about the consequences of the offense, about his or her behavior in the future, and so on – statements that can then be used to classify "criminality". Again, criminality is partly the outcome of the interview, which is a product of social collaboration. Sudnow (1965) shows how the charges of "normal" crimes are more or less routinely reduced if the suspect behaves sensibly, that is, pleads guilty in the exchange for a lesser offense charge. In the person-descriptions in plea-bargaining, the meaning of, for instance, the suspect's "priors," can take on different connotations depending on whether they are brought up by the public defender or by the prosecution attorney (Maynard, 1982). Generally, though, plea-bargaining negotiations tend to be more or less unproblematic and business-like (Maynard, 1982; Lynch, 1982).

The foregoing thus establishes how criminality is negotiated by a series of different participants in the legal process (including parents) and how these negotiations are embedded within social encounters between participants with opponent interests or with different stereotypes about such concepts as "criminality" and "sincerity."

On Combativeness, Misrepresentations, and the Social Construction of Testimony Styles: Courtroom Examinations

Within witness psychology, language use has been related to misrepresentations (see above). Hence, Muscio (1915) contrasted question types in terms of their linguistic influence on the reliability of the responses. One of his findings was that subjects are more easily influenced and less cautious when questions are posed impersonally—"was there a . . .?"—than in the second pronoun form—"did you see a . . .?" More recently, others have shown how narrative questioning tends to elicit less complete but more accurate testimonies, whereas closed questioning tends to elicit more complete but less accurate testimonies (Dent, 1982; Marquis, Marshall, & Oskamp, 1972). The problem of linguistic influences on testimonies is thus again intimately related to the recycling of evidence, that is to the production of misrepresentations.

Recently, there has also been a growing interest in interrogative style in the field of sociolinguistics and conversation analysis. The focus has been on domination and intimidation (rather than on misrepresentations). Hence, Danet has analyzed the "war of words" in courtroom examinations in terms of more or less combative or coercive question types, that is closed question types including disjunctive questions and yes/no-questions as well as declarative questions (Danet & Bogoch, 1980; Danet, Hoffman, Kermish, Rafn, & Stayman, 1976). In a case study analysis of an abortion case, coercive questions were found to be more common in the cross-examinations than in the direct examinations (Danet et al., 1976). These results were cross-validated in a later study of six trials, where it is again shown how interrogative WH-questions are indeed more common in direct examinations than in the more adversarial cross-examinations (Danet & Bogoch, 1980). Conversely, declarative questions and tags are more frequent in cross-examinations. Within an interactional perspective, it is important to situate coerciveness in the talk of specific actors. It has been shown how the questioning is more coercive in murder trials than in rape trials, and least coercive in assault cases (Danet & Bogoch, 1980). In a Swedish investigation of courtroom control, 40 trials have been intensively studied, and discourse patterns have been shown to predict verdicts—guilty versus non-guilty— as well as the severity of sentences (Adelswärd, Aronsson, Jönsson, & Linell, 1987).[1] More specifically, it is shown how serious-offense defendants are treated more strictly and less conversationally than minor-offense defendants, in that they more often:

- receive a greater proportion of 'coercive' questions;
- receive fewer acknowledgments of their prior turns;
- do not get a slot for their own narrative; and
- do not get a slot for a final word after the final speeches.

These results can be read as a manifestation of the ritual character of courtroom discourse (cf. Danet, 1980b). All the crimes—even the relatively more serious ones—concern petty theft or fraud in the Swedish investigation (no rape cases, manslaughter, or murder cases are included in the courtroom corpus). Yet, it can be seen how interrogations are not merely rational bureaucratic procedures for extracting facts. They are also societal expressive means for teaching moral lessons. It should perhaps also be pointed out that defendants do not merely react in a passive fashion to courtroom coerciveness (Adelswärd et al., 1987). Minor-offense defendants take more initiatives and more often expand their responses, talking more as in everyday conversations. It is thus not meaningful to interpret these results in terms of any unidirectional causalities. Ultimately, both parties mutually condition each other in the direction of greater informality or formality.

It should be emphasized, too, that coerciveness cannot be analyzed in terms of syntactic analyses alone. Several studies show that there is a poor match between question format and response type (e.g., Danet et al., 1976; Walker, 1987; Woodbury, 1984). Syntax-based coding schemes are insensitive to sequential implications. If a legal professional pauses before posing a follow-up question, this can allow it to be heard more like a dispute (Drew, in press). Similarly, a question that is "noncoercive" in isolation may obviously become quite coercive if repeated one or several times (Bogoch & Danet, 1984; Dunstan, 1980). Moreover, a seemingly noncoercive question may serve as a blame presequence (Atkinson & Drew, 1979). As shown by Harris (1984), accusations and information-seeking tend to overlap in courtroom interrogations. When authentic court cases are examined, it can thus be seen how several question types can be used quite flexibly, both combatively and noncombatively. For instance, declarative questions are, in fact, often ambiguous—open to negotiation (see Extract 8):

Extract 8
(Judge questioning defendant accused of having paid for a taxi with an invalid check.)

Q: So you don't remember that you called for a taxi then?
A: Yes, that much I remember. 'cause then my brother was standing beside me then and that's it, there's no more, but I don't remember that when I got to Katrineholm that I wrote um a cheque, but that (.) then.

(Adelswärd et al., 1987, p. 321)

Apparently, declarative questions need not always shape the responses in a coercive fashion. They can be taken as strong leads or as conversation-like invitations to collaborative story-telling.

In sum, it is not meaningful to analyze *coerciveness* in a mechanistic fashion. Yet, the notion of coercive questioning points to an important issue in courtroom examinations, that is, to the social construction of testimony styles. Apparently, defendants who are exposed to coercive questioning may, in turn, produce more fragmented evidence (McGaughey & Stiles, 1983; O'Barr, 1982). In some cases, adversary attorneys may quite wittingly employ coercive questioning as a means for discrediting witnesses. Yet, we have good reasons to believe that fragmented testimonies are also created less deliberately (by mistake). In such cases, testimony style is, in fact, misrepresentative of the defendant's genuine attitude (which is read/misread from his or her testimony style). Instead, the testimony style can be seen partly as a reflection of the interrogator's coercive questioning style. Similarly, persons with legal experience tend to believe that a witness is more credible if he or she is questioned more openly in that this would generally reflect a greater trust on the part of the same side attorneys (O'Barr, 1982). Directly or indirectly, low-credibility styles may thus be the artifacts of coercive questioning.

In the legal arena, "coerciveness" has been defined in terms of question types. Obviously examination and cross-examination can also be quite taxing in that attorneys employ discrediting rhetoric. Terms may be chosen in a deliberately biased way (Danet, 1980a), and attorneys may also use other means for distancing themselves from opponent witnesses. For instance, Liebes-Plesner (1984) has presented a detailed case study of how two defense lawyers seem to use discrediting rhetoric as well as sarcastic formality as ways of enraging a girl (prosecution) witness in a rape case (see Extract 9).

Extract 9
(Defense lawyer questioning prosecution witness [plaintiff] in a rape case.)

Q: Gveret Mizraxi (Madam Mizraxi)
A: Do me a favor, call me Etti
Q: Gveret Mizraxi.

(Liebes-Plesner, 1984, p. 178)

The girl is incensed at the lawyer's formal (sarcastic) address. On other occasions the same lawyer is quite colloquial (and provoking) in requests such as "save your tricks for the end". He is not consistently formal, and there is probably little doubt that he employs formal politeness for strategic purposes. Ultimately, the girl becomes openly hostile and disrespectful of the court, which can then be exploited by the defense. Notice, however, that it is the defense that has partly created this hostile testimony style.

Courtroom Deliberations, Misrepresentations, and Coparticipants' Contestations

Obviously, social interaction is constitutive of courtroom deliberations (Davis, 1980; Gerbasi, Zuckerman, & Reis, 1977). In the Swedish trial system, lay judges discuss and pronounce on defendants' guilt as well as on the type of penalty in collaboration with the judge. Normally, this discussion is viewed primarily in terms of the cumulative effect of different lay judges' sensible judgments. It is less certain whether lay judges may also trade on each others' misrepresentations. In a simulation of lay judges' deliberations, Aronsson and Nilholm (1989) have shown how participants (in 20 taped, triadic discussions of a custody case) selectively misconstrue courtroom evidence depending on their overall story schemes. In the experimental setup, one subject in each triad had received (written) background information that differed from that of the other two participants. If this person introduced such fraudulent new information into the group discussion, the other participants would not challenge it if they held views congruent with these new "facts". Moreover, they would employ this false new information in their own argumentation later on.

There was also a substantial number of spontaneous misreadings or misrepresentations of the background facts. For instance, the background material stated that a physical examination had revealed no sign of the daughter having been sexually assaulted in this custody case (which entailed a prior incest suspicion). Yet, some experimental subjects who favored the mother as custodian in fact referred to the damaging evidence of the physical examination (i.e., an inverse reading/recollection of the background material). Again, fraudulent new information of this sort was generally not contested if the coparticipants were in favor of the mother. Thus, false information was generally only detected within an adversarial context, that is if other participants in the triad held opposing attitudes (and opposing story frameworks).

Court Reporting and Misrepresentations

In the foregoing, it has been shown how evidence may become recycled at every stage of the legal process, from the very first police interrogations through the final deliberations. Ultimately, the trial is transformed into a written document, the trial record. The "verbatim" trial record provides an outward manifestation of legal order and precision, epitomizing objectivity and public control. Yet, Walker (1986) has recently documented the less-than-perfect match between trial talk and trial records. Several factors influence the final record: court reporters' model of language, the legal world's concept of what constitutes information, legal representatives' demands for editing, as well as general problems that pertain to the transformation of oral multiparty, multichannel events into written linear records. Walker's study provides a dramatic illustration of the gulf between literate practices and everyday orality and moreover shows how this gulf is problematic even for highly trained professionals whose careers are built on constructing written texts.

Procedural Rules and Everyday Interaction

Formal Procedures and Frame Conflicts

In the discussion of legal negotiations in the previous section, I have shown how testimonies may become recycled by several different actors (interpreters, court reporters, lawyers, social workers, police officers), and at several different stages. Miscommunication may also arise as the result of witnesses' misreadings of courtroom discourse. In an investigation of defendants' reconstructions of the trial, it was shown how defendants would often misunderstand courtroom discourse owing to clashes between everyday and legal framing of events (Adelswärd, Aronsson, & Linell, 1988). Three fourths of all minor-offense defendants misconstrued several aspects of the bureaucratic format, interpreting procedural rules within a frame of blame rather than within a legal frame. Thus, several defendants were upset by the fact that the judge and prosecutor would repeat questions that had been asked in the police interview (a consequence of the *rule of oral presentation*):

Extract 10
(Prosecution questioning defendant)

Q: Why didn't you say that then?
A: Well, why didn't I say that. It's all in the police report.
Q: I don't care what's in some police report.
A: No.
Q: Instead, I am asking you why.

(Adelswärd et al., 1988, p. 274)

Similarly, several defendants were quite upset by the detailed questioning (cf. the procedural rule on exhaustive presentation of evidence). In several trials, labels were negotiated in a detailed and extensive fashion. In legal terms it may be quite important if, for example, the defendant "took" or "possessed" certain goods, whether he was "pressed" or "stressed" during prior police interrogations, and so on. Such distinctions often lead to protracted or repeated question sequences, which were at times seen as "nagging" by the defendant or as a way of "rubbing it in" (Adelswärd et al., 1988).

The gap between the bureaucratic format of trials and everyday conversation thus results in various types of miscommunication. Related examples of bewildered and uncomfortable witnesses in the face of courtroom procedures can be found in other studies, even though these studies have not explicitly been conceptualized in terms of frame conflicts. For instance, Nofsinger (1983) documents how inexperienced expert witnesses may become quite confused by the court's detailed requests for exact specifications (which have already been offered from the perspective of the witness). Similarly, O'Barr and Conley (1985) demonstrate how evidentiary rules frequently lead to objections pertaining to hearsay evidence, for example (which may be quite confusing and somewhat intimidating for inexperienced witnesses). Dunstan (1980) has also reported how trials often do not run smoothly but how witnesses have to be told how to behave and how such prescriptions often are not followed. In many cases, it is first after a series of objections that the judge formulates the relevant rule (which is, in any case, quite abstract and difficult to comprehend for inexperienced witnesses).

Informal Procedures and Frame Conflicts

On the other hand, informal legal procedures may bring about other types of miscommunication, as demonstrated recently by O'Barr and Conley (1985) in a study of small claims courts. In these courts, litigants are allowed to talk quite freely, without the bureaucratic constraints of ordinary trials. O'Barr and Conley report that small claims litigants tend to feel quite satisfied with the encounter as such. Yet, their spontaneous narratives deviate from legal narratives in several ways. Small claims litigants produce an inductive type of reasoning, where agents and actions are not linked together in the coherent fashion of formal trials. In contrast, legal professionals tend to employ deductive ways of formulating a case (presenting a hypothesis, which is then substantiated in a systematic way). The litigants' everyday narratives may, in turn, result in less than satisfactory resolutions of the conflicts (which have not been distinctly presented to the court). Thus, litigants' satisfaction with the relaxed procedure is, at times, bought at the price of injustice (O'Barr & Conley, 1985). Yet, the litigants themselves may not become aware of this injustice in that justice is (mistakenly) construed in terms of everyday concepts of openness and fairness, whereas the law has to operate within the legal framing of justice.[2]

Miscommunication and Perspectivity

In frame conflicts, the participants themselves may often construe miscommunication in terms of discrediting rhetoric, evasiveness, and so forth. In the emotionally charged settings of courtrooms and legal offices, there is an interplay of blame and distrust that makes "truth" liable both to rhetorical transformations and to less deliberate (more or less purposeful) misreadings. A distinction between adversarial communication, on the one hand, and miscommunication, on the other, is thus often hard to maintain. To some extent, this distinction has to do with perspectivity (see Table 11.2).

Even from an outsider's perspective, it may often be difficult to differentiate between problematic talk in general (discrediting strategies, coerciveness, etc.) on the one hand, and miscommunication, on the other. Obviously, the analytic problem is even greater for those who hold opposing interests, and who may thus be motivated to misread testimonies in terms of opposing story frameworks. What are construed as routine adversarial procedures on the part of the court may be construed as misrepresentations by the witnesses or defendants. In all social interaction,

Table 11.2 Problematic Talk and Strategic Intent

Dialogue analysis of problematic talk	Types of problematic talk	
	MISCOMMUNICATION	Other types of problematic talk
	(no strategic intent)	(strategic intent)
Direct interactional focus	*MISUNDERSTANDINGS*	Deceitful interaction
	Frame conflicts	Coercion
	Other types of misunderstandings	Collusion
Speaker- or hearer-focus	*MISREPRESENTATIONS*	Disputatious rhetoric[a]
	Mishearings	Discrediting rhetoric
	Misreadings	Adversarial stereotyping
	Misquotes	Strategic lies
	Misattributions	Sarcastic formality
	Other types of non-deliberate misrepresentations	Strategic evasiveness
		Strategic pauses
		Strategic silence

NOTE: a. The four-part scheme represents ideal types in Weber's sense. In adversarial contexts, it may, for instance, be difficult to disentangle adversarial stereotyping (disputatious rhetoric) from nondeliberate misattributions (nonstrategic MISREPRESENTATIONS)

communication (and miscommunication) can be read from at least three perspectives: that of the speaker, that of the hearer, and that of the observer (objective or researcher perspective). In addition, court examinations always entail the audience perspective of jurors and the general public. In the literature, it has been argued that miscommunication can, at times, be traced to lawyers' audience-design strategies. That is, communication that has display functions vis-à-vis the court may be experienced as a bullying lack of understanding on the part of the defendant (even when the displays, e.g., strategic repeats, are designed to convince the audience of the defendant's relative innocence). Such an interpretation makes sense in several of the present cases of frame conflicts that pertain to legal versus everyday frames of the procedural rules (Adelswärd et al., 1988). Evidently, what is construed as normal, routine court procedure on the part of the court may be construed as misunderstandings or defamatory talk on the part of the defendants.

This review has been concerned with two principal types of miscommunication (see Table 11.2). In the first case (misunderstandings) miscommunication is directly embedded in the dialogue in question. In the latter case (different types of misrepresentations), there is a more indirect relation to ongoing or past dialogues. Yet, I have tried to show how misrepresentations can often ultimately be traced to different interactional influences. For instance, different participants' stereotypes of criminality may directly or indirectly lead to recyclings of evidence (as shown in the links between dialogues and class-bound framings of juvenile pranks/ crimes; Cicourel, 1968). In such cases, it can be seen how adversarial interests may operate on the processing of dialogues. In other cases, there may be no apparent links to adversarial interests (as in the Loftus experiments).

Moreover, indirect links to prior dialogues can be seen in studies in which misrepresentations may be traced to adversarial strategic talk. For instance, this can be seen in those cases where lawyers employ coercive questioning in ways that produce fragmented and less credible witness styles (Adelswärd et al., 1987; McGaughey & Stiles, 1983; O'Barr, 1982). Similarly, we can identify such indirect influences in cases where, for instance, defense lawyers use discrediting rhetoric or talk in ways that enrage or upset witnesses. In the case of Liebes-Plesner's (1984) alleged rape victim, it is impossible to know (with any absolute certainty) whether the witness's noncompliant and somewhat aggressive responses were those of righteous indignation or merely a revengeful attitude and contempt of the court. In the former case, miscommunication (here: the girl's misrepresentative testimony style) may be a joint accomplishment that is deeply embedded in adversarial talk.

Legal process discourse generally takes place within the dynamics of opposing story frameworks. In the present deliberately unorthodox review, I have pooled findings from experimental studies (e.g., Loftus) with conversational analyses of authentic adversarial trials. One important point to emerge, then, is that recycling of evidence operates both under adversarial (motivated) conditions, and in experimental (less motivated) conditions. This means that misleading information may become introduced in a number of ways, ranging from strategic manipulation (e.g., deliberate deceit) to "pure" mistakes and other disinterested misrepresentations.

Ultimately, human interaction is, of course, seldom completely disinterested. Within a general conflict orientation on discourse (regarding degrees of conflict as something inherent in human interaction), the present review will thus partly generalize to misrepresentations outside the legal arena. Legal setting interactions dramatize conflicts in that opposing interests form constitutive elements of legal processes. The interplay between strategic talk and nondeliberate miscommunication may often be quite similar in other social contexts. Yet, the genesis of miscommunication can perhaps be better detailed – both in authentic and in experimental settings – in the legal arena than in many other institutional contexts.

Notes

1. In the present review I refer extensively to work on Swedish District Court trials, conducted as a joint research effort at Linköping University under a grant to Karin Aronsson and Per Linell from the Bank of Sweden Tercentenary Foundation. See: Adelswärd, Aronsson, Jönsson, and Linell (1987, 1988; Aronsson, Jönsson, and Linell (1987); Aronsson and Nilholm (1989); Jönsson (1989b); and Linell (1989).

2. The present review has an explicit focus on miscommunication. There are several reviews of courtroom discourse (e.g., Atkinson, 1981; Danet, 1980b; Drew, 1985; O'Barr, 1981; Wodak, 1985) and there are also reviews of linguistic and interactional influences of testimonies (e.g., Clifford & Bull, 1978; Loftus, 1976, 1979; Yarmey, 1979).

12

Miscommunication in Organizations

Eric M. Eisenberg
Steven R. Phillips

Miscommunication in Organizations: Background

Most managers and organizational theorists view communication as extremely important in organizations, but difficult to address in any systematic way. Communication is praised or blamed although specific problems go unsolved, and opportunities for understanding the dynamics of effective communication are missed. The resultant state of affairs is frustrating to theorists and practitioners alike; like Mark Twain's comment about the weather, organizational communication is something about which everyone talks, but no one does anything.

Communication researchers are in a good position to provide a more detailed perspective on effective organizational communication, one that allows for specific analyses and actions. Such scrutiny will no doubt reveal some surprises. What is defined as problematic communication from the viewpoint of management, for example, may be seen as effective from an employee's perspective. However it is manifested, the complexities of organizational life make miscommunication inevitable.

In the sections to follow we discuss various forms of miscommunication from a variety of perspectives. Examples of organizational miscommunication occur at all levels and in all areas of companies. Here is a sampling we have encountered in our work:

AUTHORS' NOTE: The authors acknowledge Lori Roscoe and Terry Albrecht for their insightful critiques.

- In an advertising agency, a receptionist makes a mistake in recording a phone message, leading to a missed meeting and a lost contract.
- In a utility company, a depressed employee attempts to tell her boss about some personal problems, only to be told curtly "get professional help if you can't cut it around here."
- In a leasing company, the sales department withholds some details about a big deal from the legal department. The deal goes through, but five years later the secret gets out, and the company and certain individuals suffer enormously.
- In a retail tire store, a manager doesn't tell a problem employee the whole truth about her performance in a performance appraisal interview. The employee's continued poor performance negatively affects the morale of peers and subordinates, as well as the productivity of the store.
- In an aerospace firm, senior management feels ill-equipped to communicate with union employees, and hires an ad agency to do their internal communication. Employees are offended and cynical when they are told of this strategy.

Which of these examples is an example of miscommunication? Although we attempted to order them by increasing subtlety and complexity, the fact is that miscommunication can only be defined according to a specified set of criteria and in a certain context. For every communicative act, some individuals benefit, others lose; some in the short-term, some later on. No single set of criteria has emerged that allows for a simple determination of what constitutes miscommunication (or for that matter, effective communication) in organizations. Even those examples that seem the most "obvious" at first (e.g., involving lying, secrecy, or a gross lack of empathy) can be judged as effective by certain criteria and in certain contexts.

Purpose of the Chapter

After briefly introducing the concept of miscommunication and showing its importance in organizations, we describe and evaluate four major attempts at defining miscommunication. Each approach to miscommunication identifies some kind of failure. Miscommunication has been defined as the failure:

- to be understood;
- to achieve one's communicative goals;
- to be authentic, honest, and disclosive; and
- to establish an open dialogue.

Table 12.1 summarizes the key ideas associated with each perspective, linking definitions of miscommunication to more general views of organizational behavior. After reviewing these four approaches, we offer a new definition of miscommunication that both subsumes prior definitions and better accounts for organizational reality.

We conclude that any acceptable definition of miscommunication must inevitably be relative to the social context—to a theory, world view, set of values, group of stakeholders, or point in time. In our definition, *miscommunication* is the failure, in social interaction, to balance individual creative agency against the coordination and control that makes organizing possible.

The Machine Metaphor: Miscommunication as Failed Understanding

In his recent book on organizations, Morgan (1986) portrays the classical-structuralist school of organizational thought as motivated by a *machine* metaphor (see Table 12.1). Consequently, effectiveness is defined in terms of efficiency, and employees are seen as interchangeable and passive. In such a scenario, communication is regarded as the straightforward transmission of information. A manager has communicated well when he or she has transferred what is in his or her head to a subordinate, with minimal "spillage" along the way.

Axley (1984) characterized this view of communication as the *conduit* metaphor, pervasive in most discourse about organizations. Successful communication is clear and promotes understanding, and transfers necessary information for the "machine" to continue optimal operation. Miscommunication occurs when either no message is received (e.g., due to distracting physical or psychological noise) or when the message received is not understood in the way the speaker intended (e.g., the receptionist mentioned above who made a mistake with a phone message). Clarity is synonymous with competence, and ambiguity is to be avoided at all costs. Typical communication "breakdowns" from this perspective are message overload, distortion, and ambiguity (Stohl & Redding, 1987). In *message overload*, a receiver is overwhelmed by inputs and hence fails to comprehend the speaker's full intent. For example, if a secretary is simultaneously answering five phone calls and signing for a delivery, he or she may not clearly understand the boss's request. In *message distortion*, the serial transmission of information alters the original meaning so that the message does not arrive as intended. This is akin to the children's game, "Telephone," in which the first child is told a story and tries to retell the story

Table 12.1 Four Approaches to Miscommunication in Organizations

APPROACH	*KEY TERMS*	*CRITERIA FOR EFFECTIVENESS*	*VIEW OF MISCOMMUNICATION*
Classical-Structuralist	Machine Conduit Efficiency	Clarity Understanding	Failed Understanding Overload Distortion Ambiguity
Pragmatic	Individual Goals Cost/benefit analysis	Goal Achievement	Failed Goal Achievement
Human Relations	Openness Disclosure Sharing Authenticity	Open Lines of Communication Unrestricted Candor	Failed Openness Dishonesty Secrecy Lack Of Full Disclosure
Critical Theory	Dialogue Co-construction Practice Activity	Open Dialogue Individual Emancipation Reveals Domination	Failed Dialogue Hegemony Oppression

to the second child, retaining as many of the details as possible. The second child then tries to retell the story to a third child, and so forth. The final version of the story often bears only a distant resemblance to the original story. In *message ambiguity*, the failure to choose words that establish easily understood symbol-referent connections allows receivers the latitude to interpret messages in ways that differ from the speaker's intent. This definition reflects the overriding concern of the classical-structuralist school with downward communication, and specifically with orders and instructions. Although there are many occasions in organizations when clarity promotes effectiveness, there are important exceptions as well: for example, a supervisor may need to maintain confidentiality about a strategic plan. Once we look beyond the accomplishment of simple, physical tasks, clarity must always be balanced against relational and political ends, both of which are sometimes better accomplished by choosing one's words carefully.

The machine or conduit definition of miscommunication is problematic in at least two ways. First, the recipient of the message is seen as largely *passive* and as playing no significant role in the co-construction of the meaning of the message. This is in line with "personalist" views of meaning in which individuals "own" meaning and pass it around, rather than constructing it in discourse (Gergen, 1985; Holquist, 1981). *Second,* this definition assumes message senders always *intend* to be clear. Although this is usually true in the case of technical instructions, it may not always be so. For example, in the conduct of a performance review, a manager may be intentionally unclear about negative aspects of the employee's performance in order to avoid confrontation (Goodall, Wilson & Waagan, 1986). Similarly, this definition does not acknowledge that ambiguity may sometimes facilitate effective communication (Eisenberg, 1984; Levine, 1985).

The critique of the conduit metaphor in organizational communication has broader resonances in the analysis of conversation. Specifically, Grice's (1975) well-known *cooperative principles* of conversation include "avoid ambiguity," and "do not say what you believe to be false." Although Grice understood these principles to be an idealization of the communicative process, their existence does tend to minimize the fact that most people break these rules most of the time, and furthermore, *expect* others to break them in pursuit of their goals (Okabe, 1987). Simply put, competent communicators in complex organizations do much more than transfer information from point A to point B.

Others have endeavored to describe the ways organizational members deviate from cooperative principles and still succeed. In a previous paper (Eisenberg, 1984), the senior author of this chapter described some of the ways in which ambiguity may be used strategically by organizational members to accomplish important goals. Specifically, strategic ambiguity:

(1) promotes unified diversity;
(2) preserves privileged positions;
(3) is deniable; and
(4) facilitates organizational change.

An example of *unified diversity* can be found in an organization's mission statement. If made too clear, it can be divisive; like political platforms, most missions must be sufficiently abstract to allow a diversity of interpretations to coexist. Ambiguity *preserves privileged positions* in that once an employee has gained considerable stature or respect, he may be unclear in stating explicit views, relying on others to credit his past achievements and fill in the blanks. For example, if an executive has a track-record of success, she may simply say that she is going to help the organization "achieve total quality" or "put the customer first," leaving everyone to construct their own interpretations of these equivocal expressions. What makes this especially interesting is that it is unlikely that any one will question the goal or the means of achieving the goal if sufficient ambiguity exists in the credible executive's statements.

Ambiguity can also be used strategically to form in-groups, preserving privilege in a broader sense. When a group develops its own technical jargon, this technical talk is "ineffective" only from the standpoint of the outsider, who is mystified or confused. From the perspective of the insider, jargon is effective because it makes communication more efficient and builds camaraderie.

The *deniability* afforded by strategic ambiguity is especially important to managers and employees. By being less than clear, employees can protect confidentiality, avoid dysfunctional conflicts, and not reveal tactical information that might compromise the effectiveness of a decision. Finally, ambiguity can *facilitate organizational change* by allowing groups and individuals sufficient latitude to alter the focus of activity while at the same time appearing to be consistent.

The strategic use of ambiguity is but one illustration of how people make symbolic use of information in organizations (Feldman & March, 1981). Management is increasingly seen as requiring symbolic or strategic skills more akin to evangelism than accounting (Pfeffer, 1981; Pondy, 1978; Weick, 1979). Communication is not always rational in the sense of maximizing understanding, but instead involves individuals acting to maximize gains and minimize losses. Consequently, rational, *information engineering* models of effectiveness should be replaced by broader theories of symbolic information control that address the more subtle roles of tact, politeness, white lies, and agenda control. This shift toward considering individual motivations leads us naturally to the pragmatic view.

A Pragmatic View: Miscommunication as Failed Goal Attainment

This widely held perspective on communication equates effectiveness with goal attainment. In an organization, communication is considered ineffective if it fails to help an employee achieve his or her goals (see Table 12.1).

The biggest problem with such an avowedly strategic perspective is ethical relativism; if effective communication is defined as goal attainment, *who* decides which goals are worth accomplishing? Note the shift in evaluative focus from the discourse toward the correspondence between goals and accomplishments. From this angle, if an organization's Chief Executive Officer (CEO) was strategically ambiguous to escape blame for poor performance, judgments of effectiveness would not be tied to the lack of clarity in his or her language (as they would under the conduit or machine metaphor definition) but instead to whether or not the CEO was able to escape blame.

A second concern with the pragmatic perspective is determining the appropriate *time* to evaluate the effectiveness of communication. For example, if one's goal is to change the "underlying beliefs of managers and employees," how long should it take for this change to occur? A critical performance review, for example, may first prompt a defensive reaction, and only some months later show any improvement in productivity.

From this pragmatic perspective, competent communicators are adaptive and say the appropriate thing for the situation. Inappropriateness signifies a poor fit between strategy choice and goal achievement, and is synonymous with miscommunication. But inappropriate for whom? This question has important ethical implications. In a condemnation of double-talk among managers, *Fortune* magazine quoted an executive's definition of effective communication: "All you have to remember is . . . let the language be ambiguous enough that if the job is successfully carried out, all credit can be claimed, and if not, a technical alibi (can) be found" (Whyte, 1948). From a goal-oriented perspective, an employee who lies about employment history or a manager who withholds important information about the safety of working conditions might both be communicating effectively, if the goal is to succeed by hiding some uncomfortable truths. For this reason, there are serious ethical problems with a blanket endorsement of this perspective on miscommunication.

Finally, scholars are coming to see that communicators never have a single, overarching goal, and consequently, effectiveness always means balancing between multiple goals (cf. Dillard, Segrin, & Harden, 1989; O'Keefe, 1988; Phillips, 1989; Tracy & Eisenberg, 1989). A single message can serve a variety of functions. A subordinate communicating negative information about the competition to his or her boss, for example, must balance the importance of getting the information across against the face needs of the boss and his or her own personal career concerns. Performance reviews are another place where a multiple goals model applies. When appraising an employee's performance, a supervisor is challenged both to give clear feedback about the employee's weaknesses, and to maintain a positive working relationship. This calls for substantial tact and communicative skill. Consequently, many managers avoid or trivialize this activity. The performance appraisal is an archetypal example of the rule in organizational communication—the requirement to balance numerous motivations in discourse. Poor communicators fail to recognize tradeoffs and consequently ignore the face concerns of the other in getting their point across, or tip-toe through the conversation and fail to accomplish their primary goal. But although the acknowledgment of multiple goals makes the pragmatic perspective a better match to the reality of organizational communication, it fails to free us from the ethical relativism inherent in any goal orientation.

Human Relations: Miscommunication as Failed Openness

Some organizational scholars focus on the importance of *openness* and *self-disclosure* in defining organizational communication effectiveness (cf. Eisenberg & Witten, 1987). Based in the human relations movement, these authors argue that what is missing from most organizations is personal disclosure and authenticity. Furthermore, these authors propose that greater candor is tantamount to communicative effectiveness. In some organizations, openness continues to be seen as fundamental to building an effective work group (see Table 12.1).

There is, however, a tendency to overstate the applicability and positive effects of increased openness in organizations. A number of writers have critiqued the "ideology of openness" (see Brown & Rogers, this volume), offering numerous contexts in which greater openness hurts, rather than helps individuals *and* organizations (Bochner, 1984; Eisenberg & Witten, 1987; Parks, 1982). Parks (1982) maintains that people have neither the time, energy, nor sufficiently good reasons to be completely open with their colleagues. In most organizations, people are rewarded for closed, not open communication (Conrad, 1985).

A typical situation in which the use of candor might backfire is when an employee is asked for feedback on a report by their boss or close colleague. How should they respond? Too blunt a response may alienate the other person and decrease the likelihood that any suggestion will be considered. A vague response may be problematic as well, especially if the employee has a stake in making the final report as good as possible. A second example involves a senior manager preparing to quit to take a job with a competitor, but at the same time continuing daily activities in his or her current firm, including hiring and recruitment. Should the manager be honest with new recruits about the possibility of his or her departure?

These and similar questions are commonly asked in organizations, and they do not have easy answers. What *is* obvious is that simple prescriptions of clarity or openness are inadequate. Although one might *assert as a general rule* that open communication allows for smoother working relationships and better decisions, there is not clear empirical evidence documenting this claim. Furthermore, the most interesting communicative challenges at work entail deciding *how much* to reveal (or conceal), *how* to reveal, *what* to reveal, *when* to reveal, and *to whom* to reveal. While our striving for openness may be well-intentioned, most real-life communication situations present more complex social dilemmas.

Limitations to the efficacy of openness are not restricted solely to personal disclosure, but extend to more general incidences of concealment and revelation. Florida's "Sunshine Laws" are a case in point. Sunshine Laws force government agencies to open their meetings to the public. McLaughlin and Riesman (1985) conducted a case-study of public hearings to select a new president for the University of Florida. What they found did *not* provide unequivocal support for the efficacy of openness. Rather, the Sunshine Laws led to evasive, ambiguous behavior in "open" meetings, leaving the public even less informed than before. The reality of Sunshine Laws illustrates that nothing may be gained (on a practical or theoretical level) when the mismatch between theory and reality is too great.

Another reason organizational participants and theorists uncritically endorse open communication is an implicit belief in the *sharing* metaphor of social relationships (Eisenberg, 1986; Eisenberg & Riley, 1988; Krippendorff, 1985). The sharing metaphor implies that effective communication requires the cultivation of shared cognitions and emotions between interactants. Recently, this tendency has surfaced in arguments supporting the development of so-called *strong* cultures – attitudinal monoliths marked by a homogeneity of understandings, values, and beliefs (e.g., Peters & Waterman, 1982).

The tendency toward consensus models of communication is uniquely American (Moore, 1985), distinctly modern (Lyotard, 1984), and reflects a desire to resolve differences rather than learn to live with them. But shared understandings are *not* necessary for effective organization (Eisenberg & Riley, 1988; Weick, 1979); coordination of action is often more important than coordination of beliefs (Duranti, 1984; Weick, 1979). So long as organizational members agree on the implications for action of a particular communication, meanings may be *equifinal* (Donnellon, Gray, & Bougon, 1986; Gray, Bougon, & Donnellon, 1985). That is, congruent actions may result from divergent interpretations. Furthermore, not only is shared meaning unverifiable (Krippendorff, 1985) and not essential to effective organization (Weick, 1979), the lack of shared understanding may provide an atmosphere supportive of diversity and even transcendence (Eisenberg, 1990). That is, the lack of shared understanding may actually allow employees to connect and collaborate with each other in ways that would be blocked if they came to know each other better.

The emphasis on openness advanced by the human relations school was revised over time, as it became clear that most managers were asking employees to communicate openly mainly as a means of manipulation and control (cf. Eisenberg & Witten, 1987). Unrestricted self-disclosure witnessed a resurgence in the 1960s, but recent developments have caused people to be more modest in their claims about the efficacy of openness. One interesting consequence is that we are again forced to examine goals; some degree of openness may be appropriate toward one end, but not another. Furthermore, the *way* in which information is expressed (i.e., paralinguistically, nonverbally, through a communicator's style) has an effect. But just as simple endorsements of clarity are not helpful in real organizations, so too do simple prescriptions of openness reflect a naive view of what constitutes real-life organizational communication. Consequently, it is inappropriate to brand some piece of talk "miscommunication" simply because it is not open, disclosive, or honest. More must be known about the local context before such judgments can be made.

A Critical Perspective: Miscommunication as Failed Dialogue

Although arguments against blanket endorsements of clarity, goal achievement, and openness have received some attention of late, critiques of the *monologic* character of communication theory and research are relatively new (May, 1989a). In this section we first briefly narrate the transition from the monologic to the dialogic view. Then we explore the implications of the dialogic view for definitions of effective and ineffective communication.

Although most writers are explicit in their definition of communication as a transactional process, research practice typically reduces its study to monologue. Two areas of organizational research are illustrative. In the study of organizational stories (see Martin, Feldman, Hatch, & Sitkin, 1983), writers tend to see stories as canned monologues, emerging "fully cooked" from a speaker's mouth. Although this approach renders the subject easier to study, most real stories are not told this way. Instead, stories are usually co-constructed in dialogue, with "listeners" playing an active verbal and nonverbal role. The "story" gets constructed in the process (see May, 1989b; Ochs, 1988b).

Similarly, most studies of organizational compliance-gaining (see Kipnis, Schmidt, & Wilkinson, 1980) view persuasion as something one person does *to* another, despite the fact that the other may play an active role in resisting, modifying, or cooperating with the compliance-gaining attempt. This weakness is exemplified in the use of the terms *agent* and *target.* In reality, compliance-gaining can be highly interactive and requires shifting between these roles as well as the balancing of multiple goals.

The monologic view of communication is deeply rooted in personalist models of meaning, which reify individuals as "owning" meaning inside their heads (Holquist, 1981). As such, it is consistent with the conduit metaphor discussed above. What is missed most from this perspective is the socially *emergent* character of communication, effective or ineffective. Also lost is the potential for dialogue, the social co-construction of meaning over time. From a *dialogic* perspective, miscommunication is failed dialogue, or a one-sided definition of the situation; precisely the kind of situation much of our current research is unfortunately designed to study (see Table 12.1).

Because it eschews simple prescriptions of consensus and acknowledges the fluid negotiation of meaning and interpretation, the dialogic perspective is both more democratic and action-oriented than the other viewpoints we have described. It is action-oriented in the sense that it focuses on what people *do* together, whether they agree or not (cf. Eisenberg, 1990; Giddens, 1981). This move in communication studies echoes developments on a broader scale, what Ortner (1984) calls the master metaphor of *practice,* the leading theme of anthropological research in the 1980s.

This concern with practice and activity is only one connection between the dialogic perspective and its Soviet roots (e.g., Bakhtin, 1973; Vygotsky, cited in Wertsch, 1988). Another is its similarities to critical theory in general (e.g., Deetz & Kersten, 1983). Critical theorists see organizations as systems of domination in which the hegemony of taken-for-granted decision premises prevents participants from attaining their full potential. From this perspective, effective communication is *open dialogue* which creates a clearing for individual emancipation. For the critical theorist, miscommunication is any communication that oppresses individuals and supports domination (see Henley & Kramarae, this volume).

Unfortunately, in adopting a dialogic or critical perspective, the problem of ethical relativism is not solved, only dodged. Note, for example, that the locus for evaluating communicative effectiveness has shifted away from the *discourse* (because domination is usually covert) and from *explicit goals* (because participants on both sides are usually unaware of the forces of domination that are controlling them) to a *critic's judgment* of the positive or negative effects of communication on individuals. In addition to changing the locus of evaluation, we have changed the evaluator by privileging the role of the critic (Smircich & Calas, 1987).

But ethical relativism is not the only shortcoming of the dialogic perspective. Another relates to the question: *Who* is involved in the dialogue? All communication can be evaluated relative to multiple audiences, and different audiences (or stakeholders) make different assessments. This point is especially important from a dialogic perspective, where being excluded from the dialogue is the same as being disenfranchised. In a broad sense, miscommunication occurs not only when dialogue fails, but more fundamentally, when certain parties are excluded from the conversation altogether.

An Alternative Definition: Miscommunication as Failed Balance

The history of definitions of effective organizational communication is difficult to track and largely implicit. This may be because many organizational theorists and practitioners see communication as unproblematic or undifferentiated. At the same time, most people share at least an implicit appreciation for the trade-offs and subtleties required for organizational survival, and the strategic role communication can play in organizational politics. Most writers, however, are simply not accustomed to thinking about communication in this way. Instead, a dual reality is maintained; one motivated by theoretical formulations in which good communicators are open, honest, and clear; and one rooted in real life in which people are constantly adapting what they say to cope with the emerging situation. Developing useful theories of organizational communication necessitates finding a point of convergence between these two views.

Communication plays a dual role in organizing. On the one hand, communication is an expression of constraint, promoting organized action, accountability, and task accomplishment. On the other, communication expresses creativity; through interaction, individuals can exercise autonomy and exhibit innovativeness. The interplay between organized action and individual agency is present in all social organization. The individual strives to retain sufficient independence for growth and well-being, while simultaneously cooperating enough to do the job and feel a part of the group. For the organization, coordination is obviously important. But so too is individual autonomy, because it grants the organization greater flexibility, innovation, and the ability to adapt to change (Weick, 1979). The last thing an individual *or* an organization wants is employees who cooperate only according to formal rules (Katz & Kahn, 1978).

The delicate balance between individual agency and organizational constraint is enacted in communication. Every moment, in every organization, employees choose to reveal or conceal, express or protect themselves, and in so doing shape this balance. Effective communication achieves a proper balance of autonomy and control, and miscommunication is failed balance—too much freedom, and the organization becomes dysfunctional—too little freedom, the individual suffers, and the organization stagnates.

In our view of miscommunication, the locus of evaluation shifts away from goals, discourse, and the critic to a systemic or dialectical assessment. We define effective communication as discourse that promotes a balance between agency and constraint. Any assessment of miscommunication requires observers to tie a number of judgments together in determining the degree to which this balance has been achieved.

Although we feel our definition of miscommunication corresponds closely to the realities of organizational life, we have in no way escaped ethical relativism; we have simply traded one type (involving goals) for another (involving the "proper" balance between autonomy and control). Further, definitions of what counts as the "proper" balance between autonomy and control are always:

(1) *actor-bound* (i.e., more autonomy may be desired by employees but feared by management and stockholders);
(2) *time-bound* (i.e., a certain balance may be problematic in one time period and make better sense in another); and
(3) *culture-bound* (i.e., what is viewed as an appropriate degree of employee freedom in Asia may be seen as overly restrictive in the United States).

These points warrant further elaboration.

First, to say that a proper balance between autonomy and control is *actor-bound* indicates that organizational members will have differing perceptions of what constitutes the appropriate level of autonomy, and consequently, will hold different views of miscommunication. In her book on family systems, Hoffman (1981) demonstrated how the same message or action will be perceived as positive *or* negative, constructive or destructive, depending upon the system level (e.g., child, parent, grandparent) from which it is judged. For example, a cost-cutting method that saves the company money but significantly alters job descriptions may be seen as effective by senior management but ineffective by a union.

Second, the *time-bound* nature of our definition suggests that judgments of effectiveness are always historical; they are not invariant over time

(Gergen, 1985). Organizations are often thought of as having life cycles (Kimberly & Miles, 1980). At different points in an organization's life cycle, different activities are expected and desirable. Temporal differences in what counts as miscommunication are to be expected as well. For example, it would be premature to institute strict management systems or accountabilities in the entrepreneurial phase of development, just as high levels of autonomy and a low degree of control would be inappropriate in the "mature" stage. The right balance between autonomy and coordination depends in part on where an organization is in its development.

Finally, substantial work exists to illustrate the *culture-bound* nature of communication (Banks, Gudykunst, Ge, and Baker, this volume; Cushman & Kincaid, 1987). Judgments of miscommunication are culture-bound in at least three ways—national culture, organizational culture, and organizational sub-cultures. Regarding national culture, what constitutes miscommunication in one country might be construed as effective in another. For example, Pascale and Athos (1981), Hirokawa (1987), and others have noted the Asian tendency toward indirect speech and preservation of the other's "face." Japanese and Korean managers rarely say "no" directly, which leads to considerable confusion when dealing with Western cultures. Representatives of Chinese organizations focus much more on the creative side of communication than do their American counterparts. And should they enter the global marketplace, countries like Samoa or Guyana can be expected to add even more diversity. Ambiguity is critical to Guyanese communication (Williams, 1987), for example, and Samoan culture has no concept of intent or even personality (Duranti, 1984), making the Western strategy of assessing goals or motives futile.

Much has been written about how organizations *are* cultures (e.g., Frost, Moore, Louis, Lundberg, & Martin, 1985), and as such are characterized by their own unique set of attitudes and practices. Conceptions of miscommunication in one company (e.g., Apple Computers) will vary considerably from conceptions in another (e.g., IBM). Whereas some companies highly value autonomy (e.g., 3M's intrapreneurial teams), others emphasize coordination and even suppress individual expression as part of their corporate strategy (e.g., McDonald's). Finally, organizational cultures are *not* monoliths; they contain subcultures. This means that what might count as miscommunication in one part of the company may be effective somewhere else.

In sum, no adequate definition of miscommunication escapes relativism or context-dependence. The problem of defining effective communication is similar to the contemporary problem facing epistemology—what counts as firm knowledge in a post-positivist, post-modern world? According to

Rorty (1979), the best we can do is "continue the conversation"—"effectiveness" is whatever helps us to cope. Dialogue, community, and coping may be appropriate descriptors of effective communication in an increasingly complex business world, especially because any more descriptive definition necessarily privileges specific stakeholders.

McGuire's (1983) theory of contextualism provides a slightly different way of thinking about miscommunication. According to McGuire, no theory or hypothesis is ever altogether right or wrong; rather, we should proceed as if all theories are true somewhere. The purpose of research, then, is to discover the contexts in which the various theories apply. Relating back to the present argument, there may be no definitive definition of miscommunication in organizations. Instead, there is only a continual discovery of contexts wherein certain kinds of communication are more or less problematic.

13

Hot Air: Media, Miscommunication and the Climate Change Issue[1]

Allan Bell

The Nature of Miscommunication

Miscommunication is a very general label that covers a number of facets of unsuccessful communication, including terms such as misrepresentation, misunderstanding, inaccuracy, distortion, misreporting, problematic talk, and communication breakdown. This chapter first addresses theoretical and general issues of miscommunication and its place in the media. It then proceeds to examine one particular set of language data drawn from an extensive study of miscommunication in the news.

As a concept, miscommunication has been ill defined even in work to which it is supposedly central. The best that Pride (1985, p. 8) offers by way of definition is to say that it is "the term reserved for those occasions when there is reason to believe that what is communicated (perhaps registered and absorbed as knowledge) is somehow false, inadequate, distorted, etc." Milroy (1984, p. 8) takes us a good deal further, defining miscommunication as "a mismatch between the speaker's intention and the hearer's interpretation". She distinguishes misunderstanding—disparity between the speaker's and the hearer's semantic readings of the utterance—from communicative breakdown, when one of the participants observes something has gone wrong.

Misunderstanding is the commonest gloss on the concept of miscommunication. The most solidly data-based work is by Humphreys-Jones (1986) who follows a similar definition to Milroy: "incorrect understanding by one person of the intention underlying the output of another" (p. 108). Misunderstanding is a hearer-based concept, oriented to perception. But we must acknowledge that miscommunication may occur at other points of the communication situation, including at least the speaker and the message itself.

Miscommunication consists of *misunderstanding* by the hearer and/or *mispresentation* by the speaker. Such a distinction allows that it is possible for hearers to misunderstand something that was clearly and accurately expressed. Humphreys-Jones' (1986) analysis shows the lengths to which hearers can go to make an improbable reading of an utterance stick. Of course, when the speaker has in fact not represented his or her intended meaning accurately, there is enhanced scope for hearer misunderstanding. The term *mispresentation* does not necessarily imply deliberate or malicious distortion by the speaker. It could indeed involve an attempt to mislead, but it may equally be the result of ineptitude or other factors.

All this remains in the area of propositional content of utterances. This is where miscommunication is often identified, and this chapter will focus on such referential inaccuracy in media communication. We judge whether such miscommunication has occurred by comparing the content of an utterance with what the hearer declares him- or herself to have understood by it, or the speaker declares him- or herself to have meant. But miscommunication is not solely or even primarily a matter of disparate readings of an utterance. It is a much wider phenomenon involving unsuccessful interactions between people. Thus Coupland, Coupland, Giles and Henwood's (1988) discussion of miscommunication between elderly and youthful conversationalists (see Coupland, Nussbaum and Coupland, this volume) is not directly concerned with the content of what is said, but the fact that a particular interaction proved to be difficult and dissatisfying.

We can distinguish between two intersecting dimensions of miscommunication (Figure 13.1): the *referential* and the *affective* (cf. Holmes, 1989). *Referential* miscommunication occurs when the propositional content is mispresented or misunderstood. *Affective* or relational miscommunication is where the relationship between speaker and hearer is disrupted. As indicated by the crossed axes of Figure 13.1, these two dimensions are not exclusive. Holmes (1989) hypothesizes that an interaction can be high on the referential axis but low on the affective – for example, published weather forecasts. An interaction could also be high on affective but low on propositional content, for instance in greetings and formulae such as "how are you". In the media, there are formats where the affective is to the fore. Montgomery (1988), for example, examines a "DJ's" talk as "foregrounding the personal" – using talk to create a relationship with his audience. Both successful and unsuccessful communication can be plotted on these axes. If a certain kind of communication event is classed as high on the referential, any miscommunication involved in that event will be

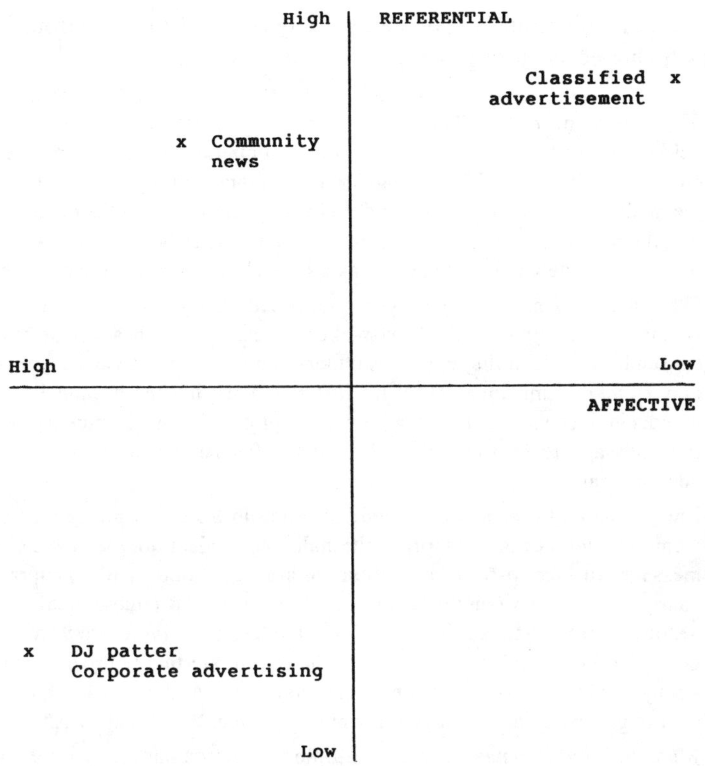

Figure 13.1 The Two Dimensions of (Mis)Communication (Following Holmes, 1989)

referential in nature. A classified advertisement in a newspaper miscommunicates through wrong information, not because it offends its readers. Conversely if an event is high on the affective axis, then miscommunication will be largely a matter of disrupted interpersonal relations.

Miscommunication in the Media

I have said that in face-to-face interaction we can locate miscommunication either with the speaker or hearer (or both). Mass communication multiplies the number of participants and in so doing multiplies the sites at which miscommunication may occur. Take the situation in which the propositional content of some situation is misreported in the news media.

The miscommunication may be cited at any or all of the numerous steps along which a news story passes:

(1) The source or newsmaker may mispresent the message. This could be deliberate, for instance in the case of a politician covering up a problem. It could be unintentional, resulting from ignorance or ineptitude in handling the media. In any case, it is a standard belief of those whom the media report that their message has been miscommunicated. Later in this chapter we will turn to examine what some newsmakers say about such mispresentations.

(2) What the newsmaker says is then interpreted by a journalist. The journalist may misunderstand the newsmaker's message. Such an error may be caused by failure in the reporter's understanding. Alternatively, the reporter may *choose* to misunderstand, for instance believing the newsmaker to be mendacious (a standard journalistic conception of those in power) and the true message to be therefore different from what the newsmaker wanted communicated.

(3) The journalist turns his or her understanding into another message, derived from but not necessarily propositionally equivalent to the newsmaker's message. In face-to-face interaction we are—for good or ill—generally in charge of our own communicative destiny. In media communication, that destiny is in the hands of others. Media messages are therefore very largely generated not by the groups or individuals who are their subject or source, but by third parties—professional communicators. At the very least, this may lead to groups being portrayed in ways other than they would wish.

(4) Most media genres pass through multiple production hands, both for editing purposes and for technical production such as typesetting or camera work. News is a classic case of multiple producers. Steps (2) and (3) above may be recycled 6 or even 10 times for a single news story. That is, the finished news message is subject to misunderstanding and mispresentation not only by the original journalist but also by the many subsequent newsworkers who handle it. We have not just one communication situation but many, embedded within each other, each with its own potential for miscommunication. The opportunities for mistransmission of the newsmaker's original message are enhanced at every step.

(5) Finally, the media message has passed through all its intermediaries and is ready for transmission to its mass audience. It is at this point that mass communication differs most radically from face-to-face interaction, because the mass audience is absent from the communicators, with limited opportunity for feedback, interchange, or correction. The audience therefore may on its part misunderstand the message communicated in the media, regardless of the accuracy of that message.

In earlier research on editing inaccuracy, I found that miscommunication of the propositional content of a media message can occur at one or more points (Bell 1983, 1984). It is also cumulative, with any instance adding to the one before, and with any miscommunication likely to be compounded at later stages of the process. The present study examines miscommunication of content through the mass media. It focuses only on the referential aspect of miscommunication. In face-to-face interaction the referential is arguably often less important than the affective. But in the media it is this aspect that receives continuing attention from researchers, newsmakers, and the public—the issue of whether the media are presenting accurate information (which is not to deny that media misinformation may have repercussions in intergroup relations, for example through inaccurate, stereotyped portrayals of minorities).

Misunderstanding the Media

Media offer a distinctive communication situation, involving a disjunction of place, and often also of time, between communicator and audience. This fracture in the communication process has significant consequences for the quality of communication. Centrally, the feedback that is an integral factor in individual spoken communication is delayed, impoverished, or lacking altogether in mass communication.

The media offer the communicator none of the opportunities for correction or clarification that are intrinsic to face-to-face conversation. The lack of two-way communication is demonstrably a contributor to the occurrence of miscommunication. Humphreys-Jones (1986) has shown that speakers usually become aware of miscommunication because of their hearer's inappropriate response. In mass communication, audiences are deprived of the usual means of inducing communicators to explain or clarify their meanings. Mass communicators are deprived of the usual access to recipients' reactions (McQuail, 1987) which could inform them that their message is being misunderstood.

Although feedback is not absent from the mass communication process, in few cases is it immediate enough for communicators to clear up on-the-spot audience misunderstanding. Apart from the phone-in radio program, most direct feedback by the audience is subject to delay—influencing subsequent but not immediate production. In addition to making contact with the media organization, the other form of feedback is through audience or circulation figures. People exercise their main influence on the media just through being the audience. In face-to-face interaction, communication breakdown between individuals is the extreme end product of miscommunication, but with the media, communication breakdown is their normal means of feedback. Dissatisfied audience members switch off, tune in elsewhere, buy another newspaper rather than contact the offending media organization.

In the absence of direct audience feedback, communicators become more reliant on monitoring their own production. Media communication is the composite product of multiple professional communicators—writers, editors, producers, technicians, and others. Many of these are employed for the exact task of clarifying other communicators' output (Bell, 1984, in press). The processes for minimizing miscommunication are therefore largely internal to media organizations. But two characteristics of media organizations and personnel promote miscommunication: They are normally ignorant of and out of touch with their audiences; and their reaction to attempted corrective feedback over errors is hostile disbelief (Burns, 1977; Schlesinger, 1987).

Research on Media Miscommunication

The label *miscommunication* has not been widely applied in media studies. Nevertheless the extent to which the media mispresent—or audiences misunderstand—content has been researched in a number of traditions. Four of these are particularly relevant here (although they are not necessarily exclusive of each other).

Analysis of media content has a long tradition in communications research. It flourished particularly in the United States from the 1930s to 1960s, producing numerous studies of many media genres, including news, soap opera, cartoon strips, and advertising. During the 1930s and 1940s, research tended to focus on propaganda. There was always concern with the way in which media could be used to present biased content in order to influence audiences. The research was traditionally quantitative or pseudoquantitative (Berelson, 1952; Budd, Thorp, & Donohew, 1967), relying on coding aspects of content into a number of discrete categories. The technique has continued to be used in one form or another, often with a focus on bias in the communication under study.

Second, what I will loosely term the ideological decoding approach has had wide currency in Europe for a number of years. Researchers have examined many media genres with a view to identifying and exposing the ideological frameworks that underpin their messages. In many instances the researchers characterize what is found as bias—that is, systematic mispresentation of groups or issues.

Some of the best known—although not necessarily the best executed—studies of this kind have been performed by the Glasgow University Media Group (1976, 1980, 1985). Initially concentrating on industrial reporting in British television news, they found that by a number of measures the coverage could be considered biased. More recently, they focused on defense news, in coverage of nuclear weapons and the peace movement, and of the 1982 Falklands/Malvinas war. Other research of this kind has also concentrated on news (e.g., van Dijk, 1988), but some studies have looked at other media genres such as advertising (Davis & Walton, 1983). Such research concentrates on media products and attempts to make inferences concerning the biases of their creators on the basis of their content. Students of the processes which produce media content (e.g., Gans, 1979; Tuchman, 1978) show convincingly that the way in which media personnel select messages to be sent is culturally and ideologically determined. Again, news and news production have been favored as a site for such studies. The routine practices of news constitute a filter that many conceivably newsworthy issues never penetrate. News is what news-workers can report on, and newsworkers largely cover what is available from a narrow network of established sources.

A third area of research applies similar assumptions to the flow rather than the generation of news. I have noted already the potential that the multiple handling of media content offers for miscommunication. Research on the "gatekeeping" performance of news editors was pioneered by White (1950). Such studies (e.g., Gieber, 1956; Hester, 1971) examine the kind of news copy an editor receives and compare it with the copy the editor sends. From imbalances in selection, the researcher draws inferences concerning the news values of gatekeepers or their institutions. The structure of such values was analyzed by Galtung and Ruge (1965), who posited that the news value of a story was enhanced by such factors as recency, unambiguity, and negativity.

News has been the focus of a large proportion of empirical research on mass media. The claim of news to cover matters of day-by-day significance, and to do so without bias or mispresentation, is doubtless a major factor in this interest. All the strands of research summarized above are essentially concerned with bias in media representations of issues, situations, and groups. Some of them focus explicitly on the stereotypical or inaccurate representation of disadvantaged groups such as ethnic minorities, women, or the aged (e.g., Hartmann & Husband, 1974). A variation on such an approach is found in Bell (1983, 1986) who examined the ways in which news stories were inaccurately edited as they were transmitted from editor to editor. Such research has the advantage of being able to treat the input text as a yardstick of accuracy, thus identifying any significant semantic mismatch between input and the editor's output as an inaccuracy.

One final strand of research is the direct study of news accuracy. Charnley (1936) pioneered this kind of investigation by clipping stories from local newspapers and sending them to sources cited in the report to identify any inaccuracies. This and subsequent studies (e.g., Blankenburg, 1970) have found on average roughly one error per story, with usually about half the stories rated fully accurate. Aware of the pitfalls of having sources as sole judges of accuracy, other researchers have developed other ways to identify inaccuracies in reporting. Lawrence and Grey (1969) interviewed the reporter as well as sending questionnaires to the reported. Scanlon (1972) had fieldworkers in effect re-cover the stories and judge the accuracy of the original report. The main data I shall use in this chapter come from an accuracy study using these methods which I conducted on New Zealand media in 1988.[2]

Most relevant research has investigated mispresentation in media messages, but some has taken account of how the audience (mis)understand these messages. Some studies have been concerned, for instance, with whether satirical programs whose clear aim is to question racial stereotyping (e.g., *All in the Family*) may be used to reinforce rather than reduce such attitudes (Vidmar & Rokeach, 1974). An early study of this kind (Cooper & Jahoda, 1947) showed that racists perceived antiracist cartoons as supporting, not negating, their own point of view. One of the findings of media effects research is that audiences tend to hear what they want to hear, interpreting content in terms of their own viewpoints.

There are some studies of the degree of misunderstanding by audiences of media content. Some of this is sponsored (unsurprisingly) by advertising interests (e.g., Jacoby & Hoyer, 1987). Van Dijk (1988) has expanded his interest in discourse analysis to news, including research on how audiences comprehend news texts. Again it becomes clear that recall of news is very imperfect, with only between 5% and 30% recalled immediately after reception. One strand of research shows how people interpret information they receive according to certain mental "scripts" or frameworks, which enable them to relate incoming information to what they already know (van Dijk, 1988). Jensen (1988) shows that "The Environment" is one over-arching script that audiences bring to bear on news. People easily mix up information from different stories with similar mental scripts. On occasions audiences will confuse events in two similar stories, for instance remembering the details of one civil disturbance as belonging to another.

The indications are, then, of considerable non-comprehension of the news. Rather surprisingly, most of this work has focused on the amount of information that is recalled. Little is said on the accuracy or otherwise of what audiences do remember. There has been little research on miscomprehension—inaccurate recall as opposed to forgetting. But Gunter's

(1987) survey concludes that the audience's recall of television news is usually inaccurate as well as poor and brief.

Media Miscommunication of Science News

As a case study, I shall take data from extensive recent research on the (mis) communication of science news in the New Zealand media (Bell, 1989). The study was in two complementary parts, covering both media reporting and public understanding of the issue. News—together with advertising—is common to all the mainline mass media of press, radio, and television. It is also a particularly apt site for examining referential miscommunication, because the genre is founded on the premise of accurate reporting of factual material. The ethos of newsworkers is that they present the facts unvarnished and the world as it is, without prejudice or interpretation. Such an ethos is of course open to question, and much of the literature cited earlier does question it and on good grounds. Nevertheless, the beliefs persist. As a subeditor who once worked for me put it "Facts are the cornflakes of journalism. There can be no dispute about a fact."

Within the news genre, the topic of science is itself particularly illuminating of the genre. The methods, timeframes, and purposes of scientific research differ widely from those of news media. The news cycle is 24 hours—the cycle of scientific research is often years. News seeks for facts as definite and unqualified as possible. The findings of science are often in news terms almost qualified to death. So when science and the news media meet, the spark of opposites should be enlightening. There have been several studies, all in the United States, on the accuracy of science news (e.g., Moore & Singletary, 1985; Pulford, 1976; Tankard & Ryan, 1974). Inaccuracies ranged from misleading headlines, misstatements of facts, omission of relevant information, sensationalizing, misquotation, and misspellings, to science-specific errors such as ignoring continuity with earlier research, overemphasizing nonscientific aspects, and treating speculation as fact.

The New Zealand Media Report on Climate Change

Climate Change includes two largely separate phenomena: the greenhouse effect and its impacts on the environment, and the depletion of the ozone layer. These were the biggest continuing science news in the New Zealand media (and in many other countries) during the late 1980s. The issues are of great importance to the future of humankind, and accurate communication and understanding of them is correspondingly significant. They are also scientifically complex.

The data consist of all New Zealand news coverage of the climate change issue for six months in 1988. The resulting sample contained 360 clips or transcripts—over 20,000 column centimeters, an average of about two stories per day in New Zealand's daily press. Clips were sent back to sources cited, mostly scientists or other specialists such as resource managers, planners, and engineers. The accompanying questionnaire asked sources to specify any points where the news story had misreported them, and elicited information on how the story came about. The response rate was 78%, giving a sample of 201 stories for which questionnaires were completed and analyzed.

Questioning quoted sources about the accuracy of a report is one method of assessing the degree of miscommunication of referential content in news media. It assumes that the source is best placed to judge a report's accuracy. That assumption is only partially warranted, because research in this tradition has shown that journalists dispute many claims made by sources (Lawrence & Grey, 1969). What a source holds to be error, the journalist often regards as point of view. The technique, then, is partial. It is however, better suited to coping with science news, which is more free of concern with personal image and advancement than, for example, political news. It is also the parallel in mass communication of the technique Humphreys-Jones (1986) adopted to identify and analyze misunderstandings in face-to-face interaction. She relied on a hearer's inappropriate response to a speaker's utterance to identify misunderstanding of speaker's intent. We use the journalist's retelling of a source's information in the form of a published story as the means to identify mispresentation, with the source as the judge of the accuracy of that retelling.

Mispresentation of Climate Change

Scientific sources were asked to rate the stories quoting them on a 5-point scale. A score of 1 signifies completely accurate reporting, a score of 5 extremely inaccurate reporting. Twenty-nine percent of the respondents gave the story reporting them a clean bill of health, assessing the report as absolutely accurate with a score of 1. The remaining 71% believed there was misreporting of some kind: 55% scored the story at 2, 9% at 3, 3% 4, and 4% scored the report as maximally inaccurate at 5. Clearly, a significant minority of stories contained no misreporting at all, and over 80% are rated no worse than slightly inaccurate. In most cases the degree of perceived inaccuracy is therefore small, but in another significant minority of stories there is severe misreporting.

Having given a story a general rating on the 1-5 scale, sources were asked to specify the kinds of inaccuracies present. Abut a third of stories contained factual inaccuracy of some kind: technical terms misused, wrong figures given, name of person or organization wrong, or some kind of misquotation. Sources had less problem with the broad structure of stories than with the detailed information. A quarter of them felt something significant had been omitted, or that there had been exaggeration or overstatement. Only one fifth believed there had been distortion in the balance of a story, with something over- or underemphasized.

Turning to specific examples of misreporting, several recurrent problems stand out. Scientists often consider headlines a particular problem, and our sources found inaccurate headlines in 12% of the press clips. Many stories that had inaccuracies in the body copy compound those with a headline which took the story from bad to worse. The main problem was overstatement, particularly on impacts of the greenhouse effect.

Source attribution was an extreme problem in one story, syndicated around seven daily newspapers, which caused the source to rate the story "extremely inaccurate". The story quoted the source at some length, partly in direct quotations. The source, however, denied having provided the quoted material. He believed that the journalist had probably obtained the material from a colleague in the same scientific organization, and then wrongly attributed it to the published source (the two share the same first name).

One obvious area of scientific inaccuracy was exaggeration. Sea level rises and other such figures were on occasion given in the wrong unit of measurement. Thus, the sea level around New Zealand was reported to be already rising at 1-2 centimeters per year when the source had (correctly) said millimeters. Another story had a source say in direct quotation that the amount of carbon dioxide in the atmosphere would increase 20-fold in the next 50 years: The scenario is for a 2-fold increase. A temperature rise prediction was reported as "four degrees Celsius in 20 years" when that is the upper limit scientists suggest for twice the length of time. These inaccuracies do not occur at random. All exaggerate and none reduce, which effectively enhances the news value of the story. Despite this, however, most media reports of potential temperature and sea level rises were within the scenarios suggested by scientists.

Time scope was an occasional problem. Quoting sea level rises without time frames sometimes made the distant future sound closer. In two cases, huge rises in sea level were mentioned—30 meters and 60 meters—without indication that they presupposed centuries-long melting of polar ice caps. Place scope was a problem in the broadcast news item that said "seven of New Zealand's eight warmest years have been in the 1980s." The meteorologist quoted the figure as a general southern hemisphere average, not specific to New Zealand. Figures for other parameters such as rises in carbon dioxide or sea level were on occasions treated as specific to New Zealand when they were global—or sometimes even northern hemisphere—averages. Such specific figures are a particularly interesting study, because they enable us to compare the levels for temperature and sea level rises publicized in the media with those volunteered by members of the public.

The other striking scientific mispresentation is some confusion between the greenhouse effect and ozone depletion. The two phenomena are largely distinct, occurring through different processes and at different heights in the atmosphere, although involving some of the same atmospheric gases. The science, however, is complex and difficult, and confusion in reporting is unsurprising. One story in the sample consisted of paragraph after paragraph mixing the two phenomena in impossible ways. The confusion in particular presents ozone depletion as the cause of the greenhouse effect (which it is not):

> The greenhouse effect is a global warming as a result of increased levels of carbon dioxide in the atmosphere, and a reduction of the ozone layer.

Notable for its level of misunderstanding and consequent mispresentation was a story in Wellington's morning daily *The Dominion* concerning a national climate change conference. The scientist quoted identified 12 inaccuracies in a few paragraphs, and rated the story very inaccurate. Under the headline DESERT-LIKE CONDITIONS PREDICTED, the first paragraph began:

> New Zealand could face a water shortage similar to Israel's by 2030 if world temperatures continued to rise . . .
>
> Every drop of water would have to be used—possibly several times.

In a country whose present average rainfall is about 1,000 mm a year, this would indeed be startling news. I need only quote the source's comment:

> The reference to Israel is quite extraordinary, since what I said is that the dry areas would need to learn to use their water more efficiently, just as Israel has done. . . . The emphasis on desert-like conditions is a gross distortion of a 2-day seminar which covered an immense range of topics.

The urge to get the most out of a story is exemplified in one particularly interesting case. A television news item said:

> A DSIR scientist is predicting more of the weather which has battered the country over recent months. . . . A simple change in weather patterns can't be ruled out, but Dr. Betteridge believes the evidence points to the greenhouse effect.

The source's comment was that the journalist had tried to push him to make a greenhouse effect interpretation of current weather conditions, which had included devastation of one region by Cyclone Bola. However, the source—official spokesperson on climate change issues for the Department of Scientific and Industrial Research—had explicitly refused. The journalist managed to get the interpretation in anyway.

The Causes of Mispresentation

These then are some of the ways in which newsmakers find that what they say is mispresented by newsworkers. It is interesting to look at the causes that sources believed underlay the problems they identified in stories. One question on the survey asked: "What do you think were the reasons any inaccuracies occurred?" The most frequent reason offered was that the issue was too complex, reflecting a pessimism on the part of specialist sources that their information can be presented accurately in the public media. As one source wrote: "'Greenhouse' in many ways is so complex it is inappropriate to news reporting formats". Some of the answers attributed problems to the constraints of journalism, saying the story was too short for the subject matter or that the journalist was in a hurry. A minority of sources were self-aware enough to admit that their own communication of information had been inadequate. A few felt they had themselves overstated things in the heat of interview or public speaking. Others volunteered that they had not explained themselves clearly enough.

Analyzing the data on how different stories came about, we can see that there is a relationship between how some stories originate and their degree of inaccuracy. Some newspapers in the sample were less accurate than others, pushing for enterprising reporting at the expense of accuracy. Figure 13.2 graphs the mean number of inaccuracies per story according to five factors in story origin. Stories initiated by the source or press officer in the source's organization averaged less than 1 inaccuracy each, while those initiated by the journalist averaged 3 inaccuracies. The difference reflects factors such as the in-house press officer's practice of having

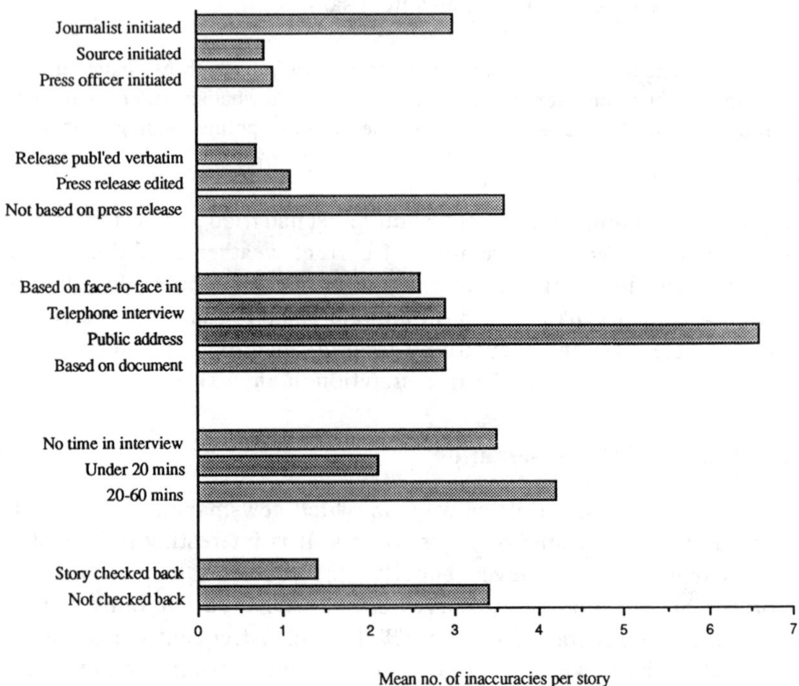

Figure 13.2 Inaccuracy Index on Climate Change Reporting

press releases checked by the source. Sources who initiate a story may also be predisposed to judge the outcome positively. Stories based on press releases were also rated more accurate than the rest even when the releases was edited heavily or added to (Figure 13.2).

Most stories had arisen from interviews, with written documents or public addresses forming the basis for others. Public addresses were very badly reported, with a mean number of over six inaccuracies per story. Because reporting speeches is a basic journalistic skill, this is a disturbing finding for the profession. It is evident that neither journalists nor sources should rely on public speeches as the sole input to a story. Interviews that were longer or conducted face-to-face did not necessarily result in more accurate stories (a finding paralleled in U.S. studies of science news such as Tankard & Ryan, 1974). Journalists are reluctant to check back copy with sources (only 14% of the stories in my sample were checked), but checked stories were twice as accurate as those not checked (Figure 13.2).

It is worth noting here the way in which news interviews are conducted, and the checks they contain – and lack – for revealing any misunderstanding by the reporter. Interviews are not conversations in which participants offer similar amounts of talk. The reporter's function is to ask questions, the source's to answer them. This produces a situation in which the journalist is usually not feeding back paraphrases of the source's information in a way that would enable the source to identify any problems in understanding. Humphreys-Jones (1986) found that 74% of realizations that there had been a misunderstanding were by the speaker not the hearer. But the news interview generally does not include restatement by the hearer-journalist of the source's information, so the source is largely unable to monitor whether there has been misunderstanding. The hearer is much less likely to come to that realization for him- or herself. This is reinforced by Milroy's (1984) finding that elliptical responses can conceal misunderstanding because they are less specific than a full utterance. The structure of turn-taking within interview situations of course ensures that ellipsis by the interviewer is a common form.

But mispresentation of information in the media is not just a matter of differing factors in the news gathering process. At one level, one can assume that these problems reflect a failure of understanding and/or expression on the part of the journalist. The newsworker who writes a story confusing the greenhouse effect and ozone depletion is presumably primarily lacking in scientific background.

Most of the mispresentations in the sample, however, cannot be put down simply to failure in comprehension. There is another factor operating here – news values. Journalists do not write articles – they write stories. Many inaccuracies serve to improve on the story, to make it sound a little better than it is. There is, for example, no instance in my sample of inaccuracy in units of measurement that *reduces* the unit, for instance from centimeters to millimeters. All go in the opposite direction, *increasing* the unit size. Mispresentations are not just a random scattering of failures to understand or report correctly. They are patterned in such a way as to enhance the news value of the story. In the terms introduced early in this chapter, mispresentation in news is a matter of referential content that is reported inaccurately. But the *reason* for this is affective: Good stories are believed to attract readers and sell newspapers. Therefore if the maximum possible is wrung from a story, more readers will be attracted; and on occasion, the maximum proves to be not permissible. The failure in referential accuracy is driven by affective motivations.

Such things do not only occur in the media. In Coupland, Coupland, Giles, and Henwood's (1988) case study of young-old miscommunication, the greatest problem for the young speaker occurred when she felt she had to mispresent her own views in the interests of keeping the conversation going. In so doing, she put the referential at the service of the affective, subordinating and even falsifying content in order to maintain a working conversational relationship.

This is not to say that journalists are consciously falsifying the news, nor is such a suggestion necessary. The excellent work by Gans (1979), Tuchman (1978), and others has made it only too clear how unconscious and ingrained are the selection processes that newsworkers follow to make their product. We have found that some stories do overstate the advance of climate change, confuse ozone and greenhouse, or misquote their sources. There are failures in the core journalistic skills of accurate quotation and reporting of basic facts. The news values that drive traditional journalism have led to instances of news staff overstating what their sources say. But striking though these examples are, they should not obliterate the fact of the scientists' own assessments across six months' coverage: that the large majority of stories are at worst only slightly inaccurate.

Climate of Opinion

We have seen the extent to which there is media mispresentation of the scientific content of the climate change issue. We are now able to turn to the receivers' side of the process and gauge to what extent the information—whether represented accurately or inaccurately—may be misunderstood by the public.

After the conclusion of the period during which media coverage was sampled, I conducted a pilot-scale survey into the level of public understanding of the issue. A sample of 61 informants representing a cross-section of New Zealand society were questioned on what they thought were the nature, causes, and effects of ozone depletion and of the greenhouse effect. Additional questions asked where their information had come from, and elicited demographic data. The sample was a quota sample, chosen to match the population proportions of the latest (1986) census on five parameters: age, gender, ethnic group, occupation, and area of residence.

As an object of study, this issue has one notable advantage: The media are the sole source of information for most of the population. All 58 informants who knew anything about the issue cited the principal daily media as a source. Eight cited friends as well as the media, and a couple mentioned other nonmedia sources. This confirms that an assessment of the public's understanding of the issue is broadly equivalent to an assessment of how they understand the media input. On most public issues, such as politics, education, or health, people will draw heavily on their own and others' experience as well as media-derived information. But for climate change, virtually all information is obtained from the media at either first- or secondhand.

Public Knowledge and Media Input

Almost everyone knew something about climate change. Of our small cross-section of New Zealand society, 93% knew about ozone depletion and 80% about the greenhouse effect. The simple fact that greenhouse means warming is well known. The nature of ozone depletion is less well known, although people know about the ozone hole. The causes of ozone depletion are much better known that the causes of the greenhouse effect. Nearly half the sample knew nothing at all about the causes of greenhouse warming. People knew a good deal about the impacts of both ozone depletion and the greenhouse effect, but often attributed rising temperatures to ozone depletion.

We were able to compare public understanding with media input on several aspects of climate change ("facts" in news terms): place and time of the ozone hole, causes of ozone depletion, temperature and sea level rises, and confusion between the greenhouse effect and ozone depletion. All mentions of these "facts" had been analyzed in the entire six-month sample of media coverage. In general we found a high level of *mis*match between largely accurate media input and exaggeration, inaccuracy, and confusion in the public mind.

A large majority of informants (52) confused ozone depletion and the greenhouse effect in some way. The main sites of confusion seemed to be that greenhouse and ozone are a single phenomenon, with ozone depletion as the cause of greenhouse warming. These are exactly the confusions that we found in the media sample, but that does not mean the media have created the public's confusion. The media are reflecting public confusion rather than vice versa. Only a small percentage of stories contained this confusion. Journalists are ordinary citizens with lay persons' understanding of atmospheric science. It is not surprising they share the public's inability to keep the two phenomena apart in their minds.

This confusion is an instance of what researchers on news comprehension have called *meltdown*. For instance, audiences have a mental "script" concerning the pattern of demonstrations or civil unrest. Information from items with similar scripts can be easily confused. Findahl and Hoijer (1981) and Jensen (1988) have both found that information about such events in one country became confused with what were perceived as similar events in another country also reported in the same news bulletin.

This process may increase over time, so that there is an increasing meltdown effect of information from one story merging into another (Woodall, Davis, & Sahin, 1983).

At one point public knowledge and media input on climate change did largely coincide. Both media and public placed the ozone hole correctly over Antarctica, with a handful of stories and informants both mentioning the lesser Arctic hole (Table 13.1). But on timing there was a complete mismatch between the coverage and the public's understanding. People said either that the hole was there all year, or that it occurred in summer—errors that did not occur in media coverage. There is no recall among our cross-section of the New Zealand public of the large number of media references to springtime. That fact seems to have been overwhelmed by another factor in the public mind. Probably awareness that summer is the time of naturally decreasing ozone and increasing ultraviolet radiation over New Zealand has been projected back on to the Antarctic situation.

Again, there is a mismatch between the balance of media reporting of the products that deplete the ozone layer and the public's understanding. News reporting closely reflects the actual ozone depleting potential of New Zealand usage. Aerosol spray cans, refrigerants, manufacture of plastic foams, and fire extinguishers contribute between 20% and 30% each, and received generally similar proportions of the mentions in the media. But people are exaggerating the contribution of spray cans three-fold (74% of public mentions), downplaying refrigeration and plastic foams, and completely ignoring fire extinguishers. Again, it is factors other than direct media input that seem to be influencing people's understanding. It seems likely that people are focusing on spray cans as the product that is most under their individual control, or they may be impressed by the obviousness of aerosols' release into the atmosphere.

Exaggerating the Greenhouse Effect

Most telling are the kinds of figures that informants suggested for potential temperature and sea level rises. The global scenarios most accepted by scientists and publicized in the media at this time were the figures derived from the 1985 scientific conference in Villach, Austria. These suggested average global temperature rises of 1.5 to 4.5 degrees Celsius by 2030, and a sea level rise of 20 to 140 cm in the same period of some 40 years. In December 1988 the New Zealand Climate Committee of the Royal Society of New Zealand published its assessment. It offered as a "most likely scenario" for New Zealand a 1.5 degrees temperature rise, and 20 to 40 cm sea level rise by 2050 (60 years). As a likely upper limit within the same period, the Committee suggested 3 degrees warming

Table 13.1 Place and Time where Ozone Hole Occurs as Mentioned by the Public (Number of References by Informants), and as Reported by the Media (Number of Stories in Which Mentioned)

	Public mentions		*Media mentions*	
	N	*Percentage*	*N*	*Percentage*
Antarctic	29	82%	67	97%
Arctic	3	9%	2	3%
New Zealand	3	9%	0	0%
Total	35	100%	69	100%
Spring	0	0%	40	87%
Summer	5	50%	0	0%
Winter	0	0%	6	13%
All year	5	50%	0	0%
Total	10	100%	46	100%

and a 30 to 60 cm sea level rise. The Committee's findings had been widely publicized less than a month before the public survey, and were probably the most recent figures in informants' minds.

We can make a comparison among the figures suggested by the public, those publicized by the media, and the scientists' original estimates. The media generally reported the scientists' figures accurately, although we have mentioned some instances of exaggeration above. Note first that three quarters of the informants could offer no specific figures for temperature rise. This lack of specific information seems at first surprising in view of the amount of coverage the issue had received, and its importance to people's lives. However, in the light of the minimal recall of news information revealed by researchers such as van Dijk (1988), Gunter (1987), and Wodak (1987), it is perhaps more surprising that so many offered a figure at all. Of those who did mention figures, half volunteered only a temperature and no time frame in which it would occur, or gave an approximate time frame but no temperature. These were excluded from the analysis.

The remaining answers, listed in Table 13.2, are those which gave both a temperature rise and a time period. Even using the most conservative basis of comparison—the upper range of the Villach estimates and informants' lowest estimates—3 out of the 11 gave answers well beyond the upper limit of scientific estimates. In one case the overestimation was by a factor of 9, in the two other cases, by a factor of 2 or 3. The other figures fell within the Villach limits, three at the upper end. It seems

Table 13.2 Estimations of Potential Temperature Rises Made by 11 Members of the New Zealand Public, Compared to the Scenario Derived from the Report of the 1985 Villach Scientific Conference and that Published in the 1988 Royal Society of New Zealand Report

	Temperature rise in degrees Celsius	*Time period (years)*	*Accuracy*
Villach	1.5-4.5	40	–
Royal Society	1.5-3.0	60	–
Informants	3-4	100-150	Low range
	0.5	20	Low range
	1-2	50-100	Low range
	2-3	50	Low range
	2	8-50	Low range
	5	50 plus	Top range
	2	10-20 plus	Top range
	1-2	10	Top range
	4	20	2x overestimate
	3	10	3x
	1-2	Each year	9x

clear then that public understanding has picked up the higher values suggested by scientists, and in many cases has actually exaggerated these considerably.

More informants gave complete information on a rise in sea level within a given time period. This probably reflects both greater attention in the media, and the obvious potential impact on an island nation such as New Zealand. Fourteen responses specified both rise and time frame (Table 13.3). Again we will use the upper limit of scientific figures for comparison. We have two informants offering figures in the lower range of scientific predictions, three in the mid range, and one at the upper limit. The other eight informants all offer figures that are beyond even the most extreme limits. In two cases the overestimation is marginal, by only 20% to 50%. But in four cases it is by a factor of 3 or 4, and in two cases it is 8 times above the maximum projection. If we compared these figures with the recent and more conservative Royal Society figures, which should have been freshest in informants' minds, the exaggeration would be many times greater.

Recalling that our media sample contained much of the input to public understanding in the months before the survey, we must conclude that public misunderstanding here considerably exceeds the balance of what was presented in the media. This is despite one story widely published in December 1988 which talked of an 8-meter sea level rise in an implied

Table 13.3 Estimates of Potential Sea Level Rises made by 14 Members of the New Zealand Public, Compared to the Scenario Derived from the Report of the 1985 Villach Scientific Conference and that Published in the 1988 Royal Society of New Zealand Report

	Sea level rise in meters	*Time period (years)*	*Accuracy*
Villach	0.2-1.4	40	–
Royal Society	0.2-0.6	60	–
Informants	1-2	100-150	Low range
	0.6	50	Low range
	1	50	Mid range
	1	50	Mid range
	1-2	50	Mid range
	1	30	Top range
	2-3	50	1.2x overestimate
	1	20	1.5x
	1	10	3x
	1	10	3x
	1	10	3x
	1.5	10	4x
	8	30	8x
	3	10	8x

time frame of 60 years. It is likely this contributed to the public's exaggeration, despite the later, equally prominent coverage given to the conservative Royal Society figures.

Conclusion

The theoretical and practical implications of our findings are considerable. We examined a number of the basic "facts" of climate change as they are represented in the news media and recalled by the public. Although serious mispresentation is rare in news coverage, there are enough instances to warrant concern over the quality of communication. We have seen how the push for news interest is in many cases the force behind specific inaccuracies. As I found in the study of editing (Bell, 1983, 1984), inaccuracies are not randomly patterned. If they were, they might be considered simply the result of failure in technical journalistic skills. On the contrary, they serve to enhance the news value of stories in which they occur. They increase news impact in areas such as immediacy (making sea level rises sound imminent), proximity (applying global figures to New Zealand), or negativity (enhancing the scale of climate change impacts).

The majority of media reporting is largely accurate, but in many cases there is conspicuous mismatch between what is reported and what the public understands. Much of the misunderstanding seems to be the public's own work. Scientists, other newsmakers—and even the public, media personnel, and researchers—have all tended to credit the media with causing any misunderstandings that the public may have. But mispresentation seems to play a smaller part in media miscommunication processes than many have assumed.

What can explain this mismatch? Two distinct strands of research indicate what may be happening here. First, much of the work on how the media affect and influence their audience indicates that people's existing attitudes are a powerful filter through which media messages must penetrate (e.g., McQuail, 1987). Early research on media effects tended to conclude that the media had a very great influence on their audience, but later findings are of a much less direct link between media input and public attitudes.

Second, research in cognitive psychology and artificial intelligence (e.g., Rumelhart, 1975) has examined how hearers understand stories. The researchers have concluded that people bring preexisting mental scripts to their comprehension, interpreting the new information in the light of quite general and fixed preconceived frameworks. Van Dijk (1988) maintains that readers have *cognitive schemata* that enable them to fill out the content of a news story from their own prior knowledge, and relate the new information to what they already know. In fact, some degree of prior knowledge is a precondition of being informed by the news at all (Wodak, 1987).

The concept of scripts or schemata by which audiences interpret news is a useful one for explaining how the audience approaches climate change. It seems likely that audience members have mental scripts which enable them to interpret information on environmental issues in the light of how previous environmental issues were experienced. Jensen (1988) calls such generalized interpretations *super-themes*. In his in-depth study of viewers' understanding of a Danish television news broadcast, the salience of environment as a super-theme was shown by an environmental interpretation being projected on to two stories to which it was marginal, as well as on to two centrally environmental topics. The phenomenon of meltdown has already been noted in the confusion of the greenhouse effect with ozone depletion. The public's interpretation of incoming information in the light of their existing (lack of) knowledge is clearly a powerful filter.

Although we have found that specific information is misunderstood, yet undoubtedly a general message of concern is getting through to people. That is, the referential content may not be accurately recalled but, on the affective dimension, general concern about global climate changes is being generated. Does it matter that people misunderstand the specifics if they get the general drift? Yes, because some of the misunderstandings affect individual or political action on the issues. A person who thinks high ultraviolet radiation is the same as high temperature may not take precautions when ultraviolet is high but temperature less so. And someone who thinks ozone depletion is the cause of the greenhouse effect may believe wrongly that not using spray cans will stop global warming. People who are magnifying in their own minds scientific scenarios of temperature or sea level rise are likely, if and when the rises do not occur, to turn against the scientists and journalists who they regard as the source of those messages.

Our study leads to a number of specific recommendations by which media presentation and public understanding can be improved (see Bell, 1989). I believe news media should take into account the ways in which a story is open to public misunderstanding, and present it in such a way as to minimize confusion, exaggeration, or other forms of misunderstanding. For example, the tendency in broadcast news to link stories on supposedly related themes has been shown to lead to meltdown, to confusion between stories rather than clarification. Journalists also need reminding of a number of their basic professional skills. Some of this goes against long-entrenched news values on which journalists have been trained to operate—getting the most out of a story—but such values are called into question when they lead to misreporting or misunderstanding.

There are also steps scientists can take to promote accurate communication. They can play a more active part in interviews, checking out journalists' understanding while an interview is still in progress. They can emphasize the causes rather than exaggerating the impacts of climate change. The public's tendency to misunderstand is not an excuse for scientists to give up trying to communicate. Our findings show that a proportion of the information is remembered accurately. This study points to some ways in which scientists and journalists can work together to better inform the public about such technical issues.

Notes

1. The data in the latter part of this paper was collected for a project on media coverage and public understanding of the climate change issue in New Zealand. I gratefully acknowledge the support of the Department of Scientific and Industrial Research, Head Office (where

I work as a journalist and media consultant), and of the Ministry for the Environment. Detail of project methodology, findings, and recommendations is contained in Bell (1989). I am indebted to Jenny Neale for advice on survey design and methodology, to Andrew Matthews for scientific input, to Peter Clare for patient computer programming and processing, and to Susan Jordan and the other research assistants who labored on the project. Thanks to Victoria University's Stout Research Centre and Department of Linguistics for hospitality to me as an honorary research fellow. I thank Janet Holmes for comments on an earlier draft of the paper, and the editors of this volume whose commission led me into an absorbing and timely research project.

2. Research relevant to media miscommunication has focused overwhelmingly on the propositional content of the media, and little on affective miscommunication. Affective miscommunication between media and audiences is of supreme interest to media personnel and advertisers – "why don't they like what we are doing?" It is not obvious, however, that it offers much to researchers seeking to understand the media or miscommunication as a phenomenon. This seems to be a natural and inevitable consequence of the necessary lack of genuine relationship between media and their audience. Where most studies have looked for bias in media products, some interesting work has been more concerned with technical nonfluencies. Goffman's (1981) long essay on radio uses a corpus of bloopers to examine the "ways of our errors" and illuminate the nature of broadcast communication. But Goffman is less concerned with the miscommunicative aspects of such on-air lapses than with the light they cast on frame space, footing, and other communicative and interactional concerns.

14

Miscommunication at the Person-Machine Interface

Ronan G. Reilly

Introduction

The perspective of miscommunication can be applied to a variety of communicative modes at the person-machine interface. For example, we might apply it to the inappropriate use of command languages, or problems in the use of modern interface metaphors such as the "desk top" metaphor used in some personal computers. Although we will briefly deal with these broader issues, the primary focus of the chapter will be on the topic of robust natural language processing by computer.

The chapter is divided into four main sections. The first provides some definitions and a broad taxonomy of miscommunication. The second section examines the constraints that the current state of interface technology puts on person-machine interaction, and how these can influence the ease and reliability of communication. The third section looks at current research on computer-based natural language understanding, focusing in particular on models of dialogue understanding. The final section examines computational techniques for dealing with various types of miscommunication at the level of knowledge and belief.

Some Definitions

By the term *miscommunication*, I mean any form of misunderstanding or misinterpretation that ultimately leads to a disruption in the flow of dialogue and to explicit corrective action by the dialogue participants. The term ill-formedness, on the other hand, entails computational considerations. Ill-formedness usually refers to any input that the language understanding system cannot deal with in a straightforward manner. An utterance can be anything from lexically ill-formed (e.g., involving a misspelled word or a typographical error) to pragmatically ill-formed (e.g., a request for information to which the user is not entitled). One could define an ill-formed input as any utterance that requires correction and/or elaboration in order to be interpreted. Obviously, not all ill-formed input will lead to miscommunication. Misspellings and mispronunciations, for example, can often be processed without any disruption of the dialogue. In contrast, all miscommunications are caused by, or manifested as, ill-formed utterances (semantically and pragmatically ill-formed utterances in the main).

In the rest of the chapter, all examples of dialogue will assume two participants, *User* and *System*. It is important to note that some of the responses attributed to the system in the examples will exceed the capabilities of current implementations. They are intended to illustrate desired performance from future systems, rather than the current state of the art. In addition, any reference to miscommunication and ill-formedness can be assumed to involve the user as the primary instigator rather than the system. This does not exclude cases where the system may induce some kind of failure in the user, evidence of which is then detected in a subsequent utterance. We are merely taking as our starting point the situation where the system has detected an anomaly in the user's utterance.

In the following subsections I will present a finer-grained analysis of various types of ill-formedness and the communication failures to which they may give rise. The taxonomy is partly based on the work of Ringle and Bruce (1980), who identify two main categories of miscommunication in ordinary conversation that have some relevance to failure in person-machine communication: input failures and model failures. An input failure occurs when the participant is unable to obtain a complete, or at least a coherent, interpretation for an utterance; a model failure occurs when the listener is unable to assimilate inputs to a coherent belief model as intended by the speaker.

Input Failures

It is possible to distinguish between four levels of input failure (Ringle & Bruce identify only the first three):

(1) Perceptual failures: A word or phrase is not clearly perceived and no interpretation results. An analogue of this in the context of the person-machine interface would be a failure to understand a mistyped or misspelled word;
(2) Lexical failures: A word or phrase is clearly perceived but the participant either fails to produce the correct semantic interpretation or is unable to produce any interpretation at all. The computational analogue of this type of failure would be when a word is encountered that is not in the system's lexicon. It is obvious that in the context of keyboard input, the distinction between type (1) and (2) failures is not clearcut;
(3) Syntactic failures: Individual words and phrases are correctly perceived and interpreted, but the participant's intended meaning is misconstrued. This is probably the most common type of error to occur with a natural language interface. Such failures are likely to be due to a combination of ungrammatical input on the part of the user and an inadequate coverage of possible utterances by the system's parser; and
(4) Dialogue failures: This type of failure occurs when an utterance cannot be incorporated into the recipient's ongoing model of the dialogue. Such failures might occur, for example, if the system is unable to find a suitable referent for a pronoun.

Model Failure

Whereas input failures are local in origin, model failures are global in nature. They involve a failure of a dialogue participant to successfully map an utterance onto his or her belief model. Unfortunately, model failures are extremely difficult to study in naturalistic dialogue because there is no way to accurately assess a participant's belief model. They are, however, a likely cause of person-machine miscommunication given the novel nature of this type of communicative environment.

Somewhat along the lines of Webber and Mays (1983), I will distinguish between three types of model failure that are relevant to person-machine communication. These are assertional failure, explicit terminological failure, and implicit terminological failure.

Assertional failure occurs when the user assumes some fact to be true in the domain of discourse, when it is not. There is, nevertheless, no reason why the fact might not be true at some future time. An example of this from a college records domain is:

(D1)

User: How many males in the 3yr degree course?
System: There were none this year.

Explicit terminological failure occurs when a user of a system assumes that some fact is true or derivable, when this can never be the case. Again, in the context of a college records database, the query:

(D2)

User: How many students teach courses?
System: None. Students don't teach courses.

is an example of an explicit terminological failure. The reason why the request fails is not just because the data base contains no information about students who teach, but because it can never contain such facts. The request violates the system's domain, or terminological, knowledge.

An implicit terminological failure occurs when a request from the user is not answerable from within the system's knowledge base. An example of such a query is:

(D3)

User: Why was there such a large intake of females in 1980?
System: I don't know.

In any language understanding system there will be a boundary to the knowledge that the system can use to answer a query. All that can be done is to provide a facility for responding somewhat more gracefully than in (D3).

Current State of Interface Technology

Person-machine dialogue is supported physically by the input and output devices used by the computer system. In this section, I will look more closely at the possibilities available for using different kinds of input-output technology. The adoption of appropriate technology facilitates development of an optimum dialogue medium that can minimize the extent and frequency of communication failure.

The approach taken here is to recognize that input and output devices are normally linked together in functional sequences, and to describe the more common combinations. Gardiner and Christie (1987) liken these functional sequences to biological species that have developed as an adaptation to their environment; we can consider particular combinations or "species" of input-output interaction similarly to be evolving as an adaptation to the electronic office environment.

Keyboard Input

Keying input through a keyboard and seeing the output from a visual display unit (VDU) is the dominant form of user interface to a computer system. This species has the advantage that it is very familiar to many users, its main disadvantage is that it does not make full use of the wide range of communication "channels" (e.g., speech, gesture) that form a natural part of human communication in other contexts. The limitation is further exacerbated by the type of display normally used, which precludes very high resolution graphics and so severely limits visual communication from the machine to the human.

Menu Selection

The most common method of interaction within this class uses a keyboard for input, a VDU for output, and a menu from which the user can select the appropriate option. Traditional systems have relied on a numeric keypad by which the user indicates the number of the menu item he or she wishes to select. More recently, a different approach to selection has been developed, using a cursor controlled by a hand-held "mouse" or other pointing device which transmits x-y coordinates to the system. The cursor is movable and allows the user to indicate the desired display options. The cursor remains in position until moved by the user with the selection device or moved by the system in response to some user action.

Alongside the development of selection devices, there have been developments in display technology (including the bit-mapped display) to produce increasingly high resolution. This has led to the development of graphics displays and complementary interaction methods to enable the manipulation of graphical images. The combination of the mouse selection device and graphics display has been incorporated in a new style of interface, a kind of simulated desktop, an example of which can be found running on the Apple Macintosh computer.

This environment is ideal for inexperienced users because they are provided with familiar images and are guided through each stage of the interaction by an appropriate set of menu options presented as a list. The use of icons representing familiar objects and incorporated into a spatial representation of the user's normal environment (e.g., desktop, office) facilitates the use of existing psychological frames of reference. Add to this an integrated set of "tools" which allow the user to perform tasks avoiding computer jargon, and we have an interface that gives some protection against low-level miscommunication caused by various types of input failure. A thoroughgoing menu-driven interface constrains the scope of person-machine communication, however, and precludes the full use of natural language (see below). The items on the menu and the actions that the user can perform must be specified in advance by the system designer. This is acceptable in a narrow domain, but becomes unnecessarily restrictive the more functionality the user requires. It is no surprise that powerful operating systems such as Unix (a trademark of AT&T) do not lend themselves to menu-like implementation, but are mediated by a sophisticated command language.

Tactile Input

Touching what we see is one of our most basic forms of communication. It provides a natural and direct means of indicating selection and choice and is the means by which we operate many of the mechanisms available to us through switches, knobs, and other forms of control. Technologies have been developed to detect touch and these are combined with display devices to provide a mode of interaction that gives the user direct control. The touch may be via a stylus but is more usually the user's finger.

Given that it is a normal part of human communication in many contexts, touch is relatively easy to incorporate into communication with a machine. By providing redundant and/or unambiguous information to the system, it can do much to reduce the probability of communication failure resulting from a misinterpretation by the machine of a command given by the user.

Speech

Speaking is the most natural form of human communication using the medium of natural language. The ultimate goal of speech technology is the support of continuous spoken utterances from any speaker using an unlimited vocabulary. The current state of speech processing, however, is still a long way from achieving this target. Most current speech-understanding systems have limited ability to deal with continuous speech. Moreover, there is generally a trade-off between continuous speech understanding and the ability to deal with more than one speaker.

In the area of speech generation, three technologies are currently used to generate speech from a computer system. These are digital compression, phoneme synthesis, and prerecorded speech. With digital compression a set of spoken words is digitally encoded, compressed, and stored. This technique models the human vocal tract by simulating the parameters used in producing speech. Phoneme synthesis involves concatenating phonemes, the basic unit of speech sound. Prerecording involves recording spoken sentences or phrases in full and storing them for later "generation".

This technology is continually improving but the following general points apply. Digital compression tends to result in only moderate intelligibility, lacking in intonation. Phoneme synthesis is the most flexible technique but tends to sound unnatural and is often of low intelligibility because it lacks prosodic information. Prerecorded speech is the most natural but is the most limited in flexibility because all the words and sentences have to be spoken in advance in order to make the recordings.

Vision

Vision is used by us to locate items of interest and take in information about our environment, whether that information is moving images, other people, or text. It is therefore normally considered an input medium to the user. It can also be considered as an input to the system insofar as information located with the user's eyes can be used as a control action by the system. Looking provides an alternative modality in system communication to support other modes.

There is a technology available that is able to detect the user's direction of gaze. It uses an infrared light source to detect the movement of the eye between the pupil center and the cornea. The signals are picked up by a TV camera and computer-analyzed. It can be used in conjunction with a display of objects by the user to indicate selection. Feedback is provided to the user either by a cursor that follows the user's gaze or by a change in the display field.

Humans can exert very fine control over their eye movements, and in principle can use this to send very precise locational information to the system. In some cases, this could form a natural component in person-machine communications, as it does in normal interpersonal communications where direction of gaze can elicit appropriate behavior from the other person. However, it could also be potentially disrupting if not implemented appropriately. Much perceptual processing of the environment seems to be geared toward maintaining a subjectively stable perceptual field despite changes occurring at the retina. Violating this principle by linking eye movements (and the associated changes at the retina) too directly or inappropriately to changes in the environment (the display) could be expected to disrupt communication in some cases.

Gesture

Gesturing, ether pointing or gesticulating, with the hands is another form of human communication. It is generally used in conjunction with speaking to indicate the desired item from a group, such as in "I'll have that one". As such it minimizes the amount of voice communication required and increases the efficiency of communication.

Gesturing is another form of selecting and touching, although the technologies are not as well developed as for these other forms of communication. Its experimental use to date has been to supplement speech recognition, where deficiencies in the technology can be compensated by the additional information provided by gesturing. For example, if a user points to something and says "that," the speech recognition device only has to recognize a single word. In the absence of gesturing, the recognition device would have to interpret a lengthy description (Bolt 1980).

Multimedia Interaction

User input and output would benefit from devices supporting the whole range of human communication involving keying, selecting, touching, speaking, looking, and gesturing for input—and seeing and hearing for output. The essence is to enable the user to use any of the devices without constraint, according to the user's preferences and skill and the demands of the task. Where different devices are used to achieve the same action, the effects should be consistent across the range of devices. This so-called *modeless* interaction is an essential prerequisite for effective multimedia uses.

Future Developments

Multimedia interaction in principle matches to the greatest extent the richness of normal person-person communication. However, just as in normal person-person communication, it requires the system to integrate a large amount of information from a variety of different sources, and to do so very quickly in real time. This is a problem given the current state of development of technology, and a problem that is exacerbated by the requirement to load the user down with various sensing devices so that the system can pick up the necessary information. Developments in either or both of these areas would be a useful step forward in facilitating person-machine communication and reducing communication failure. In particular, such developments will help to minimize the occurrence of various types of low-level miscommunication caused by input ill-formedness. They will, however, provide little support for dealing with the more difficult problems of model failure. For this we need more sophisticated dialogue systems of the sort to be described in the next section.

Computational Approaches to Natural Language Dialogue Understanding

Early Approaches

Early natural language interfaces (as well as many current ones) were generally question-answering systems on well established rigid data bases. Some of them, such as PARRY (Colby 1975) and SHRDLU (Winograd, 1972), tried to model more complex conversations. The three major achievements of these and other earlier systems were the solution of simple anaphora, simple ellipsis, and the ability to explain and paraphrase.

More recently many research projects have attempted to tackle the computational modeling of natural language dialogue in all its complexity. An important motivation for this is to increase the robustness of the interface. One possible approach to developing a robust interface might be to append as a separate module a set of rules or heuristics designed to deal with miscommunication when and if it occurs. This approach, however, implicitly assumes that miscommunication is in some way outside the normal course of communicative events. I maintain that this is not the case. Contrary to our phenomenological experience of dialogue as a smooth and effortless form of communication, when viewed at the level of the individual utterance it is inherently ambiguous. Even if individual utterances meet criteria of syntactic well-formedness (something that is regularly not the case), many will still be found to be ambiguous when considered in isolation from the communicative and environmental context in which they occur. Obviously, something interposes itself between the utterance and its interpretation, resulting in our phenomenological experience of smooth communication. These interposed elements are the structures and meta communicative functions of dialogue, not optional extras. This is why natural language interfaces that do not have dialogue capabilities have an unsatisfactory "feel", and why no amount of grammatical enhancements will improve the situation.

Dialogue Models

Computational research on dialogue can be seen to have two main strands; one dealing with the structural or *syntactic* aspects of dialogue, and the other more concerned with modeling the content or *semantics* of dialogue. As theoretical enterprises, these have remained quite separate until now, having their intellectual roots in two different traditions; computational linguistics and artificial intelligence models of planning, respectively. Recently, however, some attempts have been made to integrate the two essentially complementary perspectives (Allen, 1988; Grosz & Sidner, 1987). The following paragraphs will examine a number of ideas that are the basis of current approaches to research on natural language dialogue interfaces.

The work of Reichman (1984), Grosz (1981), and Sidner (1983) is often described as a discourse-linguistic approach, with the implication that it is primarily concerned with the structural or syntactic properties of the dialogue. A major success of the discourse-linguistic approach has been to show that there are surface qualities of certain dialogues that cannot be explained at a sentential level, but that are explicable at a discourse level. Grosz (1981), for example, has found that when participants in a tasks-oriented dialogue complete discussion of some subtask and return to the larger task in which the subtask was embedded, they will often use a pronominal form to reference something in this larger task even in those cases where a seeming contender for the pronominal is found in the linearly closer discussion of the subtask. Grosz notes that it is the underlying hierarchical structure of the dialogue that explains why no ambiguity arises; after completion of a subdiscussion its elements are no longer available for pronominal reference. This is, therefore, a truly discourse-linguistic phenomenon.

A common emphasis in the discourse-linguistic approach is the representation of the discourse as a network or hierarchical structure in which each node of the structure represents a distinct discourse element. A central discourse element of Reichman's (1984) model is that of context space. A *context space* is a frame-like structure which is active at a given point in a dialogue or discourse. The categorization of different types of context space and their component parts mirror the different units and phenomena found in a discourse world. In a given context space there are slots for foci, goals, speakers, and so on. Conversational moves involve making transitions from one context space to the next. It is possible to interrupt a context space, and then return to it. This reflects a common phenomenon in naturally occurring dialogue in which topics are developed, suspended, and resumed without need for explanation or even comment.

An advantage of Reichman's proposal is that the rules embodied in a context space network are independent of particular participant beliefs, world knowledge, attitudes, and personal motivation. In focusing on the detailed specification of dialogue rules, the undeniably crucial role of dialogue content is not ignored. Rather, by distinguishing between structure and content, the mutual interdependence of these two facets of the process is highlighted. As Litman (1983) points out, however, Reichman's model could benefit from further informalization and from more contact with surface phenomena. For example, more attention could be given to the recognition of communicative goals from the surface structure of the utterance.

Hobbs and his colleagues (Hobbs, 1978; Hobbs & Robinson, 1979; Hobbs & Evans, 1980) have applied a plan-based approach to the modeling of free-flowing video-taped conversation. Planning has a long tradition in artificial intelligence (Newell & Simon, 1972; Fikes & Nilsson, 1971; Fikes, Hart, & Nilsson, 1972). In general, most of the earlier work was concerned with the execution of plans by robots in limited microworlds. Hobbs, and a number of others, have applied the planning approach to the comprehension and production of discourse.

Although Hobbs and Evans' (1980) model of conversation is not implemented in any comprehensive way, their use of framework in the microanalysis of conversation has raised a number of issues which have implications for the implementation of dialogue systems. They show that even in a short fragment of a conversation that participants seek to satisfy many goals, at many different levels, in a highly structured, ongoing, changing plan.

Although neither an implemented system nor a detailed design for one, Cohen and Perault's (1979) work forms the basis for a number of important task-oriented dialogue systems. They present a planning framework within which speech acts can be modeled. Their approach also forms the basis for the modeling of indirect speech acts by Allen (1982). Cohen and Perault view speech acts as operators that act on the models that speakers and hearers have of each other. They recast Searle's (1969) approach in terms of these operators. They attempt, in effect, to define a competence theory of speech acts. However, they limit their analysis to two speech acts, which they claim are prototypical of Searle's, requesting and informing. They are primarily concerned with the production of speech acts, rather than their recognition. Allen (1982), however, has extended Cohen and Perault's formulation to include recognition.

James Allen (1982) has proposed a dialogue system called ARGOT. This is based on earlier work he did on a system that simulated a clerk in an information booth in a train station(Allen, 1979). It was plan-based, and could answer questions about train departure and arrival times and their locations. Although limited in a number of crucial ways, it provided, among other things, an important insight into the nature of indirect speech acts. A significant design characteristic of ARGOT is the explicit separation of task level goals from communicative goals. At the task level the system is concerned with the recognition of the particular task the user is intent on performing. In order to help the user achieve his or her objectives the system must detect obstacles that will hinder the successful completion of the task. At the communicative level there are goals that deal with the introduction of a new topic, clarification or elaboration of the previous utterance, modification of the current topic, and so on.

An important disadvantage of the planning approach as exemplified by Allen and Perault (1980) and Cohen and Perault (1979) is that it encounters difficulty when clarification subdialogues are encountered or when there is a change in topic. Litman and Allen (1984) propose a model based on a hierarchy of plans and metaplans that can cope with what Sidner and Israel (1981) call debugging subdialogues, as well as other forms of clarification and topic shifts.

Computational Strategies for Dealing with Communication Failure

Input failures

A number of researchers (Tennant, Ross, Saenz, Thompson, & Miller, 1983; Thompson, Ross, Tennant, & Saenz, 1983; and Tennant, Ross, & Thompson, 1983) have argued that unconstrained natural language dialogue is unsuitable for use in a person-machine interface because of the inability of naive users to assess the linguistic and conceptual coverage that the interface provides. In many cases the user will overestimate the linguistic abilities of a system. Tennant et al. (1983) argue that if the system is unable to understand user inputs, then the user will infer that many other sentences cannot be understood.

The solution that Tennant et al. employ is to use what they call menu-based natural language understanding. Instead of having to type input at a keyboard, the user constructs a phrase by using a mouse to choose fragments from a menu displayed on a high resolution bit mapped screen (they call their system NLMenu). As the construction of the phrase proceeds, the menu options change to indicate possible continuations. With this method it is impossible for the user to input sentences that cannot be parsed by the system. The main advantages of this type of system are: (1) the fact that there is no possibility of lexical-level input failures; (2) the explicitness of its linguistic and conceptual coverage prevents syntactic/semantic input failures; and (3) it has a lower computational requirement than conventional natural language systems.

There are a number of disadvantages with this type of system: (1) Menu searching becomes more cumbersome the larger the domain; and (2) there is no provision for interaction involving ellipsis and anaphoric reference, a characteristic of human dialogue. This type of interaction can be almost as economical, in typing terms, as a menu-based system. Furthermore, by taking a minimalist approach to linguistic coverage Tennant et al. exclude linguistic devices that might give the system some indication of the user's ultimate goal in the particular interaction. For example, there is no facility in NLMenu for indicating a shift in focus (Sidner, 1979) or for detecting clue words that might indicate a change in goal (Reichman, 1984). In general, there are no metalinguistic facilities available to the user, and it is difficult to envisage how they might be implemented. Perhaps for these reasons Tennant et al do not model the user's goals or plans. Each sentence is treated in isolation, and is parsed into a retrieval or update request using a type of Montague semantic grammar. Thus, the price paid for insuring against input failure is perhaps to make the system less capable of dealing with various types of model failure.

If we provide system with a grammar giving good coverage, and eschew the solution suggested by Tennant et al. we then have the considerable problem of dealing with the wide variety of grammatical ill-formedness that one encounters when users are given a free communicative rein (see Reilly & MacAogåin, 1988, for some empirical data on this). At the input failure level, and in particular when dealing with syntactic ill-formedness, there are now a number of reliable techniques for dealing with, inter alia, fragmentary input, spurious constituents, violation of syntactic/semantic constraints, and ellipses. In many of these cases, particularly with respect to ellipses, we are dealing with a linguistically valid utterance, but one that must be treated as if it were ill-formed. A comprehensive account of various robust parsing techniques can be found in Carbonell and Hayes (1983) and Weischedel and Sondheimer (1983). Due to limitations of space I will not go into their details here, but rather will concentrate on thr more problematic issue of model failure, and techniques for coping with it.

Model Failures

Put simply, there are two ways of dealing with the problem of user model failure in dialogue. The first is to prevent failure from occurring in the first place by ensuring that the system communicates felicitously; the second is to repair the failure with as little disruption as possible when it does occur.

Joshi, Webber, and Weischedel (1984) have noted that in person-machine interaction it is obviously necessary that the system respond in a truthful manner to user requests, but that this is not a sufficient condition for error-free communication. The aim of the system should be to prevent the user from drawing false inferences from responses. As they point out, the problem with this proposal is that it is neither feasible nor desirable to predict all the possible inferences that a user might draw from an utterance. Joshi et al. explore ways to constrain the system's reasoning in a principled way. Their aim is (1) to characterize cases in which the system can anticipate the user drawing false inferences, (2) to develop a formal method for computing the projected inferences that a user might draw, and (3) to enable the system to modify its responses to defuse possible false inferences.

There are two main differences between their proposal and the work done on cooperative responses by, for example, Kaplan (1979). The first is that it is not assumed that there is any divergence between the domain beliefs of the system and those of the user. In other words, we are talking about assertional rather than terminological failures. Second, it is assumed that the user draws a false conclusion from the system's response because the system's behavior is not in accord with the user's expectations. This may or may not involve the attribution of a false domain model to the user by the system.

Joshi et al. (1984) consider two classes of false conclusions: (1) false conclusions drawn by standard default reasoning, and (2) false conclusions drawn in a task-oriented context based on the user's expectations of how a cooperative expert will respond. In the first case it is proposed that the user attempts to derive what information is implicit in the system's utterance. This is done, in part, by contrasting what was made explicit with what might have been made explicit. Joshi et al. propose that the user applies some default rule if the system does not explicitly override its application. For example, if we are discussing a particular bird, a default rule that might apply is that unless otherwise stated assume that the bird can fly. It is common practice for dialogue participants, when dealing with an exceptional case (e.g., a flightless bird), to explicitly block such default inferences. The following exchange from Joshi et al. (1984, p. 135) is another example of a blocking response (assume that most associate professors are tenured):

(D4)

User: Is Sam an associate professor?
System: Yes, but he doesn't have tenure.

If the system knows that Sam does not have tenure, and also knows that the user is unaware of this, then a simple answer of "Yes" by the system could lead the user to assume falsely by default reasoning that Sam was tenured.

In the case of responses by experts on a particular topic, Joshi et al. argue along the same lines as Allen and his co-workers, that the system should try to uncover the plans of the user in order to provide an optimally helpful response. The user generally expects an answer to a more general question than the one asked. If a user asks the system "How can I do X?", he or she is anticipating a response to the more general question of "How can I achieve my goal?"

There is still the issue of how to constrain the extent of a helpful response to a user. Joshi et al. suggest an application of focusing theory (Sidner, 1979; Grosz, 1977) to get around the problem. They propose that at any given time in the discourse a section of the knowledge base is in focus. They claim that this subset of the knowledge base, and only this, forms the basis for blocking responses by the system.

In the section dealing with the nature of miscommunication in dialogue systems, model failure was classified into three broad categories: assertional failure, explicit terminological failure, and implicit terminological failure. In this part of the chapter I will discuss the work of Goodman (1983) and McCoy (1985) in the context of the assertional failure, and the work of Carberry (1984) which addresses the issue of explicit terminological failure.

Goodman has studied miscommunication in the instructional dialogues used by Grosz (1977) in which an expert tells an apprentice how to construct a toy water pump. He has noted that a frequent source of error in this type of dialogue is the description used by a speaker to identify an object in the world. The description can be imprecise, confused, ambiguous, or overly specific. Goodman proposes that the primary means for repairing faulty descriptions is by relaxation (reduction in specificity) of parts of the description.

Goodman observed that different linguistic structures are used to convey different elements of a description. Relative clauses are used to provide complex information, prepositional phrases are used to express simpler information, and adjectives are used to express simple perceptual features. Goodman has found that participants in a dialogue tend to relax their descriptions (when a problem has arisen) in the following order: adjectives, then prepositional phrases, and finally relative clauses and predicate complements.

The perceptual features of an object are used in a description to provide a means for distinguishing one from another. Goodman has observed that the features most likely to be relaxed are those that require the least active consideration, for example the color or shape of an object. Features that require more active consideration on the part of the listener (such as relative size, distance, or weight) are usually the last features to be relaxed.

According to Goodman, people tend to be casual with less active features and more careful with active ones. As a result, the main cause of reference failure is found to be the inaccurate use of less active features.

The main aim of Goodman's work is to try to incorporate in a computer-based system the tolerance for inaccurate description which he has observed to be used by human participants in dialogue. He considers one of the main techniques used is a relaxation of certain parameters of the description in a principled way.

McCoy (1985) deals with a problem related to that of object description, namely misconceptions concerning the properties of objects. When a user interacts with a data base or an expert system, he or she may attribute a property or property value to an object that the object does not have. She gives the following example of how a current data base system and a human might respond to the following request containing a property misconception (the objects and properties known to the data base are capitalized):

(D5)

User: Give me the HULL-NO of all DESTROYERS whose MAST-HEIGHT is above 190.

In the hypothetical data base DESTROYERS cannot have that value for MAST-HEIGHT. Upon encountering such a query, a conventional system might give the response:

System: There are no DESTROYERS in the data base with a MAST-HEIGHT above 190. Would you like to try again?

As McCoy (1985) points out, however, this is not the way most humans would respond. A human respondent would attempt to get at the root of the misconception manifested in the utterance. In the data base there is an object similar to DESTROYER that has the value of MAST-HEIGHT given. Therefore, the user's misconception may have resulted from a confusion of the two objects. Hence, a reasonable response would be:

System: All DESTROYERS in the data base have a MAST-HEIGHT between 85 and 90. Were you thinking of an AIRCRAFT-CARRIER?

The strategy adopted here is to deny implicitly the property/value given, to give the corresponding correct information, and to suggest an alternative query that might satisfy the user's goal.

The above exchange highlighted a confusion of objects by the user; it is also possible to confuse the attributes of the objects. Take, for example, the following exchange:

(D6)

User: Give me the HULL-NO of all DESTROYERS whose MAST-HEIGHT is above 3500.

System: ALL DESTROYERS in the data base have a MAST-HEIGHT between 85 and 90. Were you thinking of DISPLACEMENT?

This last response is similar to the one given above, except that the second query contains an attribute rather than an object confusion.

In order to develop a system capable of dealing with these types of misconception in a human-like manner it is necessary to devise a similarity metric for objects. McCoy (1985) points out, however, that it is not sufficient to develop a metric, the metric has to be sensitive to context. Objects considered similar under one set of circumstances might be dissimilar under another. McCoy proposes the notion of object perspective to provide a contextually sensitive measure of similarity. An object is represented in a hierarchical inheritance structure. In some contexts the superordinate (e.g., mammal is a superordinate property of human) of the object may be salient, in others it may not. When an object is viewed from a particular perspective, the perspective acts as a filter on the properties that the object may inherit from its superordinate. A number of perspectives are defined a priori for each domain that give salience values (e.g., high, medium, or low) for the attributes of each object in the domain. Properties of objects given a high salience value will be propagated through the inheritance network, those given a low rating will be suppressed. The key aspect of McCoy's proposal is that the perspective filter is orthogonal to the generalization hierarchy of object attributes. There is still, however, the problem of selecting the appropriate perspective for a particular context. McCoy gives no indication of how this might be achieved.

Carberry (1984) describes an approach to repairing a class of explicit terminological failure which she calls pragmatic overshoot. The main aim of her work is to develop a system that can offer a limited response to a pragmatically ill-formed query making use of the current context and the ill-formed utterance. The aim of the response would be to help satisfy the user's perceived goal. Her main contention is that by using the user's inferred plan, it is possible to choose a substitute for the proposition that gave rise to the pragmatic overshoot. The problem then arises of how to choose the right substitute. Initially a suggestion mechanism generates possible substitutions by examining the current context model. The erroneous proposition can represent either a nonexistent attribute or entity set relationship, or a function applied to an inappropriate set of attribute values. A selection mechanism then chooses, on the basis of three criteria, the most appropriate substitution to be used in the formulation of a revised query. The criteria are: (1) that the revised query interrogates an aspect of the current focused plan, (2) that the revised query interrogates a level of the plan hierarchy not much higher than the currently focused level, and (3) that the revised query interrogates a level of the plan hierarchy not much lower than the currently focused level.

In some respects Carberry's approach, especially in the context of attribute substitution, is similar to McCoy's. However, McCoy (1985) uses a filter to select the correct attribute, whereas Carberry uses a proximity metric. McCoy's is a more general approach because the filter can be of an arbitrary nature. Carberry's although less general, is a more psychologically plausible approach; but altogether a bad thing, given that the aim of both systems is to approximate the cooperativeness of a human respondent.

General Conclusions

An essential first step in tackling any problem is to provide an accurate characterization of it. This is what I have attempted to do in the first section of the chapter. It is safe to say that much of the progress in the area of robust person-machine communication, both in hardware and software, has been in alleviating the effects of input-level failures. Although the problems of input-level syntactic ill-formedness should not be underestimated, the major challenges for builders of natural language interfaces are in the area of model failure. Successful systems will have to have access to, and be able to reason with, knowledge relating to the domain of application. I have argued in this chapter that the best communication medium within which to do this is natural language dialogue, and that the best framework for reasoning with the contents of dialogue is a planning one.

15

Misunderstanding and Its Remedies: Telephone Miscommunication

Kent Drummond
Robert Hopper

> Rhetoric, I shall urge, should be a study of misunderstanding and its remedies. (Richards, 1936)

The focus of the present study is, as Richards urges, an examination of misunderstanding and its remedies – in this case, during telephone conversations. We would not argue that our approach to misunderstanding is "rhetorical" in the sense of being recognizable to experts in rhetorical theory. Yet our presumption is that the actors who experience misunderstandings and their remedies are acting rhetorically. Rather than being led by a theory of how actors do rhetoric, we proceed by examining naturally occurring instances in which parties to telephone conversations either prevent misunderstandings before they occur, or explicitly acknowledge and resolve them once they have occurred.

Telephone Talk Versus Face-to-Face: Is There a Difference?

Although it would be exciting to inform readers otherwise, the fact remains that telephone speech is, for the most part, speech-as-usual. Certainly, telephone speaking shows some unique characteristics that facilitate its study. Equally certainly, telephone speaking is a common enough human endeavor to merit study, even if no other speaking were like it at all. Descriptions of telephone speaking have proven surprisingly robust, however, in generalizing to face-to-face conversation. Therefore, we claim to describe not only telephone speaking, but human speech communication.

Let us consider some contrasts and similarities between telephone speaking and face-to-face interaction.

Contrasts

First, telephone conversation is constrained to sounds, which focuses our attention on what is most essential about speech communication. In addition, telephone conversation is limited to two parties, which targets our attention to what is specifically dialogic in conversation: that is, how speech action emerges across turns of speaking partners. Monologue can be understood with reference to theories of meaning, whereas dialogue may be understood as sequential action.

Both of these contrasts provide some methodical simplifications for inquiry. Specifically, telephone speech implies that the researcher, most of the time, need not deal with multiple parties (although this is changing with recent technological advances) and that video records are not essential to examining the moment-by-moment unfolding of the interaction (again, this will change as teleconferencing grows in popularity). A third simplification results from the fact that, in contrast to most face-to-face speaking, telephone encounters begin and end at definite moments. When two people face each other, they may drift in and out of conversation; telephone encounters begin precisely when the telephone rings, and they end when the two parties hang up (Schegloff, 1968, 1979a). In sum, there are certain contrasts between telephone conversation and face-to-face conversation. These very contrasts, however, make telephone conversation an excellent site for the study of dialogic speech communication.

Similarities

Given these contrasts, one might argue that telephone speaking seems quite different from face-to-face speaking. However, face-to-face and telephone speaking are more alike than different. Researchers who have compared telephone speech to face-to-face speech have presumed and/or predicted contrasts between telephone speaking and face-to-face speaking. These predictions have not been supported. We review these studies to assert the crucial similarities between telephone speech and face-to-face speaking.

A number of researchers have contrasted face-to-face speech events versus sound-only events in terms of certain discourse features such as turn lengths, interruptions, and pause lengths (Cook & Lalljee, 1972; Rutter & Stephenson, 1977; and see especially the review in Rutter, 1987). In each of these studies, investigators predicted differences in discourse features due to communicative "disadvantages" in the sound-only condition. For example, Cook and Lalljee (1972) argued that because gaze seems important to turn-taking in face-to-face conversation, sound-only partners must take turns differently:

> If gaze direction plays such an important role in social encounters, it follows that interactions where gaze signals cannot be used will be different. That is, conversations over the telephone and in similar circumstances will differ from face-to-face interactions. (Cook & Lalljee, 1972, p. 212)

Cook and Lalljee (1972) predicted eight feature-count differences between sound-only and face-to-face interaction, all of which would show some cue deficit or indication of problems in sound-alone conditions.

The expectation of communicative deficit on the phone is displayed most clearly in Rutter's term *cuelessness* (Rutter, 1987, pp. 126-131). Telephone communication, argues Rutter, lacks visual cues, hence it is "cueless" compared to face-to-face conversation. Yet Rutter's own data scarcely support his cueless characterization. Rather, in study after study he reports failure to find features that differentiate face-to-face from sound-alone speech. Rutter's summary reads: "By the late 1970s the conclusion was emerging that visual cues were rather less important for turn-taking and synchronization than had been thought . . ." (1987, p. 126). Cook and Lalljee (1972) were more candid: "The results of the study are very disappointing so far as confirming hypotheses or finding significant differences goes" (p. 214).

Cook and Lalljee (1972) found only one clear difference between the conditions: There were *fewer* interruptions on the telephone. Quite aside from problems of coding associated with the notion of interruption, however, (see Drummond, 1989), the direction of the obtained difference is contrary to prediction. In short, numerous studies have failed to predict differences in speech cues.

Further controlled comparisons could perhaps resolve some problems of studies to date, but given the failure of past predictions, one should not expect important differences in discourse feature-counts to appear. Research designed to contrast telephone and face-to-face conversation has instead displayed their essential similarity. Telephone speaking displays a rich and full communicative ecology. To be sure, visual cues are absent, but what those cues accomplish in face-to-face encounters does not go un-done over the telephone. For example, in face-to-face conversation we use visual cues to recognize our acquaintances, In telephone conversation, this identification work is accomplished through brief voice-samples at the opening of each call.

Telephone conversation is pure speech communication. It is, in many ways, quite like communication in most other settings. What may be described in telephone speech may (until shown otherwise) be held to be the case of many other speech contexts.

To summarize: Telephone conversation is worth studying on its own merits, as a primary site of contemporary speech communication. Additionally, telephone conversation occurs within certain constraints (e.g., in sounds, in dyads) that make it a felicitous case for studying interaction. Finally, descriptions of telephone conversation may generalize to conversation in other contexts.

Telephone Miscommunication

Rather than further investigate what possible differences may exist between face-to-face and telephone interaction, we propose to display a sector of research from a different perspective in which evidence concerning *miscommunication* has begun to accumulate. As it happens, the observations from this research have been gleaned from the telephone medium.

Thus far, it appears that the means by which participants prevent and resolve misunderstandings in telephone talk may be said to constitute a kind of machinery designed to achieve those ends. Sacks (1987), for example, argued that:

> There is a separate machinery designed for dealing with misunderstandings, and it draws attention to things that are not otherwise much focused on in conversation, apparently secondary bits of talk trying to "get things right." Now we know that the "misunderstanding machinery" is itself "formal", in the sense that it operates without regard to disagreements; it operates in lots of places where there is one or another sort of local failure of misunderstanding. (p. 66)

Sacks's reference to machinery for dealing with misunderstandings apparently invokes what conversation analysts have come to call procedures for conversational repair (Schegloff, Jefferson, & Sacks, 1977). In this view, repair was described as having a two-part sequence of initiation and outcome which could be performed by the speaker of the "repairable" or by another. Further, they argued that there are structural constraints favoring self-repair over other-repair at each sequential slot in a repair sequence.

Subsequent research in this tradition (Jefferson, 1975, 1987; Schegloff, 1979b) has explored structural aspects of repair phenomena. Schegloff (1987a) and Moerman (1988) have argued that repair phenomena show similar formats across languages; hence repair phenomena may achieve the status of conversational-linguistic universals.

Studies based on repair may be contrasted with certain other studies based on difficulties of *meaning* (Morris & Hopper, 1980; McLaughlin, Cody, & O'Hair, 1983). Although the structure of the repair or alignment is acknowledged as important in these latter studies, the *source* of misunderstanding is seen to be primarily semantic in nature, and to be a *mistake*. On the *conversational repair* view favored here, the word *repairable* is used to refer to the place where actors locate the problems as having begun. Frequently, one finds no particular defect in such turns, though some correction or improvement may be developed in the process of conversational repair.

In sum, we propose to describe certain "misunderstandings" in terms of the repair phenomena utilized therein. In particular, we address relationships between the *distance* from repairable to repair-initiation. Briefly, as this distance increases, the term "misunderstanding" becomes a better and better descriptor for what occurs. When repairable and repair-initiation become distant in time and speaker's subsequent turns, it gets harder to make repairs. There may be many reasons for such difficulties, but the simplistic formulation we offer here is that, as the repair-initiation occurs further from the repairable, the *problem of location* grows increasingly difficult. The problem of location involves this: If you want to initiate a correction or repair of any sort based on something somebody said, then in order to effect any repair, you must first reach alignment with partners about *when-where-in-time* the trouble occurred (e.g., in what words, in what discourse particles, in what turn). This locating work is quite easy when done quickly, but more difficult in direct proportion to delay.

This position was suggested in an essay by Moerman and Sacks:

> Understanding matters as a natural phenomenon in that conversational sequencing is built in such a way as to require that participants must continually, there and then—without recourse to follow up tests, mutual examination of memoirs, surprise quizzes and other ways of checking on misunderstanding—demonstrate to one another that they understood or failed to understand the talk they are party to. (in Moerman, 1988, p. 185)

The most important phrase in this passage is "there and then," for it suggests a *distance principle* is indeed applicable to examining instances of potential and acknowledged misunderstanding. This position can best be defended with reference to the notion of *repair-initiation opportunity space,* which provides a metric for measuring the *time* or *distance* from repairable to repair-initiation—and hence a metric for comparing how the problem of locating the repairable material is accomplished at each of the slots in the model of repair-initiation opportunity space.

In brief, our position is that repairing speech is always risky, a violation of "let it pass," and in general likely to cause trouble. Still, the trouble of leaving things unrepaired is also routine and must be dealt with. Conversational repair phenomena have evolved to deal with these problems, and their formats are specifically abbreviated, routine, and non-metacommunicative in their claims because they need to solve problems without creating too many new problems in the resolving.

These procedures (machineries) work best cross small distances. As the repair-initiation opportunity space moves along, the problems get larger. The big-long ones we call "misunderstanding."

Repair-Initiation Opportunity Space

The distance principle is based on the notion of repair-initiation opportunity space formulated by Schegloff et al. (1977). According to this formulation, the repair-initiation opportunity space is three turns long, consisting of four positions and beginning at the trouble-source turn.

Speaker A: P1 (repairs occur immediately by current speaker: self-initiation)
Speaker A: P2 (repairs occur in the turn's transition space: self initiation)
Speaker B: P3 (problems of hearing and/or understanding located by next speaker: other-initiation)
Speaker A: P4 (problems of reference or sequential implicitiveness identified by first speaker, indexing T1)

We claim that as the distance from the repairable increases, so does the work required both to locate the problem, and to get it remedied.

Repair-Initiation at P1

When repair is initiated at P1, the distance between the initiation of repair and the repairable is short. Quite often, current speakers locate trouble *as it occurs* and initiate the repair immediately.

Repair initiations at P1 may be accomplished through several means, including cut-offs, sound stretches, and dysfluent particles. Note the following excerpt from a telephone conversation between two female friends in their mid-teens:

Extract 1
A20.2

M: I 'ont kno:w- you know it just really never worked
o- I mean we- hhh we had so: much f- okay well- hh
pt hh he was- (.) its like he has a reputation I
mean I kne:w him and stuff hhhhh but has a
reputation of being you know (0.2) go out with a
girl once eh- o:ne I mean one night
E: [Uh huh
M: [And then] never talk to her again

Speaker M's speech is replete with these self-corrections, most of which are cut-offs. Note the immediate adjacency of the repair-initiations to their repairables. There is no need for these self-correction gambits to locate the trouble, because the trouble-locating "is compacted into the repair-candidate itself" (Schegloff et al., 1977, p. 376). The trajectory is short for repairs of this type.

Interestingly, although this segment contains only two of what structural linguists would call complete sentences, speaker M conveys much information here, and conveys it in an understandable way.

Repair-Initiation at P2

Repair-initiations at P2 occur at transition-relevant places (TRPs) during which speaker change may, but need not necessarily, occur. Here, a greater proportion of the repair-initiation opportunity space is in most cases lengthened over that in P1. Observe the following sequence of P2 repair-initiations:

Extract 2
A20.2

M: I'll probly do a little more studying tonight
hu:m or tommo:row during my classes I'm notorious for that.
(.)
M: study during my classes
(0.2)
M: my other clâsses
(0.3)
E: Oh heck yea::h.

In this instance, speaker M self-initiates repair at P2 on two separate occasions: once at line 3 and once at line 5. The pauses at lines 2, 4, and 6 represent transition-relevant places, but speaker change does not occur at the first two. Instead, the current speaker continues speaking after brief pauses. What she accomplishes after the first two TRPs are two separate repairs of the previous utterance. The first self-repair, at line 3 "study during my classes") clarifies the "that" in the prior utterance "I'm notorious for that." The second self-repair, at line 5 ("my other clâsses") clarifies *which* classes she studies for, that is, classes other than the one in which she studies.

Note also the different emphases on the same word, "classes" at line 3 and 5. At line 3, the "a" in "classes" is stressed, and in line 5, the "a" is both stressed and inflected upward. This technique shows recipient design (Sacks & Schegloff, 1979), in which members' use of successive, try-marked recognitionals eventually achieves confirmed hearing. Here, M appears to be try-marking "classes" in pursuit of recognition on the part of E, which she finally obtains.

The problem of locating-what-needs-repair is more severe at P2 than at P1, for the next utterance must show itself to have corrective functions, as well as locate that which is to be corrected. In Extract 2, these functions are both performed by partial repetition.

That a succeeding turn unit is largely composed of a repeat marks it as possibly problem-centered (Schegloff et al., 1977). At the same time, this device also locates the problem as having occurred at the point in the first turn that is later repeated. The repeat of "during my classes" is preceded by the word "studies" as an added hint to gain recognition. Moerman (1988) describes this process as adding a "one-bit piece of information about the referent person [in this instance, object] that the recipient can use to recognize him by" (p. 35).

Repair-Initiation at P3

When repair is initiated at P3, the distance between the initiation of repair and the repairable is longer than either P1 or P2 repair-initiations. Thus, problems of hearing or understanding must be located by a next speaker. This may be done in a number of ways.

Extract 3
A10.8

50. **S:** pt Well no:w tha- now that Frosty's over (.) I
51. c'n start studyin'
52. **J:** Fro:sty is over?
53. (1.0)
54. **S:** U:h Fro:sty was on t'nigh'

In Extract 3, S explains to J that he (S) can return to his homework now that "Frosty's over." But this utterance is problematic for J, as evidenced by the partial repeat she offers at line 52:

"Frosty is over?" "Partial" is an especially apt description here because the way J performs this utterance is different in a number of ways from S's rendition. J not only stresses the "o" in "Frosty" as S does, she stretches it as well. She also removes the contraction from "Frosty's" to say "Frosty is." And finally, she try-marks the end of the utterance, which is highly typical of other-repair initiations. The effect of J's re-doing of "Frosty's over" is to elongate that part of S's "whole" utterance that is problematic for her. Like a bookmark, J's repair initiation marks the place in S's speech that he will need to come back to in order to provide clarification.

As evidenced here, however, repair-initiations at P3 are riskier than those at P2 or P1. More conversational distance has been covered, and the challenge of problem-location looms larger. The one-second pause at line 53 and the stretched "U:h" at line 54 constitute a classic dispreferred turn shape on the part of S. There is a hesitancy on the part of S here, but with respect to what? J has located the problem in S's prior utterance through her repair-initiation at line 52. But precisely *what* about the phrase "Frosty's over" is problematic, it is not possible to say. Did J not hear the phrase correctly, and did this prompt her to repeat it, as a guess? Or does she not know who Frosty is? Or does she not know what "over" means in this instance. Any one of these problem types is plausible. And it is this ambiguity that makes the repair itself more difficult to accomplish.

So, for example, if J had said at line 52: "Now that what?" or "Who's Frosty" or "What do ya mean, Frosty's over", S would have had more of a clue as to what J's difficulty was. As shown, J's repair initiation took none of these forms. S's hesitation displays a difficulty with J's difficulty.

Nevertheless, after the pause and the "U:h," S displays what he thought J's repair initiation was about: the use of "over" immediately after Frosty. S's clarification involves both a where ("on") and a when ("tonight") to further describe Frosty, and in responding to J's initiation he offers a candidate repair. We will return to this example shortly to show how sufficient J finds this repair, but up to this point, the sequence has followed a canonical repair sequence for P3.

Note that the term "misunderstanding" would not easily apply to any of the examples shown thus far. Yet, as the distance between repair-initiation and repairable increases, we notice greater difficulty, for repair initiator, in indexing the repairable, as well as greater difficulty, for first speaker, in "making sense" of the initiation. As we move to P4, it stands to reason that such difficulties will increase further.

Repair-Initiation at P4

In canonical fourth position repairs, speaker A requests information of speaker B (first position); B responds to that request (second position); and speaker A finds that response insufficient (third position), often "accusing" B of misunderstanding the original request: "No, I don't mean X, I mean Y." An idealized version appears below:

Speaker A:	T1 (Often, a request for information)
Speaker B:	T2 (A response to that request)
Speaker A:	T3 (A statement of response insufficiency, and a re-doing of the original request)

Consider this example between a mother and daughter:

Extract 4
FO1.8

147.	**M:**	=How are things goin' with her- uh-
148.		her and Jeff?
149.	**D:**	Fine (0.4) just fine, we haven't see much
150.		of h[er we
→151.	**M:**	[I don't mean your Jeff, I mean
→152.		Jeff Over[man
153.	**D:**	[Oh not very good, Jeff's going
154.		camping with that bitch (1.0) that's . . . .

In Extract 4, the mother asks a question of the daughter. The daughter is in the act of completing her response at line 150 when the mother overlaps at line 151. In this case, the overlap is not a deep one, as a transition-relevance place was occurring on the overlapped syllable. Nevertheless, the mother prevents the daughter from continuing her response here, and the floor is open for the mother to perhaps restate her question. But she does not do so. Rather, she locates, *by the placement of her overlap within the daughter's stream of talk,* the point in the daughter's response she has found problematic. In other words, it was not until the daughter had constructed the utterance "we haven't seen much of h- " that the mother could have known that the daughter had the wrong Jeff in mind. Here also, as in the previous examples, appears an explicit statement of what was meant: "I don't mean your Jeff, I mean Jeff Overman." The formulation "I don't mean X, I mean Y" has been used to describe sequences of this type (Schegloff, 1987), but in this case, a more precise description would be "I don't mean aX, I mean Xb," where a and b are coefficients around X.

The problem of locating the repairable is more difficult at fourth position repairs to the extent that they usually involve meta-talk such as "what I meant was" or "I didn't understand you." Due to their explicit quality, we choose the term *announcements* to describe their appearance, and we note that these *announcements of misunderstanding* may take different forms, depending on who is attributed with the misunderstanding. Like repair, announcements of misunderstanding may take the forms of self- and others-.

Announcements of Misunderstanding

We distinguish between self-attributed misunderstanding announcements (SAMAs) and other-attributed misunderstanding announcements (OAMAs). In the example just discussed, the mother makes an other-attributed misunderstanding announcement: "I don't *mean* your Jeff, I mean Jeff *Over*man." In the following example, the daughter produces a self-attributed misunderstanding announcement:

Extract 5
F01.8

D: What were you doin' in Hilda's.
M: h I wadn't in Hilda's they did the style show.
(.)
M: for us,
D: (uh-h)
M: at our ^club.
→ **D:** W'what club is thi:s?=
M: =The Republican ladies' club had
their luncheon style show t'da-
D: ^O:h well- I didn't under- I- I (.)
was confu:sed ^I see (.)
D: Well how ^fu:n.

First, SAMAs appear to have a "premonitory" feature, which takes the form of a question posed by the recipient of a story or some stream of information. While we might characterize these questions simply as other-initiated repairs, they eventuate in admissions of misunderstanding, or self-attributed misunderstanding announcements. Note line 20: (D: "w'what club is this?"). The daughter produces a repair relevant to the last word of the mother's prior utterance: (M: "at our ^clu:b."). "Club" is apparently the repairable item for the daughter; her repair displays how it is so; that is, *which* club. The mother then supplies the answer in line 21:

21. M: =The Republican ladies' club had

At the daughter's prompting, the mother supplies "what club."

The daughter's subsequent response constitutes the heart of the SAMA:

→**23. D:** ^O:h well- I didn't under- I- I (.)

First, note that the '^O:h' is produced at a higher pitch, and it is stretched. These features mark what Heritage (1984, p. 312) has described as a change-of-state on the part of the daughter—in this case, a counterinforming. What follows is an explicit admission of her misunderstanding: (D: I didn't under- I- I (.) was confu:sed ^I see). Having admitted her misunderstanding, the daughter reorients to the mother's narrative by offering an assessment of the day's activities: (D: 'well how ^fu:n.').

Once the SAMA has been performed, relevant topic talk resumes.

Stacked Repairs: Unsatisfied Initiations

Occasionally, repair initiators themselves constitute sources of trouble. When this occurs, we may find repairs stacked upon repairs, the resolution of which is quite protracted. The following example involves confusion about Frosty the Snowman:

Extract 6
A10.8

46. J: . . . if if I need any help can I call you
47. S: yeah hm I'll be here
48. J: hhheh huh huh
49. (0.4)
50. S: pt Well no:w tha- now that Frosty's over (.) I
51. c'n start studyin'
52. J: Fro:sty is over?
53. (1.0)
54. S: U:h Fro:sty was on t'nigh'
55. (0.8)
56. J: Who's Frosty.

57. (1.2)
58. **S:** Who: is Fro:sty?
59. (1.3)
60. **J:** Fro:sty the Sno:wman?
61. (0.4)
62. **S:** ↑ Yes: Frosty the Snowman=
63. ='Ow many [other Frosty's do you know
64. **J:** [↑O:h was o::n »I thought you
65. said he was o:ve:r: hh huh hh [hh]
66. **S:** [we]ll he's over
67. no: [w]
68. **J:** [hh] «I thought you meant» he was over at your
69. ↑hou::se hh huh [huh huh]
70. **S:** [(hhh)]
71. **J:** huh hh
72. **S:** Oh my de:ar it's too: warm
73. **J:** Well ye:ah (.) u:h Frosty was o:ver-
74. **S:** h[e'd] me:lt in the house he[re]
75. **J:** [huh] [((#]beep #))
76. (0.5)
77. **J:** hh huh I'll talk to you later=
78. **S:** =Okay bye bye=
79. **J:** =By:e.

This is, of course, a more complete instance we cited earlier as being typical of third position repairs. It was—for the amount we included. However, listening to the remainder of the story, we hear that S's repair at line 54 prompted another repair-initiation from J at line 56 (note also another pause at line 55, suggesting possible trouble). But this time, instead of S supplying a repair to J's initiation, he stacks another repair onto hers, modifying her utterance in exactly the same way she had modified his at line 52!

At the line 60, J offers yet another repair-initiation, again after a pause, but in that initiation she offers a candidate answer as well—an answer that turns out to be correct.

This complex repair sequence would appear to be at an end, but some unusual aftershocks remain. Again we hear the announcements of misunderstanding (self-attributed) on the part of J at lines 64 and 67: "I thought you said" changes to "I thought you meant." In addition, there is an extended laughter sequence involving both participants. They engage interactively in "play," extending the fantasy of Frosty making a personal appearance. And finally, they accomplish a relatively hasty exit from the conversation. The call-waiting signal at line 76 is usually occasion for more extended talk as the called party asks his current conversational partner to "hold the phone" (see Hopper, in press). These features of aftershock are typical of protracted misunderstanding sequences.

Although we do not intend to make the claim that all instances of misunderstanding involve explicit statements to that effect, we point out that such statements regularly accompany repair sequences that completely occupy the repair-initiation opportunity space. It is in this way that such sequences become misunderstandings not only for us as observers, but for the conversational participants as well.

Afterword

Our goal here has been to present a body of research concerning telephone miscommunication which, while small, is probably not medium-dependent but applicable to a wide variety of media and situations. Nor is conversational repair the only indication that something has "gone wrong" over the telephone. Problems due to wrong numbers, answering machines that malfunction, and the complexities arising from call-waiting all must be considered in the near future. Given the novelty of the bulk of telephone technology—as well as the attendant opportunities for miscommunication—it seems premature to set standards for effectiveness in, say, "accomplishing" a call waiting; research in telephone miscommunication therefore contrasts with, for example, research on medical interviews as presented by West and Frankel elsewhere in this volume. Rather, our position at this point is descriptive as opposed to prescriptive, observational as opposed to suggestive.

Previous research suggests, however, that individuals learn to communicate more smoothly—and rapidly—over new media. Short, Williams, and Christie (1976) have shown that individuals learn to determine more accurately which communication media are effective for which tasks, and subsequent research by Williams (1978) supports this finding. As telephone-related technologies such as teleconferencing, teleducation, and telemedicine proliferate, we suggest that seemingly universal phenomena such as conversational repair be examined in these new channels to determine if their accomplishment, for the first time, is significantly impacted by the media in which they appear.

Appendix: Transcription Symbols

The following transcription conventions were drawn up by Kent Drummond and Robert Hopper, and relate most directly to symbols used for the characterization of spontaneous speech in their chapter. Other contributors, however,select from these or broadly similar conventions in their transcription or data-extracts.

Symbol	Meaning
[]	Brackets are used to indicate overlapping utterances. Left brackets note the beginning of the overlap, and right brackets close or end the overlap.
=	The "equal" sign indicates two contiguous utterances that do not overlap. Ordinarily these appear between speakers.
CAPS	Capital letters are used to show extreme loudness, as well as the first letter of each turn unit.
stress	Underlining indicates stress/emphasis.
stre:tch	Colon indicates the extension (stretching) of the sound that follows it.
nôt	A carat precedes an upward shift in pitch. It can appear at word beginning or any point within words. (In some transcripts this appears as an upward arrow.)
we-	Hyphen following a sound indicates a cut-off, a definite stopping of sound, a glottal stop.
?	A question mark is used to indicate rising pitch at word or phrase ending, *not* necessarily a question.
.	Period indicates sliding or falling pitch at the end of a word or phrase.
°	A degree sign preceding or following a word or phrase indicates that it was said more quietly than the surrounding talk.
( )	Single parentheses enclosing words or blank space are used to indicate doubtful hearings.

(0.7)	Single parentheses enclosing numbers indicate pauses in conversation. Numbers express seconds and tenths of seconds. Micro-pauses are expressed as (.).
Ye(h)s	Within speech laughter is shown by (h).
hhh	The h's indicate audible outbreaths.
·hhh	A superscripted period with h's indicates in-breaths.
pt	This symbol indicates an audible lip smack.

References

Adelman, R. D., Greene, M. G., & Charon, R. (in press). Issues in elderly patient physician interaction. *Ageing and Society.*

Adelswärd, V., Aronsson, K., Jönsson, L., & Linell, P. (1987). The unequal distribution of interactional space: Dominance and control in courtroom interaction. *Text, 7,* 313-346.

Adelswärd, V., Aronsson, K., & Linell, P. (1988). Discourse of blame: Courtroom construction of social identity from the perspective of the defendant. *Semiotica, 71,* 261-284.

Ainlay, S., Becker, G., & Coleman, L. (1986). *The dilemma of difference: A multidisciplinary view of stigma.* New York: Plenum.

Aiu, P. (1988). *Chinese beliefs about talk: Pursuing a cross-cultural model.* Unpublished master's thesis, University of California, Santa Barbara.

Aiu, P. (1990, March). *They listen but they do not hear: The legal system's treatment of native Hawaiian sacred land claims.* Paper presented at the First International/Intercultural Conference, Fullerton, CA.

Allen, J. (1979). Recognizing intentions from natural language utterances. In M. Brady & R. C. Berwick (Eds.), *Computational models of discourse* (pp. 107-166). Cambridge: MIT Press.

Allen, J. F. (1982). *ARGOT: A system overview* (Tech. Rep. No. 101). Rochester, NY: University of Rochester, Department of Computer Science.

Allen, J. (1987). *Natural language understanding.* Menlo Park, CA: Benjamin/Cummings.

Allen, J. F., & Perault, C. R. (1980). Analyzing intentions in utterances. *Artificial Intelligence, 15,* 143-178.

Allport, G. (1954). *The nature of prejudice.* Garden City, NY: Doubleday.

Althusser, L. (1971). *Lenin and philosophy and other essays.* New York: Monthly Review Press.

Altman, B. (1981). Studies of attitudes toward the handicapped: The need for a new direction. *Social Problems, 28,* 321-337.

Altman, I., & Taylor, D. A. (1973). *Social penetration: The development of interpersonal relationships.* New York: Holt, Rinehart & Winston.

Altman, I., Vinsel, A., & Brown, B. (1981). Dialectical conceptions in social psychology: An application to social penetration and privacy regulation. In L. Berkowitz (Ed.), *Advances in experimental social psychology, 14* (pp. 107-160).

Andenaes, J. (1968). The legal framework. In N. Christie (Ed.), *Scandinavian studies in criminology* (pp. 9-17), Vol. 2. Oslo: Universitetsforlaget.

Anthony, W. (1969). The effects of contact on an individual's attitude toward disabled persons. *Rehabilitation Counseling Bulletin, 12,* 169-171.

Ardener, E. (1975). The "problem" revisited. In S. Ardener (Ed.), *Perceiving women.* London: Malaby Press.

Ardener, S. (Ed.). (1975). *Perceiving women.* London: Malaby Press.

Argyle, M. (Ed.). (1981). *Social skills and work.* London: Methuen.

Aries, E. (1987). Gender and communication. In P. Shaver & C. Hendrick (Eds.), *Sex and gender*. Newbury Park, CA: Sage.

Aronsson, K., Jönsson, L., & Linell, P. (1987). The courtroom hearing as a middle ground: Speech accommodation by lawyers and defendants. *Journal of Language and Social Psychology, 6*, 99-116.

Aronsson., K., & Nilholm, C. (1989). *On memory and the collaborative construction and deconstruction of custody case arguments*. Unpublished manuscript, Linköping University.

Asch, A. (1984). The experience of disability: A challenge for psychology. *American Psychologist, 39*, 529-536.

Ashburn, G., & Gordon, A. (1981). Features of a simplified register in speech to elderly conversationalists. *International Journal of Psycholinguistics, 8*, 7-31.

Atchley, R. C. (1980). *The social forces in later life*. Belmont, CA: Wadsworth.

Atkinson, J. M. (1981). Ethnomethodological approaches to socio-legal studies. In A. Podgorecki & C. J. Whelan (Eds.), *Sociological approaches to law* (pp. 201-223). London: Croom Helm.

Atkinson, J. M., & Drew, P. (1979). *Order in court: The organization of verbal interaction in judicial settings*. London: Macmillan.

Atkinson, J. M., & Heritage, J. (Eds.), (1984). *Structures of social action: Studies in conversation analysis*. Cambridge UK: Cambridge University Press.

Austin, D. R. (1985). Attitudes toward old age: A hierarchical study. *The Gerontologist, 25*, 431-434.

Axley, S. R. (1984). Managerial and organizational communication in terms of the conduit metaphor. *Academy of Management Review, 9*, 428-437.

Baer, J. (1976). *How to be an assertive (not aggressive) woman in life, in love, and on the job: A total guide to self-assertiveness*. New York: New American Library.

Bakhtin, M. (1973). *Marxism and the philosophy of language*. New York: Seminar Press.

Banks, F. R., & Keller, M. D. (1971). Symptom experience and health action. *Medical Care, 9*, 498-502.

Barbarin, O. (1986). Family experience of stigma in childhood cancer. In S. Ainlay, G. Becker, & L. Coleman (Eds.), *The dilemma of difference—A multidisciplinary view of stigma*. New York: Plenum.

Barbato, C. A., & Feezel, J. D. (1987). The language of aging in different age-groups. *The Gerontological Society of America, 27*(4), 527-531.

Bard, M. (1970). The price of survival for cancer victims. In A. L. Strauss (Ed.), *Where medicine fails* (pp. 99-110). Chicago: Aldine.

Barker, R. G., Wright, B., Myerson, L., & Gonick, M. A. (1953). *Adjustment to physical handicap and illness: A survey of social psychology of physique and disability* (Bulletin 55). New York: Social Science Research Council.

Barnett, G. A., & Kincaid, D. L. (1983). Cultural convergence: A mathematical theory. In W. Gudykunst (Ed.), *Intercultural communication theory: Current perspectives*. Beverly Hills, CA: Sage.

Barnlund, D. (1975). *The public and private self in Japan and the United States: Comparative styles of two cultures*. Tokyo: Simul Press.

Barnlund, D., & Araki, S. (1985). Intercultural encounters: The management of compliments by Japanese and Americans. *Journal of Cross-Cultural Psychology, 16*, 9-26.

Bartlett, F. C. (1932). *Remembering: A study in experimental and social psychology*. Cambridge, UK: Cambridge University Press.

Baughman, L. (1988). Graduate paper, Department of Speech Communication, University of Illinois, Urbana-Champaign.

Bavelas, J. B. (1983). Situations that lead to disqualification. *Human Communication Research, 9,* 130-145.

Bavelas, J. B. (1985). A situational theory of disqualification: Using language to "leave the field." In J. Forgas (Ed.), *Language and social situations* (pp. 189-211). New York: Springer.

Bavelas, J. B., & Chovil, N. (1986). How people disqualify: Experimental studies of spontaneous written disqualification. *Communication Monographs, 53,* 70-74.

Bavelas, J. B., & Smith, B. J. (1982). A method for scaling verbal disqualification. *Human Communication Research, 8,* 214-227.

Baxter, L. A. (1979). Self-disclosure as a relational disengagement strategy: An exploratory investigation. *Human Communication Research, 5,* 215-222.

Baxter, L. A. (1987). Self-disclosure and relationship disengagement. In V. J. Derlega & J. H. Berg (Eds.), *Self-disclosure: Theory, research, and therapy* (pp. 155-174). New York: Plenum.

Baxter, L. A. (1988). A dialectical perspective on communication strategies in relationship development. In S. Duck (Ed.), *Handbook of personal relationships* (pp. 257-273). London: John Wiley.

Baxter, L. A., & Wilmot, W. (1984). "Secret tests": Social strategies for acquiring information about the state of a relationship. *Human Communication Research, 11,* 171-201.

Bazakas, R. (1979). *The interpersonal impact of coping, dependency, and denial: Self-preservation by the disabled.* Unpublished doctoral dissertation, Department of Education, New York University.

Beach, W. A. (1985). Temporal density in courtroom interaction: Constraints on the recovery of past events in legal discourse. *Communication Monographs, 52,* 1-19.

Becker, G., & Arnold, R. (1986). Stigma as a social and cultural construct. In S. Ainlay, G. Becker, & L. Coleman (Eds.), *The dilemma of difference—A multidisciplinary view of stigma.* New York: Plenum.

Becker, M. H. (1974). *The health belief model and personal health behavior.* Thorofare, NJ: Charles B. Stack.

Becker, M. H., Haefner, D. P., Kasi, S. V., Kirscht, J. P., Maiman, L. A., & Rosenstock, I. M. (1977). Selected psychosocial models and correlates of individual health-related behaviors. *Medical Care, 15,* 27-46.

Becker, M. H., & Maiman, L. A. (1975). Sociobehavioral determinations of compliance with health and medical care recommendations. *Medical Care, 13,* 10-24.

Beckman, H. B., & Frankel, R. M. (1984). The effect of physician behavior on the collection of data. *Annals of Internal Medicine, 101,* 692-696.

Beckman, H. B., & Frankel, R. M. (1985). Soliciting the patient's complete agenda: A relationship to the distribution of concerns. *Clinical Research, 33,* 714A.

Beckman, H. B., Kaplan, S., & Frankel, R. M. (1989). Outcome-based research on doctor-patient communication: A review. In M. Stewart & D. Roter (Eds.), *Communicating with medical patients* (pp. 223-227). Newbury Park, CA: Sage.

Beebe, L., & Takahashi, T. (1989a). Do you have a bag?: Social status and patterned variation in second language acquisition. In S. Gass, C. Madden, D. Preston, & L. Selinker (Eds.), *Variation in second language acquisition: Discourse and pragmatics* (pp 103-125). Clevedon, UK: Multilingual Matters.

Beebe, L., & Takahashi, T. (1989b). Sociolingustic variation in face threatening speech acts: Chastisement and disagreement. In M. Eisenstein (Ed.), *The dynamic interlanguage: Empirical studies in second language variation.* New York: Plenum.

Beebe, L., Takahashi, T., & Uliss-Weltz, R. (1990). In R. Scarcella, E. Andersen, & S. Krashen (Eds.), *On the development of communication competence in second language.* Rowley, MA: Newbury House.

Belgrave, F. Z., & Mills, J. (1981). Effect upon desire for social interaction with a physically disabled person of mentioning the disability in different contexts. *Journal of Applied Social Psychology, 11,* 44-57.

Bell, A. (1983). Telling it like it isn't: Inaccuracy in editing. *International News Gazette, 31,* 185-203.

Bell, A. (1984). Good copy—bad news: The syntax and semantics of news editing. In P. Trudgill (Ed.), *Applied sociolingusitcs* (pp. 73-116). London: Academic Press.

Bell, A. (1989). *Hot news: Media reporting and public understanding of the climate change issue in New Zealand* (Project report to the Department of Scientific and Industrial Research and Ministry for the Environment). Wellington: Victoria University, Department of Linguistics.

Bell, A. (in press). *The language of news media.* Oxford, UK: Basil Blackwell.

Belsey, C. (1980). *Critical practice.* London: Methuen.

Bengston, V. L., Reedy, N. M., & Gordon, C. (1985). Aging and self-conceptions, personality processes and social contexts. In J. E. Birren & K. Warner Schaie (Eds.), *Handbook of psychology and aging* (pp. 544-593). New York: Van Nostrand Reinhold.

Bennett, R., & Eckman, J. (1973). Attitudes toward aging. In C. Eisdorfer & P. Lawton (Eds.), *The psychology of adult development and aging* (pp. 575-597). Washington, DC: American Psychological Association.

Bennet, W. L. (1978). Storytelling in criminal courts. *Quarterly Journal of Speech, 64,* 1-22.

Bennet, W. L., & Feldman, M. S. (1981). *Reconstructing reality in the courtroom: Justice and judgement in American culture.* New Brunswick, NJ: Rutgers University Press.

Berelson, B. (1952). *Content analysis in communication research.* Glencoe, IL: Free Press.

Berger, C. R. (1979). Beyond initial interaction: Uncertainty, understanding and the development of interpersonal relationships. In H. Giles & R. N. St. Clair (Eds.), *Language and social psychology* (pp. 122-144). Oxford, UK: Basil Blackwell.

Berger, C. R. (1986). Uncertain outcome values in predicted relationships: Uncertainty reduction theory then and now. *Human Communication Research, 13,* 34-38.

Berger, C. R., Bradac, J. J. (1982). *Language and social knowledge: Uncertainty in interpersonal relationships.* London: Edward Arnold.

Berger, C. R., & Calabrese, R. J. (1975). Some explorations in initial interaction and beyond: Toward a developmental theory of interpersonal communication. *Human Communication Research, 1,* 99-112.

Berger, C. R., & Douglas, W. (1981). Studies in interpersonal epistemology III: Anticipated interaction, self-monitoring, and observational context selection. *Communication Monographs, 48,* 183-196.

Berger, C. R., Gardner, R. R., Clatterbuck, G. W., & Schulman, L. S. (1976). Perceptions of information sequencing in relational development *Human Communication Research, 3,* 29-46.

Berger, C. R., & Kellerman, K. A. (1983). To ask or not to ask: Is that a question? In R. N. Bostrom (Ed.), *Communication yearbook 7* (pp. 342-368). Beverly Hills, CA: Sage.

Berger, C. R., & Perkins, J. W. (1978). Studies in interpersonal epistemology I: Situational attributes in observational context selection. In B. D. Rubin (Ed.), *Communication yearbook 2* (pp. 171-184). New Brunswick, NJ: Transaction Press.

Berger, P. L., & Kellner, H. (1964). Marriage and the social construction of reality. Diogenes, 46, 1-25.

Berger, P., & Luckmann, T. (1967). *The social construction of reality.* Harmondsworth, UK: Penguin.

Berk-Seligson, S. (1987). The intersection of testimony styles in interpreted judicial proceedings: Pragmatic alterations in Spanish testimony. *Linguistics, 25,* 1087-1125.

Berk-Seligson, S. (1988). The impact of politeness in witness testimony: The influence of the court interpreter. *Multilingua, 7,* 439-441.

Berk-Seligson, S. (1989). The role of register in the bilingual courtroom: Evaluative reactions to interpreted testimony. In I. Wherritt & O. Garcia (Eds.), U.S. Spanish: The language of Latinos. *International Journal of the Sociology of Language, 79,* 79-92.

Berkowitz, N. H., Malone, M. F., Klein, M. W., & Eaton, A. (1963). Patient follow-through in the out-patient department. *Nursing Research, 12,* 16-22.

Berkson, G. (1977). The social ecology of defects in primates. In S. Chevalier-Skolnikoff & F. E. Poirier (Eds.), *Primate bio-social development: Biological, social and ecological determinants.* New York: Garland Publishing.

Berman, L., & Sobkowska-Ashcroft, I. (1986). The old in language and literature. *Language and Communication, 6*(1/2), 139-145.

Billig, M., Condor, S., Edwards, D., Gane, M., Middleton, D., & Radley, A. (1990). *Ideological dilemmas.* London: Sage.

Bishop, D., & Rosenbloom, L. (1987). Classification of childhood language disorders. In W. Yule & M. Rutter (Eds.), *Language development and disorders.* Oxford, UK: MacKeith Press.

Blank, M., Gessner, M., & Esposito, A. (1979). Language without communication: A case study. *Journal of Child Language, 6,* 329-352.

Blankenburg, W. B. (1970). News accuracy: some findings on the meaning of errors. *Journal of Communication, 20,* 375-386.

Blewitt, L. (1988). Metaphor and conflict in feminist organizations. *Women and Language, 11*(1), 40-43.

Blood, D. (1962). Women's speech characteristics in Cham. *Asian Culture, 3,* 139-143.

Blum-Kulka, S. (1983). Interpreting and performing speech acts in a second language—a cross-cultural study of Hebrew and English. In N. Wolfson & E. Judd (Eds.), 36-55.

Blum-Kulka, S. (1987, October). *A unique type of code switching: The interlanguage of Hebrew-English bilinguals.* Paper presented at the Variation in Second Language Acquisition Conference, University of Michigan.

Bochner, A. P. (1978). On taking ourselves seriously: An analysis of some persistent problems and promising directions in interpersonal research. *Human Communication Research, 4,* 179-191.

Bochner, A. P. (1982). On the efficacy of openness in close relationships. In M. Burgoon (Ed.), *Communication yearbook 5* (pp. 109-124). New Brunswick, NJ: Transaction Press.

Bochner, A. P. (1984). The functions of human communication in interpersonal bonding. In C. Arnold & J. Bowers (Eds.), *Handbook of rhetoric and communication theory* (pp. 544-621). Boston: Allyn & Bacon.

Bochner, S. (1983). Doctors, patients and their cultures. In D. Pendleton & J. Hasler (Eds.), *Doctor-patient communication* (pp. 127-138). London: Academic Press.

Boggs, S. (1985). *Speaking, relating, and learning: A study of Hawaiian children at home and at school.* Norwood, NJ: Ablex.

Bogoch, B., & Danet, B. (1984). Challenge and control in lawyer-client interaction: A case study in an Israeli legal aid office. *Text, 4,* 249-275.

Bohannan, P. (Ed.). (1967). *Law and warfare.* Garden City, NY: Natural History Press.

Boon, J. A. (1986). Symbols, sylphs, and Siwa: Allegorical machineries in the text of Balinese culture. In V. W. Turner & E. M. Bruner (Eds.), *The anthropology of experience*. Urbana: University of Illinois Press.

Botwick, J. (1984). *Aging and behavior* (3rd ed.). New York: Springer.

Bouchez, C. (1987, October 7). Male vs. female. *Chicago Tribune*, sec. 2, p. 4.

Bourhis, R. Y., & Giles, H. (1977). The language of intergroup distinctiveness. In H. Giles (Ed.), *Language, ethnicity and intergroup relations* (pp. 119-136). London: Academic Press.

Bourhis, R. Y., Giles, H., & Rosenthal, D. (1981). Notes on the construction of a subjective vitality questionnaire for ethnolinguistic groups. *Journal of Multilingual and Multicultural Development, 2*, 145-155.

Bowman, J. T. (1987). Attitudes toward disabled persons: Social distance and work competence. *Journal of Rehabilitation, 53*, 41-44.

Boyle, C. M. (1970). Differences between doctors' and patients' interpretations of some common medical terms. *British Medical Journal, 2*, 286-289.

Bradac, J., & Mulac, A. (1984). A molecular view of powerful and powerless speech styles: Attributional consequences of specific language features and communicator intentions. *Communication Monographs, 51*, 307-319.

Brannigan, A., & Lynch, M. (1987). On bearing false witness: Credibility as interactional accomplishment. *Journal of Contemporary Ethnography, 16*, 115-146.

Brickman, P., Rabinowitz, V. C., Karuza, J., Jr., Coates, D., Cohn, E., & Kidder, L. (1982). Models of helping and coping. *American Psychologist, 37*, 369-384.

Brooks, L. (1974). Interactive effects of sex and status on self-disclosure. *Journal of Counseling Psychology, 21*, 469-474.

Brown, G., & Yule, G. (1983). *Teaching the spoken language*. Cambridge, UK: Cambridge University Press.

Brown, J. R. (1988). *The political, economic and intertextual nature of conversation: Developing a critical vocabulary of everyday life*. Paper presented at the annual meeting of the Speech Communication Association, New Orleans, LA.

Brown, P. (1980). How and why are women more polite: Some evidence from a Mayan community. In S. McConnell-Ginet, R. Borker, & N. Furman (Eds.), *Women and language in literature and society* (pp. 111-136). New York: Praeger.

Brown, P., & Levinson, S. (1978). Universals in language usage: Politeness phenomena. In E. N. Goody (Ed.), *Questions and politeness: Strategies in social interaction* (pp. 56-289). Cambridge, UK: Cambridge University Press.

Brown, R. (1973). *A first language*. Cambridge, MA: Harvard University Press.

Brown, R. (1977). Introduction. In C. E. Snow & C. A. Ferguson (Eds.), *Talking to children: Language input and acquisition* (pp. 1-27). Cambridge, UK: Cambridge University Press.

Brown, R., & Gilman, A. (1960). The pronouns of power and solidarity. In T. A. Sebeok (Ed.), *Style in language*. Cambridge: M.I.T. Press.

Buck, R. (1984). *The communication of emotion*. New York: Guilford.

Budd, R. W., Thorp, R. K., & Donohew, L. (1967). *Content analysis of communications*. New York: Macmillan.

Bunzel, J. H. (1972). Note on the history of a concept: Gerontophobia. *The Gerontologist, 12*, 116-203.

Burns, T. (1977). *The BBC: Public institution and private world*. London: Macmillan.

Butler, P. E. (1976). *Self-assertion for women: A guide to becoming androgynous*. New York: Canfield.

Butler, R. N. (1969). Age-ism: Another form of bigotry. *The Gerontologist, 9*, 243-246.

Button, G., & Lee, J. R. E. (Eds.). (1987). *Talk and social organization.* Clevedon, UK: Multilingual Matters.

Butturff, D., & Epstein, E. (Eds.). (1978). *Women's language and style.* Akron, OH: L&S Books.

Buzolich, M., & Wiemann, J. M. (1988). Turn taking in atypical conversations: The case of the speaker/augmented-communicator dyad. *Journal of Speech and Hearing Research, 31,* 3-18.

Caesar-Wolf, B. (1984). The construction of "adjudicable" evidence in a West German civil hearing. *Text, 4,* 193-223.

Cahill, S. E. (1981). Cross-sex pseudocommunication. *Berkeley Journal of Sociology, 26,* 75-88.

Caldwell, M. A., & Peplau, L. A. (1982). Sex differences in same-sex friendships. *Sex Roles, 8,* 721-732.

Caporael, L. (1981). The paralanguage of caregiving: Baby talk to the institutionalized aged. *Journal of Personality and Social Psychology, 40* (5), 876-884.

Caporael, L., & Culbertson, G. H. (1986). Verbal response modes of baby talk and other speech at institutions of aged. *Language and Communication, 6*(1/2), 99-112.

Caporael, L. R., Lucaszewski, M. P., & Culbertson, G. H. (1983). Secondary baby talk: Judgments by institutionalized elderly and their care givers. *Journal of Personality and Social Psychology, 44*(4), 746-754.

Carbaugh, D. (1989). Fifty terms for talk: A cross-cultural study. In S. Ting-Toomey & F. Korzenny (Eds.), *Language communication and culture: Current directions.* Newbury Park, CA: Sage.

Carberry, S. (1984). Understanding pragmatically ill-formed input. *Proceedings of Coling84* (pp. 200-206). Stanford University.

Carbonell, J. G., & Hayes, P. J. (1983). Recovery strategies for parsing extragrammatical language. *American Journal of Computational Linguistics, 9,* 123-146.

Carroll, R. (1988). *Cultural misunderstandings: The French-American experience.* Chicago: University of Chicago Press.

Carroll, T. J. (1961). *Blindness: What it is, what it does, and how to live with it.* Boston: Little, Brown.

Cartwright, A. (1964). *Human relations and hospital care.* London: Routledge & Kegan Paul.

Cartwright, A., Lucas, S., & O'Brien, M. (1974). *Exploring communications in general practice: A feasibility study.* Report to the Social Science Research Council, Institute for Social Studies in Medicine, London

Carver, C. S., & de la Garza, N. H. (1984). Schema-guided information search in stereotyping of the elderly. *Journal of Applied Social Psychology, 14,* 69-81.

Chaiklin, H., & Warfield, M. (1973). Stigma management and amputee rehabilitation. *Rehabilitation Literature, 34,* 162-166.

Chamberlain, A. (1912). Women's language. *American Anthropologist, 14,* 579-581.

Charnley, M. V. (1936). Preliminary notes on a study of newspaper accuracy. *Journalism Quarterly, 13,* 394-401.

Chelune, G. J. (1975). Self-disclosure: An elaboration of its basic dimensions. *Psychological Reports, 36,* 79-85.

Cherry, L. (1979). The role of adults' requests for clarification in the language development of children. In R. O. Freedle (Ed.), *New directions in discourse processing* (Vol. 2, pp. 273-286). Norwood, NJ: Ablex.

Chinn, P. C., Winn, J., & Walters, R. H. (1978). *Two-way talking with parents of special children: A process of positive communication.* St. Louis: C. V. Mosby.

Cicourel, A. (1968). *The social organization of juvenile justice.* New York: John Wiley.

Cicourel, A. (1975). Discourse and texts: Cognitive and linguistic processes in studies of social structure. *Versus: Quaderni di Studi Semiotici, 12,* 33-84.

Cicourel, A. (1980). Language and social interaction. *Sociological Inquiry, 50,* 1-30.

Cicourel, A. (1983). Hearing is not believing: Language and the structure of belief in medical communication. In S. Fisher & A. D. Todd (Eds.), *The social organization of doctor-patient communication* (pp. 221-239). Washington, DC: Center for Applied Linguistics.

Cixous, H. (1976). The laugh of the Medusa (K. Cohen & P. Cohen, Trans.). *Signs, 1,* 875-893.

Clancy, P. (1986). The acquisition of communicative style in Japanese. In B. Schieffelin & E. Ochs (Eds.), *Language socialization across cultures.* Cambridge, UK: Cambridge University Press.

Clifford, B. R., & Bull, R. (1978). *The psychology of person identification.* London: Routledge & Kegan Paul.

Clyne, M. (1977). Intercultural communication breakdown and communication conflict: Towards a linguistic model and its exemplification. In C. Molony, H. Zobl, & W. Stolting (Eds.), *Duetsch im Kontact mit Anderen Sprachen* (pp. 129-146). Kronberg, West Germany: Scriptor Verlag.

Coates, J. (1986). *Women, men and language.* London: Longman.

Coburn, D., & Pope, C. (1974). Socioeconomic status and preventive health behavior. *Journal of Health and Social Behavior, 15,* 67-78.

Cogswell, B. E. (1977). Self-socialization: Readjustment of paraplegics in the community. In J. Stubbins (Ed.), *Social and psychological aspects of disability.* Baltimore, MD: University Park Press.

Cohen, A., & Olshtain, E. (1981). Developing a measure of socio-linguistic competence: The case of apology. *Language Learning, 31,* 113-134.

Cohen, G., & Faulkner, D. (1986). Does "elderspeak" work? The effect of intonation and stress on comprehension and recall of spoken discourse in old age. *Language and Communication, 6*(1/2), 91-98.

Cohen, P. R., & Perault, R. C. (1979). Elements of a plan-based theory of speech acts. *Cognitive Science, 3,* 177-212.

Cohen, R. (1987). Problems of intercultural communication in Egyptian-American diplomatic relations. *International Journal of Intercultural Relations, 11,* 29-47.

Colby, K. (1975). *Artificial paranoia.* Oxford, UK: Pergamon.

Cole, M., John-Steiner, V., Scribner, S., & Souberman, E. (Eds.), (1978). *Mind in society: The development of higher psychological processes.* Cambridge, MA: Harvard University Press.

Coleman, L. (1986). Stigma: An enigma demystified. In S. Ainlay, G. Becker, & L. Coleman (Eds.), *The dilemma of difference—A multidiscinplinary view of stigma.* New York: Plenum.

Conant, S. & Budoff, M. (1983). Patterns of awareness in children's understanding of disabilities. *Mental Retardation, 21,* 119-125.

Connolly, J. H. (1986). Intelligibility: A linguistic view. *British Journal of Disorders of Communication, 21,* 371-376.

Conrad, C. (1985). *Strategic organizational communication.* New York: Holt, Rinehart & Winston.

Conti-Ramsden, G., & Gunn, M. (1986). The development of conversational disability: A case study. *British Journal of Disorders of Communication, 21,* 339-352.

Cook, M., & Lalljee, M. (1972). Verbal substitutes for verbal signals in interaction. *Semiotica, 6,* 212-221.

Coope, J., & Metcalfe, D. (1979). How much do patients know? A MCQ paper for patients in the waiting room. *Journal of the Royal College of General Practitioners, 29,* 482-488.

Cooper, E., & Jahoda, M. (1947). The evasion of propaganda: How prejudiced people respond to anti-prejudice propaganda. *Journal of Psychology, 23,* 15-25.

Corsaro, W. (1977). The clarification request as a feature of adult interactive styles with young children. *Language in Society, 6,* 183-207.

Coser, R. L. (1958). Authority and decision making in a hospital: A comparative analysis. *American Sociological Review, 23,* 56-63.

Coser, R. L. (1962). *Life in the ward.* East Lansing: Michigan State University Press.

Coupland, J., Coupland, N., Giles, H., & Wiemann, J. (1988). My life in your hands: Processes of self-disclosure in intergenerational talk. In N. Coupland (Ed.), *Styles of discourse* (pp. 201-253). London: Croom Helm.

Coupland, J., Coupland, N., & Grainger, K. (in press). Intergenerational discourse: Contextual versions of aging and elderliness. *Ageing and Society.*

Coupland, N., & Coupland, J. (1990). Language and alter life: The diachrony and decrement predicament. In H. Giles, & P. Robinson (Eds.), *Handbook of language and social psychology* (pp. 451-468). Chichester: John Wiley.

Coupland, N., Coupland, J., & Giles, H. (1989). Telling age in later life: Identity and face implications. *Text, 9*(2), 129-151.

Coupland, N., Coupland, J., & Giles, H. (in press). *Sociolinguistics and the elderly: Discourse, identity and aging.* Oxford, UK: Basil Blackwell.

Coupland, N., Coupland, J., Giles, H., & Henwood, K. (1988). Accommodating the elderly: Invoking and extending a theory. *Language in Society, 17*(1), 1-41.

Coupland, N., Coupland, J., Giles, H., Henwood, K., & Wiemann, J. (1988). Elderly self-disclosure: Interactional and intergroup issues. *Language and Communication, 8*(2), 109-133.

Coupland, N., Giles, H., & Benn, W. (1986). Language, communication and the blind: Research agenda. *Journal of Language and Social Psychology, 5,* 52-63.

Covey, H. C. (1988). Historical terminology used to represent older people. *The Gerontologist, 28,* 291-297.

Cozby, P. C. (1972). Self-disclosure, reciprocity, and liking. *Sociometry, 35,* 151-160.

Cozby, P. C. (1973). Self-disclosure: A literature review. *Psychological Bulletin, 79,* 73-91.

Crago, M. (1988). *Cultural context in communicative interaction of Inuit children.* Unpublished doctoral dissertation, McGill University, Montreal.

Crano, W. D., & Meese, L. A. (1982). *Social psychology: Principles and themes of interpersonal behavior.* Homewood, IL: Dorsey Press.

Crocker, J., Thompson, L., McGraw, K. M., & Ingerman, C. (1987). Downward comparison, prejudice, and evaluations of others: Effects of self-esteem and threat. *Journal of Personality and Social Psychology, 52,* 907-916.

Crockett, W. H., Press, A. N., & Osterkamp, M. (1979). The effects of deviations from stereotyped expectations upon attitudes toward older persons. *Journal of Gerontology, 34,* 368-374.

Croog, S. H. (1961). Ethnic origins, educational level, and responses to a health questionnaire. *Human Organization, 20,* 65-69.

Culbertson, G. H., & Caporael, L. (1983). Baby talk speech to the elderly: Complexity and content of messages. *Personality and Social Psychology Bulletin, 9,* 305-312.

Curra, J. (1975). *The sociology of social deviance, social behaviorism, and the concept of consensus: Labelling theory and "behind."* Unpublished doctoral dissertation, Department of Sociology, Purdue University.

Cushman, D., & Kincaid, L. (1987). Introduction and initial insights. In L. Kincaid (Ed.), *Communication theory: Eastern and western perspectives* (pp. 1-10). San Diego, CA: Academic Press.

Cutler, A. (Ed.). (1982). *Slips of the tongue and language production.* Amsterdam: Mouton de Gruyter.

Daly, J. A., & McCroskey, J. C. (Eds.). (1984). *Avoiding communication.* Newbury Park, CA: Sage.

Daly, M. B., & Hulka, B. S. (1975). Talking with the doctor, 2. *Journal of Communication, 25,* 148-152.

Danet, B. (1980a). "Baby" or "fetus"? Language and the construction of reality in a manslaughter trial. *Semiotica, 32,* 187-219.

Danet, B. (1980b). Language in the legal process. *Law & Society Review, 14,* 55-64.

Danet, B., & Bogoch, B. (1980). Fixed fight or free-for-all? An empirical study of combativeness in the adversary justice system. *British Journal of Law and Society, 7,* 36-60.

Danet, B., Hoffman, K. B., Kermish, N. C., Rafn, H. J., & Stayman, D. G. (1976). An ethonography of questioning in the courtroom. In R. W. Shuy & A. Shnukal (Eds.), *Language use and the uses of language* (pp. 222-234). Washington, DC: Georgetown University Press.

Darrough, W. D. (1984). In the best interest of the child: Negotiating parental cooperation for probation placement. *Urban Life, 13,* 123-153.

Davies, P., & Mehan, H. (1988). Professional and family understanding of impaired communication. *British Journal of Disorders of Communication, 23,* 141-151.

Davis, F. (1960). Uncertainty in medical prognosis: Clinical and functional. *American Journal of Sociology, 66,* 41-47.

Davis, F. (1963). *Passage through crisis.* Indianapolis: Bobbs-Merrill.

Davis, F. (1977). Deviance disavowal: The management of strained interactions by the visibly handicapped. In J. Stubbins (Ed.), *Social and psychological aspects of disability.* Baltimore, MD: University Park Press.

Davis, H., & Walton, P. (Eds.). (1983). *Language, image, media.* Oxford, UK: Basil Blackwell.

Davis, J. H. (1980). Group decision and procedural justice. In M. Fishbein (Ed.), *Progress in social psychology* (Vol. 1, pp. 157-229). Hillsdale, NJ: Lawrence Erlbaum.

Davis, M. (1966). Variations in patients' compliance with doctors' orders: Analysis of congruence between survey responses and results of empirical investigations. *Journal of Medical Education, 41,* 1037-1048.

Davis, M. (1968). Variations in patients' compliance with doctors' advice. An empirical analysis of patterns of communication. *American Journal of Public Health, 58,* 274-288.

Davis, M. H., & Franzoni, S. L. (1987). Private self-consciousness and self-disclosure. In V. L. Derlega & J. Berg (Eds.), *Self-disclosure: Theory, research, and therapy* (pp. 59-71). New York: Plenum.

Deakins, A. (1987, October). The *tu/vous* dilemma: Gender, power and solidarity. Paper presented at the conference on Communication, Language, and Gender, Milwaukee, WI.

Deegan, M. J. (1977). The nonverbal communication of the physically handicapped. *Journal of Sociology and Social Welfare, 4,* 735-748.

Deetz, S. (1982). Hermeneutics and research in interpersonal communication. In J. J. Pilotta (Ed.), *Interpersonal communication: Essays in phenomenology and hermeneutics.* Washington, DC: Center for Advanced Research in Phenomenology and University Press of America.

Deetz, S. A., & Kersten, A. (1983). Critical models of interpretive research. In L. L. Putnam & M. E. Pacanowsky (Eds.), *Communication and organization: An interpretive approach* (pp. 147-171). Beverly Hills, CA: Sage.

DeFrancisco, V. L. (1989). *Marital communication: A feminist qualitative analysis.* Unpublished doctoral dissertation. University of Illinois at Urbana-Champaign.

Dent, H. R. (1983). The effects of interviewing strategies on the results of interviews with child witnesses. In A. Trankell (Ed.), *Reconstructing the past: The role of psychologists in criminal trials* (pp. 279-297). Stockholm: Norstedt.

DePaulo, B. M. (in press). Nonverbal behavior and self-presentation: A developmental perspective. In R. S. Feldman & B. Rimé (Eds.), *Fundamentals of nonverbal behavior.* Cambridge, UK: Cambridge University Press.

DePaulo, B. M., & Coleman, L. (1986). Talking to children, foreigners and retarded adults. *Journal of Personality and Social Psychology, 51,* 945-959.

DePaulo, B. M., & Coleman, L. (1987). Verbal and nonverbal communication of warmth to children, foreigners, and retarded adults. *Journal of Nonverbal Behavior, 11,* 75-88.

DePaulo, B. M., & Kirkendol, S. E. (1989). The motivational impairment effect in the communication of deception. In J. Yuille (Ed.), *Credibility assessment.* Dordrecht, The Netherlands: Kluwer Academic Publishers.

DePaulo, B. M., Kirkendol, S. E., Tang, J., & O'Brien, T. (1988). The motivational impairment effect in the communication of deception: Replications and extensions. *Journal of Nonverbal Behavior, 12,* 177-202.

DePaulo, B. M., Nadler, A., & Fisher, J. D. (1983). *New directions in helping, Volume 2: Help-seeking.* New York: Academic Press.

DePaulo, B. M., Stone, J. I., & Lassiter, G. D. (1985). Telling ingratiating lies: Effects of target sex and target attractiveness on verbal and nonverbal deceptive success. *Journal of Personality and Social Psychology, 48,* 1191-1203.

DePaulo, B. M., Tang, J., & Stone, J. I. (1987). Physical attractiveness and skill at detecting deception. *Personality and Social Psychology Bulletin, 13,* 177-187.

DeVito, J. A. (1983). *The interpersonal communication book* (3rd ed.). New York: Harper & Row.

Dillard, J. P., Segrin, C., & Harden, J. M. (1989). Primary and secondary goals in the production of interpersonal influence messages. *Communication Monographs, 56,* 19-38.

DiMatteo, M. R., & DiNicola, D. D. (1982). *Achieving patient compliance: The psychology of the medical practitioner's role.* Elmsford, NY: Pergamon.

Dinkel, R. (1944). Attitudes of children toward supporting aged parents. *American Sociological Review, 9,* 370-379.

Donnellon, A., Gray, B., & Bougon, M. G. (1986). Communication, meaning, and organized action. *Administrative Science Quarterly, 31,* 43-55.

Drew, P. (1985). Analyzing the use of language in courtroom interaction. In T. A. Van Dijk (Ed.), *Handbook of discourse analysis.* (Vol. 3, pp. 133-147). London: Academic Press.

Drew, P. (in press). Disputes in courtroom cross-examinations: "Contrasting versions" in a rape trial. In P. Drew & J. Heritage (Eds.), *Talk at work.* Cambridge, UK: Cambridge University Press.

Druian, P. R., & DePaulo, B. M. (1977). Asking a child for help. *Social Behavior and Personality, 5,* 968-1000.

Drummond, K. (1989). A backward glance at interruptions. *Western Journal of Speech Communication, 58,* 150-166.

Duff, P. (1986). Another look at interlanguage talk: Taking task to task. In R. Day (Ed.), *Talking to learn: Conversation in second language acquisition* (pp. 147-181). Rowley, MA: Newbury House.

Dunkel-Shetter, C., & Wortman, C. (1982). The interpersonal dynamics of cancer: Problems in social relationships and their impact on the patient. In H. S. Friedman & M. R. DiMatteo (Eds.), *Interpersonal issues in health care* (pp. 60-100). New York: Academic Press.

Dunstan, R. (1980). Context for coercion: Analyzing properties of courtroom "questions". *British Journal of Law and Society, 7,* 61-77.

Duranti, A. (1984). Intentions, self, and local theories of meaning: Words and actions in a Samoan context. *Center for Human Information Processing, 122,* 1-20.

Duranti, A. (1988). Intentions, language and social action in a Samoan context. *Journal of Pragmatics, 12,* 13-33.

Edelsky, C., & Adams, K. (in press). Creating inequality: Breaking the rules in debates. *Journal of Language and Social Psychology.*

Edelsky, C., & Rosegrant, T. (1981). *Interactions with handicapped children: Who's handicapped?* Sociolinguistic Working Paper No. 9.

Edwards, J. (1985). *Language, society and identity.* Oxford, UK: Basil Blackwell.

Ehrenhaus, P. (1983). Culture and the attribution process: Barriers to effective communication. In W. B. Gudykunst (Ed.), *Intercultural communication theory: Current perspectives.* Beverly Hills, CA: Sage.

Eisenberg, E. M. (1984). Ambiguity as strategy in organizational communication. *Communication Monographs, 51,* 227-242.

Eisenberg, E. M. (1986). Meaning and interpretation in organizations. *Quarterly Journal of Speech, 72,* 88-113.

Eisenberg, E. M. (1990). Jamming: Transcendence through organizing. *Communication Research, 17*(2), 139-164.

Eisenberg, E. M., & Riley, P. (1988). Organizational symbols and sense-making. In G. Goldhaber & G. Barnett (Eds.), *Handbook of organizational communication* (pp. 131-150). Norwood, NJ: Ablex.

Eisenberg, E. M., & Witten, M. (1987). Reconsidering openness in organizational communication. *Academy of Management Review, 12,* 418-426.

Eiser, J., Sutton, S., & Wober, M. (1978). Smokers' and non-smokers' attributions about smoking: A case of actor-observer differences. *British Journal of Social and Clinical Psychology, 17,* 189-190.

Ekman, P. (1985). *Telling lies.* New York: Norton.

Elling, R., Wittemore, R., & Green, M. (1960). Patient participation in a pediatric program. *Journal of Health and Human Behavior, 1,* 183-191.

Ellis, D. G. (1982). The epistemology of form. In C. Wilder & J. H. Weaklund (Eds.), *Rigor and imagination: Essays from the legacy of Gregory Bateson* (pp. 215-230). New York: Praeger.

Emery, O. (1986). Linguistic decrement in normal ageing. *Language and Communication, 6*(1/2), 47-64.

Emry, R., & Wiseman, R. L. (1987). An intercultural understanding of able-bodied and disabled persons' communication. *International Journal of Intercultural Relations, 11,* 7-27.

Engel, G. L. (1977). The need for a new medical model: A challenge for biomedicine. *Science, 196,* 129-136.

Erickson, W. (1979). Talking down: Some cultural sources of miscommunication in interracial interviews. In A. Wolfgang (Ed.), *Nonverbal behavior: Applications and cultural implications* (pp. 99-126). New York: Academic Press.

Etter-Lewis, G. (1987, June). *Fussin'*. Paper presented at the National Women's Studies Association, Atlanta, GA.

Farina, A., Allen, J. G., & Saul, B. B. (1968). The role of the stigmatized person in affecting social relationships. *Journal of Personality and Social Psychology, 36,* 169-182.

Faris, J. C. (1966). The dynamics of verbal exchange: A Newfoundland example. *Anthropologica, 8*(2), 235-248.

Fasteau, M. F. (1974). *The male machine.* New York: McGraw-Hill.

Fedigan, L. M., & Fedigan, L. (1977). The social development of a handicapped infant in a free-living troop of Japanese-Monkeys. In S. Chevalier-Skolnikoff & F. E. Poirier (Eds.), *Primate bio-social development: Biological, social and ecological determinants.* New York: Garland Publishing.

Feldman, M., & March, J. (1981). Information in organizations as signal and symbol. *Administrative Science Quarterly, 26,* 171-186.

Ferguson, C. A. (1977). Babytalk as a simplified register. In C. Snow & C. Ferguson (Eds.), *Talking to children: Language input and acquisition* (pp. 209-235). Cambridge, UK: Cambridge University Press.

Ferguson, C. A. (1981). "Foreigner talk" as the name of a simplified register. *International Journal of the Sociology of Language, 28,* 9-18.

Fikes, R., & Nilsson, N. (1971). STRIPS: A new approach to the application of theorem proving to problem solving. *Artificial Intelligence, 2,* 189-208.

Fikes, R. E., Hart, P. E., & Nilsson, N. J. (1972). Learning and executing generalized robot plans. *Artificial Intelligence, 3,* 251-288.

Findahl, O., & Hoijer, B. (1981). Media content and human comprehension. In K. E. Rosengren (Ed.), *Advances in content analysis* (pp. 111-132). Beverly Hills/London: Sage.

Fine, M., & Asch, A. (1988). Disability beyond stigma: Social interaction, discrimination, and activism. *Journal of Social Issues, 44,* 3-22.

Fisher, B. A. (1978). *Perspectives on human communication.* New York: Macmillan.

Fisher, B. A. (1985). Pragmatics of meaning. In J. R. Cox, M.O. Sillars, & G. B. Walker (Eds.), *Argumentation and social practice: Proceedings of the fourth SA/AFA conference on argumentation* (pp. 511-522). Annandale, VA: Speech Communication Association.

Fisher, S., & Todd, A. D. (1986). *Discourse and institutional authority: Medicine, education, and law.* Norwood, NJ: Ablex.

Fishman, P. M. (1983). Interaction: The work women do. In B. Thorne, C. Kramarae, & N. Henley (Eds.), *Language, gender and society.* Rowley, MA: Newbury House. (Reprinted from *Social Problems*, 1977, *25*, pp. 397-406)

Fitts, F. T., & Ravdin, I. S. (1953). What Philadelphia physicians tell patients with cancer. *Journal of the American Medical Association, 153,* 901-904.

Fitzpatrick, M. A. (1984). A typological approach to marital interaction: Recent theory and research. In L. Berkowitz (Ed.), *Advances in experimental social pychology, 19* (pp. 1-264). New York: Academic Press.

Fitzpatrick, M. A. (1987). Marriage and verbal intimacy. In V. J. Derlega & J. H. Berg (Eds.), *Self-disclosure: Theory, research and therapy* (pp. 131-154). New York: Plenum.

Fitzpatrick, M. A. (1988). A typological approach to marital interaction. In P. Noller & M. A. Fitzpatrick (Eds.), *Perspectives on marital interaction* (pp. 98-120). Clevedon, UK: Multilingual Matters.

Fox, R. (1959). *Experiment perilous.* New York: Free Press.

Francis, V., Korsch, B. M., & Morris, M. J. (1969). Gaps in doctor-patient communication: Patients' response to medical advice. *New England Journal of Medicine, 280,* 535-540.

Frank, G. (1988). Beyond stigma: Visibility and self-empowerment of persons with congenital limb deficiencies. *Journal of Social Issues, 44,* 95-116.

Frankel, R. M. (1983). The laying on of hands: Aspects of the organization of gaze, touch, and talk in a medical encounter. In S. Fisher & A. D. Todd (Eds.), *The social organization of doctor-patient communication* (pp. 19-54). Washington, DC: Center for Applied Linguistics.

Frankel, R. M. (1984). From sentence to sequence: Understanding the medical encounter through microinteractional analysis. *Discourse Processes, 7,* 135-170.

Frankel, R. M. (in press). Talking in interviews: A dispreference for patient-initiated questions. In G. Psathas (Ed.), *Interactional competence.* New York: Irvington.

Frankel, R. M., & Beckman, H. B. (1989, February). *Communication aspects of malpractice.* Paper presented at the Midwinter Meeting of the International Communication Association, Monterey, CA.

Franklyn-Stokes, A., Harriman, J., Giles, H., & Coupland, N. (1988). Information seeking across the life span. *Journal of Social Psychology, 128*(3), 419-421.

Freemon, B., Negrete, V. F., Davis, M. S., & Korsch, B. M. (1971). Gaps in doctor-patient communication: Doctor-patient interaction analysis. *Pediatric Research, 5,* 298-311.

Freidson, E. (1960). Client control and medical behavior. *American Journal of Sociology, 65,* 374-382.

Freidson, E. (1961). *Patients' views of medical practice—A study of subscribers to a pre-paid medical plan in the Bronx.* New York: Russell Sage.

Freidson, E. (1970). *Profession of medicine: A study of the sociology of applied knowledge.* New York: Harper & Row.

Frost, P., Moore, L., Louis, M., Lundberg, C., & Martin, J. (1985). *Organizational culture.* Beverly Hills, CA: Sage.

Furnham, A., & Lane, S. (1984). Actual and perceived attitudes towards deafness. *Psychological Medicine, 14,* 417-423.

Furnham, A., & Pendred, J. (1983). Attitudes towards the mentally and physically disabled. *British Journal of Medical Psychology, 56,* 179-187.

Galanis, C. M., & Jones, E. E. (1986). When stigma confronts stigma: Some conditions enhancing a victim's tolerance of other victims. *Personality and Social Psychology Bulletin, 12,* 169-177.

Gallagher, T. (1981). Contingent query sequences within adult-child discourse. *Journal of Child Language, 8,* 51-62.

Galtung, J., & Ruge, M. H. (1965). The structure of foreign news. *Journal of Peace Research, 2,* 64-91.

Gan, H. H. (1979). *Deciding what's news.* New York: Pantheon.

Garai, J. E., & Scheinfeld, A. (1968). Sex differences in mental and behavioral traits. *Genetic Psychology Monographs, 77,* 169-299.

Gardiner, M., & Christie, B. (1987). Communication failure at the person-machine interface: The human factors aspects. In R. Reilly (Ed.), *Communication failure in dialogue and discourse* (pp. 309-324). Amsterdam: North-Holland.

Gardner, C. B. (1980). Passing by: Street remarks, address rights, and the urban female. *Sociological Quarterly, 50*(3-4), 328-356.

Garfinkel, H. (1967). *Studies in ethnomethodology.* Englewood Cliffs, NJ: Prentice-Hall.

Gass, S., & Varonis, E. (1984). The effect of familiarity on the comprehensibility of non-native speech. *Language Learning, 34,* 65-89.

Gass, S., & Varonis, E. (1985a). Task variation and nonnative/nonnative negotiation of meaning. In S. Gass & C. Madden (Eds.), *Input in second language acquisition* (pp. 149-161). Rowley, MA: Newbury House.

Gass, S., & Varonis, E. (1985b). Variation in native speaker speech modification to non-native speakers. *Studies in Second Language Acquisition, 7,* 37-57.

Gass, S., & Varonis, E. (1986). Sex differences in NNS/NNS interactions. In D. Day (Ed.), *Talking to learn* (pp. 327-351). Rowley, MA: Newbury House.

Gass. S., & Varonis, E. (1988). *Conversational interactions and the development of an L2.* Paper presented at the annual meeting of Teachers to Speakers of Other Languages, Chicago.

Gass, S., & Varonis, E. (1989). Incorporated repairs in NNS discourse. In M. Eisenstein (Ed.), *The dynamic interlanguage: Empirical studies in second language variation.* New York: Plenum.

Geertz, C. (1986). Making experiences, authoring selves. In V. W. Turner & E. M. Bruner (Eds.), *The anthropology of experience.* Urbana: University of Illinois Press.

Gerbasi, K. C., Zuckerman, M., & Reis, H. T. (1977). Justice needs a new blindfold: A review of mock jury research. *Psychological Bulletin, 84,* 323-345.

Gergen, K. (1985). The social constructionist movement in modern psychology. *American Psychologist, 40,* 266-275.

Gibbons, F. X. (1986). Stigma and interpersonal relations. In S. Ainlay, G. Becker, & L. Coleman (Eds.), *The dilemma of difference—A multidisciplinary view of stigma..* New York: Plenum.

Gibbons, F. X., Stephen, W. G., Stephenson, B. O., & Petty, C. R. (1980). Reactions to stigmatized others: Response amplification vs. sympathy. *Journal of Experimental Social Psychology, 16,* 591-605.

Giddens, A. (1981). *A contemporary critique of historical materialism.* Berkeley: University of California Press.

Gieber, W. (1956). Across the desk: A study of 16 telegraph editors. *Journalism Quarterly, 33,* 423-432.

Gilbert, S. J., & Hornstein, D. (1975). The dyadic effects of self-disclosure: Level versus valence. *Human Communication Research, 2,* 347-355.

Gilbert, S. J., & Whiteneck, G. G. (1976). Toward a multidimensional approach to the study of self-disclosure. *Human Communication Research, 2,* 347-355.

Giles, H. (1973). Accent mobility: A model and some data. *Anthropological Linguistics, 15*(2), 87-105.

Giles, H. (Ed.), (1977). *Language, ethnicity, and intergroup relations.* London: Academic Press.

Giles, H., Bourhis, R. Y., & Taylor, D. M. (1977). Towards a theory of language in ethnic group relations. In H. Giles (Ed.), *Language, ethnicity, and intergroup relations* (pp. 307-348). London: Academic Press.

Giles, H., & Byrne, J. (1982). An intergroup approach to second language acquisition. *Journal of Multilingual and Multicultural Development, 3,* 17-40.

Giles, H., Coupland, J., & Coupland, N. (Eds.). (1991). *Contexts of accommodation: Developments in applied sociolinguistics.* Cambridge, UK: Cambridge University Press.

Giles, H., & Coupland, N. (1991). *Language: Contexts and consequences.* Monterey: Brooks/Cole.

Giles, H., Coupland, N., Henwood, K., & Coupland, J. (1990). The social meaning of RP: An intergenerational perspective. In S. Ramsaran (Ed.), *Studies in the pronunciation of English: A commemorative volume in honor of A. C. Gimson* (pp/ 191-210). London: Croom Helm.

Giles, H., Coupland, N., & Wiemann, J. M. (in press). "Talk is cheap. . . " but "my word is my bond": Beliefs abut talk. In K. Bolton & H. Kwok (Eds.), *Sociolinguistics today: International perspectives.* London: Routledge & Kegan Paul.

Giles, H., Hewstone, M., Ryan, E. B., & Johnson, P. (1987). Research on language attitudes. In U. Ammon, N. Dittmar, & K. J. Mattheier (Eds.), *Sociolinguistics* (Vol. 1, pp. 585-597. Berlin: Walter de Gruyter.

Giles, H., & Johnson, P. (1981). The role of language in ethnic group relations. In J. C. Turner & H. Giles (Eds.), *Intergroup behavior* (pp. 199-243). Chicago: University of Chicago Press.

Giles, H., & Johnson, P. (1987). Ethnolinguistic identity theory: A social psychological approach to language maintenance. *International Journal of the Sociology of Language, 68,* 69-99.

Giles, H., Mulac, A., Bradac, J., & Johnston, P. (1987). Speech accommodation theory: The first decade and beyond. In M. L. McLaughlin (Ed.), *Communication yearbook 10* (pp. 13-48). Newbury Park, CA: Sage.

Giles, H., & Powesland, P. F. (1975). *Speech style and social evaluation.* New York: Academic Press.

Giles, H., & Robinson, P. W. (Eds.). (1990). *Handbook of language and social psychology.* London: John Wiley.

Giles, H., & Wiemann, J. M. (1987). Language, social comparison and power. In C. Berger & S. Chaffee (Eds.), *The handbook of communication science* (pp. 350-384). Newbury Park, CA: Sage.

Glaser, B. G., & Strauss, A. (1965). Temporal aspects of dying as a nonscheduled status passage. *American Journal of Sociology, 71,* 45-69.

Glasgow University media group (1976). *Bad News.* London: Routledge & Kegan Paul.

Glasgow University media group (1980). *More bad news.* London: Routledge & Kegan Paul.

Glasgow University media group (1985). *War and peace news.* Milton Keynes, UK: Open University Press.

Gleason, J., & Greif, E. (1983). Men's speech to young children. In B. Thorne, C. Kramarae, & N. Henley (Eds.), *Language, gender and society* (pp. 140-150). Rowley, MA: Newbury House.

Goffman, E. (1959). *The presentation of self in everyday life.* Englewood Cliffs, NJ: Prentice-Hall.

Goffman, E. (1961). *Encounters.* Indianapolis: Bobbs-Merrill.

Goffman, E. (1963a). *Behavior in public places.* New York: Free Press.

Goffman, E. (1963b). *Stigma: Notes on the management of spoiled identity.* Englewood Cliffs, NJ: Prentice-Hall.

Goffman, E. (1967). *Interaction ritual: Essays on face-to-face behavior.* Garden City, NY: Anchor.

Goffman, E. (1974). *Frame analysis: An essay in the organization of experience.* New York: Harper & Row.

Goffman, E. (1981). *Forms of talk.* Philadelphia: University of Pennsylvania Press.

Gold, D., Andres, D., Arbuckle, T., & Schwartzman, A. (1988). Measurements and correlates of verbosity in elderly people. *Journal of Gerontology: Psychological Sciences, 43*(2), 27-33.

Golde, P., & Kagan, N. E. (1959). A sentence completion procedure for assessing attitudes toward old age. *Journal of Gerontology, 14,* 355-363.

Golinkoff, R. (1986). "I beg your pardon?" The preverbal negotiation of failed messages. *Journal of Child Language, 13,* 455-476.

Goodall, H., Wilson, G., & Waagen, C. (1986). The performance appraisal interview: An interpretive reassessment. *Quarterly Journal of Speech, 72,* 74-87.

Goodman, B. (1983). Repairing miscommunication: Relaxation in reference. *Proceedings IJCAI, 83,* 134-138.

Goodstein, L. D., & Reinecker, V. M. (1974). Factors affecting self-disclosure: A review of the literature. In B. A. Maher (Ed.), *Progress in experimental personality research* (pp. 49-77). New York: Academic Press.

Goodwin, M. (1980). Directive-response speech sequences in girls' and boys' task activities. In S. McConnell-Ginet, R. Borker, & N. Furman (Eds), *Women and language in literature and society* (pp. 157-173). New York: Praeger.

Goody, E. (1978). Towards a theory of questions. In E. Goody (Ed.), *Questions and politeness* (pp. 231-260). Cambridge, UK: Cambridge University Press.

Gottman, J. (1979). *Marital interaction: Experimental investigations.* New York: Academic Press.

Gough, H. G., & Hall, W. B. (1975). The prediction of academic and clinical performance in medical school. *Research in Higher Eduction, 3,* 301-314.

Gowman, A. G. (1957). *The war blind in the American social structure.* New York: American Foundation for the Blind.

Graddol, D., & Swann, J. (1989). *Gender voice.* Oxford, UK: Basil Blackwell.

Graham, S. (1984). Communicating sympathy and anger to black and white children: The cognitive (attributional) consequences of affective cues. *Journal of Personality and Social Psychology, 47,* 40-54.

Gray, B., Bougon, M., & Donnellon, A. (1985). Organizations as constructions and destructions of meaning. *Journal of Management, 11,* 83-98.

Greene, M. G., Adelman, R., Charon, R., & Hoffman, S. (1986). Ageism in the medical encounter: An exploratory study of the doctor-elderly patient relationship. *Language and Communication, 6*(1/2), 113-124.

Greene, M. G., Adelman, R., Charon, R., & Friedmann, E. (1989). Concordance between physicians and their older and younger patients in the primary care medical encounter. *The Gerontologist, 29,* 808-813.

Greenfield, S., Kaplan, S., & Ware, J. E. (1985). Expanding patient involvement in care: Effects on patient outcomes. *Annals of Internal Medicine, 102* 520-528.

Grice, H. P. (1957). Meaning. *Philosophical Review,* 67.

Grice, J. P. (1975). Logic and conversation. In P. Cole & J. Morgan (Eds.), *Syntax and semantics, Vol. 3: Speech acts* (pp. 41-58). New York: Academic Press.

Grigsby, J. P., & Weatherly, D. (1983). Gender and sex-role differences in intimacy of self-disclosure. *Psychological Reports, 53,* 891-897.

Grimshaw, A. (1980). Mishearings, misunderstandings, and other nonsuccesses in talk: A plea for redress of speaker-oriented bias. *Sociological Inquiry, 50,* 31-74.

Grosz, B. (1977). *The representation and use of focus in dialogue understanding.* Unpublished doctoral dissertation, University of California, Berkeley.

Grosz, B. (1981). Focusing and description in natural language dialogues. In A. Joshi, B. Webber, & I. Sag (Eds.), *Elements of discourse understanding* (pp. 84-106). Cambridge, UK: Cambridge University Press.

Grosz, B., & Sidner, C. L. (1985). *The structures of discourse structure.* (Tech. Rep. No. CSLI-85-39). Stanford, CA: Stanford University, Center for the Study of Language and Information.

Grosz, B., & Sidner, C. L. (1987). *Plans for discourse.* (Tech. Rep. No. TR-11-87). Cambridge, MA: Harvard University, Center for Research in Computing Technology.

Gudykunst, W. B. (1989a). Cultural variability in ethnolinguistic identity. In S. Ting-Toomey & F. Korzenny (Eds.), *Language, communication, and culture: Current directions.* Newbury Park, CA: Sage.

Gudykunst, W. (1989b). Culture and the development of interpersonal relationships. In J. Anderson (Ed.), *Communication yearbook 12* (pp. 315-354). Newbury Park, CA: Sage.

Gudykunst, W. B., & Kim, Y. Y. (Eds.). (1984). *Methods for intercultural communication research.* Beverly Hills, CA: Sage.

Gudykunst, W. B., & Ting-Toomey, S. (1990). Ethnic identity, language and communication breakdowns. In H. Giles & P. Robinson (Eds.), *Handbook of language and social psychology* (pp. 309-328). London: John Wiley.

Guggenbuhl-Craig, A. (1980). *Eros on crutches: On the nature of the psychopath.* Dallas, TX: Spring.

Gumperz, J. J. (1977). Sociocultural knowledge in conversational inferences. In M. Saville-Troike (Ed.), *Georgetown University roundtable on languages and linguistics 1977: Linguistics and anthropology* (pp. 191-211). Washington, DC: Georgetown University Press.

Gumperz, J. J. (1978). The conversational analysis of interethnic communication. In E. L. Ross (Ed.), *Interethnic communication: Proceedings of the Southern Anthropological Society.* Athens: University of Georgia Press.

Gumperz, J. J. (1982a). *Discourse strategies.* Cambridge, UK: Cambridge University Press.

Gumperz, J. J. (1982b). Fact and inference in courtroom testimony. In J. J. Gumperz (Ed.), *Language and social identity* (pp. 163-195). Cambridge, UK: Cambridge University Press.

Gumperz, J. J. (Ed.) (1982c). *Language and social identity.* Cambridge, UK: Cambridge University Press.

Gumperz, J. J., Jupp, T. C., & Roberts, C. (1979). *Cross-talk: A study of cross-cultural communication.* London: National Centre for Industrial Language Training in association with the BBC.

Gumperz, J. J., & Tannen, D. (1979). Individual and social differences in language use. In C. Fillmore, D. Kempler, & W. S-Y. Wang (Eds.), *Individual differences in language ability and language behavior* (pp. 305-325). New York: Academic Press.

Gunter, B. (1987). *Poor reception: Misunderstanding and forgetting broadcast news.* Hillsdale, NJ: Lawrence Erlbaum.

Habermas, J. (1970). Toward a theory of communicative competence. In H. P. Dreutzek (Ed.), *Recent sociology no. 2: Patterns of communicative behavior* (pp. 115-148). New York: Macmillan.

Hacker, H. M. (1981). Blabbermouths and clams: Sex differences in disclosure in same sex and cross-sex friendship dyads. *Psychology of Women Quarterly, 5,* 385-401.

Hall, E. T. (1976). *Beyond culture.* Garden City, NY: Doubleday.

Hall, E. T., & Hall, M. R. (1987). *Hidden differences: Doing business with the Japanese.* Garden City, NY: Doubleday.

Halliday, M. A. K. (1978). *Language as social semiotic.* London: Edward Arnold.

Hansell, M., & Ajirotutu, C. S. (1982). Negotiating interpretations in interethnic settings. In J. Gumperz (Ed.), *Language and social identity* (pp. 85-94). Cambridge, UK: Cambridge University Press.

Harragan, B. L. (1977). *Games mother never taught you.* New York: Rawson Associates.

Harris, R. J. (1973). Answering questions containing marked and unmarked adjectives and adverbs. *Journal of Experimental Psychology, 97,* 399-401.

Harris, R. J., Ross Teske, R., & Ginns, M. J. (1975). Memory for pragmatic implications from courtroom testimony. *Bulletin of the Psychonomic Society, 6,* 494-496.

Harris, S. (1984). Questions as a mode of control in magistrates' courts. *International Journal of Sociology of Languages, 49,* 5-27.

Hartmann, P., & Husband, C. (1974). *Racism and the mass media.* London: Davis-Poynter.

Hastorf, A. H., Wildfogel, J., & Cassman, T. (1979). Acknowledgement of handicap as a tactic in social interaction. *Journal of Personality and Social Psychology, 37,* 1790-1797.

Hatch, E. (1983). *Psycholinguistics.* Rowley, MA: Newbury House.

Hawes, L. C. (1989). Power, discourse, and ideology: The micropractices of common sense. In J. A. Anderson (Ed.), *Communication yearbook 12* (pp. 60-75). Newbury Park, CA: Sage.

Hawkins, B. (1985). Is an "appropriate response" always so appropriate? In S. Gass & C. Madden (Eds.), *Input in second language acquisition* (pp. 162-178). Rowley, MA: Newbury House.

Heath, S. (1983). *Ways with words: Language, life and work in communities and classrooms.* Cambridge, UK: Cambridge University Press.

Henley, N. M. (1977). *Body politics: Power, sex, and nonverbal communication.* Englewood Cliffs, NJ: Prentice-Hall.

Henley, N. M. (1980). Assertiveness training in the social context. *Assert,* 30, 1-2.

Henning, M., & Jardim, A. (1977). *The managerial woman.* Garden City, NY: Doubleday.

Heritage, J. (1984). A change-of-state token and aspects of its sequential placement. In J. M. Atkinson & J. Heritage (Eds.), *Structures of social action.* Cambridge, UK: Cambridge University Press.

Hermann, T. (1983). *Speech and situation.* Berlin: Springer-Verlag.

Hester, A. (1971). An analysis of news flow from developed and developing nations. *Gazette, 17,* 29-43.

Hetherington, R. W., & Hopkins, C. E. (1969). Symptom sensitivity: Its social and cultural correlates. *Health Services Research, 4,* 63-70.

Hewstone, M., & Brown, R. (Eds.). (1986). *Contact and conflict in intergroup encounters.* Oxford, UK: Basil Blackwell.

Hewstone, M., & Giles, H. (1986). Social groups and social stereotypes in intergroup communication: A review and model of intergroup communication breakdown. In W. B. Gudykunst (Ed.), *Intergroup Communication* (pp. 10-26). London: Edward Arnold.

Hiatt, M. (1977). *The way women write.* New York: Teachers College Press.

Hickson, D. J., & Thomas, M. W. (1969). Professionalization in Britain: A preliminary measurement. *Sociology, 3,* 37-54.

Higgins, P. (1978). *Encounters between the disabled and the nondisabled: Bringing the impairment back in.* Orangeburg: University of South Carolina. (ERIC Document Reproduction Service No. ED 163 710)

Hinde, R. A. (1978). Interpersonal relationships: In quest of a science. *Psychological Medicine, 3,* 378-386.

Hinnenkamp, V. (1987). Foreigner talk, code switching, and the concept of trouble. In K. Knapp, W. Enninger, & A. Knapp-Potthoff (Eds.), *Analyzing intercultural communication* (pp. 137-180). Berlin: Mouton de Gruyter.

Hippocrates (1923). *On decorum and the physician.* London: Heinemann Medical Books.

Hirokawa, R. (1987). Communication within the Japanese business organization. In L. Kincaid (Ed.), *Communication theory* (pp. 137-150). San Diego, CA: Academic Press.

Hirschman, L. (1973, December). *Female-male differences in conversational interaction.* Paper presented at the meeting of the Linguistic Society of America, San Diego, CA.

Hobbs, J. (1978). *Why is discourse coherent?* (SRI Technical Note 176) Menlo Park, CA: SRI International.

Hobbs, J., & Evans, D. A. (1980). Conversation as planned behavior. *Cognitive Science, 4,* 349-377.

Hobbs, J., & Robinson, J. (1979). Why ask? *Discourse Processes, 2,* 311-318.

Hobbs, J. R., & Agar, M. H. (1985). *The coherence of incoherent discourse* (Report No., CSLI-85-38). Stanford, CA: Stanford University, Center for the Study of Language and Information.

Hockett, C. (1958). *A course in modern linguistics.* New York: Macmillan.

Hoffman, L. (1981). *Foundations of family therapy: A conceptual framework for systems change.* New York: Basic Books.

Hofstede, G. (1980) *Culture's consequences.* Beverly Hills, CA: Sage.

Hoijer, H. (1954). The Sapir-Whorf hypothesis. In H. Hoijer (Ed.), *Language in culture* (pp. 92-105). Chicago: University of Chicago Press.

Holmes, J. (1989). Politeness strategies in New Zealand women's speech. In A. Bell & J. Holmes (Eds.), *New Zealand ways of speaking English.* Clevedon, UK: Multilingual Matters.

Holquist, M. (1981). The politics of representation. In S. J. Greenblat (Ed.), *Allegory and representation: Selected papers from the English Institute, 1979-1980*; New Series, no. 5 (pp. 163-183). Baltimore, MD: Johns Hopkins University Press. (Reprinted in *The Quarterly Newsletter of the Laboratory of Comparative Human Cognition, 5,* 2-9.)

Hopper, R. (1987). *Hold the phone: An examination of call-waiting.* Paper presented at the Institute for Ethnomethodology and Conversation Analysis, Boston.

Hopper, R., Koch, S., & Mandelbaum, J. (1986). Conversation analysis methods. In D. G. Ellis & W. A. Donohue (Eds.), *Contemporary issues in language and discourse processes.* Hillsdale, NJ: Lawrence Erlbaum.

Houston, C. S., & Pasanen, W. E. (1972). Patients' perceptions of hospital care. *Hospitals, 46,* 70-74.

Hugh-Jones, P., Tanser, A. F., & Whitby, C. (1964). Patient's views of admission to a London teaching hospital. *British Medical Journal, 2,* 660-664.

Humphreys-Jones, C. (1986). Make, make do and mend: The role of the hearer in misunderstandings. In G. McGregor (Ed.), *Language for hearers* (pp. 105-126). Oxford, UK: Pergamon.

Hymes, D. (1972). Models of the interaction of language and social life. In J. Gumperz & D. Hymes (Eds.), *Directions in sociolinguistics.* New York: Holt, Rinehart & Winston.

Innes, J. M. (1977). Does the professional know what the client wants? *Social Science and Medicine, 11,* 635-638.

Inui, T. S., & Carter, W. B. (1985). Problems and prospects for health services research on provider-patient communication. *Medical Care, 23,* 521-538.

Inui, T. S., & Carter, W. B. (1989). Design issues in research on doctor-patient communication. In M. A. Stewart & D. Roter (Eds.), *Communicating with medical patients* (pp. 197-210). Newbury Park, CA: Sage.

Irigaray, L. (1980). When our lips speak together (C. Burke, Trans.) *Signs, 6,* 66-79.

Jacoby, J., & Hoyer, W. D. (1987). *The comprehension and miscomprehension of print communications: An investigation of mass media magazines.* Hillsdale, NJ: Lawrence Erlbaum.

Jefferson, G. (1975). Error correction as an interactional resource. *Language in Society, 2,* 181-199.

Jefferson, G. (1984). On the organization of laughter in talk about troubles. In J. M. Atkinson & J. Heritage (Eds.), *Structures of social action: Studies in conversation analysis* (pp. 346-369). Cambridge, UK: Cambridge University Press.

Jefferson, G. (1987). On exposed and embedded correction. In G. Button & J. R. E. Lee (Eds.), *Talk and social organizations* (pp. 86-100). Clevedon, UK: Multilingual Matters.

Jefferson, T. (1988). On the sequential organization of troubles-talk in ordinary conversation. *Social Problems, 35,* 418-441.

Jensen, K. B. (1988). News of social resource: A qualitative empirical study of the reception of Danish television news. *European Journal of Communication, 3,* 275-301.

Jespersen, O. (1922). The woman. In *Language: Its nature, development and origins.* London: Allen and Unwin.

Johnson-Laird, P. N. (1983). *Mental models.* Cambridge, UK: Cambridge University Press.

Jones, E. E., Farina, A., Hastorf, A. H., Markus, H., Miller, D., & Scott, R. (1984). *Social stigma: The psychology of marked relationships.* New York: Freeman.

Jönsson, L. (1988a). *On being heard in court trials and police interrogations* (Linköping Studies in Arts and Science 25). Linköping University.

Jönsson, L. (1988b). Polisförhöret som kommunikationssituation (Studies in Communication 23). Linköping University, Department of Communication Studies.

Joshi, A., Webber, B. L., & Weischedel, M. (1984). Preventing false inferences. *Proceedings of Coling84* (pp. 134-138). Stanford University.

Jourard, S. (1959). Healthy personality and self-disclosure. *Mental Hygiene, 43,* 499-507.

Jourard, S. (1971a). *Self-disclosure: an experimental analysis of the transparent self.* New York: John Wiley.

Jourard, S. (1971b). *The transparent self* (2nd ed.). New York: Van Nostrand Reinhold.

Jourard, S., & Lasakow, P. (1958). Some factors in self-disclosure. *Journal of Abnormal and Social Psychology, 56,* 91-98.

Kalcik, S. (1975). " . . . Like Anne's gynecologist or the time I was almost raped": Personal narratives in women's rap groups. In C. R. Farrer (Ed.), *Women and folklore.* Austin: University of Texas Press.

Kaplan, J. (1979). *Cooperative responses from a portable natural language database query system.* Unpublished doctoral dissertation, University of Pennsylvania.

Kashyap, L. (1986). The family's adjustment to their hearing-impaired child. *The Indian Journal of Social Work, 47,* 311-317.

Kastenbaum, R. (1964). *New thoughts on old age.* New York: Springer.

Katz, D., & Kahn, R. L. (1978). *The social psychology of organizations.* New York: John Wiley.

Katz, I. (1981). *Stigma: A social psychological analysis.* Hillsdale, NJ: Lawrence Erlbaum.

Katz, I., & Glass, D. C. (1979). An ambivalence-amplification theory of behavior toward the stigmatized. In W. G. Austin & S. Worchel (Eds.), *The social psychology of intergroup relations.* Monterey, CA: Brooks/Cole.

Keenan, E. O. (1976). The universality of conversational implicature. *Language in Society, 5,* 67-80.

Kellermann, K. (1986). Anticipation of future interaction and information exchange in initial interaction. *Human Communication Research, 13,* 41-75.

Kemper, S. (1986). Imitation of complex syntactic constructions by elderly adults. *Applied Psycholinguistics, 7,* 27-28.

Key, M. R. (1975). *Male/female language.* Metuchen, NJ: Scarecrow Press.

Kim, Y. Y. (1986). Introduction: A communication approach to interethnic relations. In Y. Y. Kim (Ed.), *Interethnic communication: Current research.* Newbury Park, CA: Sage.

Kim, Y.Y. (1988). *Communication and cross-cultural adaptation.* Clevedon, UK: Multilingual Matters.

Kimberly, J. R., & Miles, R. H. (1980). *The organizational life cycle: Issues in the creation, transformation, and decline of organizations.* San Francisco, CA: Jossey-Bass.

Kincey, J. A., Bradshaw, P. W., & Ley, P. (1975). Patients' satisfaction and reported acceptance of advice in general practice. *Journal of the Royal College of General Practitioners, 25,* 558-566.

King, J. (1983). Health beliefs in the consultation. In D. Pendleton & J. Hasler (Eds.), *Doctor-patient communication* (pp. 109-125). London: Academic Press.

Kipnis, D., Schmidt, S., & Wilkinson, I. (1980). Intraorganizational influence tactics: Explorations in getting one's way. *Journal of Applied Psychology, 65,* 440-452.

Kirscht, J., & Rosenstock, I. (1977). Patient adherence to antihypertensive medical regimens. *Journal of Community Health, 3,* 115-124.

Kite, M. E., & Johnson, B. T. (1988). Attitudes to older and younger adults: A meta-analysis. *Psychology and Aging, 3,* 233-244.

Kleck, R. E. (1968). Physical stigma and nonverbal cues emitted in face-to-face interaction. *Human Relations, 21,* 19-28.

Kleck, R. E., Ono, H., & Hastorf, A. H. (1966). The effects of physical deviance upon face-to-face interaction. *Human Relations, 19,* 425-436.

Kleck, R. E., & Strenta, A. (1980). Perceptions of the impact of negatively valued physical characteristics on social interaction. *Journal of Personality and Social Psychology, 39,* 861-873.

Knapp, D. A., Knapp, D. E., & Engle, J. (1966). The public, the pharmacist and self medication. *Journal of the American Pharmacology Association, 56,* 460-462.

Knapp, K., & Knapp-Potthoff, A. (1987). Instead of an introduction: Conceptual issues in analyzing intercultural communication. In K. Knapp, W. Enninger, & A. Knapp-Potthoff (Eds.), *Analyzing intercultural communication.* Berlin: Mouton de Gruyter.

Kochman, T. (1981). *Black and white styles in conflict.* Chicago: University of Chicago Press.

Komarovsky, M. (1967). *Blue-collar marriage.* New York: Random House.

Komarovsky, M. (1974). Patterns of self-disclosure in male undergraduates. *Journal of Marriage and Family, 36,* 677-686.

Korsch, B. M., Freeman, B., & Negrete, V. F. (1971). Practical implications of doctor-patient interaction analysis for pediatric practice. *American Journal of Diseases of Children, 121,* 110-114.

Korsch, B. M., Gozzi, E., & Francis, V. (1968). Gaps in doctor-patient communication I: Doctor-patient interaction and patient satisfaction. *Pediatrics, 42,* 855-871.

Korsch, B. M., & Negrete, V. F. (1972). Doctor-patient communication. *Scientific American, 227*(2), 66-74.

Kramarae, C. (1977). Perceptions of female and male speech. *Language and Speech, 20,* 151-161.

Kramarae, C. (1981). *Women and men speaking.* Rowley, MA: Newbury House.

Kramarae, C., Schulz, M., & O'Barr, W. (Eds.). (1984). *Language and power.* Beverly Hills, CA: Sage.

Krashen, S. (1980). The input hypothesis. In J. Alatis (Ed.), *Georgetown Roundtable on Languages and Linguistics 1980: Current issues in bilingual education.* Washington, DC: Georgetown University Press.

Krause, N. (1986). Social support, stress and well being among older adults. *Journal of Gerontology, 41,* 512-519.

Kreps, G. L. (1986). Health communication and the elderly. *World Communication, 15*(1), 55-70.

Krippendorf, K. (1985). *On the ethics of constructing communication.* Presidential address, annual meeting of the International Communication Association, Honolulu, HI.

Kubey, R. W. (1980). Television and aging: Past, present and future. *The Gerontologist, 20,* 16-35.

Kupst, M. J., Dresser, K., Schulman, J. L., & Paul, M. H. (1975). Evaluation of methods to improve communication in the physician-patient relationship. *American Journal of Orthopsychiatry, 45,* 420-429.

Kynette, D., & Kemper, S. (1986). Aging and the loss of grammatical forms: A cross-sectional study of language performance. *Language and Communication, 6,* 65-72.

Labov, W., & Fanshel, D. (1977). *Therapeutic discourse.* New York: Academic Press.

Ladieu, G., Hanfmann, E., & Dembo, T. (1947). Studies in adjustment to visible injuries: Evaluation of help by the injured. *Journal of Abnormal Psychology, 42,* 169-192.

Lakoff, G. (1987). *Women, fire, and dangerous things: What categories reveal about the mind.* Chicago: University of Chicago Press.

Lakoff, R. (1973). Language and woman's place. *Language in Society 2,* 45-79.

Lakoff, R. (1975). *Language and woman's place.* New York: Harper & Row.

Lane, C. (1985). Mis-communication in cross-examinations. In J. B. Pride (Ed.), *Cross-cultural encounters: Communication and miscommunication* (pp. 196-211). Melbourne: River Seine Productions.

Langer, E. J., Taylor, S. E., Fiske, S. T., & Chanowitz, B. (1976). Stigma, staring, and discomfort: A novel stimulus hypothesis. *Journal of Experimental and Social Psychology, 12,* 451-463.

Lawrence, G. C., & Grey, D. L. (1969). Subjective inaccuracies in local news reporting. *Journalism Quarterly, 46,* 753-757.

Leech, G. N. (1983). *Principles of pragmatics.* London: Longman.

Levin, J., & Levin, W. C. (1980). *Ageism: Prejudice and discrimination against the elderly.* Belmont, CA: Wadsworth.

Levin, J., & Levin, W. C. (1981). Willingness to interact with an old person. *Research on Aging, 3,* 211-217.

Levin, W. C. (1988). Age stereotyping: College student evaluations. *Research on Aging, 10,* 134-148.

Levine, D. (1985). *The flight from ambiguity.* Chicago: University of Chicago Press.

Levinson, S. (1983). *Pragmatics.* Cambridge, UK: Cambridge University Press.

Levitin, T. E. (1975). Deviants as active participants in the labeling process: The visibly handicapped. *Social Problems, 22,* 548-557.

Ley, P. (1980). Giving information to patients. In J. R. Eiser (Ed.), *Social psychology and behavioral medicine* (pp. 339-373). London: John Wiley.

Ley, P. (1983). Patients' understanding and recall in clinical communication failure. In D. Pendleton & D. Hasler (Eds.), *Doctor-patient communication* (pp. 89-107). London: Academic Press.

Ley, P., & Spelman, M. S. (1965). Communications in an outpatient setting. *British Journal of Social and Clinical Psychology, 4,* 114-116.

Ley, P., & Spelman, M. S. (1967). *Communicating with the patient.* London: Staples Press.

Leyser, Y., & Abrams, P. D. (1982). Teacher attitudes toward normal and exceptional groups. *The Journal of Psychology, 110,* 227-238.

Liebes-Plesner, T. (1984). Rhetoric in the service of justice: The sociolinguistic construction of stereotypes in an Israel rape trial. *Text, 4,* 173-192.

Lind, E. A., & O'Barr, W. M. (1979). The social significance of speech in the courtroom. In H. Giles & R. N. St. Clair (Eds.), *Language and social psychology* (pp. 66-87). Oxford, UK: Basil Blackwell.

Linell, P. (in press). Accommodation on trial: Processes of communicative accommodation in courtroom interaction. In H. Giles, J. Coupland, & N. Coupland (Eds.), *Contexts of accommodation.* Cambridge, UK: Cambridge University Press.

Litman, D. (1983). *Discourse and problem solving* (Tech. Rep. No. 139). Rochester, NY: University of Rochester, Department of Computer Sciences.

Litman, D. J., & Allen, J. F. (1984). A plan recognition model for clarification subdialogues. *Proceedings of Coling84* (pp. 302-311). Stanford University.

LoCastro, V. (1987). Aizuchi: A Japanese conversational routine. In L. E. Smith (Ed.), *Discourse across cultures: Strategies in world Englishes.* Englewood Cliffs, NJ: Prentice-Hall.

Lock, A. (1981). *The guided reinvention of language.* London: Academic Press.

Loftus, E. (1975). Leading questions and the eyewitness report. *Cognitive Psychology, 7,* 560-572.

Loftus, E. (1976). Language and memories in the judicial system. In R. W. Shuy & A. Shnukal (Eds.), *Language use and the uses of language* (pp. 257-268). Washington, DC: Georgetown University Press.

Loftus, E. (1979). *Eyewitness testimony.* Cambridge, MA: Harvard University Press.

Loftus, E., Altman, D., & Geballe, R. (1975). Effects of questioning upon a witness's later recollections. *Journal of Police Science and Administration, 3,* 162-165.

Loftus, E. F., & Palmer, J. C. (1974). Reconstruction of automobile destruction: An example of the interaction between language and memory. *Journal of Verbal Learning and Verbal Behavior, 13,* 585-589.

Loftus, E., & Zanni, G. (1975). Eyewitness testimony: The influence of the wording of a question. *Bulletin of the Psychonomic Society, 5,* 86-88.

Long, B. H., Ziller, K. C., & Thompson, E. E. (1966). A comparison of prejudices: The effects upon friendship ratings of chronic illness, old age, education and race. *Journal of Social Psychology, 70,* 101-109.

Long, M. (1980). *Input, interaction and second language acquisition.* Unpublished doctoral dissertation, University of California, Los Angeles.

Long, M. (1983). Linguistic and conversational adjustments to non-native speakers. *Studies in Second Language Acquisition, 5,* 177-193.

Long, M. (1985). Input and second language acquisition theory. In S. Gass & C. Madden (Eds.), *Input in second language acquisition* (pp. 377-393). Rowley, MA: Newbury House.

Longmore, P. K. (1985). A note on language and the social identity of disabled people. *American Behavioral Scientist, 28,* 419-423.

Lorber, J. (1975). Women and medical sociology: Invisible professionals and ubiquitous patients. In M. Millman & R. M. Kanter (Eds.), *Another voice: Feminist perspectives on social life and social science* (pp. 75-105). Garden City, NY: Anchor.

Louis Harris & Associates. (1982). Views of informed consent and decision-making: Parallel surveys of physicians and the public. In President's Commission for the Study of Ethical Problems in Medicine and Biomedical and Behavioral Research, *Making health care decisions* (pp. 17-316). (Vol. 1: Report), Washington, DC: Government Printing Office.

Lucker, G. W., Rosenfield, D., Sikes, J., & Aronson, E. (1976). Performance in the interdependent classroom: A field study. *American Educational Research Journal, 13,* 115-123.

Lynch, M. E. (1982). Closure and disclosure in pre-trial argument. *Human Studies, 5,* 285-318.

Lyotard, J. F. (1984). *The postmodern condition: A report on knowledge.* Minneapolis: University of Minnesota Press.

Maccoby, E. E., & Jacklin, C. B. (1974). *The psychology of sex differences.* Stanford, CA: Stanford University Press.

MacKinnon, C. (1987). Feminism, Marxism, method, and the state: Toward feminist jurisprudence. In S. Harding (Ed.), *Feminism and methodology.* Bloomington: Indiana University Press.

Maiman, M. H., & Becker, L. A. (1974). The health belief model: Origins and correlates in psychological theory. *Health Education Monographs, 2,* 336-353.

Makas, E. (1988). Positive attitudes toward disabled people. *Journal of Social Issues, 44,* 49-62.

Malinowski, B. (1978). *Coral gardens and their magic: Vol. 2. The language of magic and gardening.* New York: Dover.

Maltz, D. N., & Borker, R. A. (1982). A cultural approach to male-female miscommunication. In J. J. Gumperz (Ed.), *Language and social identity* (pp. 195-216). Cambridge, UK: Cambridge University Press.

Markova, I. (1990). Language and communication in mental handicap. In H. Giles & P. W. Robinson (Eds.), *Handbook of language and social psychology* (pp. 363-380). London: John Wiley.

Marlos, E. (1981). Why answer? A goal-based analysis of a speech event. In D. Sankoff (Ed.), *Variation omnibus* (pp. 293-312). Carbondale, IL: Linguistic Research.

Marquis, K. H., Marshall, J., & Oskamp, S. (1972). Testimony validity as a function of question form, atmosphere and item difficulty. *Journal of Applied Social Psychology, 2,* 167-186.

Martel, M. U. (1968). Age-sex roles in magazine fiction. In. B. L. Neugarten (Ed.), *Middle age and aging.* Chicago: University of Chicago Press.

Martin, J., Feldman, M., Hatch, M., & Sitkin, S. (1983). The uniqueness paradox in organizational stories. *Administrative Science Quarterly, 28,* 438-453.

May, S. (1988, November). *The modernist monologue in organizational communication research.* Paper presented at the annual meeting of the Speech Communication Association, New Orleans, LA.

May, S. (1989a, May). *The modernist monologue in organizational communication research: The text, the subject and the audience.* Paper presented at the Annual Meeting of the International Communication Association, San Francisco, CA.

May, S. (1989b, November). *Performing narratives of work: Evoking the elderly self.* Paper presented at the Speech Communication Association, San Francisco, CA.

May, S. (in press). Agency and constraint in organizational stories. *Western Journal of Speech Communication.*

Mayer, J. E. (1967). Disclosing marital problems. *Social Casework, 48,* 342-351.

Maynard, D. W. (in press). Bearing bad news in clinical settings. *Progress in communication sciences.*

Maynard, D. W. (1982). Person-descriptions in plea bargaining. *Semiotica, 42,* 195-213.

Maynard, D. W. (Ed.). (1988). *Language, interaction and social problems [Special issue]. Social Problems, 35*(4), 311-334.

McCall, G. J., & Simmons, J. L. (1978). *Identities and interactions* (2nd ed.). New York: Free Press.

McConnell-Ginet, S., Borker, R., & Furman, N. (1980). *Women and language in literature and society.* New York: Praeger.

McCoy, K. F. (1985). The role of perspective in responding to property misconceptions. *Proceedings IJCAI 85.*

McGaughey, K. J., & Stiles, W. B. (1983). Courtroom interrogation of rape victims: Verbal response mode use by attorneys and witnesses during direct examination vs. cross-examination. *Journal of Applied Social Psychology, 13,* 78-87.

McGuire, W. J. (1983). A contextualist theory of knowledge: Its implications for innovations and reform in psychological research. In L. Berkowitz (Ed.), *Advances in experimental social psychology, 16* (pp. 1-47). New York: Academic Press.

McIntosh, J. (1974). Processes of communication, information seeking and control associated with cancer. *Social Science and Medicine, 8,* 167-187.

McKinlay, J. B. (1973). Social networks, lay consultation and help-seeking behavior. *Social Forces, 51,* 275-291.

McKinlay, J. B. (1975). Who is really ignorant – Physician or patient? *Journal of Health and Social Behavior, 16,* 3-11.

McLaughlin, M., Cody, M., & O'Hair, D. (1983). The management of failure accounts: Some contextual determinants of accounting behavior. *Human Communication Research, 7,* 14-36.

McLaughlin, J., & Riesman, D. (1985). The shady side of sunshine. *Teacher's College Record, 87,* 471-494.

McNamee, S. (1988). Accepting research as social intervention: Implications of a systemic epistemology. *Communication Quarterly, 36,* 50-68.

McQuail, D. (1987). *Mass communication theory: An introduction* (2nd ed.). London: Sage.

McTear, M. F. (1978). Some sources of confusion in foreign language teaching sequences: The rules of the game. *The 4th AILA Congress.* Stuttgart: Hochschul Verlag.

McTear, M. F. (1985a). *Children's conversation.* Oxford, UK: Basil Blackwell.

McTear, M. F. (1985b). Pragmatic disorders: A case study of conversational disability. *British Journal of Disorders of Communication, 20,* 123-142.

McTear, M. F. (1989). Semantic-pragmatic disability: A disorder of thought? In D. M. Topping, D. C. Crowell, & V. N. Kobayashi (Eds.), *Thinking across cultures.* Hillsdale, NJ: Lawrence Erlbaum.

Meehan, A. J. (1981). Some conversational features of the use of medical terms by doctors and patients. In P. Atkinson & C. C. Heath (Eds.), *Medical work: Realities and routines* (pp. 107-127). Farnborough, UK: Gower.

Mest, G. M. (1988). With a little help from their friends: Use of social support systems by persons with retardation. *Journal of Social Issues, 44,* 117-126.

Millar, F. E., & Rogers, L. E. (1976). A relational approach to interpersonal communication. In G. R. Miller (Ed.), *Explorations in interpersonal communication* (pp. 87-103). Beverly Hills, CA: Sage.

Millar, F. E., & Rogers, L. E. (1987). Relational dimensions of interpersonal dynamics. In M. Roloff & G. R. Miller (Eds.), *Interpersonal processes: New directions in communication research* (pp. 87-103). Newbury Park, CA: Sage.

Millar, F. E., & Rogers, L. E. (1988). Power dynamics in marital relations. In P. Noller & M. A. Fitzpatrick (Eds.), *Perspectives on marital interaction* (pp. 78-97). Clevedon, UK: Multilingual Matters.

Miller, G. A. (1973). *Communication, language, and meaning: Psychological perspectives.* New York: Basic Books.

Miller, G. R., & Steinberg, M. (1975). *Between people: A new analysis of interpersonal communication.* Palo Alto, CA: Science Research Associates.

Miller, L. C., Berg, J. H., & Archer, R. L. (1983). Openers: Individuals who elicit intimate self-disclosure. *Journal of Personality and Social Psychology, 44,* 1234-1244.

Miller, L. C., & Reed, S. J. (1987). Why am I telling you this? Self-disclosure in a goal-based model of personality. In V. L. Derlaga & J. H. Berg (Eds.), *Self-disclosure: Theory, research, and therapy* (pp. 35-58). New York: Plenum Press.

Mills, J., Belgrave, F. Z., & Boyer, K. (1984). Reducing avoidance of social interaction with physically disabled person by mentioning the disability following a request for aid. *Journal of Applied Social Psychology, 14,* 1-9.

Milmoe, S., Rosenthal, R., Blane, H. T., Chafetz, M. E., & Wolf, I. (1967). The doctor's voice: Postdictor of successful referral of alcoholic patient. *Journal of Abnormal Psychology, 72,* 78-84.

Milroy, L. (1984). Comprehension and context: Successful communication and communicative breakdown. In P. Trudgill (Ed.), *Applied sociolinguistics* (pp. 7-31). London: Academic Press.

Mishler, E. G. (1984). *The discourse of medicine: Dialectics of medical interviews.* Norwood, NJ: Ablex.

Moerman, M. (1988). *Talking culture, Ethnography and conversation analysis.* Philadelphia: University of Pennsylvania Press.

Montgomery, M. (1988). D-J talk. In N. Coupland (Ed.), *Styles of discourse* (pp. 85-104). London/New York: Croom Helm.

Moody, P., & Gray, R. (1972). Social class, social integration and the use of preventive health services. In E. G. Jaco (Ed.), *Patients, physicians and illness* (2nd ed.) (pp. 250-261). New York: Free Press.

Moore, B., & Singletary, M. (1985). Scientific sources' perceptions of network news accuracy. *Journalism Quarterly, 62,* 816-827.

Moore, M. (1985). Culture as culture. In P. Frost, L. Moore, M. Louis, C. Lundberg, & J. Martin (Eds.), *Organizational culture* (pp. 373-378). Beverly Hills, CA: Sage.

Morgan, G. (1986). *Images of organization.* Beverly Hills, CA: Sage.

Morris, G. H., & Hopper, R. (1980). Remediation and legislation in everyday talk. *Quarterly Journal of Speech, 66,* 266-274.

Muehlenhard, C. L., & Hollabaugh, L. C. (1988). Do women sometimes say no when they mean yes? The prevalence and correlates of women's token resistance to sex. *Journal of Personality and Social Psychology, 54,* 872-879.

Muscio, B. (1915). The influence of the form of the question. *British Journal of Psychology, 8,* 351-389.

Nadler, A., Sheinberg, L., & Jaffe, Y. (1981). Coping with stress in male paraplegics through help-seeking: The role of acceptance of physical disability in help-seeking and receiving behaviors. In C. Spielberger, I. Sarason, & N. Milgram (Eds.), *Stress and anxiety,* (vol. 8). Washington, DC: Hemisphere.

Naylor, P. (1979, July). *Legal testimony and the non-native speaker of English: Linguistic and cultural interference in interethnic communication.* Paper presented at the First International Conference on Language and Social Psychology, University of Bristol, England.

Nebes, R. D., & Andrews-Kulis, M. S. (1976). The effect of age on the speed of sentence formation and incidental learning. *Experimental Aging Research, 2,* 315-331.

Neisser, U. (1982). John Dean's memory: A case study. In U. Neisser (Ed.), *Memory observed: Remembering in natural contexts* (pp. 139-159). San Francisco: Freeman.

Newell, A., & Simon, H. (1972). *Human problem solving.* Englewood Cliffs, NJ: Prentice-Hall.

Newport, E. (1976). Motherese: The speech of mothers to young children. In N. Castellan, D. Pisoni, & G. Potts (Eds.), *Cognitive theory,* vol. 2. Hillsdale, NJ: Lawrence Erlbaum.

Ng, S. H. (1990). Language and control. In H. Giles & P. W. Robinson (Eds.), *Handbook of language and social psychology* (pp. 271-285). London: John Wiley.

Nguyen, T., Heslin, R., & Nguyen, M. L. (1975). The meanings of touch: Sex differences. *Journal of Communication, 25,* 92-103.

Nichols, P. C. (1983). Linguistic options and choices for black women in the rural south. In B. Thorne, C. Kramarae, & N. Henley (Eds.), *Language, gender and society* (pp. 54-68). Rowley, MA: Newbury House.

Nofsinger, R. E. (1983). Tactical coherence in courtroom conversation. In R. Craig & K. Tracy (Eds.), *Conversational coherence: Structure and strategy* (pp. 243-258). Beverly Hills, CA: Sage.

Nolan, C. (1981). *Dam-burst of dreams.* Athens: Ohio University Press.

Nolan, C. (1987). *Under the eye of the clock.* New York: St. Martin's Press.

Norman, A. (1987). *Aspects of ageism: A discussion paper.* London: Centre for Policy on Ageing.

Novack, D. H., Plumer, R., Smith, R. L., Ochitill, H., Morrow, G. R., & Bennett, J. M. (1979). Changes in physicians' attitudes toward telling the cancer patient. *Journal of the American Medical Association, 241,* 897-900.

Nuessel, F. H. (1982). The language of ageism. *The Gerontologist, 2,* 273-276.

Nuessel, F. H. (1984). Ageist language. *Maledicta, 8,* 17-28.

Nussbaum, J. F. (1985). Successful aging: A communication model. *Communication Quarterly, 33,* 262-269.

Nussbaum, J. F., Thompson, T., & Robinson, J. D. (1989). *Communication and aging.* New York: Harper & Row.

O'Barr, W. (1981). The language of the law. In C. A. Ferguson & S. Brice Heath (Eds.), *Language in the USA* (pp. 386-406). Cambridge, UK: Cambridge University Press.

O'Barr, W. (1982). *Linguistic evidence: Language, power and strategy in the courtroom.* New York: Academic Press.

O'Barr, W. M., & Conley, J. M. (1985). Litigant satisfaction versus legal adequacy in small claims court narratives. *Law & Society Review, 19* 661-701.

O'Keefe, B. (1988). The logic of message design: Individual differences in reasoning about communication. *Communication Monographs, 55,* 80-103.

Ochs, E. (1982). Talking to children in Western Samoa. *Language in Society, 11,* 77-104.

Ochs, E. (1988a). *Culture and language development: Language acquisition and language socialization in a Samoan village.* Cambridge, UK: Cambridge University Press.

Ochs, E. (1988b). *Language, affect, and knowledge.* Cambridge, MA: Oxford University Press.

Ochs, E., & Schieffelin, B. (1984). Language acquisition and socialization: Three developmental stories and their implications. In R.Shweder & R. LeVine (Eds.), *Culture theory: Essays on mind, self, and emotion* (pp. 276-320). Cambridge, UK: Cambridge University Press.

Okabe, K. (1987). Indirect speech acts of the Japanese. In L. Kincaid (Ed.), *Communication theory* (pp. 127-136). San Diego: Academic Press.

Oken, D. (1961). What to tell cancer patients: A study of medical attitudes. *Journal of the American Medical Association, 175,* 1120-1128.

Olshtain, E. (1983). Sociocultural competence and language transfer: The case of apology. In S. Gass & L. Selinker (Eds.), *Language transfer in language learning* (pp. 232-249). Rowley, MA: Newbury House.

Olshtain, E., & Cohen, A. (1983). Apology: A speech act set. In N. Wolfson & E. Judd (Eds.), *Sociolinguistics and language acquisition* (pp. 303-325). Rowley, MA: Newbury House.

Olshtain, E., & Cohen, A. (1987). *The learning of complex speech act behavior.* Paper presented at the Colloquium on TESOL and Sociolinguistics, TESOL, Miami.

Ortner, S. (1984). Theory in anthropology since the sixties. *Comparative Studies in Society and History, 26,* 126-166.

Osterweis, M., Bush, P. J., & Zuckerman, A. E. (1979). Family context as a predictor of individual medicine use. *Social Science and Medicine, 13A,* 287-291.

Palmore, E. B. (1971). Attitudes toward aging as shown by humor. *The Gerontologist, 11,* 181-186.

Palmore, E. B. (1982). Attitudes toward the aged: What we know and need to know. *Research on Aging, 4,* 333-348.

Parks, M. R. (1982). Ideology in interpersonal communication: Off the couch and into the world. In M. Burgoon (Ed.), *Communication yearbook 5* (pp. 79-107). New Brunswick, NJ: Transaction Books.

Parks, M. R., & Adelman, M. B. (1983). Communication networks and the development of romantic relationships: An expansion of uncertainty reduction theory. *Human Communication Research, 10,* 55-79.

Pascale, R., & Athos, A. (1981). *The art of Japanese management.* New York: Simon & Schuster.

Pearce, W. B., & Sharp, S. K. (1973). Self-disclosing communication. *Journal of Communication, 23,* 409-425.

Pederson, D. M., & Breglio, V. J. (1968). The correlation of two self-disclosure inventories with actual self-disclosures: A validity study. *Journal of Psychology, 69,* 291-298.

Pederson, D. M., & Higbee, K. L. (1969). Personality correlates of self-disclosure. *Journal of Social Psychology, 68,* 81-89.

Pelligrino, E. D. (1974). Educating the humanist physician. *Journal of the American Medical Association, 227,* 1288-1294.

Pendleton, D. A. (1983). Doctor-patient communication: A review. In D. Pendleton & D. Hasler (Eds.), *Doctor-patient communication* (pp. 5-53). London: Academic Press.

Pendleton, D. A., & Bouchner, S. (1980). The communication of medical information in general practice consultation as a function of patients' social class. *Social Science and Medicine, 14A,* 669-673.

Penelope, J. (1986). Heteropatriarchal semantics: Just two kinds of people in the world. *Lesbian Ethics, 2,* 58-80.

Penman, R. (1980). *Communication processes and relationships.* New York: Academic Press.

Peters, T. J., & Waterman, R. H., Jr. (1982). *In search of excellence.* New York: Harper & Row.

Petronio, S., Martin, J., & Littlefield, R. (1984). Prerequisite conditions for self-disclosing: A gender issue. *Communication Monographs, 51,* 268-273.

Pfeffer, J. (1981). Management as symbolic action. In B. Staw & L. L. Cummings (Eds.), *Research in organizational behavior, 3* (pp. 1-52). Greenwich, CT: JAI Press.

Phillips, S. R. (1989). *Electronic persuasion: The uses of electronic mail for interpersonal influence in organizations.* Unpublished doctoral dissertation, University of Southern California.

Phillips, S. U. (1985). Reported speech as evidence in an American trial. In D. Tannen & J. A. Alatis (Eds.), *Georgetown University Round Table on Languages and Linguistics* (pp. 154-170). Washington, DC: Georgetown University Press.

Pica, T. (1987). Second language acquisition, social interaction, and the classroom. *Applied Linguistics, 8,* 3-21.

Pica, T. (1988). Interlanguage adjustments as an outcome of NS-NNS negotiated interaction. *Language Learning, 38,* 45-73.

Pica, T., Holliday, L., Lewis, N., & Morgenthaler, L. (1989). Comprehensible output as an outcome of linguistic demands on the learner. *Studies in Second Language Acquisition, 11,* 63-91.

Piner, K. E., & Kahle, L. R. (1984). Adapting to the stigmatizing label of mental illness: Foregone but not forgotten. *Journal of Personality and Social Psychology, 47,* 805-811.

Plaja, A. D., Cohen, L. M., & Samora, J. (1968). Communication between physicians and patients in outpatient clinics, social and cultural factors. *Milbank Memorial Fund Quarterly, 46,* 161-214.

Planalp, S., & Honeycutt, J. M. (1985). Events that increase uncertainty in personal relationships. *Human Communication Research, 11,* 593-604.

Planalp, S., Rutherford, D. K., & Honeycutt, J. M. (1988). Events that increase uncertainty in personal relationships II: Replication and extension. *Human Communication Research, 14,* 516-547.

Pondy, L. (1978). Leadership is a language game. In M. Lombardo & M. McCall (Eds.), *Leadership: Where else can we go?* (pp. 87-99). Durham, NC: Duke University Press.

Potter, J. (1988). Cutting cakes: A study of psychologists' social categorizations. *Philosophical Psychology, 1,* 17-33.

Potter, J., & Wetherell, M. (1986). *Discourse and social psychology: Beyond attitudes and behavior.* London: Sage.

Pratt, L., Seligmann, A., & Reader, G. (1957). Physicians' views on the level of medical information among patients. *American Journal of Public Health, 47,* 1277-1283.

President's Commission for the Study of Ethical Problems in Medicine and Biomedical and Behavioral Research (1982). *Making health care decisions,* vol. 1, Report. Washington, DC: Government Printing Office.

Price, D. (1989). *Before the bulldozer: The Nambiquara Indians and the World Bank.* Cabin John, MD: Seven Locks.

Pride, J. B. (Ed.). (1985). *Cross-cultural encounters: Communication and mis-communication.* London: Academic Press.

Prutting, C. A., & Kirchner, D. M. (1987). A clinical appraisal of the pragmatic aspects of language. *Journal of Speech and Hearing Disorders, 52,* 105-119.

Pulford, D. L. (1976). Follow-up study of science news accuracy. *Journalism Quarterly, 53,* 119-121.

Quint, J. C. (1964). Mastectomy—Symbol of cure or warning sign? *General Practice, 29,* 119-124.

Quint, J. C. (1965). Institutionalized practices of information control. *Psychiatry, 28,* 119-132.

Ragan, S. L., & Hopper, R. (1984). Ways to leave your lover: A conversation analysis of literature. *Communication Quarterly, 32,* 310-317.

Raphael, W. (1969). *Patients and their hospitals.* London: King Edward's Fund.

Rapin, I., & Allen, D. (1983). Developmental language disorders: Nosologic considerations. In U. Kirk (Ed.), *Neuropsychology of language, reading and spelling.* New York: Academic Press.

Rausch, H. L., Barry, W. A., Hertel, R. K., & Swain, M. A. (1974). *Communication, conflict, and marriage.* San Francisco: Jossey-Bass.

Rawlins, W. K. (1983a). Negotiating close friendship: The dialectic of conjunctive freedoms. *Human Communication Research, 9,* 255-266.

Rawlins, W. K. (1983b). Openness as problematic in on-going friendships: Two conversational dilemmas. *Communication Monographs, 50,* 1-13.

Rawlins, W. K. (1989). A dialectical analysis of the tensions, functions, and strategic challenges of communication in young adult friendship. In J. A. Anderson (Ed.), *Communication yearbook 12,* (pp. 157-189). Newbury Park, CA: Sage.

Redding, W. C. (1972). *Communication within the organization.* New York: Industrial Communication Council.

Reddy, M. J. (1979). The conduit metaphor: A case of frame conflict in our language about language. In A. Ortony (Ed.), *Metaphor and thought* (pp. 284-324). Cambridge, UK: Cambridge University Press.

Redlich, F. C. (1945). The patient's language: An investigation into the use of medical terms. *Yale Journal of Biology and Medicine, 17,* 427-453.

Rehbein, J. (1987). Multiple formulae: Aspects of Turkish migrant workers' German in intercultural communication. In K. Knapp, W. Enninger, & A. Knapp-Potthoff (Eds.), *Analyzing intercultural communication.* Berlin: Mouton de Gruyter.

Reichman, R. (1984). Extended person-machine interface. *Artificial Intelligence, 22,* 157-218.

Reilly, R. G. (Ed.). (1987). *Communication failure in dialogue and discourse.* Amsterdam: North-Holland.

Reilly, R. G., & MacAogåin, E. (1988). Poorly formed input and miscommunication in natural-language keyboard dialogue: An exploratory study. *Computers in Human Behavior, 4,* 275-283.

Richards, I. A. (1936). *The philosophy of rhetoric.* Oxford, UK: Oxford University Press.

Ringle, M. H., & Bruce, B. C. (1980). Conversation failure. In W. G. Lehnert & M. H. Ringle (Eds.), *Strategies for natural language processing* (pp. 203-222). Hillsdale, NJ: Lawrence Erlbaum.

Ritchie, J. B. (1987, June 7). Metaphors in harmony. *Baltimore Sun.* Perspective, 5B.

Robinson, J. D. (1989). Mass media and the elderly: A uses and dependency interpretation. In J. F. Nussbaum (Ed.), *Life-span communication: Normative processes* (pp. 319-337). Hillsdale, NJ: Lawrence Erlbaum.

Rodin, J. (1978). Somatopsychics and attribution. *Personality and Social Psychology Bulletin, 4,* 531-538.

Rogers, L. E., & Millar, F. E. (1988). Relational communication. In S. Duck (Ed.), *Handbook of personal relationships* (pp. 289-305). London: John Wiley.

Rogers, L. E., Millar, F. E., & Bavelas, J. B. (1984). Methods of analyzing marital conflict discourse: Implication of the systems approach. *Family Process, 24,* 53-72.

Rogoff, B. (1989). *Apprenticeship in thinking.* Oxford, UK: Oxford University Press.

Rommetveit, R. (1989). Psycholinguistic hermeneutics and cognitive science. In J. Björgen (Ed.), *Basic issues in psychology: A Scandinavian contribution* (pp. 195-210). London: Sigma.

Rook, K. S. & Pietromonaco, P. (1987). Close relationships: Ties that heal or ties that bind? *Advances in Personal Relationships, 1,* 1-35.

Rorty, R. (1979). *Philosophy and the mirror of nature.* Princeton, NJ: Princeton University Press.

Rosaldo, R. (1989). *Culture and truth: The remaking of social analysis.* Boston: Beacon.

Rosenstock, I. L. (1974). Historical origins of the health belief model: Origins and correlates in psychological theory. *Health Education Monographs, 2,* 336-353.

Rosenthal, R., & Jacobson, E. (1968). *Pygmalion in the classroom: Teacher expectation and intellectual development.* New York: Holt, Rinehart & Winston.

Rosenthal, R., & Rubin, D. B. (1978). Interpersonal expectancy effects: The first 345 studies. *The Behavioral and Brain Sciences, 3,* 410-415.

Roter, D. (1977). Patient participation in the patient-provider interaction: The effect of patient question asking on the quality of interaction, satisfaction and compliance. *Health Education Monographs, 5,* 281-312.

Roth, J. A. (1963a). Information and the control of treatment in tuberculosis hospitals. In E. Freidson (Ed.), *The hospital in modern society* (pp. 293-317). New York: Free Press.

Roth, J. A. (1963b). *Timetables.* Indianapolis: Bobbs Merrill.

Rubin, K. H., & Brown, J. (1975). A life-span look at person perception and its relationship to communicative interaction. *Journal of Gerontology, 30,* 461-468.

Rubin, L. B. (1976). *Worlds of pain: Life in the working-class family.* New York: Basic Books.

Rubin, Z., Hill, C. T., Peplau, L.A., & Dunkel-Schetter, C. (1980). Self-disclosure in dating couples: Sex roles and the ethic of openness. *Journal of Marriage and Family, 42,* 305-317.

Rumelhart, D. E. (1975). Notes on a schema for stories. In D. G. Bobrow & A. Collins (Eds.), *Representation and understanding* (pp. 211-236). New York: Academic Press.

Rutter, D. (1987). *Communicating by telephone.* Elmsford, NY: Pergamon.

Rutter, D. R. (1984). *Looking and seeing.* Chichester: John Wiley.

Rutter, D. R., & Stephenson, G. M. (1977). The role of visual communication in social interaction. *European Journal of Social Psychology, 7,* 29-37.

Ryan, E. B. (in press). Language issues in normal aging. In R. Lubinski (Ed.), *Communication and dementia: Research and clinical implications.* Toronto: B. C. Decker.

Ryan, E. B., & Johnston, D. G. (1987). The influence of communication effectiveness on evaluations of younger and older adult speakers. *Journal of Gerontology, 42,* 163-164.

Sabsay, S., & Platt, M. (1985). Weaving the cloak of competence: A paradox in the management of trouble in conversations between retarded and nonretarded interlocutors. In S. Sabsay & M. Platt (Eds.), *Social setting, stigma, and communicative competence: Explorations of the conversational interactions of retarded adults* (pp. 95-116). Amsterdam: John Benjamins.

Sackett, D. L., & Snow, J. C. (1979). The magnitude of compliance and non-compliance. In R. B. Haynes (Ed.), *Compliance in health care* (pp. 11-22). Baltimore, MD: Johns Hopkins University Press.

Sacks, H. (1972). *Adjacency pair organization.* Unpublished lecture notes, University of California, Irvine.

Sacks, H. (1987). On the preferences for agreement and contiguity in sequences in conversation. In G. Button & J. R. E. Lee (Eds.), *Talk and social organization* (pp. 54-69). Clevedon, UK: Multilingual Matters.

Sacks, H., & Schegloff, E. A. (1979). Two preferences in the organization of reference to persons in conversation and their interaction. In G. Psathas (Ed.), *Everyday language: Studies in ethnomethodology.* New York: Irvington.

Sacks, H., Schegloff, E. A., & Jefferson, G. (1974). A simplest systematics for the organization of turn-taking for conversation. *Language, 50,* 696-735.

Safilios-Rothschild, C. (1970). *The sociology and social psychology of disability and rehabilitation.* New York: Random House.

Samora, J., Saunders, L., & Larson, R. (1961). Medical vocabulary knowledge among hospital patients. *Journal of Health and Human Behavior, 2,* 83-89.

Sanders, G. F., & Pittman, J. F. (1988). Attitudes of youth toward known and general target elderly. *The Journal of Applied Gerontology, 6,* 464-475.

Sarbaugh, L. (1984). An overview of selected approaches. In W. Gudykunst & Y. Y. Kim (Eds.), *Methods for intercultural research.* Beverly Hills, CA: Sage.

Sattel, J. (1983). Men, inexpressiveness, and power. In B. Thorne, C. Kramarae, & N. Henley (Eds.), *Language, gender, and society* (pp. 118-124). Rowley, MA: Newbury House.

Saville-Troike, M. (1985). The place of silence in an integrated theory of communication. In D. Tannen & M. Saville-Troike (Eds.), *Perspectives on silence* (pp. 3-20). Norwood, NJ: Ablex.

Scanlon, T. J. (1972). A new approach to study of newspaper accuracy. *Journalism Quarterly, 49,* 587-590.

Scarcella, R., & Higa, C. (1981). Input, negotiation and age differences in second language acquisition. *Language Learning, 31,* 409-437.

Schachter, J. (1986). Three approaches to the study of input. *Language Learning, 36,* 211-225.

Scheer, J., & Groce, N. (1988). Impairment as a human constant: Cross-cultural and historical perspectives on variation. *Journal of Social Issues, 44,* 23-38.

Scheff, T. J. (1974). The labeling theory of mental illness. *American Sociological Review, 39,* 444-452.

Scheflen, A. (1965). Quasi-courtship behavior in psychotherapy. *Psychiatry, 28,* 245-257.

Schegloff, E. A. (1968). Sequencing in conversational openings. *American Anthropologist, 70,* 1075-1095. (Reprinted in J. J. Gumperz & D. Hymes, [Eds.], *Directions in sociolinguistics* (pp. 346-380). New York: Holt, Rinehart & Winston, 1972)

Schegloff, E. A. (1979a). Identification and recognition in telephone conversation openings. In G. Psathas (Ed.), *Everyday language: Studies in ethnomethodology.* New York: Irvington.

Schegloff, E. A. (1979b). The relevance of repair to syntax-for-conversation. *Syntax and Semantics,* 261-286.

Schegloff, E. A. (1982). Discourse as an interactional achievement: Some uses of "uh huh" and other things that come between sentences. In D. Tannen (Ed.), *Georgetown University Roundtable on Language and Linguistics; 1981, Analyzing discourse: Text and talk* (pp. 71-93). Washington, DC: Georgetown University Press.

Schegloff, E. A. (1987a). Between macro and micro: Contexts and other connections. In J. Alexander, B. Giesen, R. Munch, & N. Smelser (Eds.), *The micro-macro link* (pp. 207-234). Berkeley: University of California Press.

Schegloff, E. A. (1987b). Some sources of misunderstanding in talk-in-interaction. *Linguistics, 25,* 201-218.

Schegloff, E. A., Jefferson, G., & Sacks, H. (1977). The preference for self-correction in the organization of repair in conversation. *Language, 53,* 361-382.

Schegloff, E. A., & Sacks, H. (1973). Opening up closings. *Semiotica, 8,* 289-327.

Schieffelin, B. (1990). *The give and take of everyday life: Language socialization among the Kaluli.* New York: Cambridge University Press.

Schieffelin, B., & Ochs, E. (1986). Language socialization. In B. Siegel (Ed.), *Annual review of anthropology* (pp. 163-191). Palo Alto, CA: Annual Reviews.

Schieffelin, B., & Ochs, E. (1988). *Micro-macro interfaces: Methodology in language socialization research.* Paper presented in Special Session "Methodology in Psychological Anthropology," American Anthropological Association annual meetings, Phoenix, AZ.

Schlenker, B. R. (1980). Identities, identifications, and relationships. In V. Derlega (Ed.), *Communication, intimacy, and close relationships.* New York: Academic Press.

Schlesinger, P. (1987). *Putting "reality" together: BBC news* (2nd ed.). London: Methuen.

Schoene-Seifert, B., & Childress, J. F. (1986, March/April). How much should the cancer patient know and decide? *CA—A Cancer Journal for Clinicians, 36,* 85-94.

Schulz, R., & Decker, S. (1985). Long-term adjustment to physical disability: The role of social support, perceived control, and self-blame. *Journal of Personality and Social Psychology, 48,* 1162-1172.

Schur, E. (1983). *Labeling women deviant: Gender, stigma, and social control.* Philadelphia: Temple University Press.

Scollon, R., & Scollon, S. B. K. (1981). *Narrative, literacy and face in interethnic communication.* Norwood, NJ: Ablex.

Scollon, S. (1982). *Reality set, socialization and linguistic convergence.* Unpublished doctoral dissertation, University of Hawaii, Manoa.

Scott, R. A. (1969). *The making of blind men: A study of adult socialization.* New York: Russell Sage.

Searle, J. (1969). *Speech acts: An essay in the philosophy of language.* Cambridge, UK: Cambridge University Press.

Seeman, M., & Evans, J. W. (1961). Stratification and hospital care—I: The performance of the medical intern. *American Sociological Review, 26,* 67-80.

Seeman, M., & Evans, J. W. (1962). Alienation and learning in a hospital setting. *American Sociological Review, 27,* 772-782.

Seggie, I. (1983). Attribution of guilt as a function of ethnic accent and type of crime. *Journal of Multilingual and Multicultural Development, 4,* 197-206.

Seligmann, A. W., McGrath, N. E., & Pratt, L. (1957). Level of medical information among clinic patients. *Journal of Chronic Diseases, 6,* 497-509.

Selinker, L., & Gass, S. (1984). *Workbook in second language acquisition.* Rowley, MA: Newbury House.

Shands, H. C., Finesinger, J. E., Cobb, S., & Abrams, R. D. (1951). Psychological mechanisms in patients with cancer. *Cancer, 4,* 1159-1170.

Short, J., Williams, E., & Christie, B. (1976). *The social psychology of telecommunications.* Chichester: John Wiley.

Shotter, J., & Gergen, K. J. (Eds.). (1989). *Texts of identity.* London: Sage.

Shuy, R. (1970). Sociolinguistic research at the Center for Applied Linguistics: The correlation of language and sex. *Industrial Days of Sociolinguistics.* Rome: Istituto Luigi Sturzo.

Shuy, R. (1976). The medical interview: Problems in communication. *Primary Care, 3,* 365-386.

Shuy, R. (1986). Some linguistic contributions to a criminal court case. In S. Fisher & A. D. Todd (Eds.), *Disclosure and institutional authority: Medicine, education and law* (pp. 234-249). Norwood, NJ: Ablex.

Sidner, C. L. (1979). *Toward a computational theory of definite anaphora comprehension in English discourse* (Tech. Rep. No. 537). Cambridge: MIT Artificial Intelligence Laboratory.

Sidner, C. L. (1983). Focusing in the comprehension of definite anaphora. In M. Brady & R. C. Berwick (Eds.), *Computational models of discourse* (pp. 267-330). Cambridge: MIT Press.

Sidner, C. L., & Israel, D. (1981). Recognizing intended meaning and speakers' plans. *Proceedings of 7th IJCAI.* Vancouver, Canada.

Sigall, H., & Landy, D. (1973). Radiating beauty: The effects of having a physically attractive partner on person perception. *Journal of Personality and Social Psychology, 28,* 218-224.

Sillars, A. L., Pike, G. R., Jones, T. S., & Murphy, M. A. (1984). Communication and understanding in marriage. *Human Communication Research, 10,* 317-350.

Sillars, A. L., Weisberg, J., Burggraf, C. S., & Zietlow, P. H. (1988). *Communication and understanding revisited: Married couples' understanding and recall of conversations.* Unpublished manuscript, Ohio State University.

Silver, J. M. (1979, November). Medical terms—a two-way block? *Colloquy: The Journal of Physician-Patient Communications,* 4-10.

Simmel, G. (1950). *The sociology of Georg Simmel* (Kurt Wolff, Trans.). New York: Free Press.

Simmel, G. (1955). *Conflict.* New York: Free Press.

Sinclair, J. M., & Coulthard, R. M. (1975). *Towards an analysis of discourse: The English used by teachers and pupils.* Oxford, UK: Oxford University Press.

Skipper, J. K. (1965a). Communication and the hospitalized patient. In J. K. Skipper & R. C. Leonard (Eds.), *Social interaction and patient care.* Philadelphia: J. B. Lippincott.

Skipper, J. K. (1965b). The role of the hospital nurse: Is it instrumental or expressive? In J. K. Skipper & R. C. Leonard (Eds.), *Social interaction and patient care* (pp. 40-59). Philadelphia: J. B. Lippincott.

Slater, P. E. (1964). Cross-cultural views of the aged. In R. Kastenbaum (Ed.), *New thoughts on old age* (pp. 229-236). New York: Springer.

Slavin, R. E. (1980). Cooperative learning. *Review of Educational Research, 50,* 315-342.

Smircich, L., & Calas, M. B. (1987). Organizational culture: A critical assessment. In F. Jablin, L. Putnam, K. Roberts, & L. Porter (Eds.), *Handbook of organizational communication: An interdisciplinary perspective* (pp. 228-263). Newbury Park, CA: Sage.

Smith, L. E. (Ed.), (1987). *Discourse across cultures: Strategies in world Englishes.* Englewood Cliffs, NJ: Prentice-Hall.

Smith, M. J., Reinheimer, R. E., & Gabbard-Alley, A. (1981). Crowding, task performance, and communicative interaction in youth and old age. *Human Communication Research, 7,* 259-272.

Smitherman, G. (1977). *Talkin and testifyin: The language of Black America.* Boston: Houghton Mifflin.

Snow, C. E. (1972). Mother's speech to children learning language. *Child Development, 43,* 549-565.

Snow, C. E., & Ferguson, C. A. (Eds.). (1977). *Talking to children: Language input and acquisition.* Cambridge, UK: Cambridge University Press.

Snyder, M. L., Kleck, R. E., Strenta, A., & Mentzer, S. J. (1979). Avoidance of the handicapped: An attributional ambiguity analysis. *Journal of Personality and Social Psychology, 37,* 2297-2306.

Snyder, M., Tanke, E. D., & Berscheid, E. (1977). Social perception and interpersonal behavior: On the self-fulfilling nature of social stereotypes. *Journal of Personality and Social Psychology, 35,* 656-666.

Solomon, H. (1986). Stigma and Western culture: A historical approach. In S. Ainlay, G. Becker, & L. Coleman (Eds.), *The dilemma of difference—A multidisciplinary view of stigma.* New York: Plenum.

Sontag, S. (1977). *Illness as metaphor.* New York: Farrar-Strauss-Giroux.

Spelman, M. S., Ley, P., & Jones, C. C. (1966). How do we improve doctor-patient communication in our hospitals. *World Hospitals, 2,* 126-134.

Spencer, J. W. (1983). Accounts, attitudes and solutions: Probation officer-defendant negotiations of subjective orientations. *Social Problems, 30,* 570-581.

Sperber, D., & Wilson, D. (1985). *Relevance: Communication and cognition.* Oxford, UK: Basil Blackwell.

Stalker, J. C. (1989). Communicative competence, pragmatic functions, and accommodation. *Applied Linguistics, 10,* 182-193.

Stanback, M. H. (1987, November). *Claiming our space; finding our voice: Feminist theory and black women's talk.* Paper presented at the Black and Women's Caucuses, Speech Communication Association, Boston, MA.

Stanback, M. H. (1988). What makes scholarship about black women and communication feminist communication scholarship? *Women's Studies in Communication, 11,* 28-31.

Steele, D. J., Jackson, T. C., & Gutmann, M. C. (1985). *"Have you been taking your pills?" The compliance monitoring sequence in the medical interview.* Manuscript submitted for publication.

Steele, J. L., & McBroom, W. H. (1972). Conceptual and empirical dimensions of health behavior. *Journal of Health and Social Behavior, 13,* 382-392.

Stewart, M. A., & Ryan, E. B. (1982). Attitudes toward younger and older adult speakers: Effects of varying speech rates. *Journal of Language and Social Psychology, 1,* 91-109.

Stiles, W. B. (1989). Evaluating medical interview process components: Null correlations with outcomes may be misleading. *Medical Care, 27,* 212-220.

Stiles, W. B., Putnam, S. M., Wolf, M. H., & James, S. A. (1979). Interaction exchange structure and patient satisfaction with medical interviews. *Medical Care, 17,* 667-679.

Stoeckle, J. D., Zola, I. K., & Davidson, G. E. (1964). On going to see the doctor: The contributions of the patient to the decision to seek medical aid: A selected review. *Journal of Chronic Diseases, 16,* 975-989.

Stohl, C., & Redding, W. C. (1987). Messages and message exchange processes. In F. Jablin, L. Putnam, K. Roberts, & L. Porter (Eds.), *Handbook of organizational communication: An interdisciplinary perspective* (pp. 451-502). Newbury Park, CA: Sage.

Stokes, J. P. (1987). The relation of loneliness and self-disclosure. In V. L. Derlega & J. H. Berg (Eds.), *Self-disclosure: Theory, research and therapy* (pp. 59-79). New York: Plenum.

Street, R., & Giles, H. (1982). Speech accommodation theory: A social cognitive approach to language and speech behavior. In M. Roloff & C. Berger (Eds.), *Social cognition and communication* (pp. 193-226). Beverly Hills, CA: Sage.

Strickland, B. (1978). Internal-external expectancies and health-related behaviors. *Journal of Consulting and Clinical Psychology, 46,* 1192-1211.

Suchman, E. A. (1972). Social patterns of illness and medical care. In E. G. Jaco (Ed.), *Patients, physicians and illness* (2nd ed.) (pp. 262-279). New York: Free Press.

Sudnow, D. (1965). Normal crimes: Sociological features of the penal code in a public defender office. *Social Problems, 12,* 255-276.

Sunnafrank, M. (1986). Predicted outcome value during initial interactions: A reformulation of uncertainty reduction theory. *Human Communication Research, 13,* 3-33.

Swain, M. (1985). Communicative competence: Some roles of comprehensible input and comprehensible output in its development. In S. Gass & C. Madden (Eds.), *Input in second language acquisition* (pp. 235-253). Rowley, MA: Newbury House.

Tafoya, D. W. (1983). The roots of conflict: A theory and typology. In W. Gudykunst (Ed.), *Intercultural communication theory: Current perspectives.* Beverly Hills, CA: Sage.

Tafoya, D. W. (1984). Research and cultural phenomena. In W. B. Gudykunst & Y. Y. Kim (Eds.), *Methods of intercultural communication research.* Beverly Hills, CA: Sage.

Tajfel, H. (Ed.). (1982). *Social identity and intergroup relations.* Cambridge: Cambridge University Press.

Tajfel, H., & Turner, J. C. (1979). An integrative theory of intergroup conflict. In W. G. Austin & S. Worchel (Eds.), *The social psychology of intergroup relations* (pp. 33-47). Monterey, CA: Brooks/Cole.

Takahashi, T. (1989). The influence of the listener on L2 speech. In S. Gass, C. Madden, D. Preston, & L. Selinker (Eds.), *Variation in second language acquisition: Discourse and pragmatics* (pp. 245-279). Clevedon, UK: Multilingual Matters.

Takahashi, T., & Beebe, L. (1987). The development of pragmatic competence by Japanese learners of English. *JALT Journal, 8,* 131-155.

Tankard, J. W., Jr., & Ryan, M. (1974). News source perceptions of accuracy of science coverage. *Journalism Quarterly, 51,* 219-225, 334.

Tannen, D. (1975). Communication mix and mixup or how linguistics can ruin a marriage. *San Jose State Occasional Papers in Linguistics,* 205-211.

Tannen, D. (1981a). Indirectness in discourse: Ethnicity as conversational style. *Discourse Processes, 4,* 221-238.

Tannen, D. (1981b). Review of *Therapeutic discourse* by W. Labov & D. Fanshel. *Language, 57,* 481-486.

Tannen, D. (1982). Ethnic style in male-female conversation. In J. J. Gumperz (Ed.), *Language and social identity* (pp. 217-231). Cambridge, UK: Cambridge University Press.

Tannen, D. (1987). *That's not what I meant! How conversational style makes or breaks relationships.* New York: Ballantine.

Tannen, D. (1990). *You just don't understand: Women and men in conversation.* New York: Morrow.

Tannen, D., & Wallat, C. (1982). A sociolinguistic analysis of multiple demands on the pediatrician in doctor/mother/patient interaction. In R. J. DiPietro (Ed.), *Linguistics and the professions* (pp. 39-50). Norwood, NJ: Ablex.

Tannen, D., & Wallat, C. (1983). Doctor/mother/child communication: Linguistic analysis of a pediatric interaction. In S. Fisher & A. D. Todd (Eds.), *The social organization of doctor-patient communication* (pp. 203-219). Washington, DC: Center for Applied Linguistics.

Taylor, B. (1974). Toward a theory of language acquisition. *Language Learning, 24,* 23-35.

Taylor, D. M., & Simard, L. (1975). Social interaction in a bilingual setting. *Canadian Psychological Reviews, 16,* 240-254.

Tennant, H. R., Ross, K. M., Saenz, R. M., Thompson, C. W., & Miller, J. R. (1983). Menu-based natural language understanding. *Proceedings of CHI '83.* Boston, MA.

Tennant, H. R., Ross, K. M. & Thompson, C. W. (1983). Usable natural language interfaces through menu-based natural language understanding. *Proceedings of CHI '83.* Boston, MA.

Thakerar, J. N., Giles, H., & Cheshire, J. (1982). Psychological and linguistic parameters of speech accommodation theory. In C. Fraser & K. R. Scherer (Eds.), *Advances in the social psychology of language* (pp. 205-255). Cambridge, UK: Cambridge University Press.

Thomas, J. (1983). Cross-cultural pragmatic failure. *Applied Linguistics, 4,* 91-109.

Thompson, C. W., Ross, K. M., Tennant, H. R., & Saenz, R. M. (1983). Building usable menu-based natural language interfaces to databases. *Proceedings of the Ninth International Conference on Very Large Databases.* Florence, Italy.

Thompson, T. (1981). The development of communication skills in physically handicapped children. *Human Communication Research, 7,* 312-324.

Thompson, T. (1982a). "You can't play marbles – you have a wooden hand": Communication with the handicapped. *Communication Quarterly, 30,* 108-115.

Thompson, T. (1982b). Disclosure as disability-management strategy: A review and conclusions. *Communication Quarterly, 30,* 196-202.

Thompson, T. L., & Seibold, D. R. (1978). Stigma management in normal-stigmatized interactions: Test of the disclosure hypothesis and a model of stigma acceptance. *Human Communication Research, 4,* 232-242.

Thorne, B. (1986). Girls and boys together . . . . But mostly apart: Gender arrangements in elementary schools. In W. W. Hartup & Z. Rubin (Eds.), *Relationships and development.* Hillsdale, NJ: Lawrence Erlbaum.

Thorne, B. (1990). Children and gender: Constructions of difference. In D. Rhode (Ed.), *Theoretical perspectives on sexual difference.* New Haven, CT: Yale University Press.

Thorne, B., & Henley, N. (1975). Difference and dominance: An overview of language, gender, and society. In B. Thorne & N. Henley (Eds.), *Language and sex: Difference and dominance* (pp. 5-42). Rowley, MA: Newbury House.

Thorne, B., Kramarae, C., & Henley, N. (Eds.). (1983). *Language, gender and society.* Rowley, MA: Newbury House.

Tiger, L., & Fox, R. (1971). *The imperial animal.* New York: Holt, Rinehart & Winston.

Ting-Toomey, S. (1988). Intercultural conflict styles: A face-negotiation theory. In Y. Y. Kim & W. B. Gudykunst (Eds.), *Theories in intercultural communication* (pp. 213-235). Newbury Park, CA: Sage.

Ting-Toomey, S. (1989a). Cultural and interpersonal relationship development: Some conceptual issues. In J. A. Anderson (Ed.), *Communication yearbook 12* (pp. 371-382). Newbury Park, CA: Sage.

Ting-Toomey, S. (1989b). Language, communication, and culture: An introduction. In S. Ting-Toomey & F. Korzenny (Eds.), *Language, communication, and culture: Current directions.* Newbury Park, CA: Sage.

Tolstedt, B. E., & Stokes, J. P. (1984). Self-disclosure, intimacy, and the depenetration process. *Journal of Personality and Social Psychology, 47,* 84-90.

Tracy, K. (Ed.). (1991). *Understanding face-to-face interaction: Issues linking goals and discourse.* Hillsdale, NJ: Lawrence Erlbaum.

Tracy, K., & Coupland, N. (Eds.). (1990). *Multiple goals in discourse.* Clevedon, UK: Multilingual Matters.

Tracy, K., & Eisenberg, E. M. (1989, May). *Multiple goals: Unpacking a commonplace.* Paper presented at the annual meeting of the International Communication Association, San Francisco.

Trankell, A. (1972). *Reliability of evidence. Methods for analyzing and assessing witness statements.* Stockholm: Beckmans.

Trankell, A. (Ed.). (1982). *Reconstructing the past: The role of the psychologists in criminal trials.* Stockholm: Norstedts.

Treichler, P. A., Frankel, R. M., Kramarae, C., Zoppi, K., & Beckman, H. B. (1984). Problems and problems: Power relationships in a medical encounter. In C. Kramarae, M. Schultz, & W. M. O'Barr (Eds.), *Language and power* (pp. 62-82). Beverly Hills, CA: Sage.

Treichler, P., & Kramarae, C. (1983). Women's talk in the ivory tower. *Communication Quarterly, 31,* 118-132.

Triandis, H. C., Brislin, R. W., & Hui, H. (1988). Cross-cultural training across the individualism-collectivism divide. *International Journal of Intercultural Relations, 12,* 269-289.

Tringo, J. (1970). The hierarchy of preference toward disability groups. *Journal of Special Education, 4,* 295-306.

Trosborg, A. (1987). Apology strategies in native/nonnatives. *Journal of Pragmatics, 11,* 147-167.

Tuchman, G. (1978). *Making news: A study in the construction of reality.* New York: Free Press.

Tuckett, D., & Williams, A. (1984). Approaches to the measurement of explanation and information-giving in medical consultations: A review of empirical studies. *Social Science & Medicine, 18,* 571-580.

Tuckman, B. W. (1966). Interpersonal probing and revealing and systems of integrative complexity. *Journal of Personality and Social Psychology, 18,* 133-137.

Valdman, A. (1981). Sociolinguistic aspects of foreigner talk. *International Journal of the Sociology of Language, 28,* 41-52.

van Dijk, T. A. (Ed.). (1987). *Handbook of discourse analysis* (Vols. 1-4). London: Academic Press.

van Dijk, T. A. (1988). *News as discourse.* Hillsdale, NJ: Lawrence Erlbaum.

Varonis, E. (1981). *A sociolinguistic analysis of cross-cultural communication.* Paper presented at NWAVE X, Philadelphia.

Varonis, E., & Gass, S. (1985a). Non-native/non native conversations: A model for negotiation of meaning. *Applied Linguistics, 6,* 71-90.

Varonis, E., & Gass, S. (1985b). Miscommunication in native/non-native conversation. *Language in Society, 14,* 327-343.

Verplanck, W. (1955). The control of the content of conversation: Reinforcement of statements of opinion. *Journal of Abnormal and Social Psychology, 51,* 668-676.

Vidmar, N., & Rokeach, M. (1974). Archie Bunker's bigotry: A study in selective perception and exposure. *Journal of Communication, 24,* 36-47.

Villard, K. L., & Whipple, L. J. (1976). *Beginnings in relational communication.* New York: John Wiley.

Volosinov, V. N. (1973). *Marxism and the philosophy of language.* Cambridge, MA: Harvard University Press.

Voysey, M. (1972). Impression management by parents with disabled children. *Journal of Health and Social Behavior, 13,* 80-89.

Vygotsky, L. (1978). *Mind in society: The development of higher psychological thought.* In M. Cole, V. John-Steiner, & E. Souberman (Eds.). Cambridge, MA: Harvard University Press.

Waitzkin, H. (1983). Doctor-patient communication. Clinical implications of social scientific research. *Journal of the American Medical Association, 252,* 2441-2446.

Waitzkin, H., & Stoeckle, J. D. (1976). Information control and the micro-politics of health care: Summary of an ongoing research project. *Social Science and Medicine, 10,* 263-276.

Walker, A. G. (1985). The two faces of silence: The effect of witness hesitancy on lawyers' impression. In D. Tannen & M. Saville-Troike (Eds.), *Perspectives on silence* (pp. 55-75). Norwood, NJ: Ablex.

Walker, A. G. (1986). The verbatim record: The myth and the reality. In S. Fisher & A. D. Todd (Eds.), *Discourse and institutional authority: Medicine, education and law* (pp. 205-222). Norwood, NJ: Ablex.

Walker, A. G. (1987). Linguistic manipulation, power and the legal setting. In L. Kedar (Ed.), *Power through discourse* (pp. 57-80). Norwood, NJ: Ablex.

Walker, H. L. (1973). Communication and the American health care problem. *Journal of Communication, 23,* 349-360.

Wallen, J., Waitzkin, H., & Stoeckle, J. D. (1979). Physician stereotypes about female health and illness: A study of patients' sex and the informative process during medical interviews. *Women and Health, 4,* 135-146.

Walton, H. J., Drewery, J., & Phillip, A. E. (1964). Typical medical students. *British Medical Journal, 2,* 744-748.

Watzlawick, P., Beavin, J., & Jackson, D. (1967). *Pragmatics of human communication.* New York: Norton.

Webber, B. L., & Mays, E. (1983). Varieties of user misconceptions: Detection and correction. *Proceedings of the 8th IJCAI.* Karlsruhe, Germany.

Weick, K. E. (1979). *The social psychology of organizing* (2nd ed.). New York: Random House.

Weischedel, R. M., & Sondheimer, N. K. (1983). Meta-rules as a basis for processing ill-formed input. *American Journal of Computational Linguistics, 9,* 161-177.

Weitz, S. (1972). Attitude, voice, and behavior: A repressed affect model of interracial interaction. *Journal of Personality and Social Psychology, 24,* 14-21.

Wertlieb, E. C. (1985). Minority group status of the disabled. *Human Relations, 38,* 1047-1063.

Wertsch, J. (1988, Winter). L. S. Vygotsky's "new" theory of mind. *The American Scholar,* 81-89.

West, C. (1979). Against our will: Male interruptions of females in cross-sex conversations. In J. Orasanu, M. K. Slater, & L. L. Adler (Eds.), *Language, sex and gender: Does la difference make a difference?* New York: New York Academy of Sciences.

West, C. (1983). "Ask me no questions . . . " An analysis of queries and replies in physician-patient dialogues. In S. Fisher & A. D. Todd (Eds.), *The social organization of doctor-patient communication* (pp. 75-106). Washington, DC: Center for Applied Linguistics.

West, C. (1984a). Medical misfires: Mishearings, misgivings and misunderstandings in physician-patient dialogues. *Discourse Processes, 7,* 107-134.

West, C. (1984b). *Routine complications: Troubles with talk between doctors and patients.* Bloomington: Indiana University Press.

West, C. (1984c). When the doctor is a "lady": Power, status, and gender in physician-patient encounters. *Symbolic Interaction, 7,* 87-106.

West, C., & Zimmerman, D. (1977). Women's place in everyday talk: Reflections on parent-child interaction. *Social Problems, 14,* 521-529.

West, C., & Zimmerman, D. (1987). Doing gender. *Gender & Society, 1,* 125-151.

West, C., & Zimmerman, D. H. (1983). Small insults: A study of interruptions in cross-sex conversations between unacquainted persons. In B. Thorne, C. Kramarae, & N. Henley (Eds.), *Language, gender and society* (pp. 103-117). Rowley, MA: Newbury House.

Westin, D. (1985). *Self and society: Narcissism, collectivism, and the development of morals.* Cambridge, MA: Harvard University Press.

Whalen, J., & Whalen, M. (1986). *"Doing gender" and children's natural language practices.* Working paper No. 23. Eugene: University of Oregon, Center for the Study of Women in Society.

Wheeless, V. E., & Berryman-Fink, C. (1985). Perceptions of women managers and their communicator competencies. *Communication Quarterly, 33,* 137-148.

Wheeless, V. E., Zakahi, W. R., & Chan, M. B. (1988). A test of self-disclosure based on perceptions of target's loneliness and gender orientation. *Communication Quarterly, 36,* 109-121.

White, D. M. (1950). The "Gatekeeper": A case study in the selection of news. *Journalism Quarterly, 27,* 383-390.

White, S. (1989). Backchannels across cultures: A study of Americans and Japanese. *Language in Society, 18,* 59-76.

Whyte, W. F. (1948). *Human relations in the restaurant industry.* New York: McGraw-Hill.

Wiemann, J. M. (1977). Explication and test of a model of communicative competence. *Human Communication Research, 3,* 195-213.

Wiemann, J. M., Aiu, P. D., & Busch, J. (1988, April). *Theoretical underpinnings of the beliefs about talk research program.* Paper presented at the Conference on Culture and Communication Theory, Tempe, AZ.

Wiemannn, J. M., & Bradac, J. J. (1989). Metatheoretical issues in the study of communicative competence: Structural and functional approaches. *Progress in Communication Sciences, 9,* 261-284.

Wiemann, J. M., Chen, V., & Giles, H. (1986, November). *Beliefs about talk and silence in cultural context.* Paper presented at the annual meeting of the Speech Communication Association, Chicago.

Wiemann, J. M., & Kelly, C. W. (1981). Pragmatics of interpersonal competence. In C. Wilder-Mott & J. H. Weakland (Eds.), *Rigor and imagination: Essays from the legacy of Gregory Bateson* (pp. 183-297). New York: Praeger.

Wiener, M., Devoe, S., Rubinow, S., & Geller, J. (1972). Nonverbal behavior and nonverbal communication. *Psychological Review, 79,* 185-214.

Wilden, A. (1980). *System and structure* (2nd ed.). London: Tavistock.

Williams, A., Giles, H., & Coupland, N. (1990). Communication, health, and the elderly: Frameworks, agenda and a model. In H. Giles, N. Coupland, & J. Wiemann (Eds.), *Communication, health and the elderly: Proceedings of Fulbright International Colloquium, 8* (pp. 1-28). Manchester, UK: Manchester University Press.

Williams, B. (1987). Humor, linguistic ambiguity, and disputing in a Guyanese community. *International Journal of the Sociology of Language, 65,* 79-94.

Williams, E. (1978). Teleconferencing: Social and psychological factors. *Journal of Communication, 28,* 125-131.

Wills, T. A. (1981). Downward comparison principles in social psychology. *Psychological Bulletin, 90,* 245-271.

Wilson, E. (1975). *Sociobiology: The new synthesis.* Cambridge, MA: Harvard University Press.

Wilson, T. P., Wiemann, J. M., & Zimmerman, D. H. (1984). Models of turn-taking in conversational interaction. *Journal of Language and Social Psychology, 3,* 159-183.

Winograd, T. (1972). *Understanding natural language.* New York: Academic Press.

Wiseman, R., Emry, R., Morgan, D., & Messamer, J. (1987). A normative analysis of the intercultural communication between able-bodied and disabled persons. *World Communication, 16,* 137-155.

Wodak, R. (1980). Discourse analysis and courtroom interaction. *Discourse Processes, 3,* 369-380.

Wodak, R. (1985). The interaction between judge and defendant. In T. A. van Dijk (Ed.), *Handbook of discourse analysis, Vol. 4,* (pp. 181-191). London: Academic Press.

Wodak, R. (1987). "And where is the Lebanon?" A socio-psycholinguistic investigation of comprehension and intelligibility of news. *Text, 7,* 377-410.

Woken, M., & Swales, J. (in press). Expertise and authority in native-non-native conversations: The need for a variable account. In S. Gass, C. Madden, D. Preston, & L. Selinker (Eds), *Variation in second language acquisition: Vol. 1. Discourse and pragamtics.* Clevedon, UK: Multilingual Matters.

Wolfson, N. (1989). *Perspectives: Sociolinguistics and TESOL.* Rowley, MA: Newbury House.

Wood, P. H. N., & Badley, E. M. (1980). *People with disabilities.* New York: World Rehabilitation Fund.

Woodall, W. G., Davis, D. K., & Sahin, H. (1983). From the boob tube to the black box: Television news comprehension from an information processing perspective. *Journal of Broadcasting, 27,* 1-23.

Woodbury, H. (1984). The strategic use of questions in court. *Semiotica, 48,* 197-228.

Word, C., Zanna, M., & Cooper, J. (1974). The nonverbal mediation of self-fulfilling prophecies in interracial interaction. *Journal of Experimental Social Psychology, 10,* 109-120.

Worthy, M., Gary, A. L., & Kahn, G. M. (1969). Self-disclosure as exchange process. *Journal of Personality and Social Psychology, 13,* 59-63.

Wright, B. (1960). *Physical disability –A psychological approach.* New York: Harper & Row.

Yamamoto, K. (1977). To be different. In J. Stubbins (Ed.), *Social and psychological aspects of disability.* Baltimore, MD: University Park Press.

Yarmey, D. (1979). *The psychology of eyewitness testimony.* London: Free Press.

Yousef, F. S. (1978). Communication patterns: Some aspects of nonverbal behavior in intercultural communication. In E. L. Ross (Ed.), *Interethnic communication.* Athens: University of Georgia Press.

Zborowski, M. (1958). Cultural components in responses to pain. *Journal of Social Issues, 8,* 16-30.

Zimmerman, D. H., & West, C. (1975). Sex roles, interruptions, and silences in conversations. In B. Thorne & N. Henley (Eds.), *Language and sex: Difference and dominance* (pp. 105-129). Rowley, MA: Newbury House.

Zola, I. K. (1963). Problems of communication, diagnosis and patient care: The interplay of patient, physician and clinic organization. *Journal of Medical Education, 38,* 829-838.

Zola, I. K. (1966). Pathways to the doctor—From person to patient. *Social Science and Medicine, 7,* 667-689.

Zola, I. K. (1979). Helping one another: A speculative history of the self-help movement. *Archives of Physical Medicine and Rehabilitation, 60,* 452-456.

Zuengler, J. (in press). Performance variation in NS-NNS interactions: ethnolinguistic difference, or discourse domain? In S. Gass, C. Madden, D. Preston, & L. Selinker (Eds.), *Variation in second language acquisition (Vol. 1): Discourse and pragmatics.* Clevedon: Multilingual Matters.

Index

About the Authors

Karin Aronsson (Ph.D., University of Lund, 1978) is Professor at the Department of Child Studies, Linköping University, Sweden. She writes on issues in language and social interaction. Recent publications have concerned conflicting frameworks, language and control, or politeness phenomena. Several studies concern institutional discourse (for example, pediatric encounters or courtroom discourse).

Joyce Baker is a doctoral student at Arizona State University. She completed her B.A. at the University of Hawaii and her M.A. at Arizona State University. She is interested in intergroup and cross-cultural communication phenomena. Her current research focus includes privacy regulation in Japan and the United States and cross-cultural research on relationship development.

Stephen P. Banks is Assistant Professor in the School of Communication, University of Idaho. His current research interests include critical linguistics, studies of talk in work settings, and the institutional uses of translation.

Allan Bell (Ph.D., University of Aucklan, 1977) works as a freelance journalist and researcher in sociolinguistics, with interests in media language, New Zealand English, and language style. He is an Honorary Research Fellow in the Department of Linguistics, Victoria University, Wellington. He is author of *The Language of News Media*.

Julie R. Brown (MA, University of California, Santa Barbara, 1984) is a doctoral candidate at the University of Utah and Lecturer in communication, University of California, Davis. Her research interests include the critical analysis of conversation and the political dimensions of everyday life.

Lerita M. Coleman (Ph.D., Harvard University, 1980) is an Associate Professor in the Department of Psychology at the University of Colorado. She has co-edited a book, *The Dilemma of Difference: A Multidisciplinary View of Stigma,* with Stephen Ainlay and Gaylene Becker. Her current research explores stigma and self- concept with special emphasis on self-stigmatization and communication.

Justine Coupland is Lecturer in sociolinguistics at the University of Wales College of Cardiff, and a Visiting Assistant Professor in Communication at the University of California, Santa Barbara. She is co-editor of *Contexts of Accommodation* and co-author of *Sociolinguistics and Ageing.* Her current research interests are medical discourse and interactional ritual.

Nikolas Coupland is Senior Lecturer at the University of Wales College of Cardiff, Visiting Associate Professor and Fulbright Scholar at the University of California, Santa Barbara. He is author of *Dialect in Use, Sociolinguistics and Ageing*, and *Language: Contexts and Consequences*, and editor of several other books in sociolinguistics, discourse, and gerontology.

Bella M. DePaulo (Ph.D, Harvard University, 1979) is a Professor in the Department of Psychology at the University of Virginia. She has co-edited, with Arie Nadler and Jeff Fisher, the three-volume set titled *New Directions in Helping*. She has also published in the areas of deceiving and detecting deceit, nonverbal behavior and self-presentation, and the social psychology of language.

Kent Drummond (Ph.D., University of Texas, 1990) is Assistant Professor of Communication at the University of Wyoming. His publications (*Western Journal of Speech Communication*; *Critical Studies in Mass Communication*) examine micro-details of everyday conversational activities.

Eric M. Eisenberg is Associate Professor of Communication Arts and Sciences at the University of Southern California. He specializes in organizational communication, focusing particularly on optimal work experience and the strategic uses of language.

Richard M. Frankel is an Associate Professor of Medicine at the University of Rochester School of Medicine and Dentistry and co-directs the Residency Training Program in Internal Medicine at Highland Hospital.

He has written widely on topics relating to communication between doctors and patients, and is currently doing research in a large health maintenance organization on the relationship between communication and patient dissatisfaction, including the decision to litigate.

Susan M. Gass (Ph.D., Indiana University, 1979) is Professor in the Department of English and Director of the English Language Center at Michigan State University. Her research interests include general issues of second language acquisition, focussing in particular on conversation involving non-native speakers, universal constraints on second languages, and the role of the native language. Her most recent book is with Jacquelyn Schachter, *Linguistic Perspectives on Second Language Acquisition.*

Gao Ge is a doctoral candidate in the Interdisciplinary Ph.D. program in Communication at Arizona State University. Her research interests include intercultural communication, cross-cultural communication, and interpersonal relationships.

Howard Giles obtained his Ph.D. from the University of Bristol in 1971 and subsequently became Chair of Social Psychology at that institution in 1984 before moving to the University of California, Santa Barbara, in 1989, where he is now Professor of Communication. He is founding editor of the *Journal of Language and Social Psychology* and co-founding editor of the *Journal of Asian Pacific Communication* as well as General Editor of a Sage Book Series entitled *Language and Language Behaviors.* He has published widely in the areas of language attitudes, accommodation theory, and intergenerational communication.

Nancy M. Henley is Professor of Psychology at the University of California, Los Angeles. She is author of *Body Politics: Power, Sex, and Nonverbal Communication;* co-editor, with Barrie Thorne, of *Language and Sex: Difference and Dominance;* with Clara Mayo, of *Gender and Nonverbal Behavior*; and with Barrie Thorne and Cheris Kramarae, of *Language, Gender, and Society.*

Robert Hopper (Ph.D., University of Wisconsin, 1970) is Charles Sapp Centennial Professor of Communication at the University of Texas at Austin. His current publications (*Communication Monographs*; *Journal of Language and Social Psychology*) apply conversation analysis to telephone conversation.

Florence King is Chief Speech Therapist with the Eastern Health and Social Services Board, Northern Ireland. Her main research interest is the development of communication in preschool children.

Cheris Kramarae is Professor of Speech Communication at the University of Illinois at Urbana-Champaign. She is the author or editor of nine books on women and language, including *Technology and Women's Voices*. She is a co-editor of the new journal *Discourse & Society*.

Michael F. McTear is Senior Lecturer in Information Systems at the University of Ulster, Northern Ireland. His books include *Children's Conversation*, *Understanding Cognitive Science*, and *Understanding Knowledge Engineering*. His research interests are computational pragmatics, language acquisition, and language disability.

Jon F. Nussbaum is Associate Professor at the University of Oklahoma. He is author of *Communication and Aging* and editor of *Life-span Communication: Normative Processes*. He is currently investigating the function of friendship and sibling relationships across life-span.

Elinor Ochs is Professor in the Department of TESL/Applied Linguistics at the University of California, Los Angeles. She is author of *Culture and Language Development: Language Acquisition and Language Socialization in a Samoan Village* and a specialist in cultural dimensions of language acquisition.

Steven R. Phillips received his Ph.D. from the University of Southern California with a focus on Organizational Communication. Currently at the University of Montana, his research interests include new communication technologies in organizations, retirement from organizations, diffusion of innovations, and deception detection.

Ronan G. Reilly (Ph.D., University College, Dublin, 1982) is a Research Fellow at the Educational Research Centre, St. Patrick's College, Dublin. His research interests are primarily in the area of computational models of natural language (NL) understanding. He recently completed a four-year research project, funded by the ESPRIT program of the CEG, the aim of which was the development of a robust NL interface to a database. He is currently working on developing connectionist models of various aspects of NL processing.

L. Edna Rogers (Ph.D., Michigan State University, 1972) is Professor of Communication at the University of Utah. Her research interests center on the study of social interaction processes and interaction processes and interpersonal relationships.

Evangeline M. Varonis is Lecturer in the English Department at the University of Akron. She has published articles in the areas of discourse analysis, second language acquisition, and composition. Her research interests include the negotiation of meaning between interlocutors and between author, reader, and text.

Candace West is Professor of Sociology at the University of California, Santa Cruz. She is the author of *Routine Complications: Troubles with Talk between Doctors and Patients* and numerous articles on the subject of physician-patient communication.

John M. Wiemann (Ph.D., Purdue University) is Professor of Communication at the University of California, Santa Barbara. His research interests include communicative competence, cross-cultural influences upon beliefs about talk, nonverbal communication, and communication, health, and aging. He co-edits the Sage Annual Reviews of Communication Research series (with R. Hawkins and S. Pingree). Recent books include *Advancing Communication Science* (with Hawkins and Pingree) and *Communication, Health and the Elderly* (with H. Giles and N. Coupland). He has been a W.K. Kellogg Foundation National Fellow and a Fulbright-Hays Senior Research Scholar at the University of Bristol.

NOTES

NOTES

NOTES

NOTES